Paradoxes and Inconsist...

Is law paradoxical? This book seeks to unra... It focuses on two main questions: the natu... ...oxes, and their social ramifications. In exploring the structure of legal paradoxes, the book focuses both on generic paradoxes, such as those associated with the self-referential character of legal validity and the endemic incoherence of legal discourse, and on paradoxes that permeate more restricted fields of law, such as contract law, euthanasia, and human rights (the prohibition of torture). The discussion of the social effects of legal paradoxes focuses on the role of paradoxes as drivers of legal change, and explores the institutional mechanisms that ensure the stability of the law, in spite of its paradoxical makeup. The essays in the book discuss these questions from various perspectives, invoking insights from philosophy, systems theory, deconstruction and economics.

Paradoxes and Inconsistencies in the Law

Edited by
OREN PEREZ and GUNTHER TEUBNER

HART PUBLISHING
OXFORD AND PORTLAND, OREGON
2006

Published in North America (US and Canada)
by Hart Publishing
c/o International Specialized Book Services
5804 NE Hassalo Street
Portland, Oregon
97213-3644
USA

© The editors and contributors jointly and severally 2006

The editors and contributors have asserted their right under the Copyright, Designs and Patents Act 1988, to be identified as the authors of this work.

Hart Publishing is a specialist legal publisher based in Oxford, England. To order further copies of this book or to request a list of other publications please write to:

Hart Publishing, Salter's Boatyard, Folly Bridge, Abingdon Rd,
Oxford, OX1 4LB
email: mail@hartpub.co.uk
Telephone: +44 (0)1865 245533 Fax: +44 (0) 1865 794882

WEBSITE: http//:www.hartpub.co.uk

British Library Cataloguing in Publication Data
Data Available

ISBN-13: 978-1-84113-541-0 (paperback)
ISBN-10: 1-84113-541-0 (paperback)

Typeset by Compuscript, Shannon
Printed and bound in Great Britain by
Biddles Ltd, Kings Lynn

Contents

List of Contributers vii
Introduction xi

Part I – Introduction 1

1. Law in the Air: A Prologue to the World of Legal Paradoxes
   OREN PEREZ 3

Part II – Generic Paradoxes 39

2. Dealing with Paradoxes of Law: Derrida, Luhmann, Wiethölter
   GUNTHER TEUBNER 41

3. Just-ifications of a Law of Society
   RUDOLF WIETHÖLTER 65

4. The Reference of Paradox: Missing Paradoxity as
   Real Perplexity in Both Systems Theory and Deconstruction
   JEAN CLAM 77

5. The Political Origins of the Modern Legal Paradoxes
   NIR KEDAR 101

6. The Institutionalisation of Inconsistency: From Fluid
   Concepts to Random Walk
   OREN PEREZ 119

7. Between Ritual and Theatre: Judicial Performance as Paradox
   LIOR BARSHACK 145

8. The Paradoxes of Justice: The Ultimate Difference Between
   a Philosophical and a Sociological Observation of Law
   FATIMA KASTNER 167

vi Contents

Part III – Local Paradoxes 181

9. *Expectations and Legal Doctrine*
   ERIC TALLEY 183

10. *Equality as a Paradoxical Ideal or*
    Respectful Treatment versus Equal Treatment
    YITZHAK BENBAJI 205

11. *Mediating Paradoxically: Complementing the Paradox of*
    'Relational Autonomy' with the 'Paradox of Rights' in
    Thinking Mediation
    MICHAL ALBERSTEIN 225

12. *Autopoiesis, Nihilism and Technique: On Death and*
    the Origins of Legal Paradoxes
    SHAI LAVI 247

13. *The Paradox of the Law: Between Generality and*
    Particularity—Prohibiting Torture and Practising it in Israel
    ROEI AMIT 275

Index 301

List of Contributers

Michal Alberstein

Michal Alberstein, is a lecturer in jurisprudence and conflict resolution in the faculty of law at Bar-Ilan University, where she also supervises a community mediation clinic and takes part in an interdisciplinary graduate program for conflict management and negotiation. She wrote her doctoral dissertation at Harvard law school (1996-2000) and won the Byes fellowship for excellent doctoral candidates. Her current research deals with theories of law and conflict resolution and their intellectual roots; multiculturalism and its relation to negotiation and mediation; and representations of conflict resolution in literature and film. Dr. Alberstein's book, Pragmatism and Law: From Philosophy to Disputes Resolution (UK 2002), deals with the intellectual roots of Alternative Dispute Resolution (ADR). In 2001, Dr. Alberstein was awarded the prestigious three-year Yigal Alon Scholarship, considered the most competitive scholarship for young outstanding Israeli academics.

Roei Amit

Roei Amit, received his doctorate from the Ecole des Hautes en Sciences Sociales in Paris, for his dissertation on "Constitutional Paradoxes", in 2002. He holds an LLB from the Tel-Aviv University, BA in comparative literature, and MA in poetics and semiotics from the TAU Humans Science Faculty, he collaborated with UNESCO in the domains of Human Rights and Law. He is currently teaching at the Paris Center for Critical Studies.

Lior Barshack

Lior Barshack is an associate professor at the Radzyner School of Law, The Interdisciplinary Center, Herzliya, Israel. His work focuses on law's relations to art, religion and kinship. The article in this volume forms part of a series of articles devoted to law's place in civil religion. Other articles in this series include "Notes on the Clerical Body of the Law" 24 (3) Cardozo Law Review (2003), and "Constituent Power as Body: Outline of a Constitutional Theology" Forthcoming in the University of Toronto Law Journal.

Yitzhak Benbaji

Yitzhak Benbaji is a lecturer in ethics, philosophy of criminal law and philosophy of language in the law faculty and in the philosophy department at Bar-Ilan University. He currently explores the moral basis of the right of self-defense and its relation to the just war theory (see his "Culpable Bystanders, Innocent Threats and the Ethics of Self-Defense," forthcoming in The Canadian Journal of Philosophy). In addition, he studies the political ideal of equality and its place in an adequate theory of political justice - see his "The Doctrine of Sufficiency: a Defense" forthcoming in Utilitas and his paper in the present volume. His 2001 Hebrew University dissertation won the Bernard Bloomfield Memorial Endowment prize for an outstanding dissertation and he was a fellow in the Institute for Advanced Study, Princeton in 2000-2002.

Jean Clam

Jean Clam is a CNRS (Centre National de la Recherche Scientifique) senior research fellow working in Berlin and Strasbourg. His main publications are: Droit et société chez Niklas Luhmann. La contingence des normes, Paris, Presses Universitaires de France 1997; (with Jean-Luc Gaffard), Norme, fait, fluctuation. Contributions à une analyse des choix normatifs, Genève, Droz 2001; Was heißt: Sich an Differenz statt an Identität orientieren? Zur De-ontologisierung in Philosophie und Sozialwissenschaft, Konstanz, UVK, 2002; Trajectoires de l'immatériel. Contributions à une théorie de la valeur et de sa dématérialisation, Paris, CNRS Editions 2004; Kontingenz, Paradox, Nur-Vollzug. Grundprobleme einer Theorie der Gesellschaft, Konstanz, UVK 2004.

Fatima Kastner

Dr. Fatima Kastner studies philosophy, sociology and law at the universities of Frankfurt, London and Paris. Fatima Kastner is a senior research fellow at the Hamburg Institute for Social Research and a lecturer at the institute for social sciences at the University of Hamburg. Main research fields: contemporary continental philosophy and social theory, especially systems theory and legal theory. Publications (a.o.): Ohnmachtssemantiken: Systemtheorie und Dekonstruktion. Zum Primat der Paradoxie von Luhmanns Systemtheorie und Derridas Dekonstruktion am Beispiel ihrer autologischen Rechtskonstruktionen. Frankfurt/Main 2002. Luhmanns Souveränitätsparadox. Zum generativen Mechanismus des politischen Systems der Weltgesellschaft, Hamburg 2005. Co-Editor of: Niklas Luhmann, Law as A Social System. London 2004.

Nir Kedar

Dr. Kedar teaches law and legal history at the Bar-Ilan University Faculty of Law, and is a fellow at the Ben-Gurion Research Center, at the Ben-Gurion

University of the Negev. Dr. Kedar has an LL.B. and a BA in history from Tel-Aviv University and an LL.M. and S.J. D. from Harvard University. His main fields of interest are Israeli, North-American and modern European legal history, Israeli history, comparative law, the study of legal systems and traditions and legal theory. Dr. Kedar's book on Israeli Statism and the Rule of Law will appear next year.

Shai Lavi

Shai Lavi teaches sociology of law, jurisprudence and criminal law at Tel-Aviv University. He received his Ph.D. from the Jurisprudence and Social Policy Program, University of California Berkeley. His book, The Modern Art of Dying: The History of Euthanasia in the United States (Princeton University Press, 2005) is a cultural history of dying and the rise of regulation in nineteenth- and early twentieth-century America. His more recent work is dedicated to the role of revenge in modern politics and in the formation of a national Jewish identity. He recently received the Zeltner prize for young scholars and is currently a member of the junior faculty group of the Israeli Academy for Science and the Humanities.

Oren Perez

Oren Perez is an associate professor at the faculty of law, Bar-Ilan University, Israel. He wrote his doctoral dissertation at the London School of Economics and Political Science (1997-2000) and won the Marie Curie Fellowship. His main fields of interest are environmental law, international economic law and legal theory. Two of his recent publications are 'Ecological Sensitivity and Global Legal Pluralism: Rethinking the Trade and Environment Conflict' (Hart Publishing, 2004) and 'Normative Creativity and Global Legal Pluralism: Reflections on the Democratic Critique of Transnational Law', 10(2) Indiana Journal of Global Legal Studies, (2003) 25-64.

Eric Talley

Professor of Law; Director of the Center for Law, Economics, and Organization; Director for the Olin Program in Law and Rational Choice, University of Southern California Law School. b. 1966. B.A., magna cum laude, University of California, San Diego, 1988; J.D., Stanford Law School, 1995; Ph.D., Stanford University, 1995. Articles Editor, Stanford Law Review. Lecturer in Economics, Stanford University, 1993; Assistant Professor, USC Law School, 1995-1997; Associate Professor, 1997-2000; Professor of Law since 2000; Alfred P. Sloan Fellow and Visiting Professor of Law, Georgetown University Law Center, 2000; Visiting Professor of Law, California Institute of Technology, 2001.Subjects: Contracts; Corporations; Law and Economics; Commercial Law; Law and Strategic Behavior; Quantitative Methods in the Law. Member: Phi Beta Kappa.

Recent publication: "Disclosure Norms." 149 University of Pennsylvania Law Review 1955 (2001).

Gunther Teubner

Professor of private law and legal sociology, University Frankfurt. Centennial Visiting Professor, London School of Economics. Research fields: social theory of law; comparative private law. Author: Gunther Teubner, Regime-Collisions: The Vain Search for Legal Unity in the Fragmentation of Global Law, Michigan Journal of International Law 25:4, 2004, S. 999-1045 (with Andreas Fischer-Lescano), Costituzionalismo societario 2005, Netzwerk als Vertragsverbund 2003, Il diritto policontesturale 1999, Droit et réflexivité 1994, Law as an Autopoietic System 1993. Editor/author:Constitutionalism and Transnational Governance 2004, Global Law Without A State, 1998, Environmental Law and Ecological Responsibility 1995.

Rudolf Wiethölter

Professor (em.) of Private, Commercial and Business Law, University Frankfurt. Research fields: private law and legal theory. Author: Rechtswissenschaft 1968. Interessen und Organisation der Aktiengesellschaft im amerikanischen und deutschen Recht 1961. Materialization and Proceduralization in Modern Law, in Teubner (ed), Dilemmas of Law in the Welfare State (Berlin, Walter de Gruyter, 1985); Social Science Models in Economic Law, in Daintith and Teubner (eds), Contract and Organization (Berlin, Walter de Gruyter, 1986); Proceduralization of the Category of Law, in Joerges and Trubek (eds), Critical Legal Thought (Baden-Baden, Nomos 1989).

Introduction

This book reflects our long-lasting fascination with paradoxes and their place in legal theory and practice. It emerged from a conference on 'Paradoxes and Self-reference in Law', which took place in Frankfurt on 16-17 December 2002. The conference was a joint-project of Frankfurt University and Bar Ilan Faculty of Law. The essays in the book provide a multifaceted deliberation on the theme of legal paradoxicality. We believe that this book, by taking the idea of paradox as the focal point for thinking about law, and by invoking insights from various disciplines - from philosophy to systems theory, deconstruction and economics - fills a considerable gap in the contemporary legal literature.

We would like to thank several people and organizsations whose help was crucial to the production of this book. The Florence Unger and Samuel Goldenstein, M.D. Interdisciplinary Program for Law, Rationality, Ethics and Social Justice provided financial support for the whole project. Mr Josef Buchmann, Frankfurt, provided financial support for the conference in Frankfurt. The law faculties of Bar Ilan University and Frankfurt (Goethe) University assisted in organising the joint-conference. Cordula Heldt, Clarissa Weilbächer and Peer Zumbansen provided significant help in organising the conference at Frankfurt. Yoram Egosi helped in the editing process. Robyn Frandsen provided invaluable help in the final editing of the book. Finally we would also like to thank those conference participants whose contributions did not find their way into the book, for various reasons, but who nonetheless made a significant contribution to this intellectual endeavor: Bruce Chapman, Emilios A. Christodoulidis, Heidi Li Feldman, Shachar Lifshitz and Yair Lorberbaum.

Oren Perez & Gunther Teubner.

Part I

Introduction

1

Law in the Air: A Prologue to the World of Legal Paradoxes

OREN PEREZ[*]

THE MOVIE '*Being John Malkovich*'[1] tells the story of a distinctive machine. Its hero, Craig Schwartz, accidentally stumbles into a hidden tunnel that has a unique property: by traversing this tunnel (or portal), the visitor finds himself briefly 'being' another person. As the movie progresses, we learn that this person, the 'vessel,' is John Malkovich, a famous American actor.[2] As travellers pass through the tunnel, they experience the corporeal existence of John Malkovich. They experience his 'inner' being and see the world through his eyes and mind. Some travellers even report a limited ability to control the vessel body (that is, John Malkovich) as would a puppeteer. At first sight, this portal seems quite harmless. But after reflection, one starts to sense that it conceals a deep puzzle: 'What happens when a man [the vessel] climbs through his own portal?'[3] This dilemma constitutes a classic self-referential paradox: a re-entry or reflexive enfoldment of the self. Indeed, it is difficult to imagine how this dilemma could be resolved in practice. One probable prediction involves an infinite regress, whereupon entering the portal, the individual—the object of the portal—will experience himself entering the portal, entering the portal, ad infinitum...[4]

---

[*] I would like to thank Adi Ayal, Yitzhak Benbaji, Shai Lavi, and Gunther Teubner for their comments on an earlier draft of this article.
[1] '*Being John Malkovich*' (1999), a screenplay by Charlie Kaufman.
[2] This is how Craig Schwartz describes his discovery to Maxine, his friend: 'There's a tiny door in that empty office. It's a portal, Maxine. It takes you inside John Malkovich. You see the world through John Malkovich's eyes, then, after about fifteen minutes, you're spit out into a ditch on the side of the New Jersey Turnpike.'
[3] This quote is from the script.
[4] The paradox of 'Being John Malkovich' can be resolved by denying the truth of its basic premise—the existence of such a portal. But this logical resolution of the paradox does not detract from the force of the movie's artistic treatment of the paradox of self-reference.

4   Oren Perez

The beauty of the film 'Being John Malkovich' lies in the way in which it gives the paradox of self-reference a tangible presence. For John Malkovich, the paradox of entering into one's own portal is not an abstract riddle, but a real-life dilemma with potentially harsh consequences. The paradox is reformulated as a corporeal threat. Of course, there is an easy way out—Malkovich can simply forget about the portal, or seal it somehow. But this option—choosing ignorance and simplicity over knowledge and complexity—seems somehow unsatisfactory. Indeed, in the movie, Malkovich chooses the more perilous option and enters the tunnel himself.[5]

This book follows, in a way, a similar path; it seeks to explicate the social facet of the paradoxes of law—the various ways in which these paradoxes are weaved into and influence the practice of law. The book's main thesis, which runs through its various chapters, is that the study of legal paradoxes is not simply a matter of logical or linguistic analysis. This thesis reflects the fact that law is a social system, whose essence cannot be captured by enumerating the norms and propositions which play a role in its operation. This means that the riddle of legal paradoxicality cannot be solved by relying solely on the tools of logic.[6] One needs the expertise of extra-logical fields of knowledge, such as sociology, history, systems theory, deconstruction, economics and, of course, legal theory. Building on this thesis, the book will try to decode the unique structure of legal paradoxes and to expose their place within the totality of legal praxis. The main aim of this introductory chapter is to delineate the conceptual space in which the book's different contributions make their moves. To this end, I will discuss the differences between legal and logical paradoxes, the possible usages of paradoxical arguments in legal thought, and the nature of some of the more fundamental paradoxes of law. However, within this delineated space, there remains a large area of disagreement. In that sense, the book does not offer a uniform theory, but a multifaceted deliberation on the theme of legal paradoxicality.

The chapter's first section provides a general introduction to the world of paradoxes. The second section moves into the realm of law and explores the differences between legal, logical and semantical paradoxes. It also explores some of the key paradoxes of law, which are analysed in further detail by the book's different authors. The chapter's final section describes the structure of the book and discusses the different contributions.

I. PARADOXES: A GENERAL PRIMER

Thinking about legal paradoxes requires one, first, to develop a clear understanding of the notion of 'paradox.' In order to do so, I will consider,

---

[5] For those who did not see the movie, the scene in which Malkovich enters the tunnel is reproduced in the annex to this chapter.

[6] Although, as will be indicated below, there are close links between these two fields of inquiry.

first, some general definitions of this idea, and then move to discuss a few prominent examples.

The term 'paradox' is sometimes used informally to designate a statement which conflicts with the common view.[7] Within the realm of law, this understanding can be applied to any legal claim which challenges a received legal opinion (eg, an entrenched legal doctrine), whether in the context of an adversarial process or as part of a more wide-ranging, interpretative struggle. Such interpretative struggles are quite common and usually are not perceived as a threat to the structural integrity of the law. This book is more interested in other forms of paradoxes, those which do not merely reflect a transitory interpretative dispute but expose a deeper social and linguistic problematic.

The philosophical literature offers various definitions of this more problematic understanding of paradoxes. Thus, Nicholas Rescher defines paradox (or, as he terms it, '*aporetic cluster*') as a 'set of propositions that are individually plausible but collectively inconsistent.'[8] The focus of this definition is on the *conflict*. Other philosophers emphasise the paradox's problematical *conclusion*. RM Sainsbury argues that a paradox is as 'an apparently unacceptable conclusion derived by apparently acceptable reasoning from apparently acceptable premises'. Charles Chihara provides a similar definition: a paradox is 'an argument that begins with premises that appear to be clearly true, that proceeds according to inference rules that appear to be valid, but that ends in contradiction.'[9] Another philosophical position highlights the argumentative or reasoning pattern that generates the paradox. WV Quine, for example, offers the following definition (using the term antinomy): 'An antinomy produces a self-contradiction by accepted ways of reasoning. It establishes that some tacit and trusted pattern of reasoning must be made explicit and henceforward be avoided or revised.' In a similar spirit, Robert A Koons defines paradox as 'an inconsistency among nearly unrevisable principles that can be resolved only by recognizing some essential limitation of thought or language.'[10]

It is possible, within this very general framework, to distinguish between two major types of paradoxes.[11] *Paradoxes of coherence* expose a deep

---

[7] Thus, the definition of paradox in the Oxford Dictionary opens with: 'Statement contrary to received opinion.' See *The Concise Oxford Dictionary of Current English*, 5th edn (Oxford, Oxford University Press, 1964) 880.

[8] See N Rescher, *Paradoxes: Their Roots, Range and Resolution* (Chicago, Open Court, 2001) xxi.

[9] RM Sainsbury, *Paradoxes* (Cambridge, Cambridge University Press, 1995) 1 and CS Chihara, 'The Semantic Paradoxes: A Diagnostic Investigation' (1979) 88 *Philosophical Review* 590.

[10] WV Quine, *The Ways of Paradox* (Cambridge, Mass., Harvard University Press, 1966) 7 and RA Koons, *Paradoxes of Belief and Strategic Rationality* (Cambridge, Cambridge University Press, 1992) 8.

[11] This distinction is not exhaustive, see Rescher, above n 8, at 72–73.

inconsistency in some well-defined set of sentences or propositions. (I use the term 'deep inconsistency' to distinguish such paradoxes from mere contradictions. The difference between the two terms lies in the way in which paradoxes make the contradiction appear inescapable.)[12] *Semantical paradoxes* involve the notions of truth, falsity and reference, and challenge the way we reason with these notions. These paradoxes, as will be indicated below, question the expressive capacities of natural and formal languages.[13] At first sight, semantical paradoxes may seem more challenging because of their more general scope. However, as will be indicated below, paradoxes of coherence can be ominous as well. An interesting question which comes up in both cases is how these paradoxes influence the world of action. This question is seldom considered by philosophers, but cannot of course be ignored when one is studying legal paradoxes.

Let us consider some prominent examples of these different paradox types.

Paradoxes of Coherence

Paradoxes of coherence, as noted above, expose a deep inconsistency in some well-defined set of sentences or propositions. A prominent example is the ancient paradox of omnipotence (which, as will be elaborated in section II, has close links to the legal realm). Consider the following riddle: can an omnipotent being (call it God) create a stone which s/he himself cannot move? If God cannot create this stone, then, clearly, we cannot qualify her as omnipotent, since there is something which s/he cannot do. But what if God can create this stone, as the idea of omnipotence directs us to assume? This seems to lead, once again, to contradiction, since by creating this stone, God has seemingly revoked (at least partially) his overall omnipotence. The paradox of Divine Omnipotence can be represented as the following *set* of inconsistent propositions[14]:

(1) Omnipotence means the ability to do literally anything.
(2) There is an omnipotent being (call her God).
(3) God can do literally anything (from (1) and (2)).

---

[12] See P Suber, 'The Paradox of Self-Amendment' (1990) 7 *Stanford Literature Review* 53. I will sometimes use the term 'logical paradoxes' to refer to this type of paradoxes.

[13] Another useful taxonomy is Quine's distinction between 'veridical' and 'falsidical' paradoxes (see Quine, above n 10, at 4–5). Veridical paradox is, in effect, a truth-telling argument or proof; it establishes that some proposition is true or false (eg, the Barber Paradox). Falsidical paradox, in contrast, 'is one whose proposition not only seems at first absurd but also is false, there being fallacy in the purported proof.' A typical example is Zeno's paradox of Achilles and the tortoise. I have chosen not to use Quine's taxonomy, although I will refer to its underlying rationale in the following discussion.

[14] The following account is based on the discussion in Rescher's book on Paradoxes, above n 8, at 130–33.

(4) God can create a stone which he himself cannot move (from (3)).
(5) A being which cannot do something, even due to his own prior actions, is not omnipotent (from (2)).
(6) God is not omnipotent—contrary to (1) (from (4) and (5)).

The core of the Omnipotence Paradox lies in those non-derivative propositions, which are part of the above set, that is, propositions (1) and (2). Indeed, what seems to lie at the core of this paradox is the question of the meaning of omnipotence, and the theological puzzle of whether an omnipotent being, that is, God, exists.

It is not my intention to provide a solution to this paradox (although I will provide some hints below). Rather, I want to focus on its structural features. The paradox in this case does not seem to arise from some basic limits of language or thought, but rather from a discord between what are perceived as plausible assumptions. It is a product of what Nicholas Rescher calls *cognitive* or *aporetic overcommitment*. This cognitive overcommitment, Rescher argues, is a generic property of all paradoxes: 'We regard more as plausible than the realm of fact and reality is able to accommodate, as is attested by our falling into contradiction. Paradox thus roots in an information overload, a literal embarrassment of riches.'[15] This leads Rescher to formulate a general methodology for paradox management:

> Any and every paradox can be resolved by simply abandoning some or all of the commitments whose conjoining creates a contradiction. In principle, paradox management is thus a straightforward process: to appraise the comparative plausibility of what we accept and restore consistency by making what is less plausible give way to what is more so. It is this generic and uniform structure of paradox management that makes generic and uniform approach to their rational management possible, paving the way to that single overarching discipline of *aporetics*.[16]

The application of this methodology does not necessarily lead to the complete abandonment of the 'problematic' propositions; a less drastic solution could be achieved through the introduction of *new distinctions*. Thus, for example, a possible solution to the paradox of omnipotence lies in the introduction of an alternative understanding of 'omnipotence'. According to this alternative understanding, omnipotence does not embrace the capacity to bring about any state of affairs whatsoever, *including necessary and impossible states of affairs*. The state of affairs in which there is a stone of

---

[15] *Ibid*, at 9.
[16] *Ibid*, at 10. Whether Rescher's set-theoretic methodology can be used to overcome every possible paradox is open to debate. Sorensen, for example, argues that some paradoxes, such as the Barber Paradox, cannot be described as joint inconsistencies, but should more accurately be viewed as *indivisible contradictions*—which cannot be divided into self-consistent propositional elements, see R Sorensen, *A Brief History of the Paradox: Philosophy and the Labyrinths of the Mind* (Oxford, Oxford University Press, 2003) 365.

such mass such that our omnipotent being cannot move it is an impossible state of affairs; hence, an omnipotent agent is not required to be able to bring it about; hence the paradox is resolved (and there is no need to abandon the second thesis, which is a fundamental precept of monotheistic theology).[17]

The next section considers the second type of paradoxical configurations: semantical paradoxes.

Semantical Paradoxes

Semantical paradoxes involve the notions of truth, falsity and reference. The beauty and force of these paradoxes lie in the way in which they put into question some of our deepest logical and linguistic intuitions. As will be clarified in the next section, there is no direct equivalent to semantical paradoxes in the field of law. Nonetheless, the different strategies which were invoked by philosophers in their incessant attempts to resolve these paradoxes provide interesting insights to the study of legal paradoxes.

Consider the following sentence[18]:

'K_1 *This sentence is false*' (we can also present this sentence in the following format: 'K_1 K_1 is false').

Suppose first that this sentence is true. Then, it is as it says it is—false. But, if it is false, it is what it proclaims itself to be. So it is in fact true. K_1 produces a paradoxical loop: if it is true, it is false; and if it is false, it is true. It is impossible, so it seems, to attribute a stable truth value to this sentence. One gets a similar contradiction by considering the proclamation: 'I am lying.'

The foregoing example, commonly dubbed the 'Liar Paradox,' is probably the most famous example of self-referential paradoxes.[19] However, it is

---

[17] For this solution, see J Hoffman and G Rosenkrantz, 'Omnipotence' in EN Zalta (ed), *The Stanford Encyclopedia of Philosophy*, Summer 2002 edn, available at http://plato.stanford.edu/archives/sum2002/entries/omnipotence/, and Rescher, above n 8, at 131–32. Hoffman and Rosenkrantz (*ibid*) provide further ideas for how this paradox may be resolved.

[18] I have chosen not to open the discussion of semantical paradoxes with a definition of truth and falsity because of the deep controversy that exists within philosophy with respect to the meaning of this notion. One can find within philosophy five major theories of truth: the Correspondence Theory; the Semantic Theory; the Deflationary (or Minimalist) Theory; the Coherence Theory, and the Pragmatic Theory. For a useful introduction to this debate, see B Dowden and N Schwartz 'Truth' in J Fieser and B Dowden (eds), *The Internet Encyclopedia of Philosophy* (2004), available at www.iep.utm.edu/t/truth.htm. Semantical paradoxes create a problem, though, for each of these theories. One initial assumption which I do make is that statements can be either true or false (the law of excluded middle).

[19] In the philosophical literature, one can find a distinction between the above version of the Liar Paradox and the one which uses the predicate 'not-true' (eg, '*This sentence is not-true*'), dubbed the 'strengthened liar.' Arguably, the previous formulation allows for a solution in which the liar sentence is declared neither true nor false. Reiger has put forward a convincing argument showing that the two formulations are not really different. The important thing, he notes, 'is not the difference between the simple and strengthened liars: it is the tendency for paradox to rear its ugly head the moment we have settled on any semantic category for a liar sentence,' see A Reiger, 'The Liar, the Strengthened Liar, and Bivalence' (2001) 54 *Erkenntnis* 195 at 196.

possible to construct similar paradoxes (similar in the sense that they involve the notions of *truth*, *falsity* and *reference*) which are hetero-referential rather than self-referential. Consider the following set of sentences (following Gyula Klima, I will call them the *'reciprocal liar'*)[20]:

Dworkin: 'What Raz is saying is true'
Raz: 'What Dworkin is saying is false'

Suppose, first, that what Dworkin is saying is true. It follows, then, that what Raz is saying is true as well. But if this is so, then Dworkin's statement is false, which contradicts our initial premise. Consider then a different starting point, which assumes that Dworkin's statement is false. Hence, what Raz is saying is false. What Raz proclaims, that is, that Dworkin's statement is false, is thus not true. So, Dworkin's statement is true, again contradicting our initial assumption.[21]

A common feature of both of these versions of the Liar Paradox is their *semantic instability*: their perpetual oscillation between truth and falsity. Thus, Hans Herzberger, one of the great paradoxifiers of the twentieth century, notes that, in thinking about the Liar Paradox:

> one is constantly led through some kind of reversal of perspective which might be compared with the experience of visual ambiguity. Is it a duck; or is

[20] See G Klima, 'Consequences of a Closed, Token-Based Semantics: The Case of John Buridan' (2004) 25 *History and Philosophy of Logic* 95 at 101.

[21] One can construct a liar-like paradox which is non-circular. A prominent example is the following paradox, first suggested by Stephen Yablo. Consider the following infinite sequence of sentences:

S_1 For all $k > 1$, S_k is not true
S_2 For all $k > 2$, S_k is not true

. . .

S_i For all $k > i$, S_k is not true
S_{i+1} For all $k > i+1$, S_k is not true

. . .

S_n For all $k > n$, S_k is not true

The above sequence, as was demonstrated by Stephen Yablo, is paradoxical. Consider the first sentence in the sequence, S_1. Suppose S_1 is true. It then follows that *all* the subsequent sentences are not true and so, in particular, is S_2. However, if for all $k > 1$, S_k is not true, it also follows that, for all $k > 2$, S_k is not true. But this means that S_2 is true. We thus reach a contradiction. Given the contradiction, one is tempted to conclude that our opening sentence S_1 is not true after all, which means that there is at least one true sentence in the sequence. Let the first such sentence be S_i. Given that S_i is true, it follows that, for all $k > i$, S_k is not true and, in particular, is S_{i+1}. However, if for all $k > i$, S_k is not true, it also follows that, for all $k > i+1$, S_k is not true. But this means that S_{i+1} is true, which contradicts our earlier conclusion that S_{i+1} is not true. What is interesting in the Yablo sequence is that it generates a paradox, although, at least on the face of it, it is not circular (no sentence refers either to itself or to the preceding sentences). S Yablo, 'Paradox without Self-Reference' (1993) 53 *Analysis* 251.

it a rabbit? Is it a white cross on a black background; or a black cross on a white background? It seems to switch back and forth, almost with a will of its own.[22]

What about truth-telling sentences—are these sentences paradoxical as well? Consider the following examples:

K_1 'This sentence is true'

The structure of this sentence can be used to produce a truth-telling sequence, which consists of an endless series of sentences of the following form (with each sentence belonging to the domain of its predecessor)[23]:

S_n 'S_{n+1} is true'

Initially, one may take these truth-telling sentences as unproblematic. One can simply consider them true and forget about it. Indeed, these sentences do not generate the kind of semantic instability characterising liar-like sentences. However, under close reflection this conclusion seems hasty. In both cases, the sentences involved can be assigned, consistently, with conflicting true/false values. This makes them hopelessly undetermined. The distinction between the Liar Paradox and the Truth-Teller paradox is thus:

> In the standard liar paradox, the problem is that there is no consistent assignment of truth-values. In the truth-teller paradox, the problem is that there are too many consistent assignments. An assignment must involve an arbitrary choice as to which truth-value should be assigned.[24]

As Herzberger notes, these sentences are 'semantically pathological in having their content somehow left undetermined.'[25]

One thing which is common to these different semantic paradoxes is their *groundlessness*.[26] This reflects the intuition that the 'truth of a sentence must be grounded in something outside the sentence itself.'[27] The paradoxicality of the liar and truth-telling sentences can be explained either in the fact that they include themselves in their *domain* (domain being what a sentence is *about*)—as in the simple liar and the simple truth-teller—or

---

[22] H Herzberger, 'Naive Semantics and the Liar Paradox' (1982) 79 *Journal of Philosophy* 479 at 482.

[23] This example is taken from H Herzberger, 'Paradoxes of Grounding in Semantics' (1970) 67 *Journal of Philosophy* 145 at 150.

[24] R Sorensen, *Vagueness and Contradiction* (Oxford, Clarendon Press, 2001) 167.

[25] Herzberger, above n 23, at 150.

[26] *Ibid*, at 148.

[27] Sainsbury, above n 9, at 114. Herzberger offers the following definition of grounding: sentence S is groundless when 'S is the first member of some infinite sequence of sentences, each of which belongs to the domain of its predecessor'. This definition appears at the Erratum to his 1970 article, above n 23, published at (1970) 67 *Journal of Philosophy* 317.

because they form an infinite or circular sequence of 'aboutness' which does not terminate—as in the reciprocal liar and the truth-telling sequence.[28]

What is intriguing in semantical paradoxes is the fact that they use seemingly correct grammatical structures to generate deeply puzzling results.[29] The force of semantical paradoxes has motivated many philosophers to investigate these paradoxes, generating a huge body of literature.[30] A thorough discussion of this literature is beyond the scope of this chapter. Nevertheless, I would like to briefly discuss some of the attempts to resolve these paradoxes, because they could prove useful to the analysis of paradoxes in law.[31]

One of the more prominent approaches, which was first promulgated by Alfred Tarski, is based on replacing our everyday, singular understanding of truth by a multilevel linguistic framework. According to this construction, one is able to speak meaningfully about the truth of statements in one language (the 'object-language') *only* in a language that is located higher on the linguistic hierarchy and whose expressive capacities are essentially richer (the 'meta-language').[32] Tarski's framework thus assumes the existence of multiple truth predicates, hierarchically arranged, and expressed only in a language 'higher' than the language in which the referent of 'true' is expressed. The main problem with Tarski's hierarchical conception of truth is that it does not seem consistent with our basic intuitions regarding the use of natural language.

Another approach takes as given the non-hierarchical character of natural language. It proposes to resolve the riddle of the liar and its various cousins by arguing that groundless sentences are intrinsically ill-formed, and should be excluded from the realm of statements—statement being understood as a sentence that is used to *say* something true or false.[33] Groundless sentences, it is argued, while grammatically correct, fail to make any statement (or claim); they are, in other words, 'truth-incompetent.' And since these

---

[28] Herzberger, above n 23, at 147.
[29] They were thus interpreted by some as a sign of the intrinsic inconsistency of natural language, see eg, J Bromand, 'Why Paraconsistent Logic Can Only Tell Half the Truth' (2002) 111 *Mind* 748.
[30] Most of the literature considers the emantical paradoxes together with set-theoretical paradoxes (eg, Russell's Paradox), see eg, L Goldstein, 'A Unified Solution to Some Paradoxes' (1999) 100 *Proceedings of the Aristotelian Society* 53 and Herzberger, above n 23. I have chosen to focus on semantical paradoxes because they can be more naturally linked to the realm of law.
[31] For a general discussion, see eg, Sainsbury, above n 9 and Rescher, above n 8. An important solution strategy which I will not discuss is based on rejecting (some) of the assumptions of classical logic (eg, the law of excluded middle). For this approach, see eg, G Priest, 'What is So Bad about Contradictions' (1998) 95 *Journal of Philosophy* 410.
[32] A Tarski, 'The Semantic Conception of Truth and the Foundations of Semantics' (1944) 3 *Philosophy and Phenomenological Research* 341 at 350–51.
[33] Statement, following Goldstein, is understood as 'a truth-bearer, a *used* sentence—"used" not in the sense just of being uttered out loud (a pheme) or written down (a grapheme) but in the sense of being used to *say* something true or false': Goldstein, above n 30, at 54.

sentences are truth-incompetent, it makes no sense to ask whether they are true or false.[34] Laurence Goldstein argues that the reason why liar-like sentences generate such awe and confusion is not because of any deep logical problematic, but rather because of certain deep-seated beliefs and preconceptions which characterise human thought. Underlying the semantical paradoxes is our naïve intuition that 'the paradoxical sentences because they are not ungrammatical, vague or sortally suspect and encompass no false presuppositions, must yield statements when used.'[35] The analysis of these paradoxes thus seems to belong more to the realm of psychology than to the realm of logic.

The foregoing approaches introduce, in effect, though for different reasons, a general ban on self-reference and other forms of groundlessness. This ban may seem too strict and incongruent with our intuitions regarding the use of language. One alternative approach which seeks to give theoretical structure to our naïve intuitions is the model of naïve semantics, articulated by Hans Herzberger in an article from 1982. The essence of this approach is the following:

> In naive semantics, paradoxes are allowed to arise freely and to work their own way out. No semantic defences are to be set up against them. ... No effort will be made to eliminate the paradoxes, to suppress them, or in any way to interfere and take deliberate action against them. They are to unfold according to their own inner principles. In its early stages naive semantics may appear somewhat haphazard and even chaotic. Gradually some islands of stability will emerge and grow until eventually everything has resettled into a new but orderly arrangement.[36]

Instead of trying to break or suppress the semantic instability associated with semantical paradoxes—their oscillation between true and false—naive semantics calls us to embrace it. This can be achieved by exposing the pattern through which paradoxical statements change their value at different stages of evaluation.[37] Naïve semantics thus rejects any attempt to classify liar-like sentences as neither true nor false or both true and false. Their fundamental semantic character is neither a truth value nor the absence of a

---

[34] Goldstein, *ibid*, at 58.

[35] *Ibid*, at 69.

[36] Herzberger, above n 22, at 482.

[37] This valuation technique consists of two phases: 'Each statement undergoes two phases of evaluation, either of which can be trivially simple or, within fixed bounds, extremely complicated. Each statement can be assigned two characteristic ordinal numbers: a *stabilization point* and a *fundamental periodicity*. The stabilization point for a statement marks the earliest stage at which its valuations become periodic, and its periodicity marks the length of its valuational cycle', Herzberger, *ibid*, at 492. Thus, for example, the reciprocal liar that was discussed above (the Dworkin-Raz dialogue) is cyclic with periodicity 4. Starting with the assumption that Dworkin's statement is true leads you to conclude that Raz's statement is true, next that Dworkin's statement is in fact false, Raz's statement is false, returning to the original evaluation that Dworkin's statement is true. So if we attribute the values (1, 0) to (true, false) we get the following cyclical pattern: 11001100...

truth value, but a *valuational pattern*, which has certain regularities which can be established upon inspection. The diagnosis of liar-like paradoxes in naïve semantics can thus account for our feeling that natural language is inconsistent, and it can do so without any actual contradictions. By demonstrating that paradoxical sentences follow certain regularities, naïve semantics shows 'how a language could contain paradoxical statements and nevertheless have a systematic and coherent semantic structure.'[38]

II. LEGAL PARADOXES

The foregoing discussion was just a prologue to our main concern: the riddle of legal paradoxicality. Resolving this riddle requires one to make a clear distinction between legal paradoxes and logical and semantical paradoxes; it is through the elaboration of this difference that one can develop a conception of legal paradoxicality. In articulating this difference, it is necessary to clarify what exactly is the subject of the discourse of legal paradoxicality. There is, on this point, a certain amount of confusion in the legal literature. I will argue that the notion of paradox—in its philosophical and logical connotations—*does not apply to law as such*. This has to do with the fact that paradoxes are properties of sentences.[39] Because social systems, such as law, are not reducible to sentences (eg, norms), they cannot be, strictly speaking, 'paradoxical' (although they can be self-referential, self-organising or self-producing, as I will argue below).[40]

This claim raises two important questions. First, what is the referent of arguments about legal paradoxes—how are we to understand such arguments? Secondly, how do these arguments fit or relate to our understanding of law as a social phenomenon? This question requires one to relate the phenomenon of legal paradoxes to a general model of law as a societal, dynamic system, and to particular problems that occur at the border between law and society.

---

[38] Herzberger, *ibid*, at 497.

[39] I use the term 'sentence' to denote a string of words satisfying the grammatical rules of a language (see the WordNet 2.0 dictionary, available at http://wordnet.princeton.edu). This broad definition includes sentences in the form of both statements and norms. Statements (or claims), unlike norms, are truth-bearers; they can be true or false, see Goldstein, above n 30, at 54.

[40] One of the key lessons of the social analysis of law is the understanding that the essence of law cannot be captured by simply enumerating its normative content. This point has been forcefully made by Gunther Teubner and Niklas Luhmann. Describing the law as a system of rules or a system of symbols, Teubner argues, provides no answer to the dynamic property of law, to its self-regulatory capacity: 'For how are norms to produce norms or symbols to generate symbols? We can only conceive of the law producing itself if we understand it no longer as a mere system of rules but as a system of actions', G Teubner, *Law as an Autopoietic System* (Oxford, Blackwell, 1997) 18. See, further, on that point, N Luhmann, *Law as a Social System* (Oxford, Oxford University Press, 2004) 98–105, 177 and N MacCormick, 'Norms, Institutions, and Institutional Facts' (1998) 17 *Law and Philosophy* 301 at 330–31.

How, then, should we understand arguments about legal paradoxes? The first step in understanding such arguments is to identify their *proper referent*. I think that the most suitable candidate for that role is what I will call a *legal set*: a sequence of sentences which invoke, explicitly or implicitly, the legal code (the distinction between legal and illegal). A legal set may include three major types of sentences: *norms*, statements about norms (*norm-propositions*), or statements about the entire legal system (*meta-propositions*).[41] There could thus be various ways in which a legal set can be formed. One way is to extract a segment from the law's printed history (understood as the entire genealogy of rules and case law pertaining to a certain jurisdiction). But one can also form a legal set by using second-order observations of the law, for example, by giving an account of a certain theory of law.[42] A paradox arises whenever a legal set, or a portion of it, gives rise to contradiction, and when this self-contradiction is supported by apparently good reasons.[43]

Given the foregoing account, two factors emerge as unique to the phenomenon of legal paradoxes. The first concerns the structure of the legal set associated with them; the second concerns the place of legal paradoxes in the social reality of law. Legal paradoxes are distinctive, first, because of the unique composition of the legal set. Because legal sets may include both *norms* and *non-normative* statements, their contradictory form is *not* limited to conflicting attributions of truth and falsity. This is because norms are usually thought to lack truth-value. As Henrik von Wright puts it:

> Norms *as prescriptions* of human conduct ... may be pronounced (un)reasonable, (un)just, or (in)valid when judged by some standards which are themselves normative—but not true or false.[44]

What does it mean, then, for a legal set to be contradictory? I do not intend to provide here a formal account of the way in which legal-oriented sentences can relate to, or contradict, each other;[45] for my purposes, it will suffice to

---

[41] This typology also covers, I believe, targeted commands, legal rulings and legal arguments. However, if one disagrees with my interpretation, these other types can be added to the foregoing list.

[42] Theorising in law reflects either an attempt to study 'how far principles, notions, and rules for decision-making can be generalized' (Luhmann, above n 40, at 54–55) or a meta-attempt to expose the nature and general structure of the law—eg, as a social system. Legal theorising can be exercised either at the level of first-order observation (when it forms part of a decision-making process), or at the level of second-order observation (eg, as part of an academic argument). For more on the role and nature of legal theories, see DE Van Zandt, 'The Relevance of Social Theory to Legal Theory' (1989) 83 *Northwestern University Law Review* 10.

[43] As will be clarified below, I understand this definition to also include cases involving a 'truth-teller'—like problematic.

[44] GH von Wright, 'Is There a Logic of Norms' (1991) 4 *Ratio Juris* 265 at 266.

[45] This will require me to enter into the murky waters of deontic logic (see eg, von Wright, *ibid*), which is not really necessary for the arguments presented here.

give an intuitive account of what is unique in legal inconsistency, and provide a few paradigmatic examples. A legal set may be inconsistent, first, when it can be shown to contain contradictory norms. Norms or rules can be contradictory, for example, when one rule permits what another forbids, when two rules issue contradictory directives (which cannot be simultaneously complied with).[46] Another form of inconsistency, which is unique to law, arises when one can show that a legal set is inflicted by contradictory assignments of validity. Indeed, as I will argue below, the notion of validity plays a unique role within the law, something akin to the notion of truth in logic. A further form of inconsistency arises when one can find within a legal set conflicting interpretations of the same legal concept. Note, however, that since legal sets may also include 'normal' propositions, and may invoke classical reasoning patterns,[47] they can also be contradictory in the sense in which this notion is used in propositional logic (ie, through inconsistent attributions of truth and falsity).

The second distinctive feature of legal paradoxes concerns their role in the systemic structure of law. The paradoxes of law can be viewed as sentential reflections of its unique systemic structure: of its self-organising and self-producing features. A self-organizing system is a system that not only regulates or adapts its behaviour, but creates its own organisation. Another feature of self-organising systems is their capacity to maintain their internal order in spite of continuous environmental perturbations. Self-production (or *autopoiesis*) denotes the process by which a system recursively produces its own network of components (in the case of law: communication), thus continuously regenerating its essential organisation in the face of external perturbations and internal erosion.[48] Self-organising and self-producing systems are intrinsically circular and self-referential.[49]

In studying legal paradoxes, it is not enough, therefore, to identify the legal set underlying them and to expose its contradictory form. One has to explicate also the relation between these paradoxes and the systemic structure giving rise to them. This change in our mode of observation brings to the fore a whole range of new practical and theoretical questions, which arise when one studies the structure of autonomous systems. How does the law achieve stability and avoid destructive loops or operational paralysis?

---

[46] See von Wright, *ibid*, at 270–71. This form of inconsistency could give rise to conflicting normative expectations.
[47] Even if this is done only implicitly and non-exclusively.
[48] See F Heylighen, 'The Science of Self-organization and Adaptivity' in *The Encyclopedia of Life Support Systems* (EOLSS Publishers, 2001), available at www.eolss.net and F Heylighen and C Joslyn, 'Cybernetics and Second Order Cybernetics', in RA Meyers (ed), *Encyclopedia of Physical Science and Technology*, 3rd ed (New York, Academic Press, 2001) vol 4, 155–70.
[49] In mathematical terms these forms of circularity can be modelled by an equation representing how some phenomenon or variable y is mapped onto itself by a transformation or process f: $y = f(y)$. To make sense of this equation one needs to explicate what y and f stand for. For a more detailed analysis, see Heylighen and Joslyn, *ibid*, at section III(A).

How does the law, as a closed, self-referential system, respond to signals and pressures from its environment? How can an observer decode the complex non-linear dynamics which characterise self-organising systems (generated by intricate circular and feedback processes)?

Understanding the systemic facet of legal paradoxes requires, I will argue, a change in our mode of inquiry. The philosophical and logical study of paradoxes has been guided by the idea that paradoxes represent a certain malady of thought which should somehow be eliminated, prevented or resolved. Thus, Alfred Tarski has noted in one of his papers: 'The appearance of an antinomy is for me a symptom of disease.'[50] One of the main goals of logic is to free us from this disease, as Nicholas Rescher observes: the 'prime directive of rationality is to restore consistency in such situations.'[51] This approach has been adopted by some legal scholars who have studied the occurrence of paradoxes in law. Thus, for example, George Fletcher, in his article on 'Paradoxes in Legal Thought,' notes:

> This Article commits itself to logical consistency as the indispensable foundation for effective dialogue and coherent criticism. Only if we accept consistency as an overriding legal value will we be troubled by the paradoxes and antinomies that lie latent in our undeveloped systems of legal thought. Grappling with uncovered paradoxes and antinomies will impel us toward consistent theoretical structures. None of this, I submit, requires us to suppress our sensitivities to policies, principles, or other questions of value.[52]

However, recognising that the paradoxes of law—at least in some cases—are reflections of its unique systemic structure indicates that this purifying approach does not provide a suitable guide for the study of legal paradoxicality.[53] One cannot purify the law from these paradoxes, because they reflect vital steering and stabilising mechanisms, without which the law would not have been able to counteract external pressures.[54] The challenge for the legal paradoxologist is to decode the operational role of the various

---

[50] A Tarski, 'Truth and Proof' (1969) 220 *Scientific American* (June) 63 at 66.

[51] Rescher, above n 8, at 9; see also Chihara, above n 9, at 590–91.

[52] GP Fletcher, 'Paradoxes in Legal Thought' (1985) 85 *Columbia Law Review* 1263 at 1264–65.

[53] The notion of purification is invoked, for example, by Nicholas Rescher, see Rescher, above n 8, at 31. Rescher himself provides some support for the foregoing thesis in his distinction between the practical and theoretical contexts. In practical contexts, Rescher argues, 'there is a possibility of compromise—of affecting a division that enables us in some way and to some extent "to have it both ways", say, to proceed A-wise on even days and B-wise on odd ones. But we cannot rationally do this with beliefs. In theoretical contexts we must choose—must resolve the issue one way or another,' Rescher, above n 8, at 11.

[54] It is simply wrong, therefore, to view consistency, as Fletcher does, 'as an overriding legal value' (although the appearance of consistency—concealing the paradox—could have instrumental value).

paradoxes of law. The static perspective which characterises the study of paradoxes in logic is not suited for that task because it is not sensitive to the social dynamics underlying the paradoxes of law. (A notable exception is naïve semantics, which emphasises as we saw the dynamic aspect of semantical paradoxes.) Resolving the riddle of legal paradoxicality thus requires extra-logical tools: from systems theory to sociology, history and economics.[55]

In exploring this riddle, we have distinguished between *generic paradoxes* and *local paradoxes*. Generic paradoxes reflect practices which are constitutive of law, forming part of its fundamental structure. The paradoxes of validity and of the authority and the foundation of law discussed below are examples of generic paradoxes. One cannot understand the idea of law as a distinct social system without understanding these paradoxes and the social processes associated with them. Local paradoxes operate on a more limited scale, and usually emerge in response to some concrete socio-legal dilemma.

The foregoing argument should not be taken to mean, however, that legal paradoxes are necessarily 'positive' in terms of their internal operational contribution or social or moral value. By exposing and decoding certain paradoxes, one may expose a flaw in some entrenched legal doctrine or pattern of reasoning. This exposure can lead to advancement in legal theory and practice, through the development of alternative distinctions and new theories (or by rejecting unfruitful legal theories).[56] I will give an example of such a paradox below (where I explore the 'law and economic' theory of tort law). This type of paradoxical argument is invoked by Eric Talley and Yitzhak Benbaji in their contributions to this book.

To conclude this section, I want to consider some prominent examples of legal paradoxes. My primary goal in this section is to lay bare the structure of these paradoxes, and to highlight their relation to logical and semantical paradoxes. I will say relatively less about the linkage between these paradoxes and the systemic structure of the law; this second question will generally be left to the book's various chapters.

The Mark of Validity

One thing which is common to lawyers and philosophers is the search for grounding. This is especially visible with respect to the notion of validity.

---

[55] Probably the most sophisticated attempts so far to develop a systemic theory of law, which relies on these sources, can be found in the writings of Niklas Luhmann and Gunther Teubner. See, in particular, Luhmann, above n 40, and Teubner, above n 40. This book can be seen as another effort to integrate the notion of paradox into a broad, socially oriented conceptualisation of law. For a non-legal study of self-organisation see the papers by Heylighen, above n 48.

[56] The invocation of new distinctions appears as an instrument for resolving paradoxes in philosophy and law, see Rescher, above n 8, and Fletcher, above n 52, at 1269.

Validity, as it is used in legal discourse, is a property of rules (or norms) and rules only. It distinguishes between the law (rules) in force and that which is not law. In other words: 'Law which is not valid is not law.'[57] Determining the validity of norms is thus of critical importance; it is essential to the formation of normative expectations and is also a critical component of legal decision-making. But validity is not only a mark unique to law; it can only be endowed and transferred *according* to law. The concept of validity thus holds an inevitable circularity: validity can only be determined recursively, that is, by reference to valid law.[58]

The closest parallel to this legal problematic in the philosophical literature is the 'Truth-Teller' Paradox (which belongs to the family of *semantical* paradoxes).[59] Because norms cannot be evaluated through the logical prism of truth and falsity, the concept of validity can operate as a plausible alternative.[60] Consider, for example, the following set of rules:

Rule 1.1: This rule, and all the rules enumerated below, are valid.
Rule 2.1. ...
Rule 2.2 ...
Rule 2.3. ...
...
Rule 2.n. ...

This sequence of rules can have (at least) two consistent assignments of validity values. The first, in which both Rule 1.1 ('meta-rule') and all the other rules ('secondary rules') are valid, and another one, in which both the

---

[57] See Luhmann, above n 40, at 125.

[58] See Luhmann, *ibid*, at 128.

[59] While validity resembles in some aspects the notion of truth, it does not generate the same kind of paradoxes. Thus, for example, the notion of validity does not yield a paradox parallel to the liar. Consider the following example: imagine that you open the Civil Code which is in force in your country. At p 100 of the Code, you find rule 499 which states: '499. This rule is not valid.' What is the meaning of this sentence? Consider, first, the option that rule 499 is valid, that is, it represents the law in force. (This is a plausible assumption; after all, we did find this sentence in the Code.) If it is valid, then what it says is valid as well, and since it says about itself that it is not valid, this must be valid as well. Contradiction. Assume, alternatively, that rule 499 is not valid. Then, what it says about itself is indeed the case, and no contradiction arises. (Strictly speaking, if a rule is not valid, what it says is legally irrelevant.) Unlike the Liar Paradox, there is a simple way out here, which requires us to assume that rule 499 is not valid. This leaves us with the riddle of how and why this sentence was incorporated into the Code in the first place.

[60] See, on that also, V Svoboda, 'Forms of Norms and Validity' (2003) 80 *Poznan Studies in the Philosophy of the Sciences and the Humanities* 223 at 229. As in classical logic, I assume bivalence, ie, a binary distinction between valid/not-valid. However, this assumption can be relaxed; it is possible to imagine, for example, a fuzzy interpretation of validity. This may change the analysis of the paradoxes discussed in this section.

meta-rule and all the secondary rules are not valid.[61] Recall that the Truth-Teller Paradox, which was discussed in section I, generates a similar problem of multiple (consistent) assignments of truth and falsity. The foregoing paradox reflects one of the deepest dilemmas of modern law: on the one hand, we feel uncomfortable with the thought that the law validates or legitimises itself; on the other hand, this is exactly what is expected from the law according to the modern conception of validity—that is, that validity can only be endowed *according* to law. The assumption that the criteria and authority for determining the validity of norms must be instituted through valid law thus generates a vicious circularity, which seems to be logically irresolvable.

At this point, it might make sense to turn to philosophy. Maybe we can get some inspiration from the various strategies invoked by philosophers to resolve the puzzle of semantical paradoxes. Consider, first, Tarski's hierarchical conception of truth. To apply Tarski's proposal to law, one would have to assume a hierarchy of laws in which the validity of the lower-level normative layer could only be determined through the prism of a higher law. This hierarchical conceptualisation of validity is inconsistent, however, with our practical experience of law as a unitary system. Another possibility, drawing on the philosophical discussion of paradox of omnipotence, could be based on reformulating the concept of validation. But the plausibility of such a move is questionable, because it calls us, in effect, to imagine law as a system controlled from outside—as a heteronomous rather than autonomous system. This reconceptualisation conflicts, I will argue, with our intuitive perception of the law.

So perhaps we have no choice but to accept the inevitable circularity of the concept of validity. This circularity provides the law with far-reaching flexibility' giving it the power to create, legitimise and destroy normative structures in response to conflicting social pressures. Note, however, that this flexibility does not turn the law into a completely anarchic domain. Indeed, both naïve semantics and the science of self-organisation have shown us how order can emerge from ungrounded and spontaneous interactions.

Paradoxes of Authority and Foundation

One cannot think about validity without confronting the riddle of grounding. But this is not the only place in which one encounters this problematic. The

---

[61] The qualification 'at least' is necessary, because once we assume that the meta-rule is not valid, there can be multiple assignments of validity, which attribute different values to the secondary rules.

liberal concept of the constitutional state is similarly haunted by paradoxes of grounding. The liberal ethos seeks to subject the sovereign state (through its manifold institutional embodiments) to the law, and in this way to limit its powers. At the same time, however, the liberal vision of constitutionalism—because of the specific form it gives to the ideal of democracy—also conceptualises the state as the source of law.[62] These dual commitments turn liberal constitutionalism into a deeply paradoxical concept. To appreciate this problematic, one has to look more closely into the constituent elements of liberal constitutionalism. Consider first the idea of parliamentary supremacy. This idea remains relevant despite the liberal commitment to constitutional discipline, because most (if not all) constitutions include an amendment clause, which is taken to be legally supreme.[63]

As I will demonstrate below, the concept of parliamentary supremacy is inherently paradoxical; it generates the same problematic we encountered earlier in the discussion of the paradox of Omnipotence.[64] Consider the following set of propositions (which constitutes, in effect, a miniature constitutional theory). To simplify the presentation, the set depicts a legal regime without a constitution. However, a similar paradox can also be generated in the case of constitutional regimes by replacing the term 'NC Parliament' with 'Supreme Amendment Clause.'[65]

(1) Legal omnipotence means the power to enact new laws and to change existing laws, without any constraints.
(2) In non-constitutional regimes, the Parliament (henceforth 'NC Parliament') is conceived to be legally omnipotent in the foregoing sense.
(3) NC Parliament thus has the power to enact new laws and to change existing laws, without any constraints (from (1) and (2)).
(4) Being omnipotent, NC Parliament can restrict its legislative powers, for example, by enacting a constitution, which will lay out certain

---

[62] N Luhmann, *Political Theory in the Welfare State* (Berlin, de Gruyter, 1990) 187–201. For further discussion of the paradox of liberal constitutionalism see CP Manfredi, *Judicial Power and the Charter: Canada and the Paradox of Liberal Constitutionalism* (Oxford, Oxford University Press, 2001).

[63] For the idea of parliamentary sovereignty, see eg, J Goldsworthy, 'Homogenising Constitutions' (2003) 23 *Oxford Journal of Legal Studies* 483, and D Chalmers, 'The Application of Community Law in the United Kingdom, 1994–1998' (2000) 37 *Common Market Law Review* 83 at 85–94. For a judicial discussion of the paradox of parliamentary sovereignty, see eg, the decision of Judge Heshin of the Israeli Supreme Court in Case 6821/93 *Bank Hamizrachi v Migdal* (9 November 1995).

[64] In terms of the analytical distinctions introduced in section I, the paradoxes of liberal constitutionalism belong to the category of paradoxes of coherence.

[65] See Suber, above n 12. This set consists of statements about law; it can be reformulated to also include rule-like sentences.

restrictions on the capacity of the Parliament to use its legislative powers (from (3)).
(5) A constrained Parliament, even when the constraints are due to its own prior decisions, is not omnipotent (from (2)).
(6) NC Parliament is not omnipotent—contrary to (2) (from (4) and (5)).

The above formulation, by assuming that the Parliament (or, alternatively, the rule which institutes the Parliament and determines its authority) is legally omnipotent, replicates, in effect, the theological paradox of Omnipotence. One way in which the resulting paradox can be resolved is to abandon the assumption that Parliaments (or constitutional amendment clauses) are legally omnipotent. This commits us to the view that in exercising their legislative powers, parliaments are subject to some irrevocable limitations. This solution is incompatible, however, with the framework of liberal constitutionalism; one has to deal, therefore, with the logical improbability of this model.[66]

The intrinsic paradoxicality of liberal constitutionalism can also be demonstrated by exploring the role of the other type of legal authority it presupposes: the judicial system. Consider the following argument (the paradox of *interpretative authority*):

(1) Courts have the exclusive authority to decide on the validity and determine the meaning of decisions of legal authorities such as acts of parliament, secondary legislation and judicial rulings—call this authority '*interpretative authority*' (this authority is instituted by a legal act, eg, a constitution).
(2) The courts' interpretative authority is exercised whenever courts have to decide on a dispute which is brought before them.
(3) The courts' interpretative authority is constrained through certain *disciplining rules*, usually included in the same legal act through which this authority was instituted (eg, in the constitution).
(4) When there is doubt in the application of their interpretative authority, courts must refer to the disciplining rules (this requirement being part of the disciplining rules).
(5) Rules cannot determine their own correct application; hence, in referring to the disciplining rules, courts have to exercise their interpretative authority (that is, to decide on the validity and meaning of these rules).
(6) In so doing, courts can, in effect, change the content of the disciplining rules—contrary to (3).

There are various ways in which this paradox can be logically resolved (eg, abandoning or reinterpreting claims (3) or (5)). It is doubtful, however,

---

[66] As Peter Suber notes, 'There is no contradiction in assuming that such irrevocable limitations exist; there is only the difficulty of turning to legal history and finding them,' *ibid*.

whether these logico-inspired responses are consistent with the modern experience of law.[67]

The paradox of authority (much like the paradox of validity) questions the *groundedness* of law. It reflects the fact that the rules, which *govern* the way in which laws are produced, interpreted and applied, include themselves in their domain of application. Thus, the rule which institutes the Parliament and determines its authority can be invoked to change itself, and the rules, which determine and purport to limit the courts' interpretative authority, allow the courts, in effect, to redraw the boundaries of their own authority. Logic, with its purifying obsession, does not seem to offer a convincing solution to these two paradoxes. As far as I can see, the only other option is simply for us to accept them as inevitable reflections of the institutional structure of law. They are genealogical remnants of the institutional mechanisms and internal dynamics, through which modern law counteracts external disturbances and maintains its structural integrity.

Some Local Paradoxes: the 'Learned Hand' Paradox

The foregoing paradoxes form part of the very essence of law. However, paradoxes also occur in more restricted fields of law. The challenge here is similar: first, to decode their structure; secondly, to understand how these paradoxes fit into a systemic understanding of law. However, whereas in the case of the constitutional paradoxes discussed above, the strategy of 'purification' seems unfitting, it may have more value in the case of 'local' paradoxes. Decoding these paradoxes may expose fallacies in our current doctrinal conceptualisations and force us to elaborate new distinctions and to develop new theories, all of which can influence the way in which law is practised (from maintaining a practice which was thought to be illogical to the development of new practices). The book's second part discusses some examples of such paradoxes. I want to consider one example, which focuses on the economic analysis of law.

One of the fields most influenced by the thinking and methods of the 'law and economic' school is tort law. Indeed, Guido Calabresi's famous book, The Costs of Accidents: A Legal and Economic Analysis,[68] whose publication is seen as a key event in the history of the 'law and economic' school, is dedicated to the study of tort law. According to the law and economic

---

[67] Neil MacCormick provides a similar formulation for this paradox: 'The norms at the highest level exhibit a notorious self-referential character—the court holds power by the constitution, but the court has power to interpret the constitution and thereby determine what its own constitutional power is, and so on,' MacCormick, above n 40, at 330. See also, Manfredi, above n 62, at 22.

[68] G Calabresi, *The Costs of Accidents: A Legal and Economic Analysis* (New Haven, Yale University Press, 1970).

school, the principal aim of tort law 'is to minimise the social costs of a tort defined as the sum of total accident costs, administration costs, costs of properly allocating accident losses by means of insurance, and accident prevention costs of both the injurer and the victim.'[69] The basic dilemma of tort law is formulated, then, as a problem of optimisation. The challenge of the tort system thus seems to lie in devising a system of incentives adequate to induce individuals and firms (in their roles as injurers and victims) to choose optimal levels of care and activity.[70] Responding to this challenge requires the law to develop both adequate liability rules and efficient enforcement mechanisms.

One of the most important doctrinal contributions of the economic analysis of tort law is the account it provides for the concept of fault. This account is based, as will be elaborated below, on the idea of optimisation. The economic analysis of negligence is encapsulated in the famous Learned Hand Formula. According to this formula, an injurer is liable if she has neglected to exercise or purchase an additional unit of care even though her marginal cost of taking this additional unit was less than the marginal benefit to the victim (and possibly herself), represented by a reduction in the total amount of expected damages.[71] The Learned Hand Formula thus sets the level of reasonable care at the socially optimal level of care.[72] Note, however, that the concrete standard of care, relevant to a particular accident-situation, is (usually) *not* announced to the parties before the event—that is, it is not available as a legal ruling or regulatory instruction. Rather, it is assumed that the court will employ the Learned Hand Formula in each tort case in order to determine a specific optimal behavioural standard which would fit the circumstances of the case. Anticipating that, the potential injurer, it is hypothesised, will adjust her behaviour and choose an optimal

---

[69] See HB Schafer and A Schonenberger, 'Strict Liability Versus Negligence' in B Bouckaert and G De Geest (eds), *Encyclopedia of Law and Economics, Vol II, Civil Law and Economics* (Cheltenham, Edward Elgar, 2000) 598. This view was first formulated by Guido Calabresi in his *Costs of Accidents* and has since served as the basis for the economic analysis of tort law.

[70] By 'optimal levels,' I refer to those levels that minimise the sum of total accident costs.

[71] This is how Judge Posner describes the Formula in one of his rulings: 'There are various ways in which courts formulate the negligence standard. The analytically (not necessarily the operationally) most precise is that it involves determining whether the burden of precaution is less than the magnitude of the accident, if it occurs, multiplied by the probability of occurrence. (The product of this multiplication, or "discounting", is what economists call an expected accident cost.) If the burden is less, the precaution should be taken. This is the famous "Hand Formula."' See *Dula McCarty, Plaintiff-Appellant v Pheasant Run, Inc, Defendant-Appellee*, 826 F.2d 1554 at 1556. The original formula of Judge Hand used total (rather than marginal) values, but it can easily be reinterpreted in terms of the marginal argument noted above. See *United States v Carroll Towing Co* 159 F.2d 169 (2d Cir 1947) at 173. For a more formal treatment, see Schafer and Schonenberger, above n 69, at 599.

[72] At least in some accident situations, such as unilateral accidents, where only the injurer can influence the probability and size of damages. See, for further details, Schafer and Schonenberger, above n 69, at 599.

level of care.[73] Whether the Learned Hand Formula will actually result in the socially optimal level of care being taken depends, therefore, on the ability of both the injurer and the court to solve the 'level of care' optimisation problem.

One has to assume, therefore, that both the potential injurers and the judges are perfect maximisers. This assumption seems somewhat far-reaching, so let us see what happens if we relax it a bit.[74] One way in which imperfection can be introduced into the picture is by modelling the decision-making process as a costly endeavour. Decisions can be depicted as '"produced" by a decision technology with two inputs, costly information-gathering and costly deliberation.'[75] The information which must be collected in this context covers, for example, data about possible 'accident-prevention' technologies and their cost, the cost of injury to the victim (under various scenarios involving different technologies) and the causal relationship (represented in probabilities) between different technological solutions and potential injuries. Deliberation costs refer to both the cost of constructing an economic model which will accurately reflect the causal structure of an accident situation, and to the cost of solving the resulting model for an optimal level of care.

Assuming that both injurers and judges face decision costs when attempting to solve the 'level of care' problem requires us to incorporate these costs into the basic optimisation dilemma. In other words, neither the sitting judge nor the injurer solves the 'level of care' problem directly (that is, with zero deliberation costs) to get the optimal level of care x^*. They also need to determine how much (costly) effort they want to invest in information-gathering and deliberation in order to find x^*. But this augmented decision problem

---

[73] This conclusion is based on the assumption that the injurer, as a self-interested person, will choose her level of precaution to minimise her private costs, and that this reasoning—under the model's assumptions—will lead to the adoption of a socially optimal level of care. Schafer and Schonenberger provide a succinct formulation of the argument: 'Would she [the injurer] therefore want to choose a precaution level above the level of due care? No, because any care taken in excess of the standard set by the court would be more costly without reducing the costs of compensation since due care is enough to be non-liable. Would she, on the other hand, want to choose a precaution level below due care? No, because now she is running the risk of bearing the total amount of the expected damages,' ibid, at 600–1. Note that if the injurer anticipates some 'noise' in the determination of the standard of care by the court, she may rationally decide to *raise* her precaution level above the optimal one in order to minimise the risk of being declared negligent, and consequently liable for the victim's total damages. This problem has brought various scholars to argue that the dominant negligence regime should be replaced by a regime of strict liability. Thanks to Adi Ayal for this point.

[74] The following discussion highlights one aspect of the bounded rationality of legal agents. For a more general discussion of this notion, which further develops Herbert Simon's pioneering work on this subject see eg, G Gigerenzer and PM Todd, 'Fast and Frugal Heuristics: The Adaptive Toolbox' in G Gigerenzer and PM Todd, *Simple Heuristics that Make us Smart* (New York, Oxford University Press, 2000).

[75] See J Conlisk, 'Why Bounded Rationality' (1996) 34 *Journal of Economic Literature* 669 at 690.

requires in itself some non-trivial (hence, costly) deliberation and possibly information collection, generating a new problem (producing, presumably, a *different value* for x*), and so on ad infinitum. The resulting augmented problem, which incorporates the costs of 'deciding how to decide', leads therefore to an infinite regress.[76]

What are the implications of this seemingly inevitable regress? Some authors, such as Conlisk, believe that the regress problem blocks any effort to explain human behaviour through optimisation-based models. Conlisk is sceptical of the possibility to 'formulate an optimization problem which takes full account of the cost of its own solution.'[77] Starting from the supposition that legal agents should be guided by the idea of optimisation—which underlies the Learned Hand Formula—one reaches, therefore, a seemingly irresolvable regress. In this case, however, one need not accept this paradox as an intrinsic property of law. The paradox may be resolved by simply rejecting the assumptions underlying it, that is, the idea that human agents make (or should make) decisions through optimisation. Indeed, this solution has been adopted by several economists. Conlisk, for example, concludes that 'We seemingly must yield to the idea that some behavioral hypothesis, other than optimization, such as learning or adaptation, is needed to escape the regress.'[78] Or, to quote another economist, 'At some point a decision must be taken on intuitive grounds.'[79] A different type of solution to the paradox of 'deciding how to decide' could be based on an argument showing that the regress problem it generates is not intractable, because, for example, it *converges* at some point. A convincing argument of this sort will have to show, first, that there is a credible mathematical solution to the regress, and secondly, that the revised model correctly describes the reasoning of legal agents (including injurers, victims and judges).

The paradox of 'deciding how to decide' exposes, I believe, a significant 'blind-spot' in the standard economic conception of 'fault'—which is also the version that has been incorporated into the law of tort.[80] It challenges the attempt to base legal rules and legal decision-making on standard optimisation techniques. But what kinds of lessons can one draw from this paradox?

---

[76] Conlisk, *ibid*, at 687. Philippe Mongin provides a different formulation to the regress problem: 'A conveniently general formulation is to say that to optimize requires one to run a costly algorithm, that to optimally select the latter requires one to run another costly algorithm, etc.,' P Mongin, 'Does Optimization Imply Rationality?' (2000) 124 *Synthese* 73 at 95–96.
[77] Conlisk, above n 75, at 687.
[78] Conlisk, *ibid*.
[79] Leif Johansen quoted in Conlisk, *ibid*.
[80] In the USA, the 'naïve' Learned Hand Formula has been incorporated into the formal law of torts, see the discussion in SG Gilles, 'The Invisible Hand Formula' (1994) 80 *Virginia Law Review* 1015 at 1015–16. For a concrete example, see the decision in the *Dula McCarty* case, above n 71.

Giving a complete answer to this question is clearly beyond the scope of this chapter. So I will make just some very brief observations. The regress puzzle puts in a different light the tendency of courts and judges to rely on intuitive reasoning and rules of thumb in the resolution of tort cases.[81] It demonstrates that this judicial practice is not groundless, and may be a reflection of a deep dissatisfaction with the Learned Hand Formula and the economic thinking underlying it. However, exposing the Learned Hand Formula as a hollow legal construct creates a lacuna in the doctrinal conceptualisation of the notion of fault. It is quite clear that, as citizens, we would not want judges and jurors to make decisions by relying solely on their uncontrolled intuition. In that respect, the paradox of 'deciding-how-to-decide' also provides us with constructive insights. It points out the importance of developing 'rules of thumb' or heuristics, which would make it possible for both injurers and judges to make decisions about fault without relying on problematic optimisation techniques or unbounded intuition.[82] This seems like a more profitable strategy than the current, empty practice of relying on the Hand Formula.

III. THE ORGANISATION OF THE BOOK

The structure of this book follows the foregoing distinction between generic and local paradoxes. The first part of the book is devoted to the study of generic paradoxes of law, the second to the study of local paradoxes. There is, though, a close connection between the two parts. Local paradoxes constitute, in some cases, a mirror image of the more fundamental paradoxes of law. The discussion of local paradoxes thus operates as another form of observing or explicating the generic category. This mirroring of the generic in the local is emphasised, in particular, in the contributions of Shai Lavi and Roei Amit.

Gunther Teubner and Rudolf Wiethölter

Why the fascination with legal paradox? Why is it so important to reveal paradoxes in law? This is the guiding question for Gunther Teubner and Rudolf Wiethölter in their two essays which are complementary to each

---

[81] This tendency is noted, for example, by Judge Posner in his ruling in *Dula McCarty*, *ibid*, at 1557.

[82] Thus, for example, Korobkin and Ulen propose to rely on 'clinical practice guidelines' in judging the negligence of physicians, see RB Korobkin and TS Ulen, 'Law and Behavioral Science: Removing the Rationality Assumption from Law and Economics' (2000) 88 *California Law Review* 1051 at 1089–90. For a general discussion of how various heuristics can be used to improve decision-making challenges, see Gigerenzer and Todd, above n 74.

other. One answer is: revealing paradoxes is a powerful instrument of legal critique. Disclosing the ambivalences, uncertainties and paradoxes of law by formal logical operations and genealogical investigations reveals how much modern law, in its highly developed rationality, is exposed to contradiction, inconsistency, chaos and paralysis. Yet, they argue, there is a second answer. Ultimately, what creates the fascination is not the undeniable critical and destructive potential, but the productive possibilities of paradoxes in law.

For Teubner and Wiethölter, paradoxes arising from self-reference are not an end point, but the starting point for further development of the law. Not only do worlds of meaning necessarily bring out paradoxes, but paradoxes bring out new worlds of meaning. Paradoxes are not logical errors that have to be extirpated, but ubiquitous aspects in the relation between *social structures* and *legal semantics*. Teubner and Wiethölter even go so far as to suggest that paradoxes—no longer social contradictions or clashes of rationality which the sociological tradition focuses upon—constitute the central dynamics of legal change. The interplay of deparadoxification—reparadoxification, the ebb and flow between paradox and difference, show an experimenting, incremental, exploratory production of legal orders that has to stumble over contingencies. Legal paradoxes are highly ambivalent. They contain destructive, paralysing potentials, but at the same time productive, creative possibilities. The alternative is open: paralysis, or *provocation of structural innovations*?

According to Teubner and Wiethölter, this pushes the question of how to deal with paradoxes into the foreground. What insights into the dynamics of legal deparadoxification are supplied by the major strands in contemporary legal theory—critical legal theory, systems theory and legal deconstructivism? Systems theory reveals the historical rhythm of continually repeated destruction and reconstruction in legal semantics: paradoxifications provoke the search for new socially adequate distinctions, which, in turn, under particular conditions, are thrown back onto their paradoxes again. The conditions that determine the recursive revelation and concealment of the legal paradox are two: pressure of social problems and communicative plausibility. Under the pressure of social problems, new differences, in turn deconstructable, are accepted by legal communication if they are plausible, ie, compatible within the net of other valid distinctions.

Yet Teubner and Wiethölter go beyond 'cool' systems analysis. They aim at a normative theory of legal paradoxes. Plausibilities are not simply to be noted but provocatively to be doubted. And the point is not dispassionate observation, but active commitment in enhancing social problem pressure. Derrida's famous formula, 'Deconstruction is justice,' brings together the features of a normative paradoxology. The revelation of legal paradoxes is anything but mere nihilistic disintegration that is looking for just some sort of non-foundationalism, a proof of the impossibility of founding the law. For all its effort at logical and doctrinal acuteness, it is not aimed at a merely analytical dissection or logical critique of law, at an academic, non-binding criticism of concepts, constructs, norms, justice. Rather, a normative paradoxology of law emphatically raises the claim to be looking for the rightness of law. It raises drastically the expectations of the quality of legal calculations—in the face of their paradoxes. Exposing the paradoxical character of legal decisions, Teubner and Wiethölter argue, does not mean suspending the claims concerning social justice but, on the contrary, it means taking the normative requirements of justice even more seriously.

Jean Clam

Jean Clam continues the discussion of the generic paradoxicality of law by considering its articulation in the writings of Niklas Luhmann and Jacques Derrida. Paradox, Clam argues, is not an ordinary legal object. Its reference is problematic because of its evanescence. It is quite difficult to stabilise the reference to the paradox without 'theologising' it: we must abridge its unabridgeable oscillation and speak of it as theologians speak of God. Clam tries to go back to a pretheological state of the paradox and to show how, at this level, law has originally to do with paradoxity. Law is nothing other than the empowering of certain primary distinctions which then function as meaning projections giving a stable sense to the world. The experience of the contingency of such distinctions is ultimately the experience of the paradoxity of law. Reviewing the positions of both Derridean deconstruction and Luhmannian systems theory on legal paradox, Clam stresses the fact that such an experience of paradoxity is missing in both of them. In effect, in neither of these discourses is the experience articulated as one of real perplexity and endured as such. They both merely refer to it as something they presuppose, but which they are neither able nor willing to deploy.

Nir Kedar

Nir Kedar offers a historical analysis of law's foundational paradoxicality. Kedar considers two so-called legal paradoxes: the 'paradox of law's self-reference' and the 'paradox of legal generality.' He demonstrates the historical process through which these 'paradoxes' were constructed as political *ideals*, drawn from the idea of the rule of law, as a solution to the bothering conundrum of legal authority. The main part of Kedar's chapter discusses legal self-reference, arguing that it emanates in fact from the modern requirement of human (or popular) sovereignty. Seen from within the legal system, modern law is a closed, self-referring system that creates, amends, interprets and justifies itself through itself. From this internal perspective, law is amendable or justifiable only under its own authority. Kedar tracks the origins of legal self-reference, showing that the roots of this insoluble are found in the quest of modern Europe to emancipate its political and legal authority from religion, and later also from any transcendent authority (including natural law), and to establish a closed, self-contained positive legal system that does not recognise any transcendent authority as legally binding. Kedar and Clam thus offer two different meditations on the puzzle of law's groundlessness.

Kedar then deals briefly with the 'paradox of legal generality,' claiming that this paradox stems from the modern requirement of equality. Law is supposed to be general (universal) and all-inclusive, in the sense that it should be defined in a universal way and be uniformly applied. However, the goal of full equality and all-inclusiveness can never be fulfilled: every universal law is also partial, and every 'all-inclusive' social order is also exclusive. The law cannot be genuinely general and all-inclusive, since it cannot justify in legal terms the extra-legal foundation of its own authority, that is, the boundaries between the legal and the non-legal. Even if paradoxical and unattainable, Kedar argues, we should esteem the human struggle to establish a more just and justifiable social (and legal) order, founded upon liberty, equality and fraternity.

Oren Perez

Oren Perez discusses a different type of generic paradox, one which, he argues, characterises law in modern pluralistic societies. The leading role of the law in the management of modern societies depends, Perez argues, on its being perceived as a fair arbiter. In pluralistic societies, this deep societal expectation presents the law with an irresolvable dilemma that reflects competing conceptions of fairness. First, the law is expected to be *consistent*. Consistency requires avoiding incongruity or contradiction amongst legal rules, legal concepts and legal practices. This requirement reflects the idea that incoherent law-making can be a source of real injustice. In pluralistic societies, however, fairness takes on an additional meaning; for the law to be conceived as fair, it is expected also to develop *'pluralistic sensitivities.'* This expectation reflects the social complexity of pluralistic societies. Pluralistic societies are torn by deep disagreements over questions of politics and morality; they are overburdened by conflicting definitions of the good or virtuous life (or society). The concept of pluralistic sensitivity requires the law to *respect* the cultural idiosyncrasies of the different communities and discourses comprising the society in which it operates.

These two visions of fairness, Perez argues, are incongruent. The discord between these two conceptions reflects the fact that the *law* does not have at its disposal some meta-principle, which can be invoked to resolve *any possible* social dilemma while satisfying the requirements of both coherence and pluralistic sensitivity. Particularistic sensitivity may thus, at least in some cases, require the law to follow an inconsistent path. The law is then faced with an irresolvable dilemma: for it to be considered a 'fair' arbiter, it must be *simultaneously consistent and inconsistent*. This dilemma is paradoxical or self-contradictory because it is driven by *internal and conflicting* prescriptions. How can the law sustain these conflicting demands or expectations without risking its status as fair arbiter? The law, Perez argues, has institutionalised the paradox, incorporating it into 'normal' legal practice. This institutionalisation was attained through the invocation of 'fluid' or 'vague' concepts and doctrines, such as equality, reasonableness and the principles governing the practice of constitutional balancing. The use of *vague concepts* has offered the law a way to keep the paradox at bay, signalling that it can maintain its coherence despite the intense pluralism of its environment. Perez then goes on to explicate the intricate legal configurations through which vagueness operates, exposing the various facets of this mechanism.

However, while vagueness provides a certain stability to the legal system, it may fall apart in times of pluralistic stress, risking the cohesion of the legal system. Perez sketches two scenarios in which this process could unfold. The apparent fragility of *vagueness* as a strategy for handling the paradox, he says, justifies looking into alternative strategies. One such strategy is 'randomisation.' Randomness seems to offer a potential resolution to the paradox—a decision-making mechanism that enables the law to satisfy the requirements of both coherence and pluralistic sensitivity. However, a closer inspection reveals that randomisation is a precarious strategy, one whose capacity to resolve the paradox of coherence is highly limited. Ultimately, Perez says, there is no escape from the paradox of fairness, as neither vagueness nor randomisation provides a definite resolution for the dilemma underlying it. It seems that we have no choice but to deal directly with the bare paradoxicality of modern law. But perhaps our problem does not lie in the paradox, but in a certain logical and anti-paradoxical state of mind, which has become prevalent. Perhaps the dynamics which is generated by the mechanisms of deparadoxification unleashed by the paradox—in its incessant dance between universal coherence and particularistic sensitivity—actually realises the ideal of fairness, maintaining in this way the structural integrity of the law.

Lior Barshack

Lior Barshack explores the paradox of legal authority. This paradox is expressed and, at the same time, repressed through an opposition between theatre and ritual in modern court proceedings. Judicial proceedings are haunted by paradoxicality: the determination and demarcation of legality

Law in the Air: A Prologue to the World of Legal Paradoxes 31

in court are implicated in illegality. Court proceedings seem to epitomise the rule of law and simultaneously signify its suspension. For a court's decision to be valid and ritually efficacious, it has to involve at least a partial incarnation of founding sovereignty—of constituent power—which suspends the existing constitutional foundation of the court's own authority. The court, at the same time, occasions a moment of ritual immediacy and pretends merely to repeat an act of representation, to stage once more the same legal scripture. This tension between ritual and theatre, between presence and representation, seems to be particularly acute in the case of modern courts, since their sanctity—their solemnity and pomp—have been enhanced by the secularisation of political authority. Modern court proceedings conceal their antinomic undercurrent by increasingly employing theatrical, as opposed to ritual, techniques: the role of the codified and sealed script, of the distant stage and of a growing number of professional, disinterested representatives, is significantly developed.

The more court ritual derives its form and authority from legal scripture, Barshack argues, the less disruptive it is to the rule of law and the transcendence of sovereignty. The lawbook replaces the magic of decision with a 'magic of the book.' It transforms a text, and the clerical voice which pronounces it, into the exclusive media of revelation, excluding any immediate, popular embodiment of sovereignty. Barshack highlights another modern instrument of deparadoxification, which complements formalism and the confinement of sacredness to the judicial body: the growing role of lawyers. Access to the clerical, judicial body has become increasingly mediated by lawyers, which took the place of the parties subsuming the concreteness of the event under general legal categories. Conflict is not enacted by the parties but staged, transformed into an impersonal argumentation conducted by their representatives. However canonical ritual may become, it paradoxically repeats a prelegal, magical manoeuvre of normative refounding. All social dramas, including the most contemplative ones, simultaneously employ theatrical/representational and ritual/transformative means. The dramatisation of legal rights, duties and statuses in court proceedings, the staging of legally defined personas, are accompanied by a suspension of law and identity and a repetition of a founding, lawless violence that is levelled at the parties as well as the judge.

Fatima Kastner

Fatima Kastner's chapter offers yet another take on the Luhmann–Derrida nexus. The focal point of her chapter is the possibility of justice within the law, a question discussed by Teubner and Wiethölter, and also addressed by Perez and Benbaji, though her approach and conclusions differ in that she emphasises the impossibility of both attaining and grasping justice (within law). By exploring the analysis of the paradoxical foundations of law in systems theory (Luhmann) and deconstruction (Derrida), Kastner derives different visions of the difference between law and justice. She argues that, although Luhmann and Derrida both accept the latency of undecidables, contradictions, ambivalences and infinite oscillations as conditions of the legal paradox, they generate different notions and expository strategies of the specific role of the self-production process of re- and deparadoxification of law. Derrida engages in a critical epistemological debate with the Western philosophical tradition by focusing mainly on the limits of the intelligibility of the paradox. Thus, deconstruction is neither a word nor a concept, but a quasi-transcendental, generic, performative articulation of the complex set of conditions under which the concept of re- and deparadoxification of law becomes possible. Derrida's writings recognise and are motivated by that recognition—that there is an unbridgeable divide between law and justice: while the law belongs to the element of calculation, justice is incalculable; and since the idea of justice is necessarily connected with the idea of infinity, it is not deducible from established criteria and rules of the legal machine. Derrida has no easy answer to this dilemma. Justice, he argues, does not have a logical foundation, but a 'mystical' one. Its logic, therefore, is the transcendence of all discourses and the reinvention of their grounds. The question which Kastner now poses is how such an extreme experience of the 'mystical' could ever be realised, and correspondingly, how could it ever inspire legal activism? It seems, she argues, that Derrida's meditation and simultaneous performance of the paradoxical foundation of law reflect an attempt to perform, and so to invent, the 'mystical.' It is, in Derrida's own words, the search for the still-open possibilities, the yet-invisible future of imagining the 'law above other laws,' 'a law beyond legality' as the ultimate precondition of justice.

Luhmann's discontent with this deconstructive option is, of course, specifically related to the state of his own discipline—sociology. Under the conditions of functionally differentiated modern society, there is no longer a binding representation of society within society, and therefore no binding concept of justice in society as such. For Luhmann's theory of self-reference, the problem of the paradoxical foundation of law within society as a self-producing system of communication arises as a paralysing problem only for a second-order observer, not for the legal system itself. But the self-referential quality of the law has implications for the role of justice as well. From the perspective of systems theory, norms appear as purely internal creations, serving the self-generated needs of the legal system for decisional criteria without any corresponding items in its environment. Consequently, justice can only be considered as a form of self-observation within the legal system. For Luhmann, then, there is no 'law above other laws' in which justice can be imagined.

Law in the Air: A Prologue to the World of Legal Paradoxes 33

Eric Talley

Eric Talley invokes the idea of paradox to investigate a certain doctrinal form, which is prevalent in modern law. A number of important modern legal contexts are regulated by doctrines that, he argues, turn in large part on a judicial assessment of either private or social 'expectations' rather than the imposition of hard and fast imperatives. Such expectation-grounded standards have long pervaded private law contexts (eg, the enforcement of questionable warranties in contract law), and are becoming increasingly influential in both public and international legal contexts as well (eg, the doctrine of regulatory takings and the jurisdictional doctrine of minimum contacts). Of particular interest is the degree to which this doctrine uses market price as a way to reflect expectations of participants. In many respects, the use of price as an informational proxy seems both prudent and sensible. At the same time, however, this type of doctrine introduces a self-referential circularity into the law that can prove mind-numbingly difficult to navigate. Talley seeks to analyse this circularity from a game-theoretical perspective. He argues that if there is a defence to the pricing paradox, it must come from its unique ability to enhance the flexibility of a legal system to deal with future unexpected contingencies. By providing this critical flexibility, expectation-centred doctrines afford individuals the opportunity to signal credible information to courts about fluctuations in their economic environment. In such situations, the very circularity of the pricing paradox may constitute its critical strength rather than a fatal weakness (as many have alleged). Talley's chapter thus provides a concrete example to the potential value of paradoxical reasoning, spanning several different fields of law.

Yitzhak Benbaji

Yitzhak Benbaji uses the form of the paradox to expose a certain fallacy in our reading of equality. (Methodologically, his chapter follows the same route taken by Eric Talley, though they consider different legal dilemmas.) Benbaji wants to decipher why some egalitarians view certain cases of unequal treatment as wrong, even where such treatment can be rationalised on the basis of a seemingly valid moral distinction. This approach cannot be understood, he argues, through the prism of the Aristotelian concept of equality. The Aristotelian imperative prohibits disadvantaging a person on the basis of irrelevant criteria. In the legal literature, this slogan is commonly conceived as a kind of rational ideal: it allows unequal treatment, as far as such treatment can be rationalised by some *valid* objective. It seems clear, then, that the aforementioned approach cannot be explained with the tools of the Aristotelian formula. Benbaji then proceeds to consider a different notion of equality—what he calls 'comparative equality.'

As he demonstrates, the notion of 'comparative equality' is inherently paradoxical. When this notion is used to evaluate actual cases of inequality, it yields inconsistent valuations (even though all seem to be rooted in the same intuition of justice). Clearly, this makes comparative equality inappropriate as a decision-making guide. Comparative equality does not provide a reasonable justification for viewing gender-based inequality as wrongful discrimination. The only morally reasonable explanation for this view, Benbaji argues, is based on the idea that what is of genuine moral importance is *respectful treatment*, rather than equal treatment. Gender-based inequality could be labelled as morally wrong only if we found it to be disrespectful. The respectful-treatment theory's basic concern is preventing disrespectful practices—that is, practices that generate good reasons for feeling disrespected or humiliated.

Benbaji uses paradoxification as a technique for reaching a better understanding of equality. Note, however, that his substantive conclusions, which argue for the possibility of an all-encompassing concept of justice which can be employed by the law to resolve social conflicts, is disputed by other contributors to this volume, in particular Kedar, Kastner, Perez and Alberstein, who are sceptical about the possibility of attaining a single conception of 'justice' within law.

Michal Alberstein

The quest for justice is also the focal point of Michal Alberstein's chapter. The context of Alberstein's deliberations is the realm of mediation or alternative dispute resolution. She contrasts the ways in which conflicts are resolved in the realm of law and mediation. The legal discourse suggests a *conflict* notion of 'fighting for law'—promoting social struggle through the 'naming' of new legal wrongs, within both the private realm of the subjects of law and the public arena. The mediation discourse offers a *settlement* notion of 'negotiating for justice' and uses techniques and psychological and economical models to manage and settle conflicts toward a state of social harmony. Alberstein seeks to construct a mediation model which incorporates the sensitivities which these two discourses offer.

Ultimately, her solution is based on a paradoxical conception of justice and mediation. In this, Alberstein seems to reject Benbaji's linear understanding of justice and to align with the indeterminate vision articulated in the chapters of Kedar, Perez, Kastner and Teubner. Alberstein's interpretive model envisions mediation as executing two difficult-to-bridge commitments: the first is the familiar mediation effort to settle a dispute between the two parties, promoting it to a level of mutual realisation and transformation, which enables an exploration of hidden dimensions of justice; the second is the search for a genuine expression of will and a value judgment which involves an inquiry into the social law of the dispute and its determination. The *first commitment* is represented by the *pragmatic* and the *transformative* models of mediation, and represents the construction of dispute settlement as a realisation and rationalisation of chaotic worlds of desires, needs and emotions. The pragmatic problem-solving mediator aspires to achieve this rationalisation through emphasising mediation as settlement and problem solving, while the transformative mediator wishes to do so through the opportunity conflict offers for relational internal dialogue. This relational growth is the utopian horizon of mediation as aspiring to peace and harmony, through internalisation of the 'relational autonomy' paradox. The second commitment reflects the legal aspiration to resist the settlement as well as the conflict drives per se, considering each dispute as an opportunity to set new law through a pragmatic violent intervention in a world based on eternal and structural conflicts, which can never be fully resolved or rationalised. This drive internalises 'the paradox of rights'; it triggers a constant search for actual settlements, settlements between non-contemporaneous scripts and narratives, within the existing singular materialisation of reality and fiction, public and private.

Shai Lavi

Shai Lavi offers a fascinating study of the history of dying in the USA. The chapter shows how during the nineteenth century, dramatic changes took place in the way Americans died. In particular, Lavi examines how the laws of the deathbed changed from religion through medicine to positive law and policy-making. The historical account serves as a case study for the rise of law as a social system and its two paradoxes. The paradox of self-reference emerges when law becomes able to say that euthanasia, the illegal act of murder, is legal. The paradox of self-regulation emerges when law's attempt to regulate medicine becomes dependent on law's autonomy from medicine and religion.

While the inquiry takes as its departing point the autopoietic theory of law and the formulation of its two legal paradoxes, Lavi proceeds to criticise autopoiesis for offering a merely descriptive account of these paradoxes. The critique is based on the notion that truth entails more than an accurate account of reality, providing a sense of significance as well. The account shares the thought that, in our times, law has become an autopoietic system, and still wonders what is the underlying significance of this fact. Can the autopoietic existence of law be accounted for, not merely described, by autopoietic theory itself? Lavi then deals with an immediate objection to this mode of questioning: how can one search for the significance of autopoietic systems outside of any particular autopoietic system? After all, is it not the central claim of systems theory that description is nothing but another operation of systems, and consequently, that there is no truth outside of the system? Is the search for the 'essence' of the system, as distinguished from its operation and the correlative adoption of a 'totalising' standpoint from which the phenomenon of systems can be viewed, not a relic of metaphysical thinking? And if this is so, then is the attempt to search for the significance of autopoiesis not neglectful of systems theory's endeavour to free us from the oppressive heritage of metaphysics?

In response, Lavi suggests that here, as elsewhere, wilfulness does not guarantee success. After all, autopoietic theory offers its own metaphysics by assuming, first, that the essence of law is 'system,' and secondly, that this essence is characteristic not only of law but of the totality of sociological, psychological and biological phenomena. The force of Lavi's critique is thus turned against autopoietic theory itself. To think through and beyond metaphysics, one must view 'system,' not as the essence of law, but only as one possible way in which law is. Lavi then proceeds to demonstrate how underlying these paradoxes is the historical phenomenon to which Nietzsche refers as nihilism, and Heidegger as technique. By demonstrating how the generic paradoxes of law are reflected in a local field of law, Lavi offers an important complement to the first part of the book.

Roei Amit

Concluding the book is Roei Amit's chapter, 'The Paradox of the Law: Between Generality and Particularity—Prohibiting Torture and Practising it in Israel.' Amit discusses a problem which is also explored in Perez's contribution: the tension between law's claim for universality, and its aspiration (and pretence) to provide justice in concrete cases. There is a major gap, Amit argues, between what we conceive to be the meaning of the law, which by definition is general and abstract, and its concrete signification, which is realised through the act of judgment in particular and singular cases. The law acquires meaning where it is no longer general as it pretends, but rather a unique case, which in turn can never be the law. Most of the time, this problem does not attract attention, Amit argues, since the systems of judgment and of meaning are functioning 'as if' the relation between the general and particular were present and transparent.

Amit explicates this paradox though a discussion of the prohibition of torture in Israeli law. The Israeli legal system's treatment of tortures is an 'example' of a discursive mechanism, which manipulates (in the sense of 'putting into work') the paradox of the law. From a 'non-existing' phenomenon, through denial and then implied authorisation, to an explicit interdiction, but still accompanied by current practices and indifference, the meanings produced by the Israeli legal system are constantly being changed as part of a general socio-cultural context.

Amit's and Perez's contributions seem to identify a similar mechanism of concealment and evasion, one which operates at the conceptual space of the law. Their different theoretical commitments generate, though, different portraits of this mechanism.

IV. ANNEX: MALKOVICH DILEMMA

Int. Craig and Maxine's Office—Continuous
Craig and Malkovich enter. Maxine looks up, startled, but controlling it.
Maxine: Darling!
Malkovich: What the fuck is going on?
Craig: Mr Malkovich, my name is Craig Schwartz. I can explain. We operate a little business here that ... simulates, for our clientele, the experience of ... being you, actually.
Malkovich: Simulates?
Craig: Sure, after a fashion.
Malkovich: Let me try.
Craig: You? Why, I'm sure it would pale in comparison to the actual experience.
Malkovich: Let me try!
Maxine: Let him try.
Craig: Of course, right this way, Mr Malkovich. Compliments of the house.

Craig ushers Malkovich to the portal door, opens it.

Malkovich: *(repulsed by the slime)*: Jesus.

Malkovich climbs in. The door closes.

Craig: What happens when a man climbs through his own portal?
Maxine: *(shrugs)*: How the hell would I know? I wasn't a philosophy major.

Cut to: Int. membranous tunnel — day
Malkovich crawls through. It's murky. He's tense. Suddenly there is a slurping sound.
Cut to: Psychedelic montage
We see Malkovich hurtling through different environments. It is scary: giant toads, swirling eddies of garish, coloured lights, naked old people pointing and laughing, black velvet clown paintings.
Cut to: Int. restaurant—night
Malkovich pops into a chair in a swank night club. He is wearing a tuxedo. The woman across the table from him is also Malkovich, but in a gown. He looks around the restaurant. Everyone is Malkovich in different clothes. Malkovich is panicked. The girl-Malkovich across the table looks at him seductively, winks and talks.

Girl-Malkovich: Malkovich Malkovich Malkovich Malkovich...

Malkovich looks confused. The waiter Malkovich approaches, pen and pad in hand, ready to take their orders.

Waiter Malkovich: Malkovich Malkovich Malkovich?
Girl Malkovich: Malkovich Malkovich Malkovich Malkovich.
Waiter Malkovich: Malkovich Malkovich. *(Turning to Malkovich)* Malkovich?

Malkovich looks down at the menu. Every item is 'Malkovich.'

Malkovich (screams): Malkovich!

The waiter jots it down on his pad.

Waiter Malkovich: Malkovich.

Malkovich pushes himself away from the table and runs for the exit. He passes the stage where a girl singer Malkovich is singing sensuously into the microphone. She is backed by a 40s-style big band of Malkoviches.
Singing Malkovich: Malkovich Malkovich Malkovich Malkovich...

Malkovich flies through the back door.
Cut to: Ext. Ditch—day
Malkovich lands with a thud in the ditch. Craig is waiting there with his van. On its side is painted 'See The World in Malk-O-Vision' followed by a phone number. Malkovich is huddled and shivering and soaking wet.
Craig: So how was it?
Malkovich: That... was... no... simulation.
Craig: I know. I'm sorry...
Malkovich: I have been to the dark side. I have seen a world that no man should ever see.
Craig: Really? For most people it's a rather pleasant experience. What exactly did you...
Malkovich: This portal is mine and must be sealed up forever. For the love of God.
Craig: With all respect, sir, I discovered that portal. It's my livelihood.
Malkovich: It's *my* head, Schwartz, and I'll see you in court!

Malkovich trudges off along the shoulder of the turnpike.

Part II

Generic Paradoxes

2

Dealing with Paradoxes of Law: Derrida, Luhmann, Wiethölter

GUNTHER TEUBNER

Translated by Iain L Fraser

Grandiosity of law in the ruins,
(Duncan Kennedy on Rudolf Wiethölter)[1]

I. CONFLICTS OF LAWS UNDER SUSPICION OF PARADOX

TWENTY-FIVE YEARS ago, when the great paradoxologists of our times were still engaged in quite different things—Jacques Derrida was doing grammatological exercises and Niklas Luhmann was steadily reducing complexity—Rudolf Wiethölter already had that disquieting phenomenon, the paradox of law, in his sights.[2] When in 1977 he wrote a *punctatio* in the *Festschrift* for his academic teacher Gerhard Kegel, which consisted of a list of reference points for and against Kegel's concept of conflict of laws, it was still a nagging suspicion. Could it be that, instead of the social theory Wiethölter was passionately seeking *about* conflict of laws, there was only a grandiose paradox *behind* them? In 2002, in a *punctatio* for his academic disciples—*punctatio* now signifying both a non-binding, precontractual commitment and a medieval practice deriving from the

---

[1] D Kennedy, Comment on Rudolf Wiethölter, 'Materialization and Proceduralization in Modern Law' and 'Proceduralization of the Category of Law' in C Joerges and D Trubek (eds), *Critical Legal Thought: An American-German Debate* (Baden-Baden, Nomos Verlagsgesellschaft, 1989), 516. The following texts by R Wiethölter are available in English: R Wiethölter, Materialization and Proceduralization in Modern Law, in G Teubner (ed), *Dilemmas of Law in the Welfare State* (Berlin, Walter de Gruyter, 1985), 221–249; R Wiethölter, Social Science Models in Economic Law, in T Daintith and G Teubner (eds), *Contract and Organization: Legal Analysis in the Light of Economic and Social Theory* (Berlin, Walter de Gruyter, 1986), 52–67; R Wiethölter, Proceduralization of the Category of Law, in C Joerges and D Trubek (eds), *ibid*, 501–510.

[2] R Wiethölter, 'Begriffs-oder Interessenjurisprudenz—Falsche Fronten im IPR und Wirtschaftsverfassungsrecht: Bemerkungen zur selbstgerechten Kollisionsnorm', *Festschrift für Gerhard Kegel* (Frankfurt, 1977), 213–263.

Orient, of interpreting the future from points distributed randomly in the sand—his suspicion had turned into certainty. After discussing various critical, deconstructive and systems approaches, Wiethölter describes the primary task of the jurist with the riddling formula: '"administration of justice" as cultivation of law's paradox itself, of simultaneously its preservation and its treatment.'[3]

Herein, there has been an antonym substitution: no longer is identity-creating social theory the counter-concept to the concept of conflict of laws, but a confusion-creating paradox of law.[4] In this article, I wish to consider the consequences of this substitution of opposite concepts, which capture an important line of the searching and learning processes in legal theory over the last 25 years.

Detaching the specific mode of thought in conflict of laws from private international law and making it serve other areas of law, in particular a social theory of law, was the ambitious project of the Kegel *Festschrift*. The point was no longer merely to theoretically reflect conflicts between national legal systems and to cope with them in practice, but to generalise 'conflict of laws' thinking itself so as to yield results for conflicts between complexes of norms, areas of law and legal institutions, and also for those between social systems, indeed even for divergences between competing social theories. The twofold recourse to the historical experience of private international law and to competing social theories managed to establish 'conflict of laws' as the central category for a legal reconstruction of social contradictions.[5]

With this sort of generalised conflict-of-laws thinking, Wiethölter was able to build upon the classics of social theory, drawing selectively on ideas in Hegel's dialectic of negation, Marx's real social contradictions, Weber's

---

[3] R Wiethölter, 'Just-ifications of a Law of Society,' in this volume, 73.

[4] The fact that antonym substitution has to do with a relevant social process and not with a mere fallacy of thinking is stressed by Holmes, 'Poesie der Indifferenz' in D Baecker *et al* (eds), *Theorie als Passion* (Frankfurt, 1987) 15–45 at 25 *et seq*, 28.

[5] By generalising conflict of laws, Wiethölter literally made a school: R Walz, *Steuergerechtigkeit und Rechtsanwendung: Grundlinien einer relativ autonomen Steuerrechtsdogmatik* (Heidelberg 1980) 199; C Joerges, *Verbraucherschutz als Rechtsproblem: Eine Untersuchung zum Stand der Theorie und zu den Entwicklungsperspektiven des Verbraucherrechts* (Heidelberg, 1981) 123; C Joerges, 'Freiheitsrechte und politische Rechte im Privatrecht Europas: Überlegungen zu einer Konstitutionalisierung des europäischen Rechtsänderungsrechts' in C Joerges and G Teubner (eds), *Rechtsverfassungsrecht: Recht-Fertigungen zwischen Sozialtheorie und Privatrechtsdogmatik* (Baden-Baden, 2003) 183–212; G Teubner, *Law as an Autopoietic System* (London, Blackwell, 1993) ch 6; G Teubner, 'Altera Pars Audiatur: Law in the Collision of Discourses' in R Rawlings, *Law, Society and Economy* (Oxford, Oxford University Press, 1997) 149–76; KH Ladeur, 'Helmut Ridders Konzeption der Meinungs- und Pressefreiheit in der Demokratie' (1998) *Kritische Justit* 281; M Amstutz, *Evolutorisches Wirtschaftsrecht: Vorstudien zum Recht und seiner Methode in den Diskurskollisionen der Marktgesellschaft* (2001) 326.

polytheism and Simmel's productivity of conflict. Social contradictions as the driver of social dynamics was the guiding theme. But in Wiethölter's thinking, social contradictions appeared not as such, but in a specifically legal metamorphosis. In a complicated process of translation, social contradictions were transformed into conflicts of legal norms. Various social dynamics of conflict were narrowed into the constraint to take a legal decision, requiring venues, procedures and criteria. The concepts of sociology of conflict were replaced by a conflict of laws doctrine (comity, characterisation, assimilation, reference, *renvoi, ordre public,* internal and external consistency). Wiethölter built up towering hierarchies of norms, dovetailing norms of conflict and substantive norms, in turn vaulted over by still higher conflict norms and substantive norms. His was a continuing search for ultimate justifications, supreme norms, supreme courts. The 'self-justifying substantive norm' criticised by Kegel was outdone twice over, first by characterising the 'self-justifying of conflict of laws' created by Kegel himself, and then in a critique of Kegel through a 'self-justifying meta-system law.'[6] But the secret judge of the whole conflict of laws affair was to be social theory, which was in turn searching for super-theory guidance in order to resolve the conflict of differing approaches.[7]

An exemplary illustration of this conflict of laws style of thought can be found in Wiethölter's critique of the dual formula of subjective rights and legal institutions. Here, Ludwig Raiser had formulated the famous conciliatory formula, 'The private actor as administrator of the overall legal system,' which postulates that the exercise of the subjective right has to be seen as being oriented toward institutions. Law's protection of individual rights always and already serves the protection of important social and legal institutions. The formula was, provisionally, the latest and most important outcome of a long debate between various dualisms of private/public, subjective rights/objective law, entitlements/infrastructures, contract/organisation and individual/institution, and had become widely accepted in contemporary doctrine both in private law and public law.[8] For Wiethölter, however, the formula of subjective right and legal institution was by no means the solution, but in fact was the problem in the first place. It could be taken as neither a substantive nor a conflict rule; it was itself the conflict. And in 1977, the all too clear tendency was towards a left-Kegelian 'paradigm shift.' Turning away from the conciliatory formula, Wiethölter advocated a 'politicisation of private law' in the form of a 'transformation from *contractual constitutional law*, ie, classical "private law," into *organisational constitutional*

---

[6] R Wiethölter, above n 2, at 246, 248, 256.
[7] R Wiethölter, above n 2, at 229.
[8] L Raiser, 'Rechtsschutz und Institutionenschutz im Privatrecht' in *Summum Ius Summa Iniuria* (Tübingen, 1963) 145–67.

law, ie, "modern" non-private law,'[9] in which the common good resulted, not from an institution-oriented exercise of subjective rights by private actors, but from political conflicts within legally constituted social organisations.

II. CHANGING THE MODE OF THOUGHT: FROM CONFLICTS TO PARADOXES

Yet, even in 1977, nagging doubts were already visible, which later took on increasing solidity. Scarcely had Wiethölter developed his own formula of a 'self-justifying meta-system of law' than he was already bringing it under suspicion of paradox. He himself let the mutual outbidding of conflicting and substantive norms run aground on the Münchhausen trilemma of norm justification: infinite regress, arbitrary rupture or circularity.[10] The ultimate salvation was then 'social practice,' in which the hierarchical levels of conflict rules and substantive rules were blurred.[11] Behind it all, though, it became increasingly clear that what in the foreground is called conflict of laws means paradoxes of law in the background. Conflict of laws are nothing but epiphenomena of legal paradoxes. Ultimately, it is the antonym substitution already mentioned that is happening here: the pair of opposites, identity/difference, which appears in the relationship between identity-creating, theory-led decisions and difference-creating conflicts of norms, is converted into the pair of opposites, paradox/difference.

The shift becomes clear in exemplary fashion from the way Wiethölter is today reformulating the rights versus institution issue. First, the tendency to resolve conflict one-sidedly by politicising it using social theory is (implicitly) withdrawn, in its transformation from contractual constitution to organisational constitution. The conflict itself is then interpreted as an expression of an underlying paradox, a problem that cannot be got at with decisions on the basis of venues, criteria or procedures:

> It is no surprise that our legal semantics of 'legal protection' (with guatanteed subjective rights at the centre) and 'institutional protection' (with temporal, material and social infrastructural guarantees at the centre) does neither 'good' nor justice' to the contemoirary requirements of the timeless paradox of law (in brief, of a law of conflict of laws about (legally) right and wrong admitted into the law).[12]

---

[9] R Wiethölter, above n 2, at 260.
[10] R Wiethölter, above n 2, at 216; R Wiethölter, 'Zum Fortbildungsrecht der (richterlichen) Rechtsfortbildung: Fragen eines lesenden Recht-Fertigungslehrers' (1988) *Kritische Vierteljahreszeitschrift für Gesetzgebung und Rechtswissenschaft* 1.
[11] R Wiethölter, above n 2, at 213.
[12] R Wiethölter, above n 3, at 67.

These are no mere semantic adaptations to fashionable paradoxologies, but well thought-out, dense formulations expressing, word for word, the structural differences between conflict of laws and paradox. This no longer means reference to 'social practice,' but a change in thinking. In a schematic listing, this involves the following:

1. Conflicts of laws are contradictions between different claims of validity: either A or not-A; law or non-law; one norm or the other; one social model or the other. Paradoxes can, of course, emerge as contradictions, but they have a more complicated structure due to their self-referentiality or to their 'self-justification'[13]: A because not-A and not-A because A; (legally) right because wrong and wrong because right. Is the Cretan lying when he says, referring to himself, that he is lying? Is law itself just, ie, is it (legally) right/wrong to judge conflicts as right/wrong?
2. There follow differences in the consequences. Conflicts can be resolved by deciding between alternatives, or they allow for a compromise. Both ways are barred in the case of paradoxes. One cannot through decision avoid the oscillation between their poles, since each decision sets the self-referential circle off again. The situation is one of undecidability in principle. The result of paradox is paralysis.[14] This is the reason that paradoxes are ordinarily either ridiculed or tabooed.[15]
3. Conflicts require criteria, venues, procedures in order for a decision to be possible. Paradoxes cannot be got round that way. There is no *via regis* towards a 'solution' for them, at most a *via indirecta*. It is not the decision of the conflict that they call in question, but the very conflict itself. At least one has to leave the beaten track. That is what makes dealing with paradoxes so hard, and the comparison of Wiethölter with Derrida and Luhmann rewarding.

But why such fascination with paradoxes in particular? Why is a conflict of laws theory—which, after all, openly expresses a preference for the theory

---

[13] On paradoxes in a philosophical perspective see Probst and Kutschera, 'Paradox' in J Ritter/K Gründer (eds), *Historisches Wörterbuch der Philosophie* (Basel, Schwabe, 1989) 1–97. On the distinctions between contradictions and paradoxes in a pragmatic perspective, see the classic treatise by P Watzlawick *et al*, *Pragmatics of Human Communication: A Study of Interactional Patterns, Pathologies, and Paradoxes* (New York, WW Norton Books, 1967). On dealing with paradoxes in law, see GP Fletcher, 'Paradoxes in Legal Thought' (1985) 85 *Columbia Law Review* 1263; P Suber, *The Paradox of Self-Amendment: A Study of Logic, Law, Omnipotence and Change* (New York, 1990) and www.earlham.edu/~peters/writing/psa/index.htm. cf also A Ross, 'On Self-Reference and a Puzzle in Constitutional Law' (1969) 78 *Mind* 1; HLA Hart, 'Self-Referring Laws' in *Essays in Jurisprudence and Philosophy* (Oxford, Oxford University Press, 1983) 170–78.

[14] See HU Gumbrecht and LK Pfeiffer, *Paradoxien, Dissonanzen, Zusammenbrüche: Situationen offener Epistemologie* (Frankfurt, Suhrkamp, 1991).

[15] P Watzlawick, above n 13.

of rational discourse—interested in systems theory and deconstruction, which are obsessively engaged in revealing paradoxes? Derrida's thought, after all, amounts, as Habermas might polemically put it were he present, to a 'deconstructive process of the decay of private law': disclosing the ambivalences, uncertainties and paradoxes of law by formal logical operations and genealogical investigations. Is it, he might, present or absent, go on to ask, worth participating in a legal 'twilight of the gods'? And for the internal logic of systems theory, it is a downright absurd idea that at its core it poses paradoxes. This idea means a self-abandonment of its earlier guiding approaches: compatibility of structure and function, possibilities of cybernetic control, dealing with environmental complexity through requisite variety. Nothing is more anti-system than paradoxes. They lead only into contradiction, inconsistency, chaos, paralysis and horror.

Allowing in these destructive tendencies with a resigned, pessimistic, melancholic undertone perceptible more than occasionally in Wiethölter's analyses of present-day private law, to the tune of 'everything is possible, but nothing works anymore',[16] is tempting. In fact, Wiethölter had already embarked on deconstructing the law before the word 'deconstruct' even existed in Germany: his merciless revelations of ostensible uncertainties in the doctrines of private law, revelations that made him so unpopular in the profession, show this, as do his ruthless disclosure of inconsistencies in legal and social theory.[17] Another deconstructive aspect is Wiethölter's 'legal negativism',[18] his decades of consistent refusal to give specific answers to specific legal questions, be it to 'solve' cases, 'discover' doctrinal constructions or 'decide' disputed questions of legal theory. His stance of refusal illustrates, in its ascetic severity, Derrida's famous aporias of law, in which, with unsparing inevitability, every legal argument leads into a position of suspension, of *epoche*, of undecidability.[19]

Yet this interpretation is probably too facile. For ultimately, it is not their undeniable critical and destructive potential that drives the interest in paradoxes, but it is the productive possibilities of working with them that is really fascinating.[20] Herein lies, as even cultural-theory critics admit, the advance of systems theory over deconstruction in Paul de Man and his

[16] R Wiethölter, 'Zur Argumentation im Recht: Entscheidungsfolgen als Rechtsgründe?' in G Teubner (ed), *Entscheidungsfolgen als Rechtsgründe: Folgenorientiertes Argumentieren in rechtsvergleichender Sicht* (Baden-Baden, 1994) 89–120 at 100.

[17] Since R Wiethölter, *Rechtswissenschaft* (Frankfurt, 1968).

[18] Explicitly, R Wiethölter, 'Recht und Politik: Bemerkungen zu Peter Schwerdtners Kritik' (1969) *Zeitschrift für Rechtspolitik* 155 at 158.

[19] J Derrida, 'Force of Law: The Mystical Foundation of Authority' (1990) 5–6 *Cardozo Law Review* 919 at 959.

[20] K Krippendorff, 'Paradox and Information' in B Dervin and MJ Voigt, *Progress in Communication Sciences* (Norwood, NJH, Ablex, 1984) vol 5, 46–71 at 51; N Luhmann, 'Sthenography' (1990) 7 *Stanford Law Review* 133 at 135; P Watzlawick, above n 13, at ch 7.

epigones. For systems theory sees in 'the paradoxes arising from self-reference not an endpoint, but the starting-point for further evolution. That confers upon this theory, among recent post-metaphysical constructions, a relatively high degree of comprehensiveness.'[21] Not only do worlds of meaning necessarily bring out paradoxes, but paradoxes bring out new worlds of meaning. Not only do conflicts of laws produce inconsistencies, but these produce new conflicts. Paradoxes are not logical errors that have to be extirpated if one is to advance. What role they play today as a ubiquitous and central aspect of social dynamics becomes clear from the following extreme formulation: paradoxes take the place of the transcendental subject; typical structures are historically contingent phenomena.[22]

Taking the example of human rights, here is how the thought pattern of paradox-driven legal development looks.[23] The paradoxical circular relationship between society and individual (society constituting the individual person, who in turn constitutes society) is, as it were, the *a priori* that underlies all historically variable human rights concepts. Flesh-and-blood people, communicatively constituted as persons, make themselves disruptively noticeable, despite all their socialisation, as non-communicatively constituted individuals/bodies, and agitate for their 'rights.' This tension in the individual/society relationship brings out various socially adequate structures of meaning that are repeatedly deconstructed anew in historical development (schematised in historical phases: the nature of the person in the old natural law, the agreement of the individuals in the social contract, the entry of persons endowed with natural rights into the state of civilisation, the *a priori* validity of subjective rights, the political positivisation of individual fundamental rights, the scandalisation of human rights breaches in world society). Could, then, the reason for the obsessive interest be that, specifically, paradoxes—and no longer social contradictions or clashes of rationality—constitute the mover of legal development? And could the reason for Wiethölter's puzzling formula—that the administration of justice is not simply the ruling out of legal paradox for the sake of legal order but its 'preservation and treatment'—lie here?

In a comparison with the contradiction-driven dynamics in classical social theory, the specific features of a paradox-driven dynamics emerge.

---

[21] A Koschorke, 'Die Grenzen des Systems und die Rhetorik der Systemtheorie' in A Koschorke and C Vismann (eds), *Widerstände der Systemtheorie: Kulturtheoretische Analysen zum Werk von Niklas Luhmann* (Berlin, 1999) 49–60 at 56.

[22] The whole quotation reads: 'Paradoxes are the only form in which knowledge is given *unconditionally*. They take the place of the transcendental subject, to which Kant and his successors had attributed direct access to unconditioned, *a priori* valid knowledge, discernible of itself. .... This by no means rules out the possibility of asking after typical structures in which the unfoldings of paradoxes take on relatively stable forms that stand the test of history,' N Luhmann, *Die Religion der Gesellschaft* (Frankfurt, Suhrkamp, 2000) 132.

[23] N Luhmann, 'Das Paradox der Menschenrechte und drei Formen seiner Entfaltung' in N Luhmann, *Soziologische Aufklärung 6: Die Soziologie und der Mensch* (Opladen, 1995) 229–36.

The interplay of deparadoxification–reparadoxification is anything but a cumulative sequence of negations, a 'transcending' of contradiction, a progress of the spirit.[24] It is more a case of the return of the same, a continual oscillation between paradox and structure, a dialectic without synthesis. The continuous changes of paradox and difference show an experimenting, incremental, exploratory production of orders that have to stumble over contingencies. And worlds of meaning are continually afflicted by their deconstruction, which repeatedly lets chaos break back into civilisation.

By comparison with Marx's 'real contradictions,' the paradoxes also present themselves as having been turned on their heads, since they do not arise as disturbances in the ideal world of thought but as 'real paradoxes' in real society, bring the relations into a dance. However, by contrast with them, no logic of decay through the primary and secondary contradictions of the social order that would then enable the revolutionary Big Bang is implied. Real paradoxes are highly ambivalent. They contain destructive, paralysing potentials but contain at the same time productive, creative possibilities. The alternative is open: paralysis or provocation of structural innovations? It is not some sort of determinism that prevails but sheer contingency. The catastrophe, or the productive new order that is in turn threatened by catastrophe—both are equally likely. This ambivalence gives a plausible explanation for the oft-noted enormous pressure of innovation bearing upon today's societies.

At the same time, the quality of deparadoxification is also remarkably pathological. It promises no solution of the crisis, but at most its temporary postponement, concealment, invisibilisation, suppression, repression.[25] It is only a matter of time before crisis breaks out again. Not by chance does this recall theories of repression, with the repeated return of that which is repressed being manifested in symptoms. 'There is something rotten in the state of Denmark'—this is the continuing condition of such societies, even if the temporary deparadoxification seems to work well. And, in contrast to psycho-analysis, there is no promising therapy. What results from direct confrontation with the paradox is not liberation but paralysis. Our society lives at best on a rationality of repression.

The question then arises, however, whether the fascination with paradoxes is no more than an intellectual fashion, or instead has something to do with their adequacy to the object. Does the shift from contradiction theories to paradoxologies reflect the experiences of the twentieth century with totalitarianisms, two World Wars, ecological and psychic catastrophes in the midst of high civilisation? Does it offer a plausible interpretive model for the experience that even the advanced rationality patterns of economics, politics

---

[24] On the relation between Luhmann and Hegel, cf N Luhmann, *Social Systems* (Stanford, Stanford University Press, 1995) ch 9 I.

[25] See the articles in the collected volume, HU Gumbrecht and KL Pfeiffer, above n 14.

and the law are exposed to the incursions of arbitrariness, irrationality, indeed violence, in their most everyday accomplishments? And not even from outside, but from their inmost *arcana*? Does it at the same time provide a plausible interpretive model for the dominance of a cognitive style that appears no longer as the great political project, but as groping experimentation in conditions of radical uncertainty? The following argument from Jean Clam may make the current search for non-teleological strategies of deparadoxification plausible:

> The problem of the teleological form of deparadoxification is that it sets going a dynamics of radical denial of paradox (as an evil to rid the world of). Modern experience with this dynamics has shown that the more hopeful the impetus to attain or constrain the *telos*, in other words, the more thorough the destruction of the foundations of the paradox was, the stormier and more damaging was the return of the denied. De-paradoxification through utopian teleologies is close to treating original paradoxes as if they were not non-transcendable and system-generating, but reconcilable and overcomable. This then justifies shifting the certainty of reconciliation along the time dimension, which for the purpose receives a macrohistorical format. Trust in the possibility of transcending the paradox, combined with postponement of its confirmation to the distant future, protects blind rage at the paradox from possibilities of learning from failures.

III. LUHMANN: SOCIOLOGISING DECONSTRUCTION

This pushes the question of dealing with paradoxes into the foreground. However much systems theory and deconstruction analyse the syntax of paradoxes, or rewrite their semantics as a combination of textuality and society, the real question is their pragmatics.[26] Here it is no doubt Luhmann who sets the tone, against merely destructive paradoxology, against a resigned, provocative presentation of the inconsistencies, against a restriction to legal negativism:

> It could well be that our society is the outcome of a structural and semantical *catastrophe* in the sense meant by René Thom—that is, the result of a fundamental change in the form of stability that gives meaning to states and events. If this is so, the deconstruction of our metaphysical tradition is indeed something that *we* can do *now*. But if so, it would be worthwhile to choose the instruments of deconstruction with sufficient care so that by using them we

---

[26] In addition to the references in above n 13, see K Krippendorff, above n 20; for legal paradoxes, see N Luhmann, *Law as a Social System* (Oxford, Oxford University Press, 1993) at 459.

could gain some information about our postmetaphysical, postontological, postconventional, postmodern—that is, *postcatastrophical* condition.[27]

'By their fruits shall ye know them.' What insights into post-catastrophe conditions of law are supplied by Wiethölter's conflict of laws thinking by his comparison with systems theory of law and with legal deconstructivism? What standards of 'sufficient care' are to be respected in choosing instruments of deconstruction that claim to provide a gain in information for today's law? In his careful dealing with paradoxes, Wiethölter first follows in Luhmann's footsteps, in order then at particular crossroads to pursue search interests that are decidedly his own.

First Step: Paradoxification

From the outset, the second-order observer who discloses the paradoxes must choose his instruments with sufficient care. If it is supposed to be more than an informationless deconstruction of symbols, it can find out something about the sociological and historical meaning of illusions. Why does the legal system need illusions, and which ones? Luhmann shows this for the illusion of the binary legal code, which is exposed to the paradoxes of its own self-reference. Behind the distinction between (legal) right and wrong, he finds both the foundational paradox of law and the decisional paradoxes of daily legal practice, and asks after the social meaning of this context of illusion, in which the legal code, despite its manifest artificiality, has remained astonishingly stable, though the forms of deparadoxification in the programmes of law have steadily changed.[28]

Wiethölter first follows the analysis, but then looks for the central paradox of law elsewhere—not behind the legal right/wrong code, but behind the law of conflict of laws between law and non-law.[29] Now, the point is no longer the empty paradoxes of the legal system's self-reference, the mere self-legitimation problems of the Münchhausen trilemma, but the much more substantial paradoxes of the law's other-reference, the question of the law's reference to the world. By disclosing the paradox of law, Wiethölter already raises the normative question of whether and how the law does justice to the world.

Second Step: Deparadoxification

Since every, absolutely every, distinction can be paradoxified, with the result of paralysing thought and decision, it becomes a truly productive

---

[27] N Luhmann, 'Deconstruction as Second-Order Observing' (1993) 24 *New Literary History* 763 at 777.
[28] N Luhmann, above n 26, at 173.
[29] R Wiethölter, above n 3, at 71.

outcome of paradox that it provokes the counter-forces of deparadoxification. According to Luhmann, the law arrives at autopoietic system formation at all, first, by converting the dangerous paradox into a harmless difference, by misunderstanding the endless oscillation between (legally) right and wrong as a conditionable contradiction, indeed, by technicalising the paradox into a programmable binary code.[30]

Wiethölter follows the argument with polite interest. *Mit brennender Sorge* however he asks the question of how the paradoxes of the law's reference to the world can be transformed into decidable conflicts of norms. This seems to offer a more productive deployment of the paradox, since the direction of search goes not just to the conditions enabling the self-reproduction of legal practice but to 'worldly' venues, procedures and criteria for deciding the conflict. Not only: the form of the conflict itself changes with changing social conditions of deparadoxification. Hence, Wiethölter's eloquent silence on the question of naming the entities in conflict—what is clashing? Norms, principles, social models, theories, rationalities?

Third Step: Sociologising the Paradox

Here, the point is choosing the observer who carries out the deparadoxification. Luhmann chooses social communication and not individual decisions. Consistently sociologising deconstruction makes for the great difference to Derrida. Stressed by the ambivalences, uncertainties and breakdowns, social systems each find their specific new distinctions that can for a certain time keep them stable.

Wiethölter instead selects a more awkward observer's viewpoint. At first, as he sets his sights on the 'law of conflict-of-laws within the law, deciding on the conflict between law and non-law', he seems to choose the legal system as observer, internalising the opposition of law and society in a re-entry. It is here that the translation of social contradictions into decidable conflicts of norms comes about. But then comes the typical Wiethölter sleight of hand, referring to a trinitary body as observer of this re-entry, namely the magic triangle of the great social theories: critical theory, autopoiesis theory and economic institutionalism. Here is the difference between Wiethölter's normativism and Luhmann's cognitivism, for which sociology ought to confine itself to noting the conflict of laws decisions. For in the translation of legal conflicts of norms into social theory, Wiethölter scents the great opportunity to gain normative criteria.

But this is not enough. Wiethölter avoids deciding the dispute among rival social theories. Despite personal sympathies for Habermas's discourse

---

[30] N Luhmann, above n 26, at 173, for a generalisation of the argument, see N Luhmann, 'The Paradox of Observing Systems' in N Luhmann (ed), *Theories of Distinction* (Stanford, Stanford University Press, 2002) 79.

52   Gunther Teubner

theory, he scrupulously keeps all three at equal distance, shunning any too intimate contact with them like the devil dodging holy water. Not that this reduces to non-binding theoretical relativism. Nor is any claim raised to a super-theory, but only to marking out a puzzling void in the Bermuda Triangle of social theories, to creating a neutral area within the bounds of which the suspension of the rival theories' validity claims is the condition for putting the law on trial. Wiethölter sets his hopes on mutual irritation, indeed, on the chances for reciprocal learning by the rival theories involved, yet without identifying this meta-process with the rationality of discourse, of systems or of the market. This is presumably how his breathless to-and-fro translations of conflicts of laws into the language of discourse theory, of systems theory and of economic institutionalism are to be understood. In the process of translation they are to yield normative surplus-value. And it is only provisionally, only experimentally, that he recommends drawing the initial distinction at critical theory, in order in its light to join up with the other theories as subsequent distinctions. But he continually stresses the provisional nature of this decision, as he sees the theories' relation to each other as being to mutually illuminate their weak points.[31]

Fourth Step: Return of the Paradox and its Renewed Concealment

Social catastrophes come about, according to Luhmann, in the correlations between social structure and semantics, when the change in social structures ruins the semantics. Today's problems are determined by the fact that the fundamental structural change of functional differentiation has destroyed the old European semantics without residue, and that even the most hectic post-modern *polysémies* can be understood only as a restless search for socially adequate self-descriptions. Here, a historical rhythm of continually repeated destruction and reconstruction is beating: paradoxifications provoke the search for new socially adequate distinctions, which, in turn, under particular conditions, are thrown back onto their paradoxes again. But what conditions determine the recursive revelation and concealment of paradox? Systems theory identifies two: pressure of social problems and communicative plausibility. Under the pressure of social problems, new differences, in turn deconstructable, are accepted by social communication if they are plausible, ie, compatible within the net of other valid distinctions. Under different circumstances, if the pressure of social problems speaks for their maintenance, and their social plausibility is high, their ever-possible reparadoxification is effectively ruled out.[32]

---

[31] R Wiethölter, above n 10, at 25.
[32] N Luhmann, above n 26.

Wiethölter himself has always been on this sort of 'relativist' search for contemporary and socially adequate deparadoxification as entirely suitable. Yet, he cannot content himself with a 'cool' systems theory analysis that merely notes pressure from social problems and records plausibilities. Behind problem pressure and plausibility, he energetically seeks their conditions, which in ever-new coinages he terms 'surplus-value of law,' 'factor X' of judicial activism or 'non-law as law.'[33] Plausibilities are not simply to be noted, but provocatively to be doubted. And the point is not dispassionate observation, but active commitment in enhancing social problem pressure. This political loosening of socially crystallised structures seems to me to be the real message of his misleading formula of 'political theory of law', in contradistinction to a non-political social theory of law. Here, Wiethölter seems to be coming close to recent deconstructivist versions of systems theory, according to which struggling with paradoxes in all social systems (not just in institutionalised politics) has to be seen as genuinely political.[34] The 'political' thus appears outside the political system, as decision in a context of undecidability: as the resolution of breakdowns of meaning into antagonistic arrangements, enciphered à la Wiethölter as dissolution of the paradox of law into conflicts between law and non-law.

The acceptable element about systems theory is, then, to Wiethölter, the fundamental challenge from real paradoxes that inevitably recurs in structural change and calls for the construction of new social identities. Equally acceptable are the 'relativist' criteria of the topicality, material appropriateness and social adequacy of the new identities, which are thus compatible with other social distinctions and respond to the pressure of social problems.

There has to be criticism, though, of the remarkable lacuna in the architecture of systems theory, which, while setting up an impressive hierarchy of levels of reflection, ultimately fails to close it off. At the first level, basic self-reference operates (self-reference of elementary events): one legal act is referring to the next legal act, and reflexively to itself. At a second level comes reflexivity of processes: legal norming is itself normed (constitution, procedural law, secondary norms). At a third level, reflection operates first as self-referential reflection in the norm theories and validity theories of law, and secondly as reflection of system-environment relations. Here, legal theory appears as social theory, as legal theories of the person and the individual, and as ecological legal theory.[35] Thus, all the boundaries of law are reflected in legal theory—except one. What is excluded from the reflection of law are the boundaries of the meaning of law itself, the questions not as

---

[33] R Wiethölter, above n 10, at 1.
[34] U Stäheli, *Sinnzusammenbrüche: Eine dekonstruktive Lektüre von Niklas Luhmanns Systemtheorie* (Weilerswist, Velbrück Verlag, 2000).
[35] N Luhmann, above n 26, at 423.

to the meaningless, nor as to the negation of meaning which is in turn meaning, but those beyond meaning. While Luhmann asks about the law's justice to its environment, he does not ask about its justice to the world. According to Luhmann's system of law, the law does possess a contingency formula in the concept of justice, but not a transcendence formula. And this is what Wiethölter is looking for.

Systems theory needs to be criticised for the exclusive site it reserves for the reflection of transcendence. According to Luhmann, in traditional society transcendence was reflected at various loci in that society. The dimension of the religious was present everywhere, in law too (natural law and justice having had religious connotations as a matter of course). But then secularisation is supposed to be a detranscendentalisation of all social subsystems and a concentration on transcendence in only one system of meaning, that of religion.[36] But is this not at variance with the tough resistance to secularisation of social utopias (socialism, fascism, neo-liberal doctrines of salvation), palpable even, and especially, in the highly rationalised subsystems of politics, law, the economy or science? Is there not an otherwise inexplicable manifestation here of salvific doctrines, eschatological hopes, which are expressed not just in pop religion and the occult, but especially within the centres of secularised rationalities? Max Weber's characterisation of the diverse social rationalities as a new absolute polytheism attests this for theory, as the ideological wars of the twentieth century, which hardly had much to do with religion as an institution, attest to this for practice.

A parallel has to be drawn here to the differentiation of knowledge. While the production of knowledge seems to be concentrated in the knowledge system (universities), in parallel with this, production of knowledge and its reflection comes about in other social subsystems (legal theory, political theory, economic theory). And it remains subsystem-specific reflection even if it is administered at the universities in academic form. The argument against Luhmann's ignoring of justice to the world runs as follows: if the academic world, in the processes of social differentiation, has not managed to monopolise the reflection of the subsystems' relations with their environments, but instead has to leave it to them themselves, how then can religion succeed in monopolising reflection on the boundaries of meaning? The empirical test would be: at what loci in society are social utopias designed?

It is this transcendence of positivity wherein Jacques Derrida's contribution to the handling of the paradox of law lies. In his more recent analyses, he directs deconstructive thought at social institutions. His main point seems to be to go beyond the mere disruptions of deconstruction and to bring a disquieting awareness of transcendence back into the highly rationalised worlds of the economy, science, politics and law. His astonishing

---

[36] N Luhmann, above n 22, at 320.

theses have to do with the paradoxical effects of the 'pure gift' as against the profit-led economy,[37] of 'friendship' as against professionalised politics,[38] of 'forgiveness' as against secularised morality,[39] and of 'justice' as against highly technicised law.[40] All of these are excesses of reference to transcendence, reactivating utopian energies from quite different sources. How far can 'political theory of law' identify itself with this?

IV. DERRIDA: THEOLOGISING DECONSTRUCTION

Luhmann is certainly doing Derrida wrong when he accuses him of simply getting stuck in the ambivalence of deconstruction, of merely frightening people with his paradoxes, of bringing no insights into the world with his verbal acrobatics.[41] Luhmann is here constructing a false alternative between getting stuck in deconstructive ambivalence and creating systemic *eigenvalues* that does not do justice to Derrida's recent work. For since 'Force of law: the mystical basis of authority,' no one other than Derrida has been seeking practical political ways out of the paralysis of deconstruction. To put it somewhat schematically, in deconstructing law, according to Derrida, only the first stage is to reduce the law to paradoxes. In the twofold nature of deconstruction, this means first of all the paradox of decision: there is no determinable meaning of law, but only *'différance,'* continuing transformation and deferment of the meaning of law, and secondly, the paradox of ultimate justification, the founding of law upon arbitrary force. But this does not lead to a paralysis of thought; instead, it is only in these abysses that justice as a problem becomes conceivable at all: 'Justice as the possibility of deconstruction.'[42] In the next stage of deconstructive thought, this leads to a 'journey through the wilderness.' And this is indeed a reference, alienating for today's scientific style, to transcendence, mystic force, encountering the other as in Levinas's philosophy of otherness, challenging modern rationalities from 'pure' justice, gift, friendship, forgiveness. Then, however, comes the third stage, which one would not expect following a deconstruction of law and a reference to transcendence: a 'compromise' of transcendence with immanence. Here, deconstruction goes back into serious, detailed calculation of rules and legal argumentation—but in the light of the unending demands of otherness.

---

[37] J Derrida, *Given Time* (Chicago, University of Chicago Press, 1992).
[38] J Derrida, *The Politics of Friendship* (Collins (trans), London, Verso, 1997).
[39] J Derrida, 'Le siècle et le pardon' (1999) 9 *Le monde des débats*, (December), available at www.celf.fr/mdderrid.htm
[40] J Derrida, above n 19.
[41] N Luhmann, above n 27, at 765.
[42] J Derrida, above n 19, at 945.

We must, then, see in another way the difference between the systems and deconstructive ways of getting around paradox. It is not that one theory persists in paralysis while the other seeks new *eigenvalues* in deparadoxification, but that both are looking for different ways out of paradox. A more appropriate label for these directions might be sociologisation versus theologisation of paradox.[43]

How far will political theory of law go here? Wiethölter likes to cite Adorno: *'Chaos in Ordnung bringen'* ['bring chaos into order'].[44] Luhmann's deparadoxification stresses only one side of this double-meaning formula: avoid the sight of paradoxes as far as possible, and oppose the threatening chaos with a new order. Derrida, by contrast, chaoticises order, by seeking through a critique of the originating force of law to plumb the dark worlds of paradox, but then striving for compromise using the arguments and calculations of legal practice. Justice, according to Derrida, is not an objective, not a consistency formula, not a contingency formula, but 'invocation, abyss, disruption, experience of contradiction, chaos within the law.' This has thoroughly practical consequences for legal decision: changing the situation as a decision *sub specie aeternitatis*, not just *sub specie societatis*.

However much Wiethölter as a 'poietic non-systemist,' as he likes to call himself, may feel attracted by such chaoticisations of legal order, he will still not be able to fraternise with the theologisation that Derrida favours. His strictly secular understanding of state and law vis-à-vis religion requires that binding legal criteria be developed in immanence only. Specifically German experience with mysticism and religiosity in the public sphere, with neo-paganism and political theology, is likely what immunises him against a legal theology renewed in the name of deconstruction—at any rate, in the public institutions of politics and law. What Derrida fairly explicitly accuses Benjamin of, in his puzzling distinction between mystical and mythical force, which in addition is not comprehensible to man,[45] is what Wiethölter would likely bring up against Derrida himself with a *Tu quoque*: namely, through recourse to a 'mystical force,' possibly promoting complicity with the worst.

The central quotation, 'Deconstruction is justice,'[46] perhaps brings together the common features of deconstruction and political theory of law, and their differences. Both agree that deconstructive analysis is anything

---

[43] For an instructive comparison of the theories, see F Barjiji-Kastner, *Ohnmachtssemantiken: Systemtheorie und Dekonstruktion* (Frankfurt, 2002), which also contains a detailed discussion of theological and non-theological transcendence in Derrida's interpretation, with further references.

[44] R Wiethölter, above n 16, at 107.

[45] W Benjamin, 'Critique of Violence' in W Benjamin, *Selected Writings I 1913–1926* (Cambridge, Mass, Belknap Press, 1997).

[46] J Derrida, above n 19, at 945.

but mere nihilistic disintegration, that it is looking for not just some sort of *non-foundationalism*, a proof of the impossibility of founding the law, that for all its effort at logical and doctrinal acuteness it is not aimed at a merely analytical dissection or logical critique of law, at an academic, non-binding criticism of concepts, constructs, norms, justice. Both emphatically raise the claim to be looking for the rightness of law,[47] in Derrida's formulation:

> [t]o aspire to something more consequential, to change things, and to intervene in an efficient and responsible though always of course, very mediated way, not only in the profession but in what one calls the *cité*, the polis and more generally the world. Not, doubtless, to change things in the rather naive sense of calculated, deliberate and strategically controlled intervention, but in the sense of maximum intensification of a transformation in progress that is occurring specifically in 'an industrial and hyper-technologized society.'[48]

In parallel, both theories also distinguish themselves cautiously but resolutely from a power critique in the tradition that runs from Marx to Foucault. A critique of law from political economy, revealing the law to be an instrument for maintaining power, is regarded by both as obsolete, as is an obsessive micro-analysis of power. Political economy and micro-analysis of power, while useful, are not essential enough, not complex enough, not close enough to the inwardness of law. Deconstruction, by contrast, means revealing the immanent violence at the core of law itself.[49]

Admittedly, the relation of both to the modern rationality-based critique of law is more doubtful. Both are certainly engaged in disclosing the arbitrary nature of law, and criticising the lack of legitimacy of positive law. However, both take a rather sceptical stance on Habermas's project to refound law upon discursive rationality. Derrida is decisive here in his deconstruction of a communicative rationality that is blind to the unavoidable element of violence in the foundational paradox and in the decisional paradox of everyday law. The force of the founding act of law is not itself accessible to rational discourse, any more than are the uncertainties of legal decision: not foundable, not justifiable, neither just nor unjust. Wiethölter is much more cautious here, holding fast to critical theory's claim to found and legitimise law. To be sure, he distances himself from all the optimistic advocates of the possibility in principle of founding law upon rational discourse, by insisting doggedly and deconstructively on the undecidability of conflicts of laws and, hence, their paradoxicality.

Deconstruction and political legal theory definitively diverge, though, when it comes to the mystical foundation for the law's authority. Especially

---

[47] R Wiethölter, above n 10, at 1.
[48] J Derrida, above n 19, at 931.
[49] *Ibid*, at 925.

Derrida's recourse to Levinas's philosophy of otherness, which counterposes to the totality of meaning the exteriority of transcendence in which justice appears as an unending demand of the other, may perhaps be respected by political legal theory, which is explicitly concerned not with something other than law, but with a possible other of law,[50] but not followed by it. At most, it could follow the discourse of the law's transcendence as a temporalisation, a futurisation that cannot be made present, whereby justice can always only mean a postponement to the future. Derrida says 'justice remains, is yet to come, *à venir.*'[51] Wiethölter's formulation that 'law's constitution of law intends redeemable excesses of enabling, rather than unredeemed ones of promise' shows the closeness to temporalisation and the sceptical distance towards the otherness and transcendence of Levinas and Derrida.

V. WIETHÖLTER: RECIPROCITY AND (IM-)PARTIALITY

If, then, we have more or less grasped the *eigenvalues* of political legal theory by contrast with systems and deconstructive paradoxologies, what are the consequences of the shift from conflict of laws to paradox? What then happens to the predominating conflict between protection of rights and protection of institutions?

As already stated, Wiethölter not only distances himself from Ludwig Raiser's conciliatory formula of the private person as a functionary of the whole legal system, in which the protection of individual interests through subjective rights is claimed also for institutional protection, but also takes back the conflict of laws norm at which he himself had first aimed, of an 'organisational constitutional law.' Why? Because the underlying conflict is itself increasingly deconstructed. The two great deconstructors are again at work: problem pressure and communicative plausibility. Today's pressure of social problems renders the venerable distinction between protection of rights and institutional protection implausible to such an extent that it can no longer evade its reparadoxification. The law's confrontation with problems of world society, under such headings as ecological risks, consequences of reproductive medicine, or exclusion of entire population groups as an effect of worldwide functional differentiation, brings out the fact that here the law is faced with social problems that can no longer be approached through oscillation between subjective rights and institutions, guided by meta-norms.

The search for new deparadoxifications then becomes critical. Which new distinctions should be brought into the deconstructed void of the

---

[50] R Wiethölter, above n 3 72f.
[51] J Derrida, above n 19, at 969.

collision directrice between rights and institutions? Wiethölter's formulations here are extremely cautious:

> Perhaps the most exciting hope might come from a sort of 'law,' truly a 'law of the constitution' or 'law of the legal constitution,' that occupies the conflict-of-laws principles for law versus morality, law versus politics, law versus the economy etc, or more exactly and more generally, law as a 'structural coupling' of 'life-world systems': 'protection of rights' and 'protection of institutions' in contemporary translation would then become justificatory protection for the roles of freedom.[52]

Still more cautiously formulated is the attempt to establish a new leading distinction: reciprocity versus (im-)partiality. Both sides of this distinction have admittedly little to do with their traditional meaning. Reciprocity is now understood as a mutual tying down of autonomies and (im-)partiality now means engaging in autonomy under reserved control.[53]

Wiethölter thereby draws up a *punctatio,* the points of which, taken together, constitute a highly risky contractual offer. I ought perhaps in conclusion to seek to go into this offer point by point, with suggestions for supplementing the preliminary contract, leaving it to others' interpretive skills to decide whether they amount to declarations of acceptance or new offers.

Point 1: Conflicts between Law and Society

Wiethölter asks to dissolve the central law versus non-law distinction into various 'conflict of laws principles for law versus morality, law versus politics, law versus the economy etc.' This means setting law's focus definitively on a radical pluralism of social autonomies. A whole bundle of distinctions now serves for deparadoxification and becomes a substitute for deplausibilised dichotomies of private versus public, subjective rights versus objective rights, entitlements versus infrastructures, contract versus organisation, individual versus institution. What is here at the centre of the 'law of the legal constitution,' cutting across the obsolete dichotomy of private and public law, is the law's relation to extremely varied social autonomies and their intrinsic rationalities and normativities.

The consequences of this shift are hard to foresee. At any rate, it means finally taking leave of the triangle of politics/economy/law and accepting a polygon of social rationalities, all equally original, that the law has to take into account. This makes the dispute over the social primacy of any one subrationality—under headings like the economic society, the knowledge

---

[52] R Wiethölter, above n 16, at 119.
[53] R Wiethölter, above n 3, at 71.

society or the organisational society—obsolete. The equation 'private law equals economic law' has to be dissolved into the new equation 'private law equals law of society,' wherein 'law of society' from the outset implies a multiplicity of socially autonomous kinds of law. A law of the legal constitution must, from the outset, abandon the hope of a constitution of the whole of society, a locus where the total social identity can be defined, and adapt to an irreducible multiplicity of 'laws of society.' The challenge now can no longer be called 'law of economic constitution I, II, or III,' but a multiplicity of civil constitutions in which not only is a third sector of non-profit organisations and concerned citizens covered by law, but the respective intrinsic normativities of the social autonomies can assert their claims.[54]

This should be accompanied by a new weighting of the traditional sources of law, with a devaluation of legislative law corresponding to a simultaneous higher value on law-making within society as the outcome of internal social conflicts, and on judge-made law as able to sense and reflect social normativities. The priority goal for such civil constitutions would, however, have to be to focus more decisively on the legal protection of non-economic and non-political normativities in society. The law must primarily set itself the problem of 'institutional externalities,' the 'environmental damage' brought by autonomisation processes.[55]

Point 2: Sacrificium Intellectus

The shift from conflict of laws to paradox-based legal thinking, which is supposed to result in a 'contemporary translation' of the leading conflict between protection of rights and institutional protection into reciprocity versus (im-)partiality, has consequences for a style of legal thinking that academic moralists ought rightly to rebuke as intellectual dishonesty, obdurate dogmatism or at least *pensiero debole*. If, however, it is true that absolutely any distinction can be deconstructed, that absolutely any decision ends in undecidabilities, that absolutely any conflict of laws ends in paradoxes, then new distinctions that can be upheld even only temporarily, eg, reciprocity versus (im-)partiality, can be introduced only by making the sacrifice of waiving criticism.

That ought to be particularly hard for such an acute lawyer and passionate enlightener as Wiethölter. But once one has reached out only one's little finger to deconstructive, paradoxical thinking, then on pain of total

---

[54] First steps in this direction can be found in G Teubner, 'Contracting Worlds: Invoking Discourse Rights in Private Governance Regimes' (2000) 9 *Social and Legal Studies* 399.

[55] On the analysis of institutional externalities, see D Sciulli, *Theory of Societal Constitutionalism* (Cambridge, 1992); D Sciulli, 'The Critical Potential of the Common Law Tradition (1994) 94 *Columbia Law Review* 1076.

paralysis one has to make the paradoxes of the newly proposed distinctions invisible, keep their latencies latent, repress their inconsistencies, refrain from deconstructing them, set bounds on acuity, waive criticism, set up cover-ups, deceive one's students—at any rate, one must, if social problem pressure so requires and urges plausibility in the net of socially valid distinctions.

It follows from the deconstructability of all institutions that critique without a substitute proposal does not count. 'A communication may take a critical stance on any particular norm: but if it does it has to offer a substitute proposal.'[56] This is not easy to reconcile with Wiethölter's suspension of the constraint to decide. Admittedly, this *sacrificium intellectus* is different from that demanded of the theologian in the name of faith, or the lawyer in the name of legal doctrine. For pressure of social problems and plausibility are themselves not stable quantities, but historically variable, so that there can always only be contemporary, socially adequate and therefore fluctuating justice. And both are in turn exposed to public reflection and to dispute over exactly how it fits the programme of a political legal theory. It is this level of exhaustive analysis and discussion of social problems and social consistency upon which critical thinking must accordingly concentrate, in order to be able to assess whether the newly introduced distinctions like reciprocity versus (im-)partiality are speedily to be deconstructed again, or else may claim at least temporary validity. And Sisyphus must at the same time beware of letting the toilsomely raised stone, which might in the proper circumstances rest stably on the hilltop for a while, roll back down for lack of sufficient care in deconstruction.

Point 3: Blind Experimentalism

The groping character of a deparadoxification of law versus non-law that suggests new distinctions only experimentally and is exposed to the test of social compatibility, corresponds to a way of proceeding that not so long ago was 'pooh-poohed' as 'muddling through,' namely a radical incrementalism, an experimentation under extreme uncertainty, a 'blind' stumbling by the law from case to case, a stumbling of politics from scandal to scandal. This implies doing without grand designs, the implementation of big social projects—yet not doing without social theory. Theory now changes its role. It becomes comparable with the medieval divinatory practice of *punctatio*: arbitrarily setting points in the sand for venturesome interpretations and predictions, so as to find guiding benchmarks through subsequent confirmation or non-confirmation.

Legally, this heralds a reassessment of case law. The primacy of experience holds in the particular case and of the single-case law over the overly-hasty

---

[56] N Luhmann, above n 26, at 428.

generalising approach of the abstract rules. Yet, this should be accompanied by a decided politicising of case law, not just aimed at balancing individual interests in an individual case, but explicitly seen as a social experiment. If this is not to be only an empty formula for reviving the quiescent civil law, then it would have to be reflected in procedural changes to the law, changes ranging from collectivisation of the right of action via rights of public involvement and hearing or more ambitious evidential procedures to an ex post, learning way of handling judgments at law.

Point 4: Society-wide Reciprocity

This concept is as far removed from the feudal prince-vassal relation of loyalty as from the mutuality of market exchange. Seeking to set up individual contractual parity using individual judicial corrections looks like naïve recourse to outmoded concepts of *ius* in a balanced relationship between individuals. What is instead to be sought is compensation for asymmetric individual relations, restoring balanced social relations by an extremely circuitous route across several system boundaries. The point is, then, reciprocity as mutual dependence of subautonomies, something that applies not just to the autonomy of social systems but also to that of individuals, collectives, institutions and formal organisations. It is a normative concept through and through, and is therefore much closer to Durkheim's solidarity in conditions of a social division of labour than to Luhmann's concept of the structural linkage of areas of social autonomy.

Consequences of this sort of integration effort through society-wide reciprocity ought to go in the direction of greater dissociation between law and institutionalised politics. If it is true that politics has, if not lost its leading role in integrating the whole of society, then at least largely cut it back, then reciprocity can no longer be described as an exclusively political project in which the law has to follow up on legislative action, and especially omission, in thoughtful obedience, but as a project wherein the law itself must enter responsively into emerging forms of reciprocity in society. Such proponents of a normative sociology as Lon Fuller or Philip Selznick, but also François Ewald or Roger Friedland and Robert Alford, are perhaps the protagonists here of an interinstitutional 'morality' taking shape in society, the intrinsic potential of which is taken up by the law and can be built on in thoughtful obedience.[57] And at this point, quite numerous network phenomena come

---

[57] L Fuller, *The Morality of Law* (New Haven, Yale University Press, 1969); P Selznick, *Law, Society and Industrial Justice* (New York, 1969); P Selznick, *The Moral Commonwealth: Social Theory and the Promise of Community* (Berkeley, University of California Press, 1992); F Ewald, *L'État Providence* (Paris, 1986); R Friedland and R Alford, 'Bringing Society Back in Symbols, Practices, and Institutional Contradictions' in WW Powell and P DiMaggio (eds), *The New Institutionalism in Organizational Analysis* (Chicago, University of Chicago Press, 1991) 232–63.

into play, overlaying if not replacing the integrative effects of institutionalised politics. Wiethölter's scepticism over the fashionable network debate should disappear, if it could, in fact, be shown not just that networks are hybrid legal formations between law of contract and company law, but that intersystem networks, because they obey different logics of action, can contribute decisively to creating society-wide reciprocity.[58]

Point 5: Impartial Partiality

Through this openly paradoxical formula, political legal theory definitively distinguishes itself from systems or deconstructive paradoxologies. If the formula is to mean the law's relation to social autonomy, as the following quotation suggests:

> Autonomy was in fact never anywhere a guarantee of decentralized and sectoral 'general good' but itself a party, to which one can release activities only at the cost of 'objectively justified' criteria, venues kept open and fairness procedures kept to, in short, 'relative impartiality' and capacity for universalization[59]

... then the formula contains neither a sociologisation of law nor its theologisation, but a release of social potentials for normativity, a sort of maieutics.

This differs from Luhmann's systems sociology, which celebrates its impartial social theory distance, in its participant perspective on legal discourse through partiality, in a threefold sense: first, partiality for normativity criteria of the legal tradition and the further development of law, rightly demanded quite impartially from the autonomous sectors of society; secondly, partiality for normativity criteria of the autonomous sectors themselves, for which in cases of conflict the law takes sides in order to impartially resolve disputes; finally, partiality for one of Wiethölter's most remarkable puzzling formulas, for 'society as society,' which, though explicitly building on Luhmann's deconstruction of society, as it were counterfactually and utopianly clings to it.[60]

The formula also contains a demarcation from deconstruction, pointing in its concept of justice towards a transcendent otherness of law. It is here that one of Wiethölter's most radical ideas lies, which he also formulates with appropriate caution:

---

[58] For this view of networks, see KH Ladeur, 'Towards a Legal Theory of Supranationality: The Viability of the Network Concept' (1997) 3 *European Law Journal* 33; G Teubner, 'Hybrid Laws: Constitutionalizing Private Governance Networks' in RA Kagan et al, *Legality and Community: On the Intellectual Legacy of Philip Selznick* (Berkeley, Rowman, 2002) 311–31; A Windeler, *Unternehmungsnetzwerke: Konstitution und Strukturation* (Wiesbaden, Verlag, 2001).
[59] R Wiethölter, above n 10, at 21.
[60] R Wiethölter, above n 16, at 117.

Perhaps the emancipation of such law from law in the rival social theories, which, no doubt, as 'other than law' or 'other law', does not (yet) seem out of date, into an 'Other of law' contains a step towards chances of realization, and perhaps then as 'universal' general (not solely private) law. 'Law' would then not be bowing to social-theory designs, but itself be one, and therefore at any rate not 'system', not 'discourse', not an 'undertaking'.[61]

Such a far-reaching autonomisation of law, which—in total contradiction to earlier formulations—moves away from dependency on social theories and promotes law itself into a social-theory design, would indeed cross the boundaries of law, though not in the direction of a transcendence of otherness, but of the immanence of a quasi-therapeutic relationship oriented to the healing normativity of medicine, not as externalisation in the direction of public health and biopolitics, but as a 're-entry' of the logic of wounding and healing into law.[62] One question ultimately remains open about this therapeutic relationship between law and society. Which is the therapist and which the patient?

---

[61] R Wiethölter, above n 3, at 73.

[62] 'Law, which can draw its force of validity neither from eternal ideas nor from itself, verges more on "medicine" and "biology" than on theology and technology, and is—as "poiesis"— more of an "art" than a "science,"' R Wiethölter, *Verrechtlichung*, MS (Frankfurt, 1995) (on file with the author) 9.

3

Just-ifications of a Law of Society

RUDOLF WIETHÖLTER

Translated by Iain L Fraser[1]

I. PRELIMINARY

I TALKED ON THIS theme[2] on 2 November 1998, on an invitation from D Simon, at the Max Planck Institute for European Legal History, speaking freely on the basis of notes in the form of a batch of keywords. The intense and widespread interest among the 'audience' ('Friends, Romans, Countrymen') imposed—objectively—desires for the impossible on the speaker: a 'state-of-the-law message' (from the late autumn of one's professional life?); an ad hoc arbitration ruling on rival theories (the labourer's meta-critique of royal buildings?); a 'final lecture' (as a speech to the educated among the contemptuous rabble, as a reverse prophecy, as an autobiographical fragment?). The outcome then (presumably also the observed one) was: none of that, and a bit of all of it—*omnia omnes omnino*. Or (borrowing not so freely from Theodor W Adorno), I wanted to lay my cards on the table, but that is not the same as the game. Obviously, the point then is (only!?) card games. Still more briefly, my presentation was aimed at punctations,[3] richly intertwined, enciphered and riddling, in a word: 'poietically/unsystematically.'

---

[1] Translator's note: The writer engages in many kinds of wordplay, often splitting the compound words common in German into their component parts to suggest several meanings at once. Most of this is untranslatable; the flavour resembles that of the styleme of some preachers in English, who split 'atonement', say, into 'at-one-ment'. I have added the occasional note, where unavoidable, to elucidate otherwise impenetrable connections.

[2] Translator's note: Both nouns in the title are hyphenated. *Recht-fertigung* (just-ification) can be etymologised as 'making/manufacturing law/right and giving reasons.' *Gesellschaftsrecht* is the ordinary word for law of associations (company law plus partnership law). Hyphenation recalls that '*Gesellschaft*' is also the ordinary word for 'society.' I have retained the law of associations here as a nod to the author's free-association style, while elsewhere mostly using 'society.'

[3] Translator's note: lists of points; often preliminary contracts.

I have dodged the imposed temptation to submit a basic paper for Florence by submitting the naked keywords from then, now in a somewhat different garb. The 'punctation' that follows thus recreates the 1998 talk, without being it. As the form, I have chosen torsos or fragments of 'key concepts.' Keys like this count for references to others or to myself, for associations, for connections: in short, for extrapolations or further calculations, for memories and hopes, or more fashionably, for areas of experience and horizons of expectations. They aim at ('radical'!?) 'disclosures' of problems, ('cautious' and 'considerate'?) 'conclusions' to discourses, and ('provisional', 'circumspect'!?) 'resolutions' of decisions.

I wish to offer as a concurrent self-reference, or as it were a virtual appendix, two earlier papers.[4]

II. FRAGMENT 1: ACCESSIONS TO INHERITANCE

Law as one's own time grasped in thought—a Promethean reaching for the stars, today unbearable. That is, law that ought to be fixed, irrespective of not being attached to or supported on anything, whether in heaven or on earth; not to be understood from itself, nor from the so-called development of the human spirit—a logic of decay as an ideal pan-Cassandra. So, as before, we are back with Sisyphus: we are contemporaries of a legal dispute about the process of law, seen from a particular vantage point. But which one?

The Trinity developed in the eighteenth century against all intermediary ('social') powers, in political philosophy (every human being has legal capacity, but only human beings), political economy (no monopolies or privileges) and political sociology (*il n'y a que l' état et l'individu*) has enabled an art of historical development in political economy that manages to have dealings with Rousseau-type trends and at the same time philosophically idealist ones. That established historical burdens of proof for the nineteenth and twentieth centuries. 'Rule of law' (the heritage of political philosophy) and 'democracy' (the heritage of political sociology) are among the characteristic features of 'political economy' that can be continually re-related anew to each other and played off against each other. For more than 200 years, thus, the 'strong state' and the 'sound economy' have been rivalling about determining society as a society where emancipation stands for freedom from all sorts of unfreedom arising in the name of objective rationality of rule, majority will of the people or free individual rights. Since the French revolution, then, a latent undecidability has been maintained as to whether the revolutionary public would be more of an (Anglo-American-type) civil society, or

---

[4] Reprinted in *KritV* 1988, 1–28, and in G Teubner (ed), *Entscheidungsfolgen als Rechtsgründe* (1995) 89–120.

else some continental mode of state-society dichotomy (meaning a dichotomy between politics and the economy). Germany kept to the state-society model, but as it were filled in the French analytical and technical basic pattern with Anglo-American pragmatic spirit, thus feeling able to assert democracy and liberalism as a unitary construction. What was bestowed on us, though, at any rate in Germany, was only either 'society' wishing to achieve its specific partial interest position as a higher pre-state right against the state through the state, or else the 'state,' wishing to impose its own inherited rationality of power on historical developments as permanent administration from above. What got left behind along the way was 'society as society,' as a claim to bring traditions of 'democratic' universality of duties of virtue and 'liberal' universality of freedoms reconstructively into a universality of law, which, in terms of 'political economy' and at the same time 'social morality,' and despite all the ambivalences, tips over neither into the functionalisation in public and constitutional law of 'partial' law (the historical path that Kant's philosophy took politically) nor into the total, biased taking over of all legality (the historical path of the 'strong state' and the 'sound economy' to date).

What defines us in terms of 'legal science' continues to be the fight over the 'society of law' itself. The alternative, hitherto held (at least in Germany) to be unavoidable, or at any rate unexchangeable, namely between 'public' (state) law as rationally necessary and 'private' law (of civil society) as subjectively arbitrary, or else guaranteeing necessarily rational 'freedom' as law against all conceivable ('private') systems of ownership including their ('public') guarantees, cannot help us (any longer). It is no surprise that our legal semantics of 'legal protection' (with guaranteed subjective rights at the centre) and 'institutional protection' (with temporal, material and social infrastructural guarantees at the centre) does neither 'good' nor 'justice' to the contemporary requirements of the timeless paradox of law (in brief, of a law of conflict of laws about (legally) right and wrong admitted into the law).

'Society as law of society'—that is the three-front war in ('revolutionary') permanence: for 'independent' against 'feudal' power (today, allegedly, of whatever kind!), for preservation of the established against (and for establishment of what is to be preserved through) the challenging power of the unsatisfied-unpacified 'non-independent' (today, more abstractly, the world shared with others, the social sphere and posterity—'*Mit-, Um- und Nachwelt*'), for lasting and continuing transcendences of the whole as a whole by the whole (in time and space) against its—equally lasting and continuing—deconstructions. In traditional political and legal language, these fronts are called: Front 1 = 'freedom' ('economy,' 'liberalism'), Front 2 = 'equality' ('politics,' 'socialism'), Front 3 = 'Third Way' ('democratic and social state based on rule of law'). Front 3—'transcending' the other two fronts—today defines all the debates about a societal interest of law in itself that cannot (any longer) be understood and applied exclusively from the viewpoint of 'markets' and 'politics,' but will have to rearrange the 'right of action'—'admissibilities'—in the redistributions of social learning to change that are emerging in the longer term. This ideal overall front is the 'law.'

The whole of the legal world here (like the world in general) is in favour of 'modernisation.' What counts as modernisation—with and since Max Weber—is a timelessly abstractable and, at the same time, reflexibilisable triangle of demythologisations (copings with the past), differentiations (logics of the particular under reservations of the determinability of the general) and autonomies (emancipations into possible—and therefore more and different than any achieved—freedom, which has then to establish itself immediately and simultaneously against all sorts of unfreedom). Such efforts at change aim concretely at comparisons and gains in capacities for solutions to problems. In practice, the point is—so at bottom the lines of convergence of all the influential major theories (systems sociology, institutional economics, political philosophy) say—functional definitions as law-shaping postulates, which become the basis of general legislating or law-making doctrines, or more specifically, permissions for decisional freedoms under review.

Observation of the event as first interim consideration: enormous heritages that have not been entered into: so many beginnings for 'transcendings' there have never been (while there always were, though not this way).

Note:
> One man asks: 'what comes next'
> The other only 'is it right?'
> And that's what differentiates
> The free man from the slave.[5]

III. FRAGMENT 2: RIDDLING ENCHANTMENTS

With 'riddles' (aka 'problems', aka ...) of 'society' and 'law,' things seem for some time to have been bewitched: society, like law (once again, not so freely after TW Adorno), seemed once to have been overtaken, but are kept alive because the time for their realisation was missed. For all the rival social theories, 'society' and 'law' are central, yet they do not stand at the centre.

'Society,' Qua

1. Critical philosophy: not unsocial sociability, not a state of emergency or reason, not social humanity, no third-class or fourth-class conceptuality.

---

[5] Translator's note: Iambic, three tetrameters + one trimeter, rhymed *abcb*.

Instead (explicitly and comprehensively in the context of a 'critical' theory of society), efforts to extend a concept of basic antagonisms: after byways through forces of production versus relationship production, labour versus interaction versus politics, system versus life-world, we now have challenges to the institutionalised, organised manufacture of decisions by culturally mobilisable subpublics—on the discovering and learning search for a civil society that is to be created and exercised.
2. Systems sociology: the 'society of society' (Niklas Luhmann, 1997: 'Since the classics, that is, for about a hundred years now, sociology has not made any noteworthy progress in the theory of society'; 'when I was taken into the faculty of sociology of the University of Bielefeld, established in 1969, I found myself confronted with the demand to name research projects I was working on. My project, then and since, was called: theory of society; duration: 30 years; cost: none') is 'the social system itself' as the 'underlying system reference'; all in all, a 'theory of society as the proposal to describe society in society'; 'the leading question is, then, what operation this system produces and reproduces whenever it occurs. The answer ... is: communication.' (There follow 1,164 more pages).
3. Institutional economics: a constitutional monarchy without a monarch, but with a secret king, the 'law' (not so freely after G Radbruch); its 'private law of society' is not 'private,' is neither 'law' nor 'society,' but a total constitution (= society) guided by political economy (= private), defined by social philosophy in terms of content (= law).

L von Stein was unable to classify 'any concept of society yet.' Max Weber had already lost interest in it. In between had come the invention of sociology. Admittedly, it leaves 'society' lying on the left (or the right). 'Social actions,' 'social systems' take advantage of their careers as themes. For all that, the simple faith-type belief in 'state versus society' is gone forever; the 'case for both' exists (if it does?) as once did 'God' in deistic times. So *nunc et semper:* 'theory of society.'

'Law,' Qua

1. Critical philosophy: without law it does not work—and with law it does not either! The summing up in movement theory is defined 'historically and in terms of the logic of decline': pure law cannot be strong, strong law cannot stay pure. The 'traditions' that remain recall the beginnings of unavailability, and hope 'at long last' for the 'proceduralisation' dialectic of potentials that can be made actual.
2. Systems sociology: law is dead—long live law! The summing up in difference theory is defined in terms of 'Germanic inheritance law': *le mort*

saisît le vif; the dead inherits the living. No *hereditas iacens,* no interim administrations of new by old or old by new, but old by old versus new by new—'law as enforcement of law,' This looks like—both when observing the *x*th stage and in the final view—(permanently reserved!) total repudiation of inheritance. 'It may therefore very well be that the contemporary prominence of the legal system and the dependence of society itself and of most of its functional systems on the functioning of the legal code is nothing but a European anomaly that will wither away with the evolution of a world society.'

3. Institutional economics: law is (no longer) what it (anyway never) was! The summing up in enterprise theory is defined in 'conspiratorial cryptography' terms: free competition on open markets—an equation in at least four (since there are at least four 'revealed'!) unknowns.
4. 'Juridifications' (which can be joined by dejuridifications and de-dejuridifications, inclusively or successively): *Querelle des Anciens et des Modernes* in a second great edition (= 'Juridification II'; the previous stage, 'Juridification I' until the 1960s/1970s of the twentieth century, ending at the time in failure of politics and market failure as failure of law).
5. Traditional alternative: special general (especially private) law (ie, in a nutshell, 'impure' law of the sphere of circulation) and general special (especially 'private') law (ie, in a nutshell, 'situational' law of the social sphere); its exhausted energies can be summed up as follows: traditional 'formalisations' of law 'confer' their hidden materialities on citizens who are free and equal in 'money' and/or 'power' as they do their business ('wealth' as special having and being able! Correspondingly definable having and being able! Correspondingly definable inability to have and be able, or to be able to have!). 'Materialisations' on the foundations of such forms are then condemned ('cultural criticism') to swear powerlessly to ideas against realities or developments, or—in thoroughly authoritarian/totalitarian fashion—to rely on particular particularities ('interests'). Universal general (not only 'private') law is left as the unsolved riddle of the uncompleted project of modernity.
6. Observation of the event as second interim consideration: contradictions, paradoxes, agonies, as far as one can see (or can see that one does not see). Law has 'emancipated' itself radically for the whole world into self-determinacy, and is nonetheless dependent on nothing so much as on externality, normativity, structuring, if it is not to be stolen, to get lost, or be otherwise misplaced. Law now this way, now that? As if bewitched! For a social (legal) dispute about the latent, hidden, tacit 'linkage' of law in the (legal) dispute orientations of the rival social projects that have in turn left 'society' behind them and rely on 'theory of society' about the process of law—obviously—does not come about in the camps of the various parties. That is the powerlessness of all law.

Note:
'When Cicero stepped down from the rostrum,
all the people cried in delight 'no mortal speaks finer!'
when Demosthenes stepped down, what the Athenians shouted was:
'War against Philip, war!'[6]

IV. FRAGMENT 3: PROMISES OF SCEPTICISM

The short formulas for the ('bourgeois' and 'anti-bourgeois') tradition of promises which continue to dominate us are: some favour promises of a (better) future that will displace the (worse) present (and even more, the always and still worse past), others favour promises of a (better) future that is being displaced by the (worse, and made even worse by the past) present. Only, we all lack faith in salvific messages, even if they have been more fashionably formulated for some time now: ways of tying down time; to stop and to endure ... and so forth.

My vision of a productive utopia is: the constitutional law of law! Instead of 'constitution' one might also say constitutionalisation, enabling and realisation, comparison and linkage, relation or the like. The only important thing is that the point is 'conflict of laws rules' as a form (note *en passant*: PIL as a related approach, though only in spirit, not by blood!), for the sake of 'things' (as content) (note *en passant*: etymologically, thing means 'dispute'!). There are accordingly two connected—'logically-historically' determined—legal propria: 1) the uncompleted, whether in bourgeois or anti-bourgeois terms, post-feudal project of 'reciprocity'; here the point is to fasten down (aka to network, mediate, 'transcend,' etc) dependent independencies (also identifiable as independent dependencies) that can replace Immanuel Kant's 'autonomy' as—more than 'freedom' and 'equality'—determinant *materia in motu*; 2) the 'impartial partiality' (also identifiable as partial impartiality) of all law that can be unstuck only in methodological and theoretical ways; here the point is dealings with, or concessions of, autonomies (aka freedoms, experiences, caprices etc) subject to reserved review (criteria, venues/fora, procedures). The building in of law versus non-law into law by way of 'law of conflict of laws' lets 'non-law' be interpreted more briefly as eg, 'politics' (this is how 'political legal theory' wishes to be interpreted), or more specifically also as eg, 'political economy' (when one wins home to 'land' and 'house') or as 'social history' (when there is more room for memories and souvenirs) or ... (when ...).

Law of the legal constitution is 'proceduralisation,' 'just-ification,' a productive principle for 'positive law as right law,' and in its turn, thus,

---

[6] Translator's note: mostly iambic, rhymed *abba*.

similarly in dependent-independent independence-dependency, tied just as much to its own superfluousness and uselessness as to the caprice of 'Law and Justice,' always 'aimed' at the avoidances it carries with it, especially of failure 'of itself (of law).' Proceduralisation does not merely play off materiality against formality (or vice versa). It is not a continuation of traditional form-content definitions, but a resumption of materialisation definitions and their determinabilities by form. It does not have some other law, nor something other than law, in mind, but the other (one possible other) of law, its redeemable surpluses of enabling rather than its unredeemed ones of promise. Everything possible is possible! That is literally true. Or more briefly: 'justification' is the form of the thing 'proceduralisation.'

Law of the legal constitution can take on board the messages of institutional economics, to plan law as an incentive for purposes of action towards decision, no less profitably, and economically of resources, than the messages of systems sociology to keep richness of variation and sensitivity to retention always simultaneously available in the selection processes, or the messages of critical philosophy to 'try out' regulatory postulates of law of conflict of laws as law of challenge and improvement in disputes over practical suitability in application (ie, as a rule counterfactually!). And conversely, law of the legal constitution profits, in its decisive decisions as to distinctions, from the decisive strengths/weaknesses of the social-theory camps, from their blind spots, their presumptuous presumptions, their deceptions (which may take the form of blackouts or screens), especially at the—always indefinitely-definite—'lock-gates', ie, the 'boundaries' between system and environment in systems sociology, where 'structural linkages' or 'externalisations' are negotiated and decided, at the 'undertakings' in institutional economics, to which competence privileges are 'allotted,' at the 'passages' in critical philosophy, where validity and recognition are to be accomplished.

'Society,' which L von Stein was unable to 'classify,' observed, understood and explained by our classics not so much as an object but from methodological or theoretical perspectives, has so far been unable ('quite contrary to its intentions') 'to unite men without dividing them, nor divide without establishing the gaps between them' (GE Lessing). 'Coordination' and 'subordination' simultaneously: bringing chaos into order—such a society (paradoxically enough) can never be had; 'the point is' to bring it forth (again). Here, what is to be relied on is the hidden plans of the nature of law and the usage of legal reason, cultivated in conflict, which means, on the 'developmental dynamics' (aka dialectics, basic contradictions, challenges) of 'nets' (eg, globalisations) and 'caprices' (eg, individualisations).

Then, law of the legal constitution certainly is 'poietic non-system.' This formula is not intended as some sort of 'anti-podium' to Gunther Teubner's 'autopoietic system.' Yet the 'auto' (an Enigma system all by itself?) meets with 'reluctant acquiescence' (J Taubes), and the 'system' is showing traces of wear (instead of endless notes and reminders, let three suffice: for the British ideal gentleman, 'man of system' meant a doctrinarian; 'the will to system is a lack of integrity' (F Nietzsche); TW Adorno explicitly saw his *magnum opus* ('Negative Dialectics') as an 'Anti-System'). 'Poietic non-system'—that is, the 'administration of justice'[7] as cultivation of the paradox of law itself, of simultaneously its preservation and its treatment; it is spontaneous, self-conscious, self-justifying 'legal games,' it is 'medicine' (healing through operations) and 'art' (as a reminder: 'wit' = 'noting the connection between distant ideas' (Jean Paul). In brief, it is 'surprising turns,' though not as adaptability or frivolity, not as a cold shower or malice; instead, 'getting' the law is justification in application, more 'production' than 'presentation,' more context of discovery than context of justification, more question than answer, more finding possibility than seeking reality, more perception than prediction[8] (in more technical legal terms, rather querying the facts than establishing the legal consequences), and in these respects, then, 'really' a work of seeking, learning and discovery. Or in older European terms: *aisthesis* as 'receptive' basic experience and expectation of/for/in perceptions and imaginations, plus *poiesis* as 'productive' basic experience and expectation of/for/in ('critical'!) constructions, 'creations,' 'reprimands,'[9] plus *katharsis* as 'communicative' basic experience and expectation of/for/in 'movements,' changes, healings. Or more briefly: 'Lichtenberg's subjunctives' (A Schöne)—realistic thinking thanks to the capacity to imagine things might be different, and the conscience that they ought to be made better.

Observation of the event as third interim consideration: to socialise the law of society in law of justification terms into law, and justify justifications in law of association terms—perhaps (but 'perhaps' would, of course, need a separate law as social theory lecture of its own) that contains a solved riddle and at the same time the power of law. Perhaps the emancipation of such law from law in the rival social theories, which, no doubt, as 'other than law' or 'other law,' does not (yet) seem out of date, into an 'other of law' contains a step towards chances of realisation, and perhaps then as 'universal' general (not solely private) law. 'Law' would then not be bowing to social theory designs, but itself be one, and therefore at any rate not 'system,' not 'discourse,' not an 'undertaking.' The problems of connections (Does that which applies to this law apply correspondingly to 'language,' to 'corresponding' language?) are stimulating—for another talk, by another speaker.

---

[7] Translator's note: the German term *Rechtspflege*, taken literally, can be seen as meaning care/cultivation of the law.

[8] Translator's note: the two German words etymologise as 'truth-taking' and 'truth-saying.'

[9] Translator's note: the German etymologises as 'settings to rights,' and can also mean directions/corrections.

Note:
> Whether the right understanding of law
> was ever known to anyone
> is doubtful: all opinion
> will always find something wrong.
> What's doubtful, though,
> can hardly be a science.[10]

V. FRAGMENT 4: TEMPTATIONS TO PROHIBITION

It is not surprising that in the law (and not just in private law), the tracks and traces of social theories are to be found. If 'lacunae in justice' (keyword: avoiding contempt and humiliation, waste, aberrations) become the predominant theme of searching, learning and discovery, then involvements in and effects from societal infrastructures will turn the careers of legal theories around: 'preventive neglect' will replace 'elimination of consequences' ('*culpa in non faciendo*'!).

Traditional 'spatial-objective' legal thinking has for some time now been replaced by 'functional' methods. These do not combine forms, causalities, freedoms, but target relations, programme performance, networks, automatisms. In sum: it is risk prevention, compensation for special sacrifice and obligations to acquiesce that are staged by the legal dramaturgies. 'Freedom' (of processes, manufacture, organisations etc) under controls (barriers, self-restraint thresholds etc) brings the infringer (of ground rules) to the fore, not 'the injured.' Guarantees of expectations become more important than instructions to act. The 'free' are (or become) those who 'guarantee' upright, authentic, appropriate status, in short 'integrity,' and/or the findings of the transactional activities concerned. 'Freedom,' like 'procedures,' like 'controls,' has to ensure legal games that are successful because they are 'tractable.'

The development was to be seen in all fields (at any rate in private law, including labour and business law, with which I am particularly familiar): provision of goods and services, industrial disputes and conflicts of opinion, accidents, etc (or more briefly, administration of things).

The proceduralisation of just-ification is—*qua* criteria, venues, procedures—tied back to social theory instructions, particularly as regards laws of historical experience and the structural conditions of compatibilities. It is here that forecasting prerogatives (with, at the top, constitutional courts and the legislator) and corresponding error prerogatives (in some circumstances also correction obligations)—familiar to lawyers as the issues of the burdens of allegation and of proof—play their parts. One magic formula

---

[10] Translator's note: Trochaic tetrameters, rhymed *aabbcc*.

(from the German Federal Constitutional Court) that is universalisable runs: freedom, where all experiences and all insights give convincing support. Or more briefly (linking up with Fragment III): 'just-ification' is ideally justly made where the messages (as impositions, barriers, restraints) of the rival social theory projects are 'proceduralised' and 'temporalised,' ie, 'recognised,' 'understood,' 'processed.' 'The point is' to put the theoretical possibilities, in terms of movement or difference or enterprise methodologies, to the test in practice.

In the legal toolbox—and it is again hardly surprising—old-new 'figures' are making headway: unenforceable obligations, executed contracts, arbitral awards (articles 315-317 BGB[11] as an almost crystal-clear principle of discourse!?), frustration of contract (as a reminder: *promissa in se habent tacitam condicionem si maneant res quo sunt loco* (H Grotius)).

Observation of the event as fourth interim consideration: freedoms under impositions—a project that entangles prohibitions into temptations, and temptations into prohibitions. This is the practice for coping with contingencies of an 'artificial' theory 'in being'[12] ('perhaps'!?) the paradigm of a self-righteous law of the legal constitution. And it will continue, as before, to be 'Poetry and Truth.'[13]

Note:
> Motto for the First Part (this and the following relate to Goethe's *Dichtung und Wahrheit*): 'He who is not flayed does not learn [line from Menander '[Ο μὴ δαρεὶς ἄνθρωπος οὐ παιδεύεται]'.[14] This is institutional economics (insights into necessities).
> Motto for the Second Part: 'What youth desires, age receives in abundance.'[15] This is critical philosophy (better late than never).
> Motto for the Third Part: 'It is assured that trees do not grow into the sky.'[16] This is systems sociology (variation—selection—retention).
> Motto for the Fourth Part: '*Nemo contra deum nisi deus ipse.*'[17] Is this ('perhaps'!?) 'critical law' in the compromise negotiations between autopoietic System and poietic Non-system?

---

[11] Translator's note: the German Civil Code.
[12] Translator's note: English in original.
[13] Translator's note: the title of Goethe's autobiography.
[14] Translator's note: used by Goethe as epigraph to his autobiography.
[15] Translator's note: quote from Goethe's autobiography.
[16] Translator's note: also in Goethe, though possibly already proverbial.
[17] Translator's note: likewise in Goethe.

4

The Reference of Paradox: Missing Paradoxity as Real Perplexity in Both Systems Theory and Deconstruction

JEAN CLAM

I. LAW'S TEXTURE AND ITS (W)HOLENESS: THE POSSIBILITY OF A REFERENCE TO A PARADOX OF LAW

IS THERE A paradox in law, especially a fundamental, foundational one? What is not there, for sure, is a simple answer to such a simple question. Paradoxes are not to be found in law like texts, arguments, procedures, rhetorical figures, logical methods, etc are. One could try to enumerate the maximum of legal objects one is able to find in the domain of law, in an attempt to build a complete inventory of them; still, among those objects, we are not able to identify such a thing as a paradox.

Let us then start our search for a paradox of law the other way round. If it is not there, in law, so let us ask: what then is there in law? It could very well be that what is sought but cannot be found among the other constituents of law is not accidentally, but structurally, absent on the level of items, objects, constituents, components, etc of law.

I speak of texts, arguments, procedures, rhetorical figures, logical methods, etc. Those are undoubtedly legal objects, but how do we get a complete inventory of all such objects? One would have to sharpen one's intuition and try to think of together, as if they were assembled on a single spot, all those items that could be stated as components of law. A search method would have to be devised. It could be phenomenological or functional or simply empirical, taking as a clue the current use of language. All of these methods would try to find out first what is law positively.

The empiricist would start with the most conspicuous objects of law, the great volumina filling the space of law in social life. He or she would stick to the common comprehension of the legal system as a set of institutions, articulated following a hierarchical, tripolar design: sovereign/legislative, enforcing/administrative, interpreting/judicative.[1] Law originates in the first instance and undergoes a process of implementation and concretisation in social life. Its sources are univocally ordered, and collisions of rules can be avoided by looking closely at the hierarchy of norms, or establishing some conventions as to the source that should prevail in specific internormative contests.

Starting from the experience of lawful action, the phenomenologist would try to construct the legal domain from the intention directed towards the meaning of lawfulness and the filling of that intention with intuitive evidence. There is here perfect adhesion of intention and meaning to each other. Law can be deduced from its essence down into all its branches and institutions. There is an a priorical sense in which law can be unfolded from the structure of pure practical reason or pure consciousness.[2]

The functionalist would project law as a device having the function of making social expectations mutually congruent by granting lawful expectations and the orientation of social action on them a counterfactual validity, meaning a validity that would still hold when such expectations have been disappointed by the factual course of social communication. Adapted to a figure of law which is the one with which we have been familiar since the great positivisation of law in European modernity, the functionalist view of law fits extremely well into the tremendous flexibility of modern normative evolution. An underground current of constant cognitivisation pushes a great number of norms steadily towards a decline of their normative intensity.[3] The evolution of the legal system can be quite fittingly accounted for on the grounds of such a movement of cognitivisation.[4]

An empirical or historical approach would stick to the institutional entities which have mundane reality and visibility. This approach would use these entities to unfold a general description of law as something extant in

---

[1] Interpreting in the sense of applying a general norm to the single case.

[2] The German idealists elaborated such pure deductions of law in pieces of transcendental philosophy. See, on a theory of intersubjectivity, JG Fichte, 'Grundlage des Naturrechts nach Prinzipien der Wissenschaftslehre' in *Werke* (Berlin, De Gruyter, 1971); GWF Hegel, *'Phänomenologie des Geistes'* in *Werke* (Frankfurt, Suhrkamp, 1970); Hegel, *'Rechtsphilosophie'*, in *Werke* (Frankfurt, Suhrkamp, 1971). Also see J Clam, 'Choses, échange, média: Enquête sur les étapes d'une dématérialisation de la communication' in (1999) *Archives de Philosophie du droit* 43 at 97–137; V Hösle, *Hegels System: Der Idealismus der Subjektivität und das Problem der Intersubjektivität* (Hamburg, Meiner, 1988).

[3] The cognitivisation of law could be seen as weakening its autonomy. There is, however, an aspect under which such a cognitivisation can, paradoxically, enhance legal autonomy. In the reading G Teubner makes of Wiethölter in Chapter 2, impartiality can be fostered by such a cognitivisation process. In effect, part of this allows for the deconstruction of many a 'prejudice' from which law had its stricture.

[4] It has a correlate in a counter-movement of proceduralisation of the heuresis of the norm, insofar as it correlates with a tendency to juridicise whole areas of social life which can no longer count on the massivity of intuitive normation.

human societies and playing a major role in the stabilisation and legitimation of power. Such an approach is not hampered by the insistence of classical (Roman) legal theory on the abstract nature of law. Any order is an intelligible order holding as a projection of ideas on reality. Law is in its entirety condensed in its institutions and its social efficiency. These provide us with a guiding thread through any inventory of legal objects and any exploration of the meaning of law.

In all those visions, paradox would appear at certain ends of the legal domain in the form of a dysfunctional development requiring a stepping in of legal instances or the stimulation of certain processes restoring the adequacy and the performance of law.[5] What is in law are substantive, positive and contentful, sometimes also processual, magnitudes. Nowhere in the texture of law do the holes appear out of which every mesh of it is made.[6]

To let the relationship of law to paradox come to perception, an inversion is needed that absentifies presences and plenitudes (wholenesses) and presentifies absences and 'holenesses.' It makes no sense to search for paradox by constantly enlarging the inventory of the components of law and integrating into it entities which are more and more abstract. Paradox is not 'out there' in law, but at the fundament of the movement of generation of law. This inversion which places paradox at the source of law marks the beginning in legal theory of a paradoxology that has still a great deal to do to acquire its central thought figures and to be able to handle them adequately. What we can say is that legal theory is still far from mastering the specific paradoxity of law. The developing legal paradoxology often lacks the sensitivity necessary to handle abyssal structures and movements. The tendency is always to take the paradox for granted, as if it were just there in law, as if one just needed to refer to it to get sight of it.

II. PARADOX AS AN EVANESCENT OBJECT

Our thesis is that paradox is the generative process of law itself. That means that the paradoxological main proposition of systemist legal theory itself

---

[5] It is not always possible to draw with precision the boundaries between: classical legal collisions; conflicts of norms (of the norms underlying the production of laws, which could then collide with one another); inconsistency of values (determining the crystallisation of norms); divergence of orders of meaning and their rationalities (the economic, the political, the artistic,—etc); and last but not least, paradoxical intricacies of law itself. The understanding of legal collisions (*Rechtskollisionen*) is thus a very broad one by Wiethölter. Gunther Teubner shows (in Chapter 2) that a transition exists that leads from this concept to that of paradox. Wiethölter's approach works with a very diffuse idea of the contentiousness of social communication—and of meaning in general. Such a contentiousness seeks legal channels that would narrow its scope and deliver models for its resolution. However, the specifically paradoxical contentions call upon a political decision that takes place in a context of fundamental non-decidability.

[6] The idea of a '*Lückenkonfiguriertheit*'—in the sense Peter Fuchs uses this concept—fits very accurately into our context. P Fuchs, *Moderne Kommunikation: Zur Theorie des operativen Displacements* (Frankfurt, Suhrkamp, 1993) 139.

needs to be superseded: it is not just the operation of the legal system that brings legal paradox into being and to perceptibility; it is the paradox of law that brings law to operation and generates it as the field of intelligibility and inventiveness allowing social communication to be what it is. Legal paradox is at the heart of intersubjectivity as such. It yields the intricate structure or mesh along the lines of which social communication unfolds itself.[7]

Social communication, in effect, comes in process by deparadoxising the paradoxity of its own normative regulation. Paradoxisation and deparadoxisation appear as closely correlated, and in a sense as a double-sided process in which the operation of deparadoxisation sticks constantly to the preceding, unfolding operation of paradoxisation.[8] Generation of law out of its paradox must let the paradox operate very closely underneath the current operation of the legal system. This creates a temptation to objectify the generating paradox and to position it as a unitary, consistent and indicable whole just behind the ongoing processes of legal communication.

One should be very keenly aware of this temptation and always bear in mind that a paradox is a non-object, that it is the most precise instantiation of non-objectifiability. The question is, then: how can we approach such a non-object as legal paradox? How can we get sight of it and hold it within our intellective grasp?

We said that the paradox is generative of the operation of the system. How do we get to the source of the operation? The answer is that we can only get to it from the accomplished operations of the system backward to their generative matrix. That means that we have to make the experience of the operation of the system along the paths of its genesis, beginning however with the crystallised states of operation clusters, observing their internal inconsistencies, their modes of conflict with each other, and going backwards to the original perplexities that set in motion the system in its whole.

---

[7] My presentation of the generativity of paradox refers to a much detailed treatment of the question I gave in former contributions, especially J Clam, 'Die Grundparadoxie des Rechts und ihre Ausfaltung. Beitrag zu einer Analytik des Paradoxen' (2000) 21 *Zeitschrift für Rechtssoziologie* 109. Fatima Kastner (in Chapter 8) gives a different account of the generative function of paradox as 'transformational-generative mechanism' determining social evolution in all its aspects. The thesis is not excessive if one reads it properly: Social evolution is a 'creative response to the underlying paradox.' There is a paradox underlying the orders of meaning of social communication, because those orders cannot anylonger be unified in a 'heterogeneous, poly-con-structural, functionally differentiated world society'—in Kastner's words. The stress lies in Kastner's presentation on the functional differentiation, which thus seems to be at the origin of the paradoxisation of social communication.

[8] Paradox is defined by Luhmann as a '*performativer Widerspruch*' in *Organisation und Entscheidung* (Opladen, Westdeutscher Verlag, 2000) 10, 39. Luhmann adds then: '*Das Paradox aber ist der Beobachter selbst*' (at 10). Kastner underlines the temporal aspect of deparadoxisation by referring to system operativity in Luhmann's theory: the operations of the system are vanishing punctual events and can therefore deparadoxise the systemic whole somewhat in the same way as they paradoxise it, namely, by vanishing as soon as the connection to the following operation is achieved.

The Reference of Paradox: Missing Paradoxity as Real Perplexity 81

The difficulty is, therefore, that the paradox of law should be reconstructed ever anew on the basis of legal operations that bring specific perplexing intricacies to the fore. We cannot refer to it simply by naming it, supposing a knowledge of those operations and their intricacies. What we can do is only to refer to its actual unfolding, that is, to repeat such an unfolding and ascertain that we are really designating it by experiencing the perplexities that spring from it. Without the renewed authentic experience of perplexity, paradox comes only illusorily to sight.

Paradox is an evanescent object, that is, a non-object oscillating between being (experienced in real perplexity) and not being (not experienced in such a way) but constituting an illusory, nominal or conceptual reference of an unavailing linguistic or discursive indication. This entails the following conclusion: there is not always a paradox of law. Law is simply, from time to time, paradoxical. Not in the sense that it is sometimes consistent in itself, managing to skip paradoxity, and sometimes not, but in the sense that its paradoxity is not always revealed when it is indicated.

This is often the case precisely when we scientifically thematise paradox and paradoxity in law. It is like speaking of God in a theological discourse. There is a very slight guarantee that we are getting paradox in sight because we are just speaking of it or referring to lots of theoretical discourses about it (to Luhmann's, Derrida's, Wiethölter's, etc theoretisations of it). Also, when Luhmann, Derrida, Wiethölter refer to paradox, they have, a priori, no such guarantee. They must ever approach it anew in the adequate manner. That is what is exhausting about paradox—because the manner of approaching paradox can only be exhaustion (of thought, sight and discourse) through paradox.

However, one could argue that the paradoxical figures of law can be unearthed, and have so many times been unearthed and in such accurate reflections, that we could suppose a certain common experience of paradox among a special public trained to identify it. We would otherwise not be able to speak of a theory of paradox or a theoretical thematisation of paradox. Paradoxology would be a vain thing.

The solution is a theologisation of paradox. In effect, there is no abridged reference, no current grasping, no usual contact, no (theoretical) discourse of paradox without a theology of paradox. That means: paradox begins to exist as a matter for theoretical reflection when an experience of it has been had repeatedly, has been thematised, has circulated among a number of intelligences trained to accomplish the experience of paradoxity. A knowledge of paradox and its main figures condenses, then, in an abridged deixis which can only be handled by initiates to its experience, by theologians of paradox. Paradoxologists are people speaking about something that cannot be spoken about (so easily). The constraints weighing on paradoxological discourse are enormous. They have to be taken very seriously.

The paradox of paradox(ology) is that of the abridgement of the unbridgeable, the condensation and deixisation (the making deictible or indicable)[9] of the movement of deixis that makes deixis impossible. Still, when we experience such a movement, we tend to experience it as a whole and to sense its repetition, to the many forms under which it seems to be iterated in many an encounter. So we tend to identify it, to bestow unity on it and to indicate it, speak about it as 'the movement of deixis that makes deixis impossible.'

The unfolding of the reference to paradox, under these premises, entails an unfolding of the experience of paradoxity, which means the actualisation of perplexity or the perplexisation of the actual movement of thought. Going along with it would mean paralysis (Lähmung).

Nobody can choose paralysis. The only option for paralysis would be: short narrations, pieces of meditation and edification unfolding paradoxes and enduring the trajectories on which they place thought and consciousness. It is the experience of endless perplexity—on a given level of consciousness. You sit in the presence of paradox, try to get very near to it and let it work in you to transform you into an impassible interioriser of impossible noesis. Impassibility is reached only through the passibility to the experience of perplexity, through being durably passible to a movement of perplexisation of thought trajectories and withholding any attempt to put an end to it by identification and objectivation.

What we do with paradoxity is something else. We theologise it. Not in the sense of theologisation Teubner uses to characterise Derrida's unforeseeable but eventual springing from total perplexity to a reference to transcendence (Levina's other) which would bring paradox to a halt in something we cannot grasp but to which we give a sacred name: justice. We speak of it as theologians speak of God: abridging the unabridgeable out of a confidence in their capacity to re-unfold, when necessary, the experience of perplexising unabridgeability; out of their familiarity with the figures of the movement of perplexisation.

If this is the general figure of paradox, what is the special figure of the paradox of law? How do we theologise it? What is wrong with our theologisation of it?

The sense of this introductory development to the notion of legal paradox is to sharpen our perception to the non-existence, non-disposability, non-dependability of a paradox in law. We cannot do anything about paradox: we cannot identify it, erase it, alleviate it, prevent it, counter it by special measures.

What Luhmann calls deparadoxisation is the normal operation of law itself. It is simply law as springing from its paradox. Paradox is generative

---

[9] In German, one would say '*anzeigbar*'.

of law. It is the source of law, in the sense that it is a movement at the fundament of law that necessitates law's unfolding in such a way as to be the law it is. The movement of paradox—the perplexisation of normative thought through itself—sets legal deparadoxisation in motion. Perplexisation and deperplexisation are entangled movements of enfolding and unfolding, actuated at the fundament of law and bringing to operation the imperfection and the incompleteness of law.

That is why the theologisation of law (and of religion) is so fallacious; because the movement of paradoxity is so near to the movement of deparadoxisation that it comes to veil it like the movement of Being (*Seiendes*) comes to veil the movement of Be(ing) (*Sein*). It comes to appear as if the generation of law as an extensive system with appropriate structures and articulated processes would be the matter of law; as if the legal system would come into being and develop out of a rationality of its own, which would just encounter at some ends those of its ultimate usages or of the most intricate entanglements of its logic, certain difficulties denying it the attainment of perfect consistency. Law, however, is generated out of its paradox (like Being out of Be) like the actual movement, the veiled process of its generation.

That is why it is so necessary to go back ever again to the pretheologised state of the paradox, the state before the indication of the paradox as such—as an indicable perplexity. There, paradoxity should be analysed in the various movements that constitute it. There is, in effect, no guarantee that a paradox as a movement of perplexisation of thought and action is in itself unitary. On the contrary, in the case of law there are a lot of presumptions that legal perplexity is plural and that law's paradox, if unitary in its centre, is multiple in its unfolding.

There are a great number of perplexities which are specific to law, its logics and its practices. Those have been termed, in recent legal literature—and often under the influence of mainly Luhmannian systems theory—paradoxes. The detheologising trend we are adopting should help us distinguish between types of perplexity. The aim is to separate a proper use of the term paradox, indicating solely, if possible, the ground movement of perplexisation taking place in law.

III. THE FOUNDATIONAL PARADOX OF LAW

The most direct formulation of the 'Urparadox' of law, ie, of the radical paradoxity of the idea of law as the domain of normative experience inducing a recourse to external constraint (*äusserer Zwang*), is the following one[10]: self-referential orders of meaning come to being by way of an

---

[10] To get an idea of the ways by which such a formulation has been reached, refer to Clam, above n 7.

operative condensation of inaugural distinctions which 'notch' the world along a divide that separates a self-indicating self (the system) from an unmarked alien-indicated non-self. Such distinctions are 'without why' (*ohne warum*)[11]: they are a sort of 'decisions' or 'acts of violence.' They are radically contingent and cannot be ultimately justified. Every world-notching distinction wields a violence that marks contentful somethings and leaves unmarked horizons. There can be no justification for the course of the dividing frontier and the fact that those contents have come to being, whereas those non-contents have been left out.

That is why one is justified in speaking of violence: because the radical contingency of the notching has a decisional character and entails a communicative active involvement taking hold and profit of the decision that has been made. Violence founds 'law' and 'law' cannot, a posteriori, 'justify'[12] violence. This is a very general sense of the word 'law.' Every distinction, ie, every operation of meaning generation, is, though radically contingent, fundamentally binding. A projected distinction, that is, a meaning in general, is each time binding and normative. It constrains us to think along its divide and to exclude alternative distinctions.

Holding alternatives open is something we could do while thinking along a distinction. (This amounts to being aware of the contingency of the distinction, a mode of meaning projection specific to modernity and reaching a maximum of contingency-consciousness in post-modernity.) Yet what we cannot do is to think and act along different distinctions at the same time. This would let the world remain in a state of endless indeterminacy. It would prevent a univocisation of the world, which is the precondition of its attaining a minimal solidity. It would entail its dissolution all over again into unseizable, unceasingly moving fluences. Every time that a contentful something gets its contours, a distinction operates which performs a univocisation of an aspect of the world and a solidifying selection of a part of its originary possibilities.

Such an import of univocity into the world is necessarily, inevitably binding. Any 'forming' (*Formung*) is intrinsically 'binding' (*bindend*) because form cannot subsist without the supposition that its contours are holding, that it is not already in the process of dissolving. A form is something that holds together. It is a tensional concept: form is tension.[13] If the matter which is bound in the form did not lean against its envelopes, the form

---

[11] This refers to an Angelus Silesius' dictum ('*Die Ros ist ohn warum*'), which has been taken up in later German mysticism and has been commented upon by M Heidegger, *Der Satz vom Grund* (Pfullingen, Neske, 1975) 77.

[12] In the etymological sense of the word, the one which harks to the Christian doctrines of justification: *justificare*, to make just.

[13] This is a perception that comes to full recognition in the art and aesthetics of the nineteenth century. It culminates in Rilke's vision of Rodin's work. RM Rilke and A Rodin, *Augenblicke der Leidenschaft* (Frankfurt, Insel Verlag/Suhrkamp, 2000).

would not have any tension in itself, it would dissolve into less broad sub-forms or into no form at all. Any form is a norm, and inversely so.

The specific normative qualification that has to be superadded to bring forth a norm in the strictest sense can be seen as supervenient to the pure, cognitive signification from a certain point of view. Fundamentally, however, a meaning projection brings perception, thought and communication on the trajectory of alternativeless ways of viewing the world, performing a selection of its possibilities and thus excluding others. This exclusion is binding, in the sense that those who do not join in it are cut off from the world that has taken form outside of their own projection. That world mobilises dominant intersubjectivities that cannot indefinitely tolerate alternative meaning projections which are neither understood nor performed by them. It comes, ultimately, to a form of a more or less massive, more or less tolerable challenge of their world projections.

In traditional normative orders, the limits of the tolerable are very soon reached. In modern ones, cognitivisation is unremarkably but constantly at work, promoting the plausibility of alternative projections. But this smooth process is precisely a process. It is not always and already accomplished. In the time it is having its way, the valid projections preserve their validity and must therefore exclude and reject alternative ones. If world meanings are provisional, they are nonetheless firmly valid, and this means binding and exclusive during the time that this validity endures.[14]

Any contentful something is the ontologised objective correlate, or in systems theoretical terms, the onticised heteroreference of a self-referential positing of a distinction corresponding to a projection of meaning in the world (as well as into and unto it). Such a distinction is radically contingent and the question of its justifiability cannot be answered. By what right do I perform such a distinction, selecting relevant contents and excluding alternative, irrelevant non-contents? The reason or the right to draw a distinction cannot be given, and the fact that it cannot is the origin of the paradox of law.

The question of law is the question about the justification, the right (*Berechtigung*) to make decisions that have constraining consequences on others. That is what we call the fundamental or originary paradox of law. It is the unanswerable question about the right or the rightful, justifiable empowering of distinctions to univocise the world in a certain, fundamentally not alternativeless way. The paradox of law is thus originary or fundamental in a double sense: (a) it is the radix of all other legal paradoxes that we encounter along the process or the operation of law; (b) it is also

---

[14] The paradox of provisional validity is a central piece of Luhmann's sociology of law. See especially, N Luhmann, 'Die Geltung des Rechts' (1991) 22 *Rechtstheorie* 273.

the paradox lying at the fundament of all other paradoxes because it implies the non-justifiability of the violence of all other meaning-founding distinctions. The legal order of a society is the order of orders, the order which guarantees the validity of all other binding distinctions giving *Geltung* in society.[15]

It is thus possible to view legal paradox as the central paradox of the empowering of any radically contingent meaning projection and its elevation to social validity. Every time that the world emerges from its originary soft fluidity and indefinite plasticity and takes hard contours, partially univocising it, a problematics of violent origins of law is opened. Heaving up the world to significance and (relative) univocity is heaving it under the reign of a law, binding it to avert the psychosis of meaning dilution and to stick to the validity of its projections. This 'legalising' of world interpretations is violent. The violence of law and the lawfulness of violence as expressions of the radical contingency of meaning are the foundational paradox of law.

The becoming univocal of the world is its getting edges, sharp, violent edges. The fracting violence of reality is born out of the univocity of the world, a world which is no longer able to host all of its contradictory possibilities. The world does not unroll in smooth shapelessness, where forms interpenetrate without conflict, ache or harm. Univocity is bought at a high price: it is the end of hallucinatory satisfaction, of non-differentiation of self and non-self, of self and the nourishing object of satisfaction. It is the beginning of preference as depreference of all the non-preferred,[16] the advent of law with its cutting off and asunder of still fusionally interpenetrating wishes, desires, pretensions, entities. It is the end of prelapsal unsinfulness as the reign of non-limiting choices, of 'this as well as that'—in contrast with our: either this or that. This builds the immediate tensional background of law. It is nothing that can be surpassed definitively by any deparadoxising device and that can be left behind oneself. It is the urging, generative moment of all actual law. It is still present at the heart of all of its creative, dogmatic and theoretic endeavours. The short substantial stories of paradox, its living deployments, have to do with the coming to symbolic pregnancy of things like: an eating mouth, a crowded city, a buying act, a juridical prose, as well as any staging of meaning.

---

[15] I have tried in a previous work to specify the difference between the binding qualities of the (subsystemic) other orders of meaning and those of the legal system. See Clam, above n 7, at 120. I spoke of the equipollence of those orders to each other and the non-equipollence of the legal system to them.

[16] As in Simmel's analytic of value, which constitutes the introductory theory to his *Philosophie des Geldes*. See G Simmel, *Philosophie des Geldes,* 7th edn (Berlin, Duncker u Humblot, 1977).

IV. UNFOLDING OF THE URPARADOX IN PARTIAL PARADOXES

There is still a way to go from this presentation of law's paradoxity to the specific paradoxes of law that are discussed in legal theory and legal paradoxology. We have said that any reference to paradox has to be aware of its inevitable but opacifying theologisation. It should pass through a repetition of its movement, which ascertains that it has been caught in sight. Systemist paradoxology of law is not always so careful with its references to paradox, and there is a lot of ambiguity about the various uses of the term. Luhmann himself did not take pains to distinguish between the levels of paradoxity and to isolate a fundamental one from which an unfolding of the polymorphy of paradox could be developed and iterated. What he called 'Paradox' or 'Paradoxie' was, for him, sufficiently obvious, and he supposed that the concept did not require further clarification. For me, the isolation of a fundamental-generative paradox is a major stake of legal theory.

What Luhmann and other theorists often call paradox corresponds mostly to local perplexities of legal processing of environmental events, and has secondarily to do with the originary apories of law. In the following, I try to give a short inventory of partial paradoxes which can be presented as structural moments of the Urparadox.

The first paradoxical aspect has to do with the circular relationship of rule and decision. The differentiation of rule and decision is immanent to all legal systems, in particular to those which function on the basis of written rules. Such rules are thought to be central constituents of law, represented as a corpus of regular prescriptions and interdictions. Decisions are then seen as the practical aspect of law and opposed to the commanding rules which appear then as the eidetic substance of law. Deficient decisions do not imperil the validity of rules. In the same frame, decisions are represented as unable to transform the higher standing eidetic rules since these have a logical precedence on decisions. Such a conceptual frame is unable to host the paradoxical moment in the circular relationship of rules and decisions. The paradox stems from the circular mutuality that entangles them in the circulation of legal value.

The positivisation of law also builds a paradoxical moment into the centre of modern law production. The paradox of positive law is that of the conservation of strong and full legal validity, in spite of the relativity and constant transformation of law through current legal revision and reform. Positive law has its validity by means of its alterability. The paradox here is that of the grounding of validity on provisionality. Positive law is a law that can be changed at any moment without being insecurised in its validity by that prospect. Politics is the instance that promotes legal change and from whose system the directives for change are imported. It thus plays the role of a parasite of law.

88 Jean Clam

Law has to develop a representation of itself to be able to reflect its own identity within itself, and thus to ground its difference to the other subsystems of society, in particular to those whose processes are closely coupled to its own. The legal system must be able to ascribe to itself its own operations, and to distinguish them from the operations of other systems. It must build a representation of self and non-self, law and non-law. It must re-enter the difference between law and non-law in law. Law perceives its own distance from itself and introduces this perception of its non-identity into itself again, thus building its own identity by way of a reflection of the difference of self and non-self in self. This leads to the paradoxity of the autopoietical closure of law and the impossibility of law establishing contact with any object outside itself.

Another paradoxical aspect of law springs from the specifically legal problematics of the commencement of law. When and where does law begin, enter being, and what was there before it? This brings us back to the Urparadox and to the originary entanglement of law and violence. Legal philosophy and legal theory dedicate a lot of attention to the question of how law was born and what were the reasons for its advent. Natural law assumes that human subjects have rights independent of the existence of a social order which would grant those rights to them. Natural rights are absolute rights that have validity independently of any violent enforcement, but need such an enforcement to give effectiveness to their validity. This brings forth an opposition between law and order. Order always realises a certain measure of lawfulness and the establishment of a fully adequate reign of law needs to mobilise a measure of violence to destroy the subsisting order—which is always partially lawful simply on the grounds that it is an order, always securing a minimum of civility. This would then have to be destroyed if the establishment of law had to be enforced.

A further paradoxical aspect is that of the incompleteness of legal order. The topos was discussed traditionally under titles like aequitas, derogation, state of emergency, necessary illegality. The legal system cannot realise law completely. It has to introduce formalisations (of discourse, rhetorics and logic), simplifications (of the situation, motives, arguments, etc) and be sparing with its attentional resources. This disposition to reduce the relevant information and to select points of view that would facilitate legal decisions has a counterpart in the opposite disposition of constantly re-injecting material justice orientations into the formalised legal process. On the whole, then, law oscillates between the contradictory requirements of the paradox of its intrinsic incompleteness.

Luhmann's description of the working of the legal system makes clear that there can be no growth of the positive value (legal/lawful) of the binary code of the legal system without correlative growth of the other negative one (illegal/unlawful). This designates the paradox of legal ambiguity. The more efficient is the legal system in the production of positive legal values, the more irrepressible is the concomitant growth of the non-values. The paradox is conspicuous when we consider leading values of modernity like freedom, right, equality (solidarity), etc. Those are values which cannot be specified. They have a mostly paradoxical structure, being on the one hand regulating and on the other deregulating. They draw limits in order to erase them: they give prerogatives for things free from own and alien prerogatives. Values which are structured in this manner are produced simultaneously with their anti-values. Their structure flows from the Urparadox of an incomplete order—that is, from the specific paradox of law (consisting in the enfoldment of law and violence in one unique form) that unlawfulness/illegality (*Unrecht*) is always produced with law and lawfulness because the former correspond to the constitutive operation of violence within law. The anti-value to law is always realised with every distinction of a 'legal' and an 'illegal,' because the 'legal' implies an order founded on a selection which has to be enforced by an exclusion of the non-selected. Selection and exclusion are unlawful/violent because of their radical contingency and unjustifiablility. They are only a posteriori factually legalised.

Beside the structural moments we have pointed out, there are still other, somewhat secondary aspects of the paradoxical enfoldment and unfolding of law and legal order. They reveal more particularly the paradoxity of the predifferentiated and autopoietical system of modern positivised law. Such is the paradox of jurisprudence as circularity of interest and evaluation, or the paradox of the recoupling of decisions that have their orientation in the consequences of decisions with the consequences of such an orientation (on the consequences of decisions).[17] Let it be sufficient here just to indicate them without going into a detailed commentary on their figures.

The system-theoretical projection of a paradox of law entails a revision of the concept of paradox and paradoxity in general. It is inadequate to conceive of paradox as a logical contradiction, a deadlock of the movement of thought and a sort of intellectual reflection of the fact that something is impossible in the real world. Paradox is neither the fatal end nor the definitive failure of the constitution of beings. It is, on the contrary, in the Luhmannian vision, the beginning of a history, of a movement of system constitution, liable to risks and unforeseeable bifurcations.

Paradoxes are not impossibilising, but possibilising. They are the foundation of a productive genesis, launching the course of a systemic condensation. The productivity of paradoxes can be immense. The general figure of productive paradox is one we have observed in the case of law, but one that can be generalised to the whole range of systemic paradoxes. It is because force and violence are at the heart of law and cannot be separated

---

[17] On these secondary aspects, see Luhmann's posthumously edited study '*Die Rückgabe des zwölften Kamels*' in G Teubner (ed), *Die Rückgabe des zwölften Kamels. Niklas Luhmann in der Diskussion über Gerechtigkeit* (Stuttgart, Lucius & Lucius, 2000).

from its form that law sets such a tortuous genesis of legal order in motion. It is because communication takes place on the ground of incommunicability (of separate consciousnesses) that it demands the generation of deparadoxising systems.

We thus have to define a new type of non-logical, non-apophantical paradox that has to do with the observation of operations and not of propositions. Operative systems overcome in a very complex manner the deadlocks of propositional logic and its limited fields of evidence. The operation thus becomes a innovative concept of roundabout-ness. Systems must operate because they can reach what they reach for only in the roundabout way of long operative catenations excluding direct seizure, direct identification and attainment.

Systemic operating is a movement of surpassing fundamental impossibilities that cannot yield any guarantees of performance except actual ones. Nothing is ever gained permanently on the fundamental perplexity. When the system stops operating, there is nothing that can hold beside, or as a result of, its operating. There are no substantive gains of autopoietic systematicity, but only operative, actual ones. The paradox is itself nothing but a movement or an act of perplexisation: surpassing paradoxity can itself be nothing else than a movement of deparadoxisation, following the lineaments of the living paradox.

Observing paradox and its deparadoxisation can, in its turn, never live upon stable references to identifiable objects. With paradox and a truly paradoxological observation of it, we find ourselves in a post-ontological world with unfamiliar thought figures.

We will certainly have to theologise the non-object 'paradox,' in the sense that we will have to objectify it in a manner that makes its thematisation possible, while at the same time a movement of retractation of the indication is taking place. Theological indication always operates with a self-sublation, a self-rewinding of the movement of positive indication hinting at the hole in the middle of the indicated term. There are neither paradoxes nor deparadoxised entities, but only ongoing movements of perplexisation and of deperplexisation, movements which, if stopped, leave nothing behind them.

The paradoxological observation of paradox underlies the same figure: paradox cannot be observed from outside itself. When the observation ceases to accomplish the movement of paradoxical observation in the experience of perplexity, paradox slips out of sight and apprehension. That is why the theological reference to paradox is twofold: it is alternatively theologising, abridging the reference and skipping its revelation; and detheologising: re-unfolding the reference and giving way to its unobscured, unabridged movement.

The conclusion must then be: paradox is not there in law because law has already and always been deparadoxised, being itself the proper movement of deparadoxisation. We should stop speaking of a paradox of law as long as we are unable to detheologise our own indication of paradox by getting into a mode of experience in which spontaneous ontologisation of ongoing movements of world and thought processes comes to a halt. Enduring non-coherence is, then, the sole event in thought.

V. MISSING PARADOX

'The first how-question (*Wie-Frage*) is always: which paradox is being unfolded by which distinction, so that it becomes possible to work henceforth with the distinction and forget the paradox?'[18]

This is, to be sure, a sharp and clear statement about the manner in which paradoxes are and are not there. It says that every distinction is the unfolding of a paradox and, as far as this unfolding is concerned and observed, the paradox can be ignored or forgotten. Once the distinction is working, ie, processing the aspect of the world it makes meaningful, to speak of a paradox does not make sense anymore. To get sight of the paradox, one has to reconsider the distinction and try to think in a single thought the two sides which are brought to being with the effectuation of that distinction. Paradoxity is grasped when the contingency of the distinction as a definite act and event is being experienced. It is the experience of the contingency of meaning in a very special sense: meaning is the way being is what it is, affects the existing subject in its existence; such an affect is the suture of the existent to existence; the contingenciation of meaning loosens the binding of the existent to existence, sets the existent in its projectivity afloat and transforms the adhesion of the existent to being into an aching spot of disjunction.

To conceive of meaning as a difference and not as a positive content exposes all projections of meaning to fluctuation, ephemerality and indeterminacy. In effect, meaning as a fugitive event born out of the projection of a form against non-form appears as engulfed by the indeterminacy of an unmarked space or state. Such an engulfedness by the unmarked shows the distinction or the form (or meaning) it delineates unceasingly undermined by a deep dimension of insecurisation, variability and contingency from which the regime of meaning cannot take distance by itself. This sets the frame for an existential situation in which the perplexity of thinking, action and belief conjoins an extremely acute demand for orientation amid unlimited potentialities of meaning production. In effect, the contingenciation of meaning sets the stage for a dissemination and an exponential increase in

---

[18] 'Die erste Wie-Frage ist immer: Welches Paradox wird durch welche Unterscheidung entfaltet, sodass man im weiteren mit der Unterscheidung arbeiten und das Paradox vergessen kann', N Luhmann, *Organisation und Entscheidung* (Opladen, Westdeutscher Verlag, 2000) 43.

the potentialities of meaning production. Being engulfed by an indeterminacy that refluidifies all emerging determinacy meaning is produced at a frenetic pace and in huge multiplicities. The demand for orientation in it is urgent because the crystallising and structuring of semantic spaces around its emerging contents are becoming more and more impractical.

Meaning hitherto was thought as an In-side subsisting per se and associated to a substance of the world—'horse' was the form, the content, the idea realised in an individual horse and giving it its unity-and-identity, its substantiality as *per se esse*. In the new, post-ontological situation, it is thought of as a contingent, emerging effect of a notching of world indeterminacy by a distinction. Such a distinction is seen as unstable and moving because it is nothing in itself: it is nothing but a crisping of the surface of indeterminacy in which everything takes form. Forms and species (*eidè*) have no firmness in themselves. They all can be thought of in quite different ways. They can dissolve, letting other aspects of the world come forth, inducing new perceptions and interpretations of it.

Hence, engulfedness by indeterminacy does not mean that the world of firm things and substances is just surrounded by indistinct multiplicities constituting a sort of environing vagueness. The firmness of things does not come to them from themselves nor from the consistency of their eidetic content. Neither are things to be seen as correlates of subjective or intersubjective synthesis of meaning intentions positing them in a sort of thematisation which singles them out and lets them stand as the aim of an actual beam of attention. Their surroundings would then be thought of as spatial fringes and strands of self-locating nomadic centres.

This certainly is not the way an environment is related to a system in Luhmann's systems-theoretical framework. In such a framework, the engulfedness of an emerging form by world indeterminacy amounts to a sort of internal integration of indeterminacy into the operation itself of determination. It is thus impossible to split the determinate something from that which 'environs' it and which amounts to all that is left outside the form when it is drawn as a distinction, determining a contentful inside against an indeterminate outside. The determinate of the form is nothing else than that which emerges from the play of difference between marked inside and unmarked outside. The relationship of both is neither simply an analytical logical correlation—which does not add anything to the position nor the knowledge of neither sides—nor a dialectical one, which would have to be synthesised and sublimated to deliver more than the mere opposition of the terms: in such a dialectical opposition the opposed terms are both contentful contraries (like life and death, domination and servitude, etc). In the systems-theoretical framework of a protologic of determination (of being something in general or somethingness), the indeterminate term is the complementary (non-)term to the posited one (a, all of non a).

The Reference of Paradox: Missing Paradoxity as Real Perplexity

The engulfedness of determination by indeterminacy means that the latter is constitutive of the former, because determination (or form, content, inside position through distinction) is always fundamentally and structurally criterionless. There is nothing to make this carving of a form out of indeterminacy than any other one. All forms are contingency engulfed, having the unmarked-ness of non-form at the ground and at the innermost levels of their own structure. Every determinacy, every determinate state of being is double-sided: both the content crystallising Inside and the non-contentful, unmarked Outside. Stabilising any form means to re-enter into it its founding demarcation of determinacy and indeterminacy. When form reflects in itself its own contingency, ie, the in-essence in it of all that which is excluded by it, it attains a state of greater stability: the firm can only be grounded on the fluid, and its groundedness on fluidity, when re-entered in itself, gives to it systemic stability. Systemic stability is a paradoxical state of stability, not only in spite of instability, but on grounds of instability.[19]

Now, it is possible to turn all this into a fabric of discourse. That means: it is possible to start from the assumption of the contingency of all forms and their being engulfed by the movement of their own contingenciation, to refer to this contingency as a given and to suppose that paradoxity is perceived at the fundament of any position of meaning. Luhmannian systems theory has an apodictic way of positing paradox and of starting from it. According to its own practice, it just has to invoke Spencer Brown's proto-logic and repeat its axiomatic commencements, integrating them into the theory of social communication, to reach the dimension of paradoxical entanglements which render linear, transitive and cumulative structures of thought impossible. The reference to non-ontological ways of thinking and to theories of non-ontological objects is sufficient from the onset for Luhmann to place his own theory in a post-ontological setting. Luhmann does not bother to bring to the fore the experience of the real, non-elaudable perplexity which constitutes the life of paradox in thought, belief and communication. He has seldom reached, so far, the dimension of the living paradox, and his theorisation leaves it behind while working on the construction of new frameworks of thought able to handle the structure of non-self-identical objects.

The situation is fairly similar with Derrida's *différance* discourse. This is, at first glance, highly surprising. In effect, Derrida's work on *différance* is in many respects quite opposite to Luhmann's theoretical project and its lines of realisation. Unlike Luhmann, Derrida does not refer to paradox as an axiomatic position at the starting point of a logic of logic. On the contrary,

---

[19] To give an example, we could refer to law and to its systemic validity *through* provisionality—in opposition to validity *in spite* of provisionality and variability. See, especially, on this point, N Luhmann, 'Die Geltung des Rechts' (1991) *Rechtstheorie* 22.

he seems to dwell abundantly, if not exclusively, on the grounds of the paradoxical play of reference elusion, disintegrating the idea itself of a final, unitary and identical content of meaning.[20] The work of *différance* at the fundament of meaning 'disseminates' meaning into any possible direction of redetermination through the free play of the significant. The whole of Derrida's writing is the attempt to create a space in which the paradoxising dissemination of meaning can take place by embracing the movement of deconstructive writing itself. One could thus argue that Derrida represents precisely that way of thought at which we were hinting while speaking of real perplexity as the only authentic experience of paradox as a living paradox.

In fact, Derrida does not go beyond a theology of paradox, although his writing has the very appearance of a movement of detheologising paradox and of restoring its mystical sources. The reference of paradox by Derrida is as opposite to Luhmann's as possible: it is accomplished in a movement of repetitive and unending self-retractation typical of all negative theologies trying to re-instate the unseizable in its unseizability by using a style of deixis in which deixis makes the experience of its own impossibility. All structural characteristics of Derrida's discourse—as a writing of writing—seem to converge upon a figure of discourse which corresponds fairly well to the form of lived experience of last perplexity, which we identified as the sole specific feature of an adequate deixis of paradox.

What is, then, the reason to deny Derrida's decontructionist approach the recognition of truly sticking to the vertiginous requisites of paradoxity? The reason is precisely that such an external, formal sticking to perplexising entanglements is what dissimulates the non-anchoring of their deixis in the matter of paradox. In order to detheologise the discursive reference to paradox, it is not enough to place the discourse of such a reference on a complex orbit of indefinite elusion of it. Detheologising means exposure to the living substance of paradox, falling short of the formal artifices of discourse which try to reflect the entanglements and perplexities drawn by the lines of paradoxical representation.[21] Thus, behind the complex, circular, inconsistent and self-repeating figures, one would find paradox in its crude state, preceding the ab-straction, out of its matter, of its discursive figure. Paradox is originally an encountered perplexity, a black hole in which

---

[20] A very synthetic and precise presentation of 'Luhmann and Derrida' is given by F Kastner in Chapter 8. The common grounds as well as the divergences of both authors are identified with a brilliant sagacity. I refer to the developments at the beginning of her article as a complement to my own approach. I am concentrating here on the differences between Luhmann and Derrida in respect to their treatment of the paradox problematics.

[21] It is a sort of logic of negative theology not affected by that which takes place in the movement of negation of its object, but interested only in the formality of elusion. That is why the philosophical post-modern discourse on paradox seems so poor: it does not have contact with paradox itself, but only reflects the deferment effects of paradoxity.

The Reference of Paradox: Missing Paradoxity as Real Perplexity 95

thought and action are absorbed, an abyss in which they seem to be attracted and to vanish. To get entangled in a paradox is to find oneself caught in a structure in which the exertion of any effort remains out of relation to its results. Whatever the number, complexity, intensity and duration of lines of thought and action deployed in a paradoxical disposition of the world, there is no advance whatsoever toward an outcome beyond the pat outcome of paradox. Deparadoxising begins when a fulcrum is given outside of paradox and trajectories are cleared which bypass its all-absorbing and paralysing centre.

The original and specific situation of paradox with no possible knowledge of an outlet is the living matter and substance of paradox itself. Before paradox is known in its redundancies, circularities, self-engulfedness and entanglements; before their lineaments have been studied, ab-stracted and theorised as peculiar and deceiving logical figures; before familiarity has been established with them, before a special deixis has been developed which is aware of its fallacies and expert of its logical intricacies; there is only the raw matter of paradox. This matter is initially a story, a narrative setting, a situation, a schematic prosopopoiesis, building a sort of primitive scene out of which all meaning would spring. It is a sort of generative structure, generating meaning out of the perplexity and the impossibility of sticking to the material of the situation itself. Such stories are the narratives of the Fall, of the conflict of Antigone and Kreon, of the Holocaust, etc. They are about destiny and the world.[22] They are about that which is 'beyond the principle of pleasure': that which makes the intensity of the deployment of the world (*Weltvollzug*) as intensity of the being affected by the world (in existential affectability). These are the real perplexities behind the logics of circularity, self-engulfedness, self-presupposition, the logics of knottings that cannot be undone.[23]

What we are doing is thematising paradox from a point of view that would be able to appresent its most specific features and peculiarities. We

---

[22] There is the matrix of fate in which one is trapped as soon as one is born. One has to face castration in a dialectic of law and sin which are born from each other. Deparadoxisation refers only to ways of enduring paradox by establishing oneself in it, by founding the order of Law/Sin on it. The order of Law is established on the ground of the paradox of the coincidence of the coming to pass of Law and Sin.

[23] These knottings are not metaphorical of the familiar form of logical perplexity which functions as a paradigm of any dead end of thought: circularity or infinite regressivity. The topologies of the knottings at which we are hinting can be far more complex and multidimensional. Jacques Lacan has worked on a number of such nodosities and has developed a whole topology to describe and conceptualise them. See J Lacan, *Ecrits* (Paris, Seuil, 1966). See also, on this topic, J Granon-Lafont, *La topologie ordinaire de Jacques Lacan* (Paris, Points hors ligne, 1985). The playful windings of paradoxic figures along redundantly circular reflexivities and elusional deferments correspond to the abstraction of a basic topology quite remote from the real and much more complex movement of paradox. Lacan's topology tries to get as close as possible to this movement.

are trying to take into account the paradigmatic changes that have taken place in the sciences of nature and of man in the last 50 years, all of which have shown that no systematic or consistent organisation of knowledge and action was possible anylonger. Instead of the familiar figures of deductive theory and the catenating certainty of its theorems, we are confronted with theoretical incompleteness and impossibility to organise knowledge otherwise than around fundamental, paradoxical apories. Our site of vision is thus that of a highly reflexive theoretical and philosophical paradoxology. From such a vantage point, paradox has to be ultimately reconstructed as bifid non-reference. In effect, the non-referentiality of paradox is actual on two dimensions: the material or substantial, situational dimension of crude and real perplexity; the formal dimension of the abstracted lines of intrication imposed on thought and action when they get entangled into paradox.

It is quite important not to confuse this doubling of paradoxical non-referentiality, because it is along the lines of its divide that the border runs between a theologising deixis and a detheologising deixis of paradox. Paradoxic deixis remains within the limits of a theology of paradox as long as it just reflects in itself the lines of intrication (of thought and action) abstracted from the substance of the generating scene. Thus, unending elusion of reference within a discourse of *différance,* re-introducing in itself the non-reference it wants to point at, is an operative model which configures, in the operation of discourse, the figures of paradoxical incompleteness, inconsistency, circularity, etc when projected upon the grid of a figural-discursive analysis. That is why paradoxity seems here to be unveiled under the sign of playfulness. And indeed, paradox plays like this, escaping any hint at it, referring to itself as being beyond or a way short of itself. The discourse thematising the non-referentiality of paradox seems to have no other choice than to reproduce in itself the plays and playfulness of indefinite vanishing and indefinite reappearance of some obscure reference before the intention of seizing it meaningfully.

Our thesis is that, as long as such a discourse is devoted to this kind of deixis, it is operating in the second dimension of non-referentiality and entrenching itself in a theological elaboration upon paradoxity. Derrida's discourse is paradigmatic of this posture. The substance of paradox is not at stake in it. As far as paradox presses to emerge at the one or other end, Derrida does not take pains to enter into the originary dimension which precedes the grammatisation of paradox and the typification of its figures. The dimension of crude paradoxity is in effect an 'anonymous' dimension, one for which we do not have names by which we could indicate it. We use the term 'anonymous' in the sense Aristotle uses it[24] in the context of descriptions promoting to light things which hitherto have remained in a

---

[24] Or to affine expressions like *anonymôs* (*einai*).

state of indistinction. In such a state, things were not differentiated from their surroundings, have not yet been 'distinguished' and could not as such be thematised. They thus made superfluous any effort to designate them. They have remained unearthed until now, and had no features of their own, being mixed with, intertwined in, and undivided from each other.

In its originary dimension of non-referentiality, paradox dwells in a pre-grammatical state like a natural language which has never been submitted to any reflexion on its regularities and has not yielded any representation of its formal organisation. Speakers of such a language very often lack the simplest idea of words, of the existence of minimal units of discourse and the structural articulations that take place around them. They dwell in language as in myth or religion: as something they are embarked upon and that constitutes the significance of the world. It is this state of signi-fying or meaning giving that cannot be bypassed by any inquiry into significance as such. However, the tendency is, as soon as a grammar of such a language is available—be it in as indigent a state of infancy as it will—to rely on the knowledge of the forms and figures that structure significance to win cognizance of it.

An analogous tendency shapes the discourse of paradox: it lives frequently on the knowledge of the forms and figures specific of paradoxity, thematises and reproduces them in itself in a stark appresentation of it, seeing no alternative to refer to paradoxical non-referentiality other than a re-entry of non-reference in itself in a body of discourse especially designed for such descriptions. Doing so, it moves away from the living substance of paradox as a being-engulfed in a significant tale with no commencements and no outside. Such a tale is the first and last reality of paradox. Beside it, the cognizance of the figures of intrication paradox is yielding to reflexive thought is a derivative and abstract access to that ultimately grounding reality (of non-referentiality). Thought has to go back ever again to this reality and its lived perplexity. It has to return to the primitive destiny of significance in order to be nourished and nurtured by it. Our paradoxological approach—which behaves like a critique of paradoxic discourses which unacknowledgeably theologise paradox while pretending precisely to deliver a particularly sharp version of it—is able to show the doubling of thought dimension and to scrutinise the distinctive directions taken by thought at this bifurcation. It can describe and typify both strains of thought: one living in adhesion to the matter of paradox, and the other taking its cues from such a thought itself without embarking on the same venture.

Material paradoxical thought would be of a type exemplified by authors like Augustin, Levinas, Heidegger and Saussure. We insist upon including the latter in order to make clear that, not only are philosophical discourses of that type, but the analytical and strictly theoretical can also belong to it. In distinction to such a thought, there is a theoretisation of paradoxity, best exemplified by Derrida, which refers to the first type to ascertain its

98 *Jean Clam*

intention to behold paradox, but whose main preoccupation is to draw the consequences of an outletless paradoxity of any significance and any tale of meaning. It thus inaugurates a world in which meaning does not crystallise, being produced by its own fluency as an irritating, stimulating and sometimes enlightening shock of incongruent meaning-intentions. The more such a thought contains itself within the limits of performative paradoxity, the further it gets away from the material sources of semantic perplexity.[25] These sources are the knots along which any line of paradoxic thought experiencing the real perplexity of paradox has to unfold. That is why the second type of discourse can drift amazingly far away from the lived embarrassment and the authentic labour imposed by crude paradox. Simply referring to such labour and embarrassment does not help. Derrida's thought can thus be characterised, from the vantage point of a paradoxological analysis, as a discourse that does not open spaces of paradoxic thought, but only lives upon already opened spaces of such a nature. It thus has no direct contact with the substance of paradox, but has to establish such a contact through the mediation of other discourses that live in the originary perplexity of material paradox. That is how we should read Derrida's reference to Levinas in a most crucial passage of the main Derridean text on the paradox of law—as if it were possible to establish contact with the primary dimension of non-referentiality by referring from outside it to a movement of thought which is taken into the labour of its unfolding.[26] Derrida's own movement remains external to the former, being limited to the second dimension of paradoxic non-referentiality.

To conclude our paradoxological critique, we may say that neither systems theory nor deconstruction is able to provide access to the matter of paradox. They both remain, on the whole, within the limits of the theological discourse of paradox, supposing that its reference is known from the proto-paradoxic discourses of a type of thought enduring crude paradoxity and sustaining a state of pregrammatical, pretheological, mythic and situational anonymity of paradox. There are, in both systems theory and deconstruction, occasional efforts to detheologise their own reference to paradox. The development by Luhmann of a reflection upon the concept of the

---

[25] In her developments on Derrida's invention of paradoxical infrastructures, Kastner expands (in Chapter 8) upon the performative character of Derridarian paradoxity (she speaks of the 'Derridarian performance of the latency of paradoxical infrastructures'). For my part, I stress this aspect in Derrida's writing, whereas Kastner includes in this performative posture the political and ethical engagements of Derrida.

[26] There is, in fact, quite a variety of ways in which paradox can be unfolded. Paradox can be explicated by a sort of analytical unfolding, not erasing, however, its enigmaticity. On the contrary, analytical unfolding can yield a most stimulating access to paradox and function as an initiation into its material enigma. I claim that paradoxes can be unfolded analytically until such a point wherein they reveal a substantial perplexity and not only a formal, reflexive, regressive, and-so-forth perplexity.

The Reference of Paradox: Missing Paradoxity as Real Perplexity

'world' seems to us the most serious attempt to reduce the remoteness of his paradoxist theory to the very sources of paradox.[27] Such a hiatus has, in effect, been ever widening, the more Luhmann took for granted the formal intrication of paradoxical figures encountered at any end of a theoretical description of the different orders of meaning. But Luhmann understands paradox as the unity of a distinction (of a marked domain and an unmarked domain). He projects this unity as the world. And the world is unknowable. If it were knowable as the unity of the distinguished or the unity of the double-sided form, we would be able to surpass our enclosedness within a referential system, get out to the 'real world' and know objectively which distinctions really exist out there. The world for Luhmann is something like the *Ding an sich*, a sort of observation beyond the limitations of a self-referential system. The world can be seen, however, as that knot of all knots. It is the knot which exerts the quality and intensity of being. It is the radix of paradox and paradoxity. Yet, the world theme by Luhmann is not developed in a way that makes it possible to draw any other consequence for the thematic of paradox than the following: paradox cannot be supposed to be out there in law, nor can it be posited apodictically as if it were protologically self-evident; paradox has to be referred ever again to the material, deep dimension of the world as the dimension of the originary non-referentiality of what perplexes thought in its own operation.

---

[27] G Teubner tries to cope with the world-horizon of the problem of justice by introducing a distinction between an environmental justice and a world justice. Whenever the world concept is invoked by Luhmann, there is a decisive hint at a non-environmental 'beyond' (all environments). This is why I cannot follow Teubner in his understanding of world justice as a justice which is realised in the real world. There can be no transition from environment to world.

5

The Political Origins of the Modern Legal Paradoxes

NIR KEDAR

PHILOSOPHERS DO NOT like paradoxes. They are disturbed by the logical cul-de-sac and immediately embark on an attempt to solve the deadlock. Historians, on the other hand, are less afraid of paradoxes. They do not approach them therefore in the way philosophers do; they do not attempt to solve the paradox, but rather to explain its origins, its social role and its political or cultural significance. In this chapter, I wish to look at two so-called legal paradoxes: the 'paradox of law's self-reference' and the 'paradox of legal generality,' and demonstrate how these paradoxes were really constructed in the modern era as political *ideals*, drawn from the idea of the rule of law—a solution to the bothersome conundrum of legal authority.

Seen from within the legal system, modern law is self-referring—it contains several *insolubilia* (eg, the paradox of self-amendment). From a legal internal point of view, the law is a closed, self-referring and autopoietic system that creates, amends, interprets and justifies itself through itself. From this internal perspective, law is amendable or justifiable only under its own authority. The legal closed system is paradoxically self-referring, since the legal rule is used as the authority for its own amendment or justification.[1] Legal philosophers are many times bewildered by insolubles of this kind: 'If a constitution has an amendment clause (a provision describing or prescribing how to amend that constitution), then can that clause be used to amend itself? Is self-amendment paradoxical? If it is paradoxical, can it be lawful? If it is lawful, can the logic of law be logical?'[2]

---

[1] See P Suber, 'The Paradox of Self-Amendment in American Constitutional Law' (1990) 7 *Stanford Literature Review* 53; P Suber, *The Paradox of Self-Amendment: A Study of Logic, Law, Omnipotence, and Change* (New York, Peter Lang Publishing, 1990). See also A Ross, 'On Self-Reference and a Puzzle in Constitutional Law' (1969) 78.309 *Mind*, New Series 1.

[2] Suber, 'The Paradox of Self-Amendment in American Constitutional Law,' above n 1, at 53.

In this chapter, I am not disturbed by the logical insoluble or by its lawfulness. Instead, my aim is to show that what is seen as a legal paradox of self-reference is really a political *ideal*. Modern law is self-referring because modern political theory requires the law to be a closed, self-contained and autopoietic positive system that does not recognise any transcendent authority as legally binding. Modern legal theory is obsessed with the origin of law, with the question whether there is law beyond the positive law. Notwithstanding, in this chapter I will not deal with the fascinating questions of legal positivism or the relations between law and morals, but rather with the modern Western political theory that insists upon the autonomy, the positiveness and the generality (universality) of the law. Modern Western political theory prefers the institutionalised social convention called 'positive law' over the vague, intangible and foreign norms of religion, natural law or morality. Modern political theory requires modern society to constrain itself by the authority of a positive law, that bows before no extra-social transcendent authority—a positive law that is based upon written texts and upon clearly and positively identifiable social facts, such as voting in Parliaments, court decisions, etc.

The paradox of legal self-reference points indeed at the larger and bothersome problem of legal authority. From a legal internal perspective, law is a closed, self-referring system. Nevertheless, from an external point of view, the justification for obeying the authority of the legal order must emanate, in the last resort, from a transcendent—extra-legal—source. The rule of law is always the rule of man. Law does not amend or justify itself; it is people who amend or justify their laws. From an extra-legal perspective, the authority of law stems from a prelegal origin that antecedes the legal authority and is not bound by it. Yet, the one thing which the law can never justify by itself is its prelegal (and therefore, non-legal) origins. The legal order cannot justify the prelegal roots of its authority. This is the foundational problem of legal authority that Hannah Arendt has called 'the problem of beginning' and Jacques Derrida has dubbed 'the mystical foundation of authority.'[3] There is no law (no-law) before the law; and if there is, we cannot explain or legitimise it from our internal, legal standpoint. The law in itself is always a partial and imperfect justification of its own authority. The history of law is the recital of the constant struggle to just-ificate the

---

[3] H Arendt, *The Life of the Mind*, vol II: *Willing* (New York, Harcourt Brace Jovanovich, 1978) 207 ('the problem of beginning—a problem because beginning's very nature is to carry in itself an element of complete arbitrariness'); J Derrida, 'The Force of Law: The Mystical Foundation of Authority' in D Cornell, M Rosenfeld, D Carlson (eds), *Deconstruction and the Possibility of Justice* (New York and London, Routledge, 1992) 3; W Benjamin, 'Critique of Violence' in P Dametz (ed), *Reflections: Essays, Aphorisms, Autobiographical Writings* (New York and London, Harcourt Brace Jovanovich, 1978) 277. See also J Raz, *The Authority of Law* (Oxford, Clarendon Press, 1974) 1.

prelegal/non-legal origins of legal authority; it is the story of the attempts to legalise the primeval no-law.[4] Consequent paradoxical self-reference notwithstanding, the insistence of modern law upon a closed, autopoietic positive legal system should be understood as an important step in the Sisyphic quest to justify legal authority.

The problem of legal authority provokes not only the insoluble of legal self-reference, but also the legal paradox of generality (or all-inclusiveness). Modern political theory requires general equality before the law. Law is supposed to be general (universal), all-inclusive and objective in the sense that it should be defined in a universal way and uniformly applied. But the very creation of law marks a borderline between the legal and the non-legal, between what is legally justifiable and what is not.[5] The law and the application of law always includes some (people, groups, acts, situations) and excludes others. In order to be general and all-inclusive, the law must be able to justify these distinctions between the legal and the non-legal. Yet the law in-itself cannot justify these borderlines, as they are also the limits of its own authority. From the internal legal perspective, the formation of the law—ie, the decision as to what is legal and what is not—is an extra-legal, and thus a non-legal, act. In other words, law can never really be general and all-inclusive, since the law in-itself can justify in legal terms neither the foundation of its authority nor the limits between the legal and the non-legal.

To be sure, 'legal paradoxes' are not paradoxes in the strict sense: they are neither logical Paradoxes, such as 'Russell's Paradox,' nor are they semantic paradoxes, such as the 'Liar Paradox.' They do not really create a logical impasse. Legal paradoxes are not even epistemic paradoxes, like the 'Knowability Paradox' or the 'Surprise Examination Paradox.' Instead, they are really apories, riddles or perplexities. If we look at them as para-dox(ical), that is, as behaving against our (common) opinion, it is because history, not logic, labelled those legal perplexities 'paradoxes'. Notwithstanding, like the other chapters in this book, this chapter will also use the term 'paradox' when describing apories such as legal self-reference and legal generality.

The chapter has four sections. The first tracks the origins of the political ideal/paradox of legal self-reference. I argue that the roots of legal self-reference are found in the quest of modern Europe to emancipate its political

---

[4] We can say, of course, that there is really no transcendent pre-law and that every legal (and other) norm is really a human product. If this is the case, then the paradox of legal authority is really an example of a total, closed, self-referring cultural system. For further discussion, see section III below.
[5] In that sense, as Jean Clam (following Derrida) has shown, law is paradoxical in the same way meaning is paradoxical. Law, like language, is supposed to be general (universal) and objective in its essence. But like the definition of words and expressions, the delineation of the legal formulas also draws a borderline between the legal and the non-legal. See Jean Clam in chapter 4.

and legal authority from religion, and later also from any transcendent authority (including natural law), and to establish antithetically a regime of strict legal positivism. The second section demonstrates that early-modern European history was in fact complicated. On the one hand, European political culture sought to escape the transcendent by moving towards the social, the ideal towards the empirical and the positive. Yet, on the other hand, these same abandoned transcendent norms (religion, morality or natural law) were also employed by the European *tiers état* in its social struggle against the *ancien régime*. Early-modern political history can be thus described as a dialectic process of accepting and rejecting transcendent norms. The synthesis of this dialectic was the idea of the rule of law, which on the one hand insists upon legal positivism and self-rule, but on the other hand preserves a kind of transcendent authority through the all-inclusiveness of the state and the generality (universality) of law. The third section talks about the 'the paradox of legal self-reference' in light of the general problem of legal authority and the modern requirement of human (or popular) sovereignty. The fourth section briefly discusses 'the paradox of legal generality' and its relation to the idea of the rule of law and the problem of legal authority.

I. POLITICAL ORIGINS OF LEGAL SELF-REFERENCE: FROM TRANSCENDENT AUTHORITY TO HUMAN SOVEREIGNTY AND LEGAL POSITIVISM

The paradox of legal self-reference stems from the strict modern demand for legal positivism, ie, from the requirement that the law be a formal, institutionalised social convention, whose authority emanates directly from society and not from any extra-social transcendent authority. The reader should bear in mind that I do not wish to deal with problems of legal positivism, but rather to sketch the intellectual history of legal positivism, that is, the prehistory of the paradox of legal self-reference.

Beginning in the eleventh century, European political theory underwent a process of political secularisation and 'positivisation': in a long process, the authority of the state and the law was gradually perceived to be independent from religion, from morality and eventually also from natural law. This process began with the Gregorian Reforms in the eleventh century, continued throughout the late medieval ages and the early-modern times, and attained its apex with John Locke's positivist parliamentarism and with Immanuel Kant's rational theory of the state and the law.

The investiture struggle (1075–1122 AD) and the *Reformatio* of Pope Gregory VII can be seen as the first important step in the secularisation of the European legal order. These major events resulted not only in the transformation of European political consciousness, but also in the formation of two distinct legal systems: the secular, positive, legal system(s) (royal, manorial, mercantile or urban) and the religious legal system of the Catholic Canon law (called indeed the *jus novum*). Even if European monarchs still enjoyed divine legitimacy (in exchange for their recognition of the supreme moral authority of the Church), it is fair to say that the new European secular legal orders then matured into an independent field which developed its own language, reasoning, philosophy, institutions and training system.[6] Step by step, the European political and legal philosophy of the late medieval ages and the Renaissance became secular and humanistic: up until the seventeenth century, God had gradually disappeared from his role as the author of the state and the law. In the writings of Niccolò Machiavelli, the Renaissance Florentine political thinker, the political sphere is normatively and empirically autonomous. Religion and morality do not govern the state. Instead, Machiavelli conceives of the state and its legal order as human creations, and sees their purposes as social: maintaining the general order while restraining human impulses and instincts. Prudent governance and wise legislation are thus seen by him as human qualifications, based upon human virtues, while religion and morality are considered only inasmuch as they assist (or hamper) the state and the achievement of its social objectives.[7]

Sixty years after Machiavelli completed his major works, Jean Bodin published his famous *Six livres de la république* (1576), in which he introduced the concept of sovereignty, defining it as an original power which has no justification.[8] The seeds of self-reference were sown. As an original power, maintained Bodin, the sovereign is the source of all laws, and because sovereignty is an absolute and perpetual power, every command of the sovereign is law. It is a closed system: all sovereign commands are law and all laws are the creation of the sovereign. The sovereign itself, however, stands outside that closed legal system. As the absolute creator of all laws, it cannot be subject to these positive laws, and is therefore released— by law—from any obligation it may have taken on earlier. Bodin is thus the first modern positivist.

But transcendent authority continued to play a decisive role in European political and legal thought. Over the course of the sixteenth century, the idea of a transcendent—extra-social—natural law evolved anew, and gradually replaced God in authoring (and legitimising) the social order. Unlike the medieval Thomist theory of *lex naturalis*, the modern European concept of natural law was secular and even humanistic. In the writings of Bodin, even

---

[6] See H Berman, *Law and Revolution: The Formation of the Western Legal Tradition* (Cambridge, Mass, Harvard University Press, 1983) 120.
[7] See eg, N Machiavelli, *The Prince* (1513) (D Donno (trans), Toronto and New York, Bantam, 1966) 56–62.
[8] J Bodin, *Les six livres de la république* (1576) (Paris, Fayard, 1986).

the sovereign is constrained by natural law, that is, by 'natural' institutions such as the family, inheritance or property. In the early seventeenth century, the Dutch Hugo Grotius presented the definite break with the scholastic tradition, offering a theory of natural law which was based solely upon human reason and was independent from divine natural law.[9] For the first time, divine and human natural laws were divorced.

Several decades later, Samuel von Pufendorf, Benedict Spinoza and Thomas Hobbes employed the humanistic theory of natural law in order to justify the coercive power of the state. According to all three, the establishment of a strong centrist state that would guarantee peace and security was a rational imperative of the *human* natural law. Natural law was now employed in order to justify the constitution of a sovereign 'state.' It is important, however, to notice that, at that early stage, the state was the only subject of natural law. The people, according to the political theory of the time, were not considered subjects of the natural law, but only 'citizens'—the subjects of the positive law of the state. Natural law was the rational source of the sovereign state, but had no authority within the state. The creation of the state marked the borderline between natural law and positive law. The political theories of the seventeenth century expelled natural law from the state's inner legal domain, emphasising the priority of positive law. Pufendorf, the first to hold a chair of natural law in a German university, explained the constitution of the sovereign state through human natural law, maintaining that a sovereign state is inevitable, since only the sovereign state can effectively harmonise the two conflicting human (natural) impulses of sociability and self-preservation. However, in order to protect peace and security, Pufendorf also asserted that, within the civil state, the civil laws of the sovereign had precedence even over natural law.[10] In accordance with the political requirements of his time, Hobbes, too, emphasised in his *Leviathan* the necessity of sovereignty and demanded a *Machtstaat*. Rejecting transcendent legal authority, he insisted that following the civil contract, law means only positive law, and is identical with all the sovereign's measures. Likewise, Spinoza found that the creation of the state is the fulfilment of necessity and reason, but insisted upon the exclusivity of positive law inside the sovereign domain. Even the *jus divinum*, asserted Spinoza, was considered law only if it were incorporated into the positive legal order of the state.[11] It is important to bear in mind, however, that

---

[9] See H Grotius, *De Iure Belli ac Pacis* (1625) (FW Kelsey (trans), Oxford, Oxford University Press, 1925).

[10] S von Pufendorf, *Elementarum Jurisprudentiae Universalis* (1660) (WA Oldfather (trans), Buffalo, NY, Hein and Co, 1995) vol II, 150–53; Pufendorf, *De Officio Hominis et Civis Juxta Jegem Naturalem* (1673) (FG Moore (trans), Buffalo, NY, Hein and Co, 1995) vol II, 125–27.

[11] B Spinoza, *Theological Political Treaties* (1670) (S Shirley, (trans) Leiden, Brill, 1991) vol XIX, 217–29.

positive law as it was conceived by Pufendorf, Hobbes and Spinoza was not self-referring, because theoretically the state and its legal order still emanated from (and were justified by) a transcendent, supra-positive source: natural law.

Only after the establishment of the modern liberal state did natural law finally transform into the idea of the rule of *positive* law. The political theories of the eighteenth century sought not only to justify the coercive power of the sovereign state, but also to limit that sovereign power, to secure—first through natural law, but gradually through *positive* law—a sphere of individual liberty from the total power of the state. Indeed, although liberalism developed out of natural law theories, it eventually developed into strict legal positivism. Preferring the institutionalised social convention called 'positive law' over the vague, intangible and foreign norms of religion, natural law or morality, liberal theory left both God and natural law outside the positive legal order of the state. The newly constructed liberal theories still identified the positive law with the sovereign's will and measures, yet at the same time (and this is the meaning of the 'rule of law') they regarded positive law as the protector of human and civic liberties against the intrusive power of the sovereign, demanding of positive law that it both express sovereignty and check its power.

Even though he is considered the champion of natural law, John Locke actually signifies the twilight of natural law and the dawn of the rule of (positive) law. In his *Second Treatise of Government*, Locke portrays the Parliament as having a Janus face, gazing both at natural and positive law. Locke's Parliament is, in fact, the alchemist's laboratory, in which natural law is transformed into positive law:

> The great end of men's entering into society being the enjoyment of their properties in peace and safety, and the great instrument and means of that being the laws established in that society, the first and fundamental positive law of all commonwealths is the establishing of the legislative power ... This legislative is not only the supreme power of the commonwealth, but sacred and unalterable in the hands where the community have once placed it.[12]

Locke's theory corresponds with the political transformations of his time. Until the late seventeenth century, natural law was a crucial weapon in the struggle of the growing European third estate (ie, the middle classes or the bourgeoisie) against the existing political order of the *ancien régime*. However, in the late seventeenth century and during the eighteenth century, when the bourgeoisie gained more political power and especially after it succeeded in establishing the liberal states, natural law was 'positivised' and

---

[12] J Locke, *Two Treatises of Civil Government* (1690), book II, ch XI, s 134.

crystallised in the form of statutes and constitutions. We must be precise: the *values* entrenched in the natural law (the so-called 'natural rights') were written in statutes and constitutions; the *authority* of natural law was substituted by the rule of positive law. Locke, who wrote after the English Glorious Revolution, asserted that the law of the land is only the positive law created by the sovereign Parliament. Yet, Locke's positive law was different from Hobbes's and Spinoza's: now, in the liberal era, positive law was not only seen as the executing instrument of the state. As the positivised form of natural law, it was also a major restraint upon sovereignty. Natural law was replaced with the idea of the rule of law that insisted upon the certainty, the generality (universality) and the autonomy of the positive law.

On the other side of the Channel, Jean-Jacques Rousseau's idea of popular sovereignty expressed his rejection of the binding authority of any norm which is transcendent to society.[13] The people, asserted Rousseau, are the only sovereign and the only legislature. In Immanuel Kant's *Rechtslehre*, religion, morality and all 'natural' or extra-positive laws are not even considered as part of the legal order. For Kant, only positive law is valid as law. Kant's theory of law should be seen in connection to his theory of ethics, which has two elements, objective and subjective. First, he sought to discover the formal-universal (and thus objective) principle of morality—that is, the formal principle that represents an action as a duty. He found this formal-objective principle in the universality of the 'moral law' based upon his famous categorical imperative. Secondly, Kant discussed the subjective element of his theory of ethics, ie, the incentive to obey the 'law' (whether the law prescribed internal or external actions). When the incentive to conform to the law emanates *not* only for the law's own sake, but from external motives or constraints, Kant calls it 'legality' (lawfulness: *Gesetsmäßigkeit*); when the obedience to the law stems from the idea of duty embedded in the law itself, it is called 'morality' (*Moralität*). Kant indeed separates his *Metaphysics of Morals* into two parts: The Theory of Right (*Rechtslehre*), and the Theory of Virtue (*Tugendlehre*). In correspondence with this distinction between morality and legality, he further posits:

> That lawgiving which makes an action a duty and also makes this duty the incentive is *ethical*. But that lawgiving which does not include the incentive of duty in the law and so admits an incentive other than the idea of duty itself is *juridical* ... The [theory] of right and the [theory] of virtue are therefore distinguished not so much by their different duties as by the difference in their lawgiving which connects one incentive or the other with the law ...

---

[13] In a well-known statement in his *Discours sur l'inégalité*, Rousseau blames natural law theorists for casting their so-called natural law according to *what they believe* to be universal conventions. See CE Vaughan (ed), *The Political Writings of J. J. Rousseau*, (Cambridge, Cambridge University Press, 1915) vol I, 137.

Ethical lawgiving (even if the duties might be external [ie, 'duties to others']) is that which cannot be external; juridical lawgiving is that which can also be external.[14]

Kant's distinctions between legality and morality laid the theoretical basis for the divorce of law from morality. Understood separately from ethics, Kant's theory is the first systematic positive legal theory: though he acknowledges, of course, the relation of law to moral virtues and practical reason, his *legal* theory emphasises the power of the state, which creates the legal norm and which distinguishes positive law from other normative phenomena. Kant's new terminology signifies the modern positivist legal thinking, which uses the criterion of legal authority in order to differentiate between positive law and every other extra-positive (transcendent) authority. Once conjoining in a social contract, the state of nature transforms into a *Rechtsstaat* and natural law into positive law. Kant rejected as non-legal even the laws of necessity and equity, dubbing equity 'a mute divinity who cannot be heard.'[15] Like Locke, both Rousseau and Kant replaced natural law with the idea of the rule of (positive and general) law. '*La liberté consiste à ne dépendre que des lois,*' declared Voltaire.[16]

After the end of the eighteenth century, then, positive law was almost 'the only game in town' (though in the USA, natural law still played an important role until the mid-nineteenth century, when it eventually faded away as well). Modern political theory conceived of (positive) law as normatively and empirically autonomous from any non-positive authority (religion, morality, natural law and the like). Even though liberal theory did recognise the influence of these other normative systems on the content of positive law, it refused to consider them as legally binding in themselves, unless of course they were inserted into the law by some (positively) legitimate act of political or social legislation (parliamentary legislation, legitimate court judgment, legal custom, etc).[17] As we can see, modern political theory is not obsessed merely with the content of the law, but also (and perhaps mainly) with its form and with the origins of its authority. Formally, the modern law (like the modern state) does not emanate from any transcendent authority. Rather, it is considered to be the expression of the general will of society, or to be more accurate, the will of the general citizenry. Paradoxically, 'state' and 'citizenry'

---

[14] I Kant, *The Metaphysics of Morals* (1790) (M Gregor (trans), Cambridge, Cambridge University Press, 1996) 20–1.
[15] 'It also follows from this, that a *court of equity* (in a conflict with others about their rights) involves a contradiction,' *ibid* at 27.
[16] Voltaire, 'Pensées sur le gouvernement' in L Moland (ed), *OEuvres complètes de Voltaire*, 23 (Paris, Garnier, 1877–1885) 526.
[17] Again, the reader should bear in mind that I am not dealing with the problems of legal positivism, but rather with the development of the idea of the rule of law.

are of course legal concepts, defined by law. The positive law defines its origins; it draws the boundaries of citizenship and the citizenry, and formally, it even constitutes the state in a Münchhausen-like movement. Legally, there is no law above or beyond the Constitution (with a capital C, as it is written in the nomo-fanatic USA). The circle is completed: the legal order is now conceived of as an original, closed and self-referring system.

II. DIALECTICS OF ACCEPTING AND REJECTING TRANSCENDENT NORMS

The historical narrative I have presented thus far is perhaps too facile. Early-modern European society not only escaped from the transcendent by moving towards the social, but at the same time it fought the feudal and the *ancien régime*'s social reality by appealing to a higher, extra-social, transcendent 'law.' While the move away from the transcendent towards the social attempted to get rid of any meta-social authority, jettisoning both God and natural law, the battles against the existing social order employed as a political weapon exactly the same transcendent, meta-positive norms: religion, morality and eventually natural law. The following description traces this dialectic of escaping from, and to, extra-positive law.

The idea of natural law that is entangled with political power appeared in the late medieval ages. The Papal reforms in the eleventh century, which resulted in the formation of two distinct legal orders (religious and secular), created a system of mutual normative inspection, formalising Pope Gelasius's theory of the Two Swords. Furthermore, each of the two legal orders matured as an independent normative authority, entitled to inspect its constituency (the church, or the 'general' society and even the secular sovereign). As Franz Neumann rightly noticed, '[t]he Gregorian dispute was not merely a fight for power between the secular and the spiritual authorities, but the fight of a rational doctrine of Natural Law against the magic and supernatural powers of kings.'[18] Inside the Church, Catholic dogma, and later also the idea of natural law (reintroduced to the Christian world by St Thomas of Aquina), were used as a *political* weapon by oppositionist ecclesiastic groups such as the nominalists and the conciliar theorists. The holistic normative order disintegrated. Now, both inside and outside the Church, law became divided into two distinct, opposite, yet inseparable types: political law, which was regarded as the conscious creation of society or the sovereign, and the transcendent, extraordinary 'natural law,' which was expressed in universal norms, containing demands for social

---

[18] F Neumann, 'Types of Natural Law' in *The Democratic and the Authoritarian State: Essays in Political and Legal Theory* (Glencoe, III, The Free Press, 1957) 83.

justice, political liberties and equality before the law.[19] The idea of an absolute sovereign power (even inside the Church) would be forever caught up with the restricting idea of a critical rational law.

Indeed, from the sixteenth century on, natural law would become the intellectual foundation of the social and political revolutions in the West. At the beginning, the idea of natural law supported the disintegration of the feudal regime and the establishment of a strong sovereign state that would monopolise the execution of power, and would guarantee the general 'enjoyment of property in peace and safety.' Later, from the days of Locke, natural law turned into a major weapon in the struggle of the European *tiers états* against the absolute monarchies and the privileged aristocracy. From that time, natural law was applied as a higher authority that limited sovereignty, corrected the positive law, and instituted a sphere of individual liberty from the coercive power of the state. Natural law faded away after the major revolutions in Europe and America, and the foundation of the modern liberal states, when it underwent a process of positivisation—its values were crystallised in written constitutions and laws, and its inspecting authority was replaced with the rule of positive law. But natural law, to be sure, is still present in contemporary political discourse. Modern history has demonstrated that, even in the liberal era, the sovereign state and its positive law do not resolve many social injustices. Hence, there is always an actual political need to seek for an extra-social and extra-positive source of justice Indeed, even in our present positivist era, diverse (and usually deprived) social groups apply the ideas of 'natural law' and 'natural (human or social) rights' in their protest against the existing social and political orders.

European legal history is thus a dialectical oscillation between two lines of political action: the first opposing any supra-positive authority, the second embracing it. Every time transcendent authority is thought to be suspended from social history, it reappears in a new synthetic form, which already contains the seeds of its own future antithesis. The Gregorian reforms led to the formal separation of the secular legal order from the Catholic legal system, but it also constituted a mutual—religious–secular—inspecting mechanism, later giving birth to the Thomist theory of natural law that served as a rational criterion for both the Canonical and the secular positive legal orders. When God was eventually dismissed from European political theory, the idea of natural law was reintroduced (in a secularised version) in order to explain and justify the state and its positive legal order. The synthesis of the antithetic natural and political law—the *aufhebung* of natural law—was the idea of the rule of law. According to this

---

[19] See F Neumann, 'The Change of Function of Law in Modern Society' in *ibid*, at 29.

modern political idea, natural law was abolished and reformulated as positive law, and its values were preserved in positive constitutions and statutes. The idea of the rule of law entailed a somewhat paradoxical regime of 'positive transcendent law.' Even though the rule of law is, of course, the rule of *positive* law, the necessary liberal requirements of generality (universality) and autonomy of the positive law created (at least in theory) a domain of legal independence, a sphere of relative 'transcendence' within the positive legal order. The autonomy of the state and its legal order is extraordinary, both in the sense that the state and the law are conceived of as separate from the social order, and in the sense that this autonomy of the state and its legal order is an incredible phenomenon—simultaneously dependent upon, and independent from, society.

III. PARADOX OF LEGAL SELF-REFERENCE AND THE PROBLEM OF LEGAL AUTHORITY

As the previous paragraph implies, modern political theory gave birth to manifold legal paradoxes. First, the strict political requirement for legal positivism entailed the problem of legal self-reference. From a legal internal perspective, modern law is formally a self-contained system that creates itself, amends itself and justifies itself through itself. Indeed, the modern paradox of legal self-reference stems from the reluctance of modern political theory to recognise as legally binding any normative authority which is transcendent to society. In fact, the problem of self-reference concerns not only (and perhaps not mainly) the positive law, but it is actually a manifestation of the deeper problem of authority that bewilders modern society. The problem of legitimising the law is really the problem of justifying culture and the social order. In order to justify our norms and culture, we either have to accept an extra-social transcendent authority, which we can never fully justify or understand; or we have to insist upon our human and social sovereignty—and must then face paradoxes of omnipotence (eg, can an omnipotent limit its unlimited power?) and problems of self-reference.

According to our *political* theory, the justification of the social order must be introverted; it cannot emanate from an extra-social transcendent source. Law and culture must be the products of human legislation. Society, or the people, must be the fundamental sources of the laws and of the social institutions, in order to found the state and the law upon rational, stable and incontestable grounds. Authorities which theoretically transcend society (such as religion or natural law) are suspected by modern political culture as being irrational or vague, and thus as politically unstable, foreign and perilous. (Recall the European fear from the Catholic *ultra-montanisme*.)

After jettisoning both religion and natural law, society (that is, 'the people') became—according to modern liberal theory—the sole, legally legitimate legislature, subordinated only to its own will, as this will is expressed in positive law. Society is the master, and at the same time the subject, of the rule of law. But if the state, and the people or society, are at once the foundation of law and its subject, if the law is both transcendent and immanent to society, are we not captured in a paradoxical vicious circle? In modern political theory, this perplexity is usually formulated as a question of liberty: if we are sovereign, ie, if we are politically omnipotent and free to legislate our own rules, how can we by law (or otherwise) limit our potency; how can we confine our liberty? And furthermore, what is the logic of the confinement? Is the rule of law really an auto-restriction upon our free will?

This political 'paradox' of sovereignty is, of course, not a genuine logical paradox, as it does not create a logical impasse. Human or popular sovereignty does not enjoy real omnipotence, but rather indicates the human free will. If we accept (on political grounds) that sovereignty should be restricted in some events, then the 'paradoxical' question should be redefined in the following manner: how can we politically justify the specific forms of restrictions (in our case, positive law) which we agreed to cast upon our liberty? How can we justify the paradoxical ideal of the rule of (positive) law?

In modern Western political thinking, this concept of 'we' has usually been articulated in two different ways. In Europe, the question was usually in reference to the 'state.' Thus, the German hundred-year-old 'paradox of Jellinek' (named after the great legal theorist Georg Jellinek) asks: 'what does it mean for the state to be simultaneously the sovereign author of the law and a central subject of that same law?' In the Anglo-American world, where the state is conceived (at least since the days of Locke) mainly as a night-watch and not as a necessary vehicle for freedom, justice and emancipation, the question is referred not to the state but to 'society.' There, the paradox, which Roscoe Pound ascribed to the Puritans,[20] but which is really a broader liberal (or the liberal-democrat) paradox, asks the same question about society: how is it that modern society stresses its own (popular) sovereignty and self-government, yet at the same time it is overridden by its own positive law?

In any case, my aim here was not to solve the paradox of sovereignty or the insoluble of legal self-reference, but to expose their political and historical roots, and to claim that the legal or social 'paradox' of self-reference is not only an aporie but a political *ideal* as well. Thus understood, legal self-reference can be seen as an achievement in the exhausting social struggle to justify the *origins* of legal authority. The so-called paradox of legal self-reference is in fact a product of modern history (and all history is

---

[20] R Pound, *The Spirit of the Common Law* (Boston, Marshall Jones Co, 1921) 45–47.

human). It was consciously constructed as the least of many political evils. A positive law based upon institutionalised social conventions was considered *politically* as being more just and efficacious than the vague, uncertain and foreign natural law.

The paradox of sovereignty (or of omnipotence) bewildered political theory from its very beginning, but until the eighteenth century, it was not a *legal* paradox. Before the late seventeenth century, *legal* self-reference was considered neither a political ideal nor a paradoxical difficulty, because until that time European political theory was obsessed with the foundation of sovereignty and not with its limitation. The bitter social, political and religious struggles in early-modern Europe created among Europeans a yearning for peace and order. The novel idea of sovereignty expressed the urgent necessity of Europeans to create a political entity that would preside over the different churches and the opposing social groups in Europe, and to guarantee the general peace and security. At that stage, the paradox of *legal* self-reference did not exist, because formally the sovereign was not subject to the positive law, but rather was seen as the extra-legal transcendent fountain of all laws. In other words, until the late seventeenth century, self-reference did not exist in the *legal* sphere, since the law referred to the sovereign, but the sovereign was not bound by the positive law. At most, the sovereign was subject to 'natural law' or to God, but both natural law and (of course) God were authorities that were transcendent to the positive *legal* order.

Only after the state's sovereignty was no longer disputed in Europe, so that restrictions upon sovereignty could no longer entail the state's disintegration, did liberal theories emerge, requiring the limitation of the sovereign power. But even in the early liberal era, the paradox (or the ideal) of *legal* self-reference did not arise within the positive legal order as long as the main restraint upon sovereignty was natural law. *Legal* self-reference emerged only when—following the establishment of the modern liberal state—natural law was 'positivised' and its authority gave place to the rule of law. Indeed, the rule of positive law—the idea that society and the sovereign state are bound by their self-legislated, positive, autonomous and general laws—became a principal political ideal in modern Western society. Because the rule of law is so highly appreciated by modern culture, its paradoxical facet (self-reference) is nowadays usually concealed, allowing the ideals of popular sovereignty and the rule of law to be celebrated as uncontested and even as natural. Only a few perceptive theorists have attempted to find an Archimedean point for the self-referring closed legal system in rationality (as in the writings of Kant or Kelsen) or, as noted by Niklas Luhmann, in 'the future.'[21]

[21] N Luhmann, 'The Future Cannot Begin: Temporal Structure in Modern Society' in *The Differentiation of Society* (New York, Columbia University Press, 1982) 271.

IV. PARADOX OF LEGAL GENERALITY AND THE RULE OF LAW

Legal self-reference is not the only legal paradox that stems from the problem of legal authority and from the ideal of the rule of law. As we have seen, legal self-reference derives from the modern insistence upon human (or popular) sovereignty and free will. But modern political theory requires not only liberty and human sovereignty; it also demands an equal, universal and all-inclusive attitude of the law and of social institutions. Yet, the requirement of equal treatment by the law creates another legal paradox—the paradox of legal generality.

The ideal of the rule of law commands not only the positiveness and autonomy of the law, but also the generality (universality) and all-inclusiveness of law. The generality of law means that legal rules should be defined by the legislature in a universal manner and will be uniformly applied by the administration and the judiciary. Modern political theory believes that the generality of law shields the individual from the arbitrariness of the governing power by uniformly employing neutral rules that apply to the entire population (or at least to broad categories of indeterminate people). Together with the separation of powers and the independence of judges, the general law is an important postulate of the modern legal order, as it establishes both formal equality and a minimum of personal and political liberty.

Historically, the pursuit of generality, equality and all-inclusiveness stems from the liberal endeavour to challenge the early-modern European social and political order and to show that the existing social order of the time was exclusive, discriminatory and contaminated by power or prejudice. However, the pursuit of generality teaches us that the goals of full equality and all-inclusiveness can never be fulfilled. It demonstrates that there is no neutral social order, and shows that every political order is in fact also arbitrary and contingent, that every general law is really partial, and that every 'all-inclusive' social order is also exclusive. The 'all-inclusive' state and the 'general' law cannot really be universal and equal, since the men and women who make the laws and who interpret and enforce them cannot act—by definition—in a universal and all-inclusive manner. The state and the law are forever held in check by the social hierarchies and traditions from which they attempted to escape.

In its legal phase, the paradox of generality and all-inclusiveness is but another utterance of the problem of legal authority. Law, like every norm, draws boundaries between 'do' and 'do not,' between 'right' and 'wrong,' between 'legal' and 'non-legal,' between 'citizens' and 'non-citizens' (foreigners, barbarians). The law includes some and excludes others (people, acts or objects). In order to be considered as genuinely general and all-inclusive, the law must be able to explain why some are protected by the law and some are not. It must be able to justify the distinctions between what is legal and what is not. Since the delineation of the legal and the non-legal is in fact the demarcation of the limits of legal authority, we can rephrase the previous sentence in the following manner: in order to be considered genuinely general and all-inclusive, the law must be able to justify its authority. As we have seen, from a legal internal perspective, the law is a closed, self-contained system. The legal internal justification of legal authority would be, in the last resort, self-referring: 'The legal is legal because the law says so.' The determination of the legal and the non-legal must emanate, it is clear, from an extra-legal source. However, for the law, the extra-legal source of its authority is essentially non-legal. Seen from the legal internal perspective, the law stems from an inexplicable, contingent, arbitrary and perhaps even violent, preceding 'no-law' that is transcendent to the law and cannot be justified by it. The law can never really be general and all-inclusive, since it cannot justify in legal terms the foundation of its own authority: the law in-itself cannot explain the boundaries between the legal and the non-legal, nor can it justify in-itself the arbitrariness and violence (ie, the illegality) involved in the process of drawing the limits of legal authority. The paradox of legal generality and all-inclusiveness—the Sisyphic attempts of the law to be universal and all-inclusive—is in fact an expression of the foundational problem of legal authority, the 'Urparadox of law', as Jean Clam has named it.

Modern legal and political theories are forever captured in a paradoxical vicious circle, while aiming to constitute equality through the all-inclusive state and the rule of general (universal) law. They cannot—by definition—legitimate the coercive power of either the all-inclusive state or the general law; they cannot save us from the foundational problem of legal authority. Indeed, the more equality grows, the more we realise how far and unattainable are the goals of real and general equality and all-inclusiveness. The brighter our light, the more we appreciate how deep is the darkness around us.

V. CONCLUSION

What are we to learn from this historical analysis? Must we conclude that *plus ça change et plus c'est la même chose*? Perhaps the answer is 'yes.' The legal history of the last millennium shows that human society was not able to justify the foundation of law (or indeed, of politics, culture or meaning). We always end up with a transcendent, mysterious source that our laws and culture cannot justify.

Still, we can draw a different conclusion. As opposed to the pessimistic modern European philosophy—from Nietzsche to Heidegger to Derrida—we might better look at the brighter side of the paradox of legal authority, and celebrate the very brave and humane attempts to cope with it. The noble dream of the rule of law did not, and in fact could not, justify the problem of legal authority. The law can neither legalise nor really hide the prelegal/non-legal arbitrariness and violence that are involved in the process of its formation. Nevertheless, we need to appreciate the ways in which the rule of law has tried to justify the origins and the authority of the law: on the one hand, the positiveness of law attempted to ensure that the law would be legislated and applied by a self-governing sovereign society, and not by some vague, transcendent and necessarily foreign authority; on the other hand, the all-inclusive sovereign state and its independent and general legal order enabled the relative autonomy of the modern *Rechtsstaat* from the social power relations and traditional conventions, guaranteeing to a certain extent the 'rule of law and not the rule of men.' Even if paradoxical and unattainable, we should esteem the human struggles to establish a more just and justifiable social order. After all, a sincere confrontation with the problem of legal authority is preferable to a witty (but politically impotent) surrender to the paradox.

6

The Institutionalisation of Inconsistency: From Fluid Concepts to Random Walk

OREN PEREZ*

'Let the jury consider their verdict,' the King said, for about the twentieth time that day.
'No, No!' said the Queen. 'Sentence first—verdict afterwards.'
'Stuff and nonsense!' said Alice loudly. 'The idea of having the sentence first!'
'Hold your tongue!' said the Queen, turning purple.
'I won't!' said Alice.
'Off with her head!' the Queen shouted. (Lewis Carroll, *Alice's Adventures in Wonderland* (London, Penguin Books, 1865, 1994) 145)
'When I use a word', Humpty Dumpty said in rather a scornful tone, 'it means just what I choose it to mean—neither more nor less.'
'The question is,' said Alice, 'whether you can make words mean so many different things'.
'The question is', said Humpty Dumpty, 'which is to be master—that's all.'
(Lewis Carroll, *Through the Looking-Glass* (London, Penguin Books, 1872, 1994) 100)[1]

THE LAW OCCUPIES a central place in the life of modern societies. It is perceived as the ultimate arbiter of social conflicts. The leading role of the law in the management of the modern society depends, to a large extent, on its being perceived as a fair arbiter. In pluralistic societies this deep societal expectation presents the law, I want to argue, with an irresolvable dilemma. This dilemma is the focus of this chapter. In pluralistic

---

* I would like to thank Daphne Barak-Erez, Yitzhak Benbaji, Yoram Egosi and Gidon Shaviv, as well as the participants at the conference 'Paradoxes and Self-reference in Law,' Frankfurt, 16–17 December 2002, for their comments on an earlier draft of this chapter.

[1] I owe this (second) quote to Judge Heshin of the Israeli Supreme Court, who cited it in his ruling in Supreme Court Case 6339/97 *Roker v Salomon* (23 December 1999), at para 7.

societies the concept of fairness reflects two competing expectations.[2] First, the law is expected to be *consistent*. Consistency requires avoiding incongruity or contradiction amongst legal rules, legal concepts and legal practices.[3] This requirement reflects the idea that incoherent law-making can be a source of real injustice.[4] This yearning for consistency seems to echo a deeply entrenched expectation for 'equal treatment': that people who are similarly situated should be governed by the same rule (interpreted and applied uniformly). Denying or frustrating this expectation is perceived as unjust.[5] Thus, the law of Lewis Carroll's 'Wonderland,' which

---

[2] My discussion of fairness is limited in two senses. First, I am interested in the social construction of this notion and its doctrinal manifestations within the law—not in devising normative, morally driven, criteria for fairness. Secondly, I do not attempt to offer a complete characterisation of fairness (socially constructed), but rather focus on two key dimensions of this concept.

[3] In speaking about the consistency of 'the law' I do not refer to the law as a *social system*, but to its *printed history*, understood as the entire genealogy of rules and case law pertaining to a certain jurisdiction. This distinction is further elaborated in section II of Chapter 1. Legal inconsistency thus arises when there is some incongruity in this normative grid; for example, when two rules contradict each other (eg, when one rule permits what another forbids, or when two rules issue contradictory directives which cannot be simultaneously complied with), when one can find within the law contradictory interpretations of the same rule or concept (eg, the precautionary principle discussed below), or when one can point to other contradictory legal practices (eg, a reality in which courts give different damage awards to plaintiffs with similar claims). One can find in almost any legal system some meta-norms whose goal is to restore and maintain consistency, invoking different criteria, such as hierarchy (*lex superior*), temporality (*lex posterior*) and speciality (*lex specialis*). This article highlights a different mechanism for coping with inconsistency. Some authors maintain that coherence constitutes a more demanding requirement. Since there is little agreement with respect to what exactly this 'something more' amounts to, I will use these terms interchangeably. See J Dickson, 'Interpretation and Coherence in Legal Reasoning' in EN Zalta (ed), *The Stanford Encyclopedia of Philosophy* (Fall 2001 edn), available at http://plato.stanford.edu/archives/fall2001/entries/legal-reas-interpret/ at s 3.1.

[4] Thus, eg, Eisenberg *et al* note in their analysis of punitive damages: 'If damage awards and prison sentences are "predictably incoherent," then our legal system (indeed, every legal system) might be so pervasively unfair as to be indefensible,' T Eisenberg, JJ Rachlinski and MT Wells, 'Reconciling Experimental Incoherence with Real-World Coherence in Punitive Damages' (2002) 54 *Stanford Law Review* 1239 at 1240. For further discussion of the linkage between consistency and fairness see GP Fletcher, 'Paradoxes in Legal Thought' (1985) 85 *Columbia Law Review* 1263 at 1276 and SB Staar, 'Simple Fairness: Ending Discrimination in Health Insurance Coverage of Addiction Treatment' (2002) 111 *Yale Law Journal* 2321.

[5] Unequal treatment could be justified only if it is driven by a legally (and some would say, morally) valid distinction, which is universally applied (see Yitzhak Benbaji in chapter 10, section I). The linkage between consistency and fairness is driven, I believe, by two further concerns. First, inconsistency is seen as unfair because it can undermine people's reasonable reliance on previous rulings. Secondly, inconsistency is perceived as problematic because it could be a sign of a systemic disorder—of the law being, in fact, arbitrary and capricious. What is arbitrary and capricious is unprincipled. And if the law is not driven by principles it cannot be just, because justice, however defined, is surely a principle. On the linkage between consistency and fairness, see further TM Franck, *Fairness in International Law and Institutions* (Oxford, Clarendon Press, 1995) 38.

allows for ad hoc justification ('sentence first, verdict afterwards') and grants judges unlimited control over meaning ('it means just what I choose it to mean'), does not seem to cohere with our expectations of a fair system of law.

However, in pluralistic societies fairness takes on an additional meaning; for the law to be conceived as fair it is expected also to develop *'pluralistic sensitivities.'* This expectation reflects the social complexity of pluralistic societies. Pluralistic societies are torn by deep disagreements over questions of politics and morality; they are overburdened by conflicting definitions of the good or virtuous life (or society).[6] These differences trigger, and are reflected in, real-life disputes: over the allocation of public resources, over the apportionment of 'civic' duties and burdens, and over the definition and scope of various 'liberties' (eg, freedom of speech, assembly and worship). The concept of pluralistic sensitivity requires the law to *respect* the cultural idiosyncrasies of the different communities and discourses comprising the society in which it operates. The idea of respect for the different, which underlies the principle of 'pluralistic sensitivity,' has, I believe, a compelling intuitive force (although it is not easy to delineate its exact boundaries).

These two visions of fairness are, I believe, *incongruent*. The unbridgeable discord between the principles of coherence and pluralistic sensitivity reflects the fact that the *law* does not have at its disposal some meta-principle, one which can be invoked to resolve *any possible* social dilemma, while satisfying the requirements of both coherence and pluralistic sensitivity.[7] Such a meta-principle cannot be found either within the law or in society at large (eg, in morality).[8] Putting it in other words: in pluralistic societies one should

---

[6] For a discussion of the discords that haunt pluralistic societies, see eg, T McCarthy, 'Legitimacy and Diversity: Dialectical Reflections on Analytical Distinctions' (1996) 17 *Cardozo Law Review* 1083 at 1121.

[7] To illustrate this point, consider, eg, the principle of equality, interpreted as the requirement to 'ensure equal treatment for people who are similarly situated in morally relevant respects.' If the society in question is divided in its vision of 'morality,' it will also be divided in its understanding of 'equality.' What one may consider as a valid 'deviation' from the principle of equality, justified by the uniqueness of the case at hand (eg, giving special rights to gay people in view of their marginalised status), may seem unjustified by another observer (who might find this type of 'special treatment' objectionable on religious grounds). In deeply pluralistic societies, these differences cannot be completely resolved; any legal decision will thus necessarily offend one community (or world-view).

[8] Thus, it is assumed that there is no set of moral principles which can resolve, satisfactorily, any possible moral dilemma. Ruth Barcan Marcus argues that the intractability of some moral dilemmas has a dynamic force; it should motivate us 'to arrange our lives and institutions with a view to avoiding such conflicts,' Ruth Barcan Marcus, 'Moral Dilemmas and Consistency' (1980) 77 *Journal of Philosophy* 121 at 131–32. While this strategy may resolve some of our moral predicaments, it is doubtful whether it can resolve all of them.

be able to find many and competing interpretations of the 'just' law—both within and outside the law.[9]

The law is faced then with an irresolvable dilemma.[10] On the one hand, as a 'fair' arbiter, the law is expected to rule in a consistent fashion. Consistency requires the law to adopt highly precise rules for resolving disputes, and to apply these rules in a uniform and non-contradictory fashion. While this strategy could ensure the coherence of the law, it involves the risk of permanently alienating those communities whose world-views are incompatible with the chosen legal rules (given the lack of a communally agreed meta-principle, such incompatibility seems inevitable, at least for some disputes). In a deeply pluralistic society, the idea that the law should, in the name of coherence, systematically reject the claims of certain groups seems deeply problematic; indeed, it offends our intuitive understanding of fairness. The principle of 'pluralistic sensitivity' requires the law, therefore, to follow an incoherent path (at least sometimes).[11]

We can now reformulate the paradoxical dilemma faced by a law operating in a pluralistic society: its status as a 'fair' arbiter depends on its ability to be *simultaneously consistent* and *inconsistent*.[12] Note that this dilemma involves self-contradiction, because it is driven by *internal and conflicting* prescriptions. Both the aspiration for coherence and the principle of pluralistic sensitivity are assumed to be part of the normative apparatus of the law. But how can the law sustain these conflicting demands or expectations without risking its status as fair arbiter? The law, as this chapter will show, has institutionalised the paradox, incorporating it into 'normal' legal practice.

---

[9] This argument suggests therefore that (at least in pluralistic societies) the totality of legal practice cannot be cast into some all-encompassing and perfectly calibrated interpretative mould. Other opinions do exist. Kaplow and Shavell, for example, present a unified theory for just law-making based on the criterion of welfare maximisation, see L Kaplow and SM Shavell, 'Notions of Fairness Versus the Pareto Principle: On the Role of Logical Consistency' (2000) 110 *Yale Law Journal* 237 (which is a succinct summary of their thesis). Kaplow and Shavell argue that 'legal policies should be evaluated solely on the basis of their effects on individuals' well-being' and that 'no independent evaluative weight should be accorded to notions of fairness' (at 237). For a critique of Kaplow and Shavell's thesis see eg, MB Dorff, 'Why Welfare Depends on Fairness: A Reply to Kaplow and Shavell' (2002) 75 *Southern California Law Review* 847.

[10] Law is not the only social mechanism used to resolve pluralistic disputes. One important non-legal mechanism is geographical segregation. This mechanism allows communities with incompatible world-views to evade conflicts through physical separation. It was used in Israel to resolve some of the tensions between orthodox and secular Jews. It does not, however, resolve all the problems. Another mechanism is, of course, politics.

[11] Note, however, that the pluralistic fairness facilitated by incoherence is general or sequential. It ensures that the interests and world-views of certain groups will not be *systematically* disregarded. Still, in *particular* cases, there will always be *winners* and *losers*.

[12] The scope of this challenge is a function of the diversity of the society in question.

This institutionalisation was attained[13] through the invocation of 'fluid' or 'vague' concepts and doctrines, such as equality, reasonableness and the principles governing the practice of constitutional balancing. The use of *vague concepts* has offered the law a way to keep the paradox at bay, signalling that it can maintain its coherence despite the intense pluralism of its environment.

This chapter seeks to develop a better understanding of the institutional mechanisms which were utilised by the law to manage the paradox of coherence. My argument will proceed in three steps. First, I will consider in more detail the structure and systemic role of legal vagueness (section I). What interests me in this respect is, first, to unfold the way in which vagueness is used to handle the paradox, and secondly to explore the limits of this strategy as a mechanism for deparadoxification. I will argue that, while vagueness provides a certain stability to the legal system, it may fall apart in times of pluralistic stress, risking the cohesion of the legal system. I will sketch two scenarios in which this process could unfold. Second, in view of the apparent fragility of *vagueness* as a strategy for handling the paradox, I will explore an alternative strategy: 'randomisation.' Randomness seems to offer the law a method for arbitrating between conflicting claims or wants without breaching its dual commitment to coherence and pluralistic sensitivity (section II). However, a closer inspection reveals that randomisation is a precarious strategy, one whose capacity to resolve the paradox of coherence is highly limited; in section III I explore the limits of this strategy in further detail. There is, so it seems, no escape from the paradox. The final section (section IV) considers the implications of this conclusion.

I. FLUID CONCEPTS IN LEGAL DISCOURSE

Exposition: Vagueness and Fluidity in Law

Vagueness, I have argued above, plays a crucial role in managing the paradox of coherence. But what exactly are the discursive manifestations of legal vagueness? I am interested in one central manifestation: the inexactness of general legal concepts. Legal concepts are deeply fluid; their boundaries and domain of application are highly malleable. This fluidity, which implicates the law's conceptual space, is, I will argue, a dynamic, composite and highly disordered phenomenon. My purpose in this section is to provide a detailed and analytically tight description of legal inexactness. This analysis will be used in the next section to explicate my thesis about the linkage between the vagueness of law and the paradox of coherence.

---

[13] Using the term 'attained' hints at a purposive decision. However, it is probably more accurate to view this phenomenon as an emergent (non-purposive) property of legal communication.

The first step in analysing the inexactness of legal discourse is to deconstruct the notion of vagueness itself. The concept of vagueness is used to describe three distinct situations of *inexactness* in human communication.[14] The first, sometimes termed *ambiguity*, involves terms that have *multiple* meanings (eg, bank).[15] The second situation, sometimes termed *fuzziness*, involves notions that have blurred or imprecise boundaries. Think, for example, of describing patients as depressed, or of categorising industrial discharges as polluting. Fuzzy terms are often used in conjunction with gradual predicates designating a degree (eg, 'very,' 'quite,' 'almost not').[16] A third situation of inexactness involves *general* terms, that is, terms that can be applied to a variety of situations.[17] A given term can be inexact in any

---

[14] I will use the terms 'inexactness' and 'vagueness' interchangeably as general terms covering all the various instances of inexactness. The following discussion does not constitute a complete account of the concept of vagueness. See further, JA Goguen, 'The Logic of Inexact Concepts' (1969) 19 *Synthese* 325, R Sorensen, 'Vagueness has No Function in Law' (2002) 7 *Legal Theory* 387 and M Black, 'Vagueness' (1937) 4 *Philosophy of Science* 427. The philosophical debate regarding the notion of vagueness involves further questions, on which I do not intend to comment in this chapter. First, some writers argue that vagueness is an epistemic condition that reflects the ignorance of the observer of the true state of things, while others claim that vagueness is an intrinsic attribute of language, which has nothing to do with ignorance. While I am inclined toward the second view, I do not think this debate has much influence on the argument of this chapter. For an attempt to explore the relevance of this question to law, see K Greenwalt, 'Vagueness and Judicial Responses to Legal Indeterminacy' (2001) 7 *Legal Theory* 435. See also T Williamson, 'Vagueness, Indeterminacy and Social Meaning' (2001) 16 *Critical Studies* 61. Another important question is whether vagueness is only a feature of claims or representations, or whether it may also be a feature of the world itself. See G Rosen and N Smith, 'Worldly Indeterminacy: A Rough Guide' (2004) 82 *Australasian Journal of Philosophy* 185.

[15] P Parikh, *The Use of Language* (Stanford, CSLI, 2001) 3.

[16] Fuzzy set theory offers a way to 'translate' the vagueness of human language into exact terms, through the tool of membership functions. A fuzzy set A in the space of points X is characterised by a membership function $fA(x)$ which maps each point in X onto the real interval (0, 1). The value of $fA(x)$ at x represents the 'grade of membership' of x in A (which increases as $fA(x)$ increases). See LA Zadeh, 'Fuzzy Sets' (1965) 8 *Information and Control* 338. Thus, if we know the membership function of a fuzzy notion such as 'fat,' we have a systematic way to deal with this notion. This could ensure a consistent usage of this term, in the sense that if all members of a certain community use the same membership function, they should all agree on the degree of fatness of any individual in that community (eg, very fat, somewhat fat, etc). In practice, however, one can find in society conflicting applications of fuzzy terms, reflecting, in effect, incompatible membership functions (I revisit the question of incompatible membership function below). The designation of proper, and practically sensible membership functions is one of the major challenges of fuzzy set theory; see generally, D Dubois, W Ostasiewicz, and H Prade, 'Fuzzy Sets: History and Basic Notions' in D Dubois and H Prade (eds), *Fundamentals of Fuzzy Sets* (Doredrecht, Kluwer Academic Publishers, 2000), 93–105.

[17] In a way, generality is almost taken for granted because 'language would be useless if each noun referred to exactly one object,' Goguen, above n 14, at 345. Generality is, of course, an important attribute of legal norms. Thus, eg, the EU Court of First Instance provides the following definition of general terms: 'A measure is of general application if it applies to objectively determined situations and produces its legal effects with respect to categories of persons viewed generally and in the abstract.' This definition applies to many legal concepts and doctrines. See Case T-70/99 *Alpharma Inc v Council of the European Union* [2002] ECR II-3495 at para 74.

one of these ways, or in more ways than one. Thus, an ambiguous term might have several meanings that, in turn, may be fuzzy. General terms may be fuzzy (eg, the concept of 'reasonable man') and, furthermore, may be context-sensitive and, hence, ambiguous.

Legal concepts exhibit all of the aforementioned forms of inexactness. But to understand how the vagueness of law is realised in practice one has to take into account the unique structure of the law's conceptual space. First, legal inexactness, as it is encountered by legal observers who invoke legal rules or concepts, is a *composite* phenomenon. Legal rules and concepts usually come in the form of sentences, which more often than not include several inexact terms.[18] The precautionary principle, which will be discussed below is a good example of this feature of legal vagueness.

Secondly, the inexactness of law is a *dynamic* or *fluid* phenomenon. This fluidity is facilitated by two features of legal deliberation. The first is the constant *oscillation* of the law between the general and particular levels. As they move between these levels, legal concepts change their meaning. This process is not necessarily coherent. Indeed, the process by which general legal concepts change their meaning through the adjudication of particular disputes is a major source of inconsistency.[19] But the fluidity of legal concepts is also a reflection of the way in which legal principles are *played* against each other. A case in point is the practice of constitutional balancing. Consider, for example, the constitutional principle of equality (or non-discrimination). The vagueness of this concept emerges both from the *intrinsic (atomic)* inexactness of the term 'equality' and from the way in which the courts *play* this principle against other constitutional principles. This continued balancing constantly changes the meaning and domains of application of the various constitutional principles involved, turning constitutional law into a highly fluid field of meaning.

But what is probably the key for understanding the role of vagueness in managing the paradox of coherence and pluralistic sensitivity is the fact that vagueness operates as a conduit for communicative disorder.[20] Vague

---

[18] For a discussion of vague sentences, see RL Epstein, *Five Ways of Saying 'Therefore': Arguments, Proofs, Conditionals, Cause and Effect, Explanations* (Belmont CA, Wadsworth, 2002), 2–4.

[19] Note, however, that context dependence does not necessarily lead to inconsistency; a good example is indexical terms (I, there, tomorrow), which do not change their general meaning when they are applied in specific contexts. See further, Sorensen, above n 14, at 405.

[20] My claim is that vagueness allows for the possibility of communicative disorder or indeterminacy; however, I am *not* arguing that vague concepts are necessarily indeterminate. Indeed, as Timothy Endicott notes (in the context of context dependence and indeterminacy): 'Context-dependence does not necessarily lead to "subjective interpretation," because the context may give objective reasons for applying or not applying an expression to something,' T Endicott, 'Linguistic Indeterminacy' (1996) 16 *Oxford Journal of Legal Studies* 16 at 686. Similarly, fuzzy set theory provides an analytical framework for handling fuzzy notions in a consistent fashion (see above n 16).

legal concepts tend to resist systematic decoding, and their invocation in actual communication is frequently a source of indeterminacy. Thus, for example, fuzzy legal terms 'refuse' to be encapsulated into specific membership functions,[21] and constitutional balancing defies the persistent attempts of legal scholars to explain it in terms of a precise algorithm. The disorderliness of the law's conceptual space could (and does) lead to conflicting legal determinations.

It might be useful at this point to illustrate what I mean by 'disordered vagueness.'[22] Consider a simple concept such as 'colour.' To simplify things, let us assume that 'colour' is inexact in the sense (and only in the sense) of having multiple, discrete meanings. A systematic decoding of 'colour' means that the users of language have at their disposal the interpretative means to *disambiguate* the term in any possible communicative situation. I assume, in other words, that ambiguity dissolves if the particulars of the context in which a certain term is asserted, and the rules for disambiguating this term are commonly known by the speakers. This means that if 'colour' can be used either to refer to 'a particular hue, one, or any mixture, of the constituents into which light decomposes as in "spectrum," or to people of 'non-white race', language users should then be able to infer from context which of the two senses was intended.[23] If society were to follow uniform rules of disambiguation, there could therefore be no inconsistency in the interpretation of 'colour' in actual communications, despite the ambiguity of this term. To the extent that inconsistency arose, it would reflect a clear and undisputed breach of social conventions.[24]

Now assume that 'colour' cannot be systematically decoded. This condition of disorderliness could take various forms. It could reflect, for example, a disagreement over the *composition of the set of meanings* implied by the term 'colour' (eg, 'colour' might also mean 'ruddiness of face'); it could reflect disagreement over the rules that govern the disambiguation of 'colour' in specific contexts (ie, disagreement with respect to the *contextual cues* that determine which of the various meanings of the term apply); or it could reflect disagreement, uncertainty or plain ignorance about the

---

[21] For the notion of 'membership function,' see above n 16.
[22] For a legal example, see the discussion in HD Saunders and JG Genser, 'Trial and Error' (1999) 39 *Sciences* 18 at 20, of the criminal law concept of 'beyond reasonable doubt' (describing how this concept has been interpreted differently by a research group comprised of businessmen, acting as potential jurors).
[23] The quotes in the text were taken from *The Concise Oxford Dictionary of Current English*, 5th edn (Oxford, Oxford University Press, 1964) 237.
[24] Assuming no disagreements or uncertainty about the particulars of the context in which the term is used.

particulars of the context.[25] This would mean that the term colour could be subject to conflicting (but not illegitimate) interpretations in similar contexts.

A more detailed example is provided below of how legal vagueness is realised in the context of a particular legal doctrine—the precautionary principle.

Disordered Vagueness and the Paradox of Coherence

In what sense does the phenomenon of disordered vagueness allow the law to manage the paradox of coherence and pluralistic sensitivity?[26] The first thing to note is that vagueness makes inconsistency—and, consequently, the paradox—less noticeable. It allows the law to apply what looks like a single concept across diverse cases, altering at the same time the meaning of this concept at the application stage—maintaining in this way a façade of consistency. In other words, the disordered vagueness of its conceptual space allows the law to have it 'both ways.'[27] On the one hand, by insisting on using singular concepts across the board, the law *signals* a strong commitment to the ideal of coherence. On the other hand, because this commitment is maintained, first and foremost, on the top level of general concepts, it provides wide leeway for pluralistic sensitivity at the *micro-level* in which the general concepts are applied. The fluidity of its general concepts thus allows the law to navigate between, and respond to, the conflicting pressures inflicted on it by the environment.[28]

---

[25] Another example of disordered vagueness would be fuzzy terms with multiple membership functions. As noted above, membership functions determine the extent to which a certain observable (thing) is F, when F is a fuzzy term such as 'beautiful.' The existence of multiple membership functions would produce varying scales of 'beautifulness,' leading in practice to conflicting opinions with respect to the beauty of distinct observables. See further, Endicott, above n 20, at 686 and Goguen, above n 14, at 345.

[26] An alternative name for disordered vagueness, suggested by Goguen, is *ambivalence*, ibid, at 345.

[27] I assume of course that the institutionalisation of inconsistency through fluid concepts is an *implicit process*. It is never explicitly declared, because such declaration would jeopardise the very rationale of this institutionalisation.

[28] Note that this argument differs from Cass Sunstein's theory of incompletely theorised agreement, CR Sunstein, *Legal Reasoning and Political Conflict* (New York, Oxford University Press, 1996). Sunstein argues that, by basing their holdings on principles of a low level of theoretical abstraction, judges can ensure that their rulings will be consistent with numerous theories of law. This can allow the law to construct a type of 'unassuming' consensus—incompletely theorised agreement—between competing meta-theories, a consensus that is based on pragmatic considerations instead of theoretical ones. In this way, law (as well as adjudication) can ensure its viability as a mechanism of social ordering in a deeply pluralistic society. Sunstein's argument assumes, implicitly, that these competing meta-theories could agree to a particular, well-specified practical solution to a legal dilemma, even if they would remain in disagreement over the theoretical justifications of this solution. This chapter deals with the more difficult situations in which each theory leads to a completely different practical solution (holding), which cannot be resolved through low-level pragmatic reasoning.

One can question, however, the robustness of this strategy as an instrument for concealing or suppressing the paradox. A key difficulty concerns the fact that, presumably, other legal observers could pursue the same analysis presented above, and this could lead to the uncovering of the law's incoherence. If the law's coherence is exposed as nothing more than a façade, generated by a calculating and inconsistent application of vague concepts, trust will be lost and the law will risk destabilisation. (I will say more about the way in which this risk may unfold below.) It seems, then, that the apparent success of the mechanism of vagueness in unwinding the paradox of incoherence requires additional explanation. In what follows, I explore some alternative explanatory paths. This discussion will also expose the limits of vagueness as an instrument for deparadoxification.

My first observation links the seeming success of the mechanism of vagueness to the pluralistic make-up of the community observing and participating in the game of law. This community is divided in its communicative orientations and capabilities. According to this explanation, the law utilises the differences amongst the distinct observers (and participants) of legal communication: legislators, lawyers, judges, scholars and laymen. These observers differ not only in their knowledge of the law, but also in their interpretative stance towards it. The key difference is that between legal professionals and laymen. Laymen, even when they participate in legal communication (as parties to adjudication or participants in conversations about law), are, to a large extent, ignorant of the interpretative intricacies which characterise the application of general concepts. This ignorance reflects not just a lack of know-how, but also the fact that laymen usually encounter the law in very particular contexts and thus do not possess the broad perspective necessary in order to detect inconsistencies at the 'top' level of general concepts. Further, laymen generally approach the law with a pragmatic rather than an analytic stance (ie, they do not analyse their failures or successes in an analytic fashion). Together, these features cause laymen to be less sensitive to any inconsistencies that might characterise the law in general. Laymen, it is hypothesised, tend to accept at face value the claim that the law can meet, without residue, its dual commitments for coherence and pluralistic sensitivity.[29]

Another possible explanation focuses on the scope of the paradox. The capacity of the law to sustain the paradox is explained by redrawing its boundaries. One can distinguish in this context between two different points of view. The first point of view treats the incoherence of law as a temporal phenomenon, as a *transitory interpretative struggle*. Incoherence

---

[29] A possible criticism of the 'heterogeneity' argument could be based on the idea of *discursive diffusion*. Even if one accepts the claim that legal observers differ in their ability to analyse legal communication, one can still expect information to flow among various segments of society, smoothing away any individual differences. If this diffusion is intensive enough, the paradox could be exposed despite the heterogeneity of the observing community.

is tolerated because it reflects a legitimate search for meaning—not the unfairness or arbitrariness of the law. The second point of view focuses on the *topological* quality of legal incoherence; it asks the observer to evaluate any incoherence against the totality of legal communications. If such evaluation shows that the incoherence of law is limited, in fact, to a clearly *bounded* field, the phenomenon ceases to be problematic.[30] As a limited or peripheral phenomenon incoherence can be tolerated because it does not hamper the law's overall claim to coherence while signalling, nonetheless, a principled openness to pluralistic needs.

To the extent that the foregoing observations are seen as plausible descriptions of the contemporary reality of law, they go some way toward explaining how the mechanism of vagueness can succeed in keeping the paradox at bay. At the same time, however, these observations also expose the limits of the mechanism of vagueness. I have mentioned three (not necessarily overlapping) conditions for the success of this mechanism: a heterogeneous and fragmented community of legal observers, a perception of incoherence as a transient phenomenon and a limited presence of incoherence within the totality of law. While these conditions seem quite plausible, they can be breached if the ruptures within society become too intense. This could expose the paradox, leading to the destabilisation of the legal system and endangering its social standing. This process of destabilisation could transpire in at least two ways, leaving the law with only one—but not both—of the essential elements of legitimacy, either coherence or pluralistic sensitivity. The first possible scenario involves the loss of meaning: as the vagueness of law becomes more and more *disordered*[31] in response to pluralistic pressures, its concepts and doctrines could lose their force as explanatory devices. The

---

[30] One may well doubt whether the law could sustain itself as an autonomous social system if it should become completely incoherent. The legal system's main function is the facilitation of *normative expectations*, which, unlike *cognitive expectations*, need not be revised in the face of new information, N Luhmann, 'Operational Closure and Structural Coupling: the Differentiation of the Legal System' (1992) 13 *Cardozo Law Review* 1419 at 1426. But normative expectations can only arise in an environment in which legal norms are both general and consistent: generality, because norms cannot generate expectations with respect to the behaviour of others, unless they are generally applicable; consistency, because inconsistent application of the normative apparatus of the law would inevitably prevent the possibility of forming meaningful normative expectations (other than vacuous expressions such as 'people should behave lawfully').

[31] Through a process of further fuzzification or ambiguation of legal terms, accompanied by incoherent rules of application. Fuzzification means the rendering of a sharp distinction, eg, Jew/non-Jew, into a fuzzy one (which means that Jewish would become a matter of degree). Ambiguation means the injection of further meanings into a term or concept (eg, bank). Further fuzzification or ambiguation refers to the construction of more detailed scales (in the case of fuzzy notions) or additional submeanings (in the case of ambiguous concepts). When this process takes place in a communicative environment governed by messy rules of disambiguation—that is, when the use of inexact terms is governed by a variety of incompatible rules (eg, multiple membership functions in the case of fuzzy terms and varied contextual cues in the case of ambiguous terms)—the result is a more chaotic legal space.

result: such extensive disorderliness could render the top-tier conceptual level meaningless, portraying the law as an arbitrary and capricious system. This could lead to a loss of trust in the capacity of the law to produce just rulings. This scenario could probably transpire only if the intensification of vagueness spread either into several legal fields, or, alternatively, occurred in a central legal area (such as constitutional law).

A second possible scenario involves an opposite phenomenon: the *re-entry* of meaning into the disordered discourse of the courts. In this scenario, the top-tier conceptual level (despite its contradictory and disordered application in various court rulings) could, nonetheless, preserve a certain 'sharp' core in the eyes of a dominant set of legal observers. This *imposed structuring* could delegitimise the main interpreting bodies of the law—the courts—which would then be perceived as distorting the meaning of the law by refusing to apply the 'right' (ie, just) version of the law.

Before I continue, I would like to consider a different reaction to the paradox of coherence. The foregoing analysis takes the reality of the paradox as a given and focuses on the possibility of managing it in a way which will not endanger the legitimacy of law. But one can of course dispute my (contingent) claim about the existence of the paradox. Such argument can take one of the following forms. One can question either my initial assumptions about the simultaneous (normative and social) import of coherence and pluralistic sensitivity, or my thesis about the impossibility of complying with them both at the same time. Either of these alternatives leads to the resolution of the paradox. Attacking the assumptions which serve as the basis for the paradox, or the reasoning that leads to its contradictory conclusion, is a well-established practice for paradox-breakers.[32] While I maintain that the reasoning and assumptions which generate this paradox are highly plausible, I do not deny that the opposing arguments have some merit. So let us consider them in more detail.

Consider, first, the critique of the assumption regarding the simultaneous import of coherence and pluralistic sensitivity. This critique claims, in effect, that either one of these principles (or both), does not represent a valid principle of law, or that, alternatively they can be fitted into a clear priority ranking. Any of these alternatives offers a solution to the paradox. To make this argument convincing, it must be supported, I think, with an argument about the social perception of these competing values. Otherwise it will leave an unexplained cleavage between the inner structure of the law and the structure of the society it proclaims to rule. This requires an

---

[32] This strategy reflects the underlying structure of a paradoxical argument. A paradox can be defined as 'an argument that begins with premises that appear to be clearly true, that proceeds according to inference rules that appear to be valid, but that ends in contradiction.' See CS Chihara, 'The Semantic Paradoxes: A Diagnostic Investigation' (1979) 88 *Philosophical Review* 590. For a general account of this strategy, see N Rescher, *Paradoxes: Their Roots, Range and Resolution* (Chicago, Open Court, 2001) 27.

argument of the following sort. One can argue, for example, that people are not very sensitive to legal incoherence, or that people who live in pluralistic societies attach a higher value to the idea of pluralistic sensitivity and may be ready to tolerate any associated incoherence.[33] Without this kind of supplementary sociological observation the thesis about the inner structure of the law will remain unconvincing (because it will fail to explain how the law can cope with the expected social critique). As a whole I do not find this line of argument convincing, but I leave it to the reader to judge.

An alternative critique accepts the simultaneous import of coherence and pluralistic sensitivity but argues that applying them together does not create any contradictions and hence is not problematic. This critique is based on the thesis that it is possible to develop a meta-principle or meta-discourse, which could be invoked to resolve any possible social dispute. This would mean that society and law can develop a uniform understanding of a 'just' law, leading to the dissolution of the paradox. As already noted, I am sceptical about the possibility of such meta-discourse.[34]

One thing seems to be beyond doubt: vagueness is a fragile and unstable strategy. This should motivate us, so it seems, to explore alternative strategies for dealing with the paradox. In section II, I consider such an alternative strategy: 'randomisation.' But before discussing this alternative, I would like to discuss a concrete example—the precautionary principle—examining how the strategy of vagueness operates in practice. This discussion highlights the virtues and limits of this strategy.

The 'Precautionary' Principle

The precautionary principle emerged in response to a deep and persistent conflict between two competing ideologies: environmentalism and industrial capitalism. One manifestation of this conflict was a dispute over the nature and scope of risk regulation. On the one hand, in the wake of several highly publicised ecological disasters and public health scandals (such as the 1984 disaster at Bhopal, and the outbreak of 'mad cow' disease in England),[35]

---

[33] For an argument showing that people do not naturally seek coherence, see eg, CR Sunstein, D Kahneman, D Schkade and I Ritov, 'Is Incoherence Outrageous' (2002) 54 *Stanford Law Review* 1293 at 1298 (although they focus on the bounded domain of punitive damages).

[34] See above text to nn 8,9. For a different opinion, see Kaplow and Shavell, above n 9, and Benbaji, this volume.

[35] For a discussion of the Bhopal disaster, in which more than 2,000 persons died and 200,000 were injured in Bhopal, India, as a result of the accidental release of lethal gas from a chemical plant operated by a local subsidiary of the US firm Union Carbide, see S Jasanoff (ed), *Learning from Disaster: Risk Management after Bhopal* (Philadelphia, University of Pennsylvania Press, 1994). For a discussion of 'mad cow' disease, see P Brown, 'Mad-Cow Disease in Cattle and Human Beings' (2004) 92 *American Scientist* 334.

environmental groups and their supporters were demanding a more proactive risk regulation. This proactive approach was necessary, so they argued, to prevent the reoccurrence of such human and ecological disasters. On the other hand, the industrial community was arguing that this interventionist approach would prevent technological innovation and impose unbearable costs on the industrial sector. As will be indicated below, the precautionary principle sought to arbitrate between these competing world-views. Much of the principle's success (as well as its weaknesses) can be attributed to its deep fluidity.[36]

Consider the following formulation of the precautionary principle (Principle 15 of the Rio Declaration on Environment and Development (1992)):[37]

> In order to protect the environment, the precautionary approach shall be widely applied by States according to their capabilities. Where there are threats of serious or irreversible damage, lack of full scientific certainty shall not be used as a reason for postponing cost-effective measures to prevent environmental degradation.

What is the meaning of this principle? Well, it depends. Some environmentalists interpret this principle in a strong way, as *requiring regulative action* 'whenever there is a possible risk to health, safety, or the environment, even if the supporting evidence is speculative and even if the economic costs of regulation are high.'[38] This proactive interpretation of the precautionary principle can be supported by several court rulings which invoked the principle and by the adoption of the precautionary principle by numerous international instruments covering a wide range of ecological risks.[39] The industrial community rejected this interpretation. The precautionary

---

[36] The ambiguity of the precautionary principle was discussed by other writers, see eg, P Sandin et al, 'Five Charges against the Precautionary Principle' (2002) 5 *Journal of Risk Research* 287.

[37] Another prominent example is Art 3(3) of the Climate Change Convention (1992), which provides: 'The Parties should take precautionary measures to anticipate, prevent or minimize the causes of climate change and mitigate its adverse effects. Where there are threats of serious or irreversible damage, lack of full scientific certainty should not be used as a reason for postponing such measures, taking into account that policies and measures to deal with climate change should be cost-effective so as to ensure global benefits at the lowest possible cost.'

[38] CR Sunstein, 'Beyond the Precautionary Principle' (2003) 151 *University of Pennsylvania Law Review* 1003 at 1018.

[39] As for judicial rulings, see eg, in the European Union: Case T-70/99 *Alpharma Inc v Council of the European Union* [2002] ECR II-3495, and Case T-13/99 *Pfizer Animal Health v Council* [1999] ECR II-1961, upheld on appeal by order of the President of the Court of Justice in Case C-329/99 P(R) *Pfizer Animal Health v Council* [1999] ECR I-8343. In the United Kingdom, see eg, *Castle Cement v Environment Agency*, QBD (Administrative Court) [2001] 2 CMLR 19 (paras 39–40). And in the USA: *Am Trucking Ass'ns v EPA* 283 F.3d 355, 378 (D.C. Cir. 2002). Provisions which are based on the precautionary principle can be found in at least 14 international documents, Sunstein, above n 38, at 1006, 1011–20.

principle, they argued, reflects a general property of risk regulation—that it has to deal with uncertainties. As such there is nothing really novel about this principle, nor should it be interpreted as imposing more extensive burdens on industry.

These conflicting interpretations were made possible by the deeply fluid wording of the precautionary principle. The vagueness of the precautionary principle questions, as will be demonstrated below, the usefulness of this principle as a guide for decision-making; it was valuable, however, in resolving the tension between environmental groups and the business community.[40] One way in which the vagueness of the precautionary principle can be assessed is by considering the meaning of its core elements: the notions of 'threats of serious or irreversible damage,' 'lack of full scientific certainty' and 'cost-effective measures.'[41] Consider, first, the notion of 'threats of serious or irreversible damage.' This term seeks to distinguish between those risks that should be subject to precautionary action and thus deserve special regulatory attention (*exceptional risks*), and those that do not (*ordinary risks*). The problem, however, is that the meaning of the notions of *'seriousness'* and *'irreversibility'* is far from clear. Presumably, the precautionary principle should have offered us a method for distinguishing between risks according to their *level* of 'seriousness' and 'irreversibility' (particularly because almost all the risks subject to health and safety or environmental regulation are, to some extent, 'serious' and 'irreversible'). Well, it does not.

This 'silence' is problematic because contemporary risk discourse offers multiple methods for ranking risks which, in themselves, invoke deeply inexact terms. None of these methods enjoys a privileged social status; indeed, they represent totally different world-views.[42] Among the possible ranking criteria, one can mention *moral criteria* (eg, the equitability of the risk: to what extent its impacts are equally distributed, its measure of voluntariness and the extent to which those who were exposed

---

[40] The analysis of the precautionary principle ('PP') in this section is based on the assumption that the PP purports to provide guidelines for action. However, many of the formulations of this principle, including Art 15 of the Rio Declaration quoted above, are ambiguous, and can be interpreted as lacking a behavioural force (eg, one can interpret Art 15 as a discursive principle, which purports to regulate what kind of arguments can be validly made in a deliberation about risks), see Sandin, above n 36, at 289. One should not read the following text, therefore, as an interpretation of a particular formulation of the PP (eg, Art 15), but rather as an attempt to find whether it is possible to extract clear decision-making guidelines from the PP. In exploring this question, I will use the text of Art 15 of the Rio Declaration as a useful starting point.

[41] I am relying here on the text of Art 15 of the Rio Declaration. These core notions can be found, however, in other formulations of the PP.

[42] For a general discussion of the complexity of ranking risks, see eg, MW Jones-Lee, 'Safety and the Saving of Life: the Economics of Safety and Physical Risk' in R Layard and S Glaister (eds), *Cost-Benefit Analysis* (Cambridge, Cambridge University Press, 1994) and H Margolis, 'What's Special About Cancer?' in RJ Ellis and M Thompson (eds), *Culture Matters: Essays in Honour of Aaron Wildavsky* (Westview Press, 1997).

had any control over it), *psychological criteria* (the 'dread' effect or catastrophic potential of the risk in question) and *welfare-based criteria*.[43] To illustrate the differences between these attitudes toward risks, let us consider a concrete example: the risks associated with aeroplane crashes and car accidents. The risk of an aeroplane crash seems more 'serious' because it involves a larger number of casualties per accident; its catastrophic potential and 'dread' effect are therefore greater. On the other hand, car accidents cause more casualties overall than aeroplane accidents; from a total welfare perspective, then, they seem more serious. Regarding irreversibility, both accident types seem equally irreversible in terms of their consequences (death or injury). However, one can argue that the risk of an aeroplane accident is more irreversible, as it leaves its unfortunate victims a much lower chance of survival (reflecting, among others, lack of controllability).[44] So which accident type is more serious or more irreversible? The answer is not clear. The precautionary principle does not resolve this ranking puzzle.

The notion of 'lack of full scientific certainty' is equally vague. Its vagueness lies in the problematic distinction between 'full' and 'partial' scientific certainty. From the perspective of scientific methodology and philosophy of science, this distinction is nonsensical. Science, including those fields of science that serve as the basis for risk-regulation (eg, toxicology and epidemiology), is based on inductive reasoning and not on purely analytic, deductive arguments. Uncertainty is therefore an inherent attribute of science. We live in an *incompletable* (or 'open') universe,[45] whose domain of uncertainty cannot be described completely or precisely.[46] There are two aspects to this

---

[43] The most influential variant of welfare-based criteria is the economic one, which is based on the methodology of cost-benefit analysis. This technique allows the regulator to rank hazards according to the marginal benefit (in terms of improvement to human health) of investing US$1 in regulatory/precautionary action directed at that hazard. Such a comparison should lead to a ranking of hazards and regulatory options according to the relative seriousness of the hazards and the relative efficiency of possible regulatory actions (in reducing health risks), all measured in monetary terms. Theoretically, such ranking should allow the regulator to equalise, at the margin, the resources devoted to avoiding one fatality from each hazard, Jones-Lee, above n 42, at 296. This type of examination requires, of course, deep understanding of the potential damage of each hazard, and a capacity to translate this knowledge into monetary values. It also depends on one being satisfied with the philosophical soundness of the economic method. However, even if one is ideologically committed to the economic ethos, many difficulties remain. Because, by assumption, the hazards that are subject to the precautionary principle exhibit extreme levels of uncertainty, it is doubtful whether traditional cost-benefit techniques can be employed at all.

[44] Irreversibility is also a function of the resilience of the ecosystem which is the subject of a certain risk. But this notion is again vague.

[45] This notion was first introduced in K Binmore, 'De-Bayesing Game Theory' in K Binmore, A Kirman and P Tani (eds), *Frontiers of Game Theory* (Cambridge, Mass, MIT Press, 1993).

[46] In contrast, one of the features of a *completable* or *closed* universe is that it enables those who operate within it to specify, beforehand, *all* the possible outcomes of a particular action and to assign to *each* outcome a unique probability. The distinction between closed and open universes, in itself, has no privileged philosophical status. Its usefulness lies in the way in which it conforms to our experience of observing the world through different modes of inquiry.

uncertainty: (1) *ontological uncertainty*, uncertainty about the correctness of our description of reality, which reflects, among other things, the limits of the inductive method, and (2) *time uncertainty*, which refers to uncertainty about the future.[47] This *strong uncertainty* implies that our theories of the world are inherently fallible: there is always the risk that the discovery of new data will force us to revise.[48]

From this perspective, there is nothing really novel in the claim that a lack of decisive evidence of risk should *not* constitute a reason against regulation. This claim merely reflects the fact that risk regulation, to the extent that it is based on science, is always based on incomplete evidence and imperfect theories. The criterion of 'lack of full scientific certainty' thus seems to add nothing to our current regulatory practices.[49] An alternative interpretation, which may save the precautionary principle from being completely trivial, could take this element of the precautionary principle as a reference to some *minimal* level of scientific evidence (or causal explanation), which, while less than what is usually required to justify regulatory intervention, is nonetheless sufficient as grounds for action when dealing with the 'exceptional' risks covered by the precautionary principle. But this interpretation is problematic, both because it invokes the fuzzy notion of 'minimal,' and because it relies on the inexact notion of 'exceptional' risk.

Finally, there is the notion of 'cost-effective measures.' This notion is similarly inexact. The idea of 'cost-effectiveness' presupposes that it is possible to rank alternative regulatory actions by their effectiveness and efficiency in preventing harm. This assumption, however, is highly questionable. First, since the concept of harm is itself deeply contested (eg, how does one measure harm to wilderness?), any ranking scheme that will be based on a particular understanding of harm will be subject to objections. A second problem concerns the deep uncertainties which implicate many environmental risks.[50] These deep uncertainties cause experts and laymen to disagree (between them and among themselves) on the probabilities which should be attributed to different ecological hazards. These dual difficulties—the definition of harm and the assignment of proper probabilities—can generate conflicting estimations of 'cost-effectiveness.' For a typical example, consider the climate

---

[47] See S Faucheux, G Froger and G Munda, 'Toward an Integration of Uncertainty, Irreversibility, and Complexity in Environmental Decision Making' in J van den Bergh and J van der Straaten, *Economy and Ecosystems in Change: Analytical and Historical Approaches* (Cheltenham, Edward Elgar, 1997) 52.
[48] See Binmore, above n 45, at 325.
[49] Neither can this phrase be interpreted as a requirement to take measures whenever the existence of any risk cannot be completely excluded, since science, as an inductive enterprise, cannot provide such evidence.
[50] For a discussion of these two issues, see G Daily *et al*, 'The Value of Nature and the Nature of Value' (2000) 289 *Science* 395.

change debate. One line of argument, associated mainly with the industrial community and the oil-producing countries argued that no regulatory action should be taken until further studies are completed, because efficiency requires one to gain more knowledge before acting.[51] On the other hand, the environmental camp argued with similar force that, since the possible consequences of human-induced climatic changes could be so devastating, acting immediately was not only morally requisite but also economically justified.[52]

Despite its substantial fluidity, the precautionary principle was quite successful in defusing the tension over risk regulation. The principle's vagueness provided the law a wide interpretative discretion at the application stage. In some cases, this discretion was used in a pro-environmental way; in other cases, it was used as an excuse to delay action while further clarifications were being sought.[53] The deep vagueness of the precautionary principle has also made it easier for politicians and negotiators to support its inclusion in various international instruments. However, protests against globalisation, which have become widespread since the late 1990s,[54] seem to reflect (among other things) an increasing dissatisfaction with the way in which the precautionary principle has been applied, and a loss of trust in its ability to arbitrate, in a fair and balanced way, between environmental and economic perspectives.

II. RANDOM UP

[H]e very calmly rode on, leaving it to his Horse's Discretion to go which Way he pleas'd; firmly believing, that in this consisted the very Being of

---

[51] This approach was supported by the Bush Administration. See SD Murphy, 'Bush Administration Proposal for Reducing Greenhouse Gases' (2002) 96 *American Journal of International Law* 487.

[52] See eg, the report by Friends of the Earth International, 'Putting Costs into Perspective: Economic Benefits from Fighting Climate Change' (1997) *Climate Change Briefing* 3.

[53] The best example for such a delay is, of course, the Kyoto Protocol, which was signed in 1997 under the mandate of the 1992 Framework Convention on Climate Change. The Protocol introduced ambitious targets for cutting emissions for most of the developed countries, but none for the rest of the world. However, since 1997 very little has been achieved in actual terms (the Protocol has only entered into force on 16 February 2005, eight years after it was initiated), mainly because of the American refusal to ratify the protocol. One of the main reasons which were given by the USA in support of its decision was the need to extend the scientific understanding of the problem of climate change before taking very costly actions. For a discussion of the Kyoto Protocol and the American position, see eg, C Bohringer and C Vogt, 'Economic and Environmental Impacts of the Kyoto Protocol' (2003)36 *Canadian Journal of Economics* 475 and T Schelling, 'What Makes Greenhouse Sense?' (2002) 81 *Foreign Affairs* 2.

[54] For an analysis of the anti-globalisation movement, see O Perez, *Ecological Sensitivity and Global Legal Pluralism: Rethinking the Trade and Environment Conflict* (Oxford, Hart Publishing, 2004) at 1–7.

Adventures, Miguel de Cervantes. (Don Quixote (Peter Motteux (trans), New York, The Modern Library, 1950) vol 1, ch 2, 8)[55]

In times of pressure, the façade of coherence generated by the use of fluid concepts may break, threatening the law's legitimacy and endangering its stability. But what is the alternative? One possibility is to employ random selection devices. Randomness seems to offer a way out of the paradox—a decision-making mechanism that could allow the law to satisfy the requirements of both coherence and pluralistic sensitivity. The idea of using randomness to resolve legal disputes may seem, at first glance, inconsistent with the spirit of law. The appeal to randomness reflects, one can argue, a certain doctrinal void or 'loss of reason'—a victory of arbitrariness over rationality. Should not the law evolve through reason, rather than through 'random walk'? Neither of these claims provides, I will argue, a convincing reason for rejecting 'randomness.' First, as will be pointed out below, using 'randomness' as a decision-making tool requires careful, rational planning (thus the use of randomness does not reflect 'loss of reason'). Secondly, randomness (or lottery) constitutes an impartial method for arbitrating among competing claims or incommensurable world-views; in that sense, it is fair. Randomness is not, therefore, 'arbitrary' in the derogatory sense of the word.

Understanding the way in which random selection devices can be used to resolve legal dilemmas requires that I first make some brief comments about the meaning of randomness. The seemingly simple question—'What is random?'—has occupied mathematicians over the last 100 years, and remains an open question to this day.[56] No attempt will be made therefore to resolve this question here. For our purposes, it will suffice to focus on two key properties of randomness: *disorder or incompressibility* and *unpredictability*. The idea of randomness as *incompressibility* is based on the observation:

> that the information embodied in a random series of numbers cannot be 'compressed,' or reduced to a more compact form ... This 'incompressibility' is a

---

[55] I owe this quote to M Gardner, *Mathematical Circus* (Washington, DC, MAA Spectrum Book, 1992) 66.
[56] See eg, AA Muchnik, AL Semenov and VA Uspenski, 'Mathematical Metaphysics of Randomness' (1998) 207 *Theoretical Computer Science* 263 and R Nickerson, 'The Production and Perception of Randomness' (2002) 109 *Psychological Review* 330. There seems to be wide support for the proposition that randomness, as a mathematical and psychological attribute, is relative rather than absolute. The question of whether a certain phenomenon is random (eg, a sequence of numbers or symbols) is determined by the language in which this question is formulated, the horizon of patterns against which the phenomenon in question is analysed, and the identity of the observer to whom this question is directed, see G Hellman, 'Randomness and Reality' (1978) *PSA: Proceedings of the Biennial Meeting of the Philosophy of Science Association* 79; WA Dembski, 'Randomness by Design' (1991) 25 *Nous* 75 and Nickerson, *ibid* 331.

property of all random numbers; indeed, we can proceed directly to define randomness in terms of 'incompressibility': A series of numbers is random if the smallest algorithm capable of specifying it to a computer has about the same number of bits of information as the series itself.[57]

The idea of *unpredictability* reflects the basic intuition that 'looking random' means that the next element in a sequence of numbers or events is unpredictable.[58] In a 'white noise' or random series, 'each number tells you exactly nothing about what to expect for the next number.'[59]

Applying these two features of randomness to the legal context yields two conclusions. The first is that in those cases that fall under the rule of 'randomness,' the ruling of the court in one case (or the decision of a government official) will tell you nothing about the court's (or the official's) future rulings, except the assurance that they will be based on a random decision-making mechanism. Secondly, a statistical analysis of legal decisions that invoked the rule of randomness (whether judicial or administrative) should reveal no clear pattern. Using random decision devices holds several advantages for a law that operates in a pluralistic society. First, because the legal decision now depends on an external device—a random generator—the law cannot be blamed for taking 'sides' or for masking its arbitrariness through vague doctrines. The law can thus preserve its impartiality.[60] Secondly, random-guided decision-making is also fair in that it guarantees that every element of the relevant set 'ie, legal claims' has an equal chance of being selected. Randomness produces, in other words, a *fairness of equal chances*.

The mechanism of randomness seems to provide the law, therefore, with a way to circumvent the problematic tension between consistency and

---

[57] See GJ Chaitin, 'Randomness and Mathematical Proof' (1975) 232 *Scientific American* 47.

[58] See S Bassein, 'A Sampler of Randomness' (1996) 103 *American Mathematical Monthly* 483. A related question is 'unpredictable by whom?'—and this, of course, is a question which the law is bound to find interesting. See Nickerson, above n 56, at 331.

[59] I Bakshee, 'From Noise to Beauty' (2000) 29 *Science Spectra* 24 at 29. Another 'take' on the notion of unpredictability was offered by Muchnik *et al*. They explain this notion by reference to the concept of a game. Imagine a game with two players: Man and infinite binary sequence. 'Man tries to guess the values of some terms of Sequence. If he fails then he pays and if he is successful then he gets a prize. Our intuition tells us that a very random Sequence cannot be beaten,' Muchnik *et al*, above n 56, at 280.

[60] This impartiality could be accomplished by employing a random-number generator whose underlying mechanism would be controlled neither by the judge nor by the litigants. Random generator, as the name implies, is a device that generates random numbers. Generally, there are two approaches to random number generation: pseudo-random generators and physical-random generators, Jennewein *et al*, 'A Fast and Compact Quantum Random Number Generator' (2000) 71 *Review of Scientific Instruments* 1675. The first approach relies on algorithms that are implemented on a computing device; the latter measures some physical observable expected to behave randomly. Jennewein *et al* present, for example, a physical quantum random number generator based on the process of splitting a beam of photons on a beam splitter, a quantum mechanical source of true randomness.

pluralistic sensitivity. Consistency is achieved by applying the random mechanism to resolve all the cases that fall within the boundaries of random rule.[61] Pluralistic sensitivity is achieved by giving each party or point of view an *equal chance* of winning the argument—a form of *blind sensitivity*. The idea of randomness thus seems to provide the means through which the principle of 'pluralistic sensitivity' could be given an exact meaning, freeing us from its problematic elusiveness.

Modern law has been quite reluctant to incorporate the concept of randomness into its doctrinal repertoire.[62] Randomness was invoked, mainly, in cases in which a scarce good had to be allocated to multiple, equally situated claimants.[63] Thus, for example, in Israel, lottery was used as a mechanism for allocating public land. This practice was endorsed by the Israeli Supreme Court, which has repeatedly stated that the principles of fairness and equality demand that, in making decisions over the allocation of public land, the government should use either tender or lottery. These mechanisms, the court stated, ensure that the allocation process will be fair.[64] Similarly, lotteries have been used in the USA for distributing scarce medical resources (albeit in the limited context of selecting patients for receiving experimental therapies).[65]

---

[61] One may argue that the kind of consistency achieved through randomness is consistency of method or legal procedure, and not consistency of legal principles (to which I referred at the opening of this chapter). I am sceptical, though, about how far one can go with this distinction, since legal procedure is guided by substantive legal principles; in that sense, randomness is not different from so-called 'substantive' principles (eg, good faith). I explore the implications of this distinction further below.

[62] The ancients were more open to the use of random mechanisms. Thus, eg, the ancient Greeks used the mechanism of lot to appoint various public officers, JB Bury, *A History of Greece,* 1st edn (New York, The Modern Library, 1913) 178. Bury notes: 'According to men's ideas in those days, lot committed the decision to the gods, and was thus a serious method of procedure—not a sign of political levity, as we should regard it now. But a device which superstition suggested was approved by the reflexions of philosophical statesmen; and lot was recognised as a valuable political engine for security against undue influence and for the protection of minorities' (*ibid*). For an attempt to revive this ancient tradition, see eg, AR Amar, 'Choosing Representatives by Lottery Voting' (1984) 93 *Yale Law Journal* 1283.

[63] The attraction of using a random-selection mechanism in these cases was its capacity to create a sense of fairness by allocating 'equal chances to secure some (usually indivisible) good to those who have (on some independently determined basis) equal claims to it,' B Chapman, 'Chance, Reason and Rule of Law' (2000) 50 *University of Toronto Law Journal* 469 at 475.

[64] Supreme Court Case 5023/91 *Poraz v Minister of Housing* (31 March 1992), at para 11. The choice between these two mechanisms depends on the objective of the allocation. If the objective is to raise public funds, then the mechanism of tender should be preferred; if it is the allocation of land to particular communities (eg, in the context of Israel, new immigrants), then lottery should be chosen. See *Poraz, ibid*, at para 11. In the latter case, the right to participate in the lottery could be limited to a special segment of society on grounds that it deserves special treatment.

[65] See MH Shapiro, 'On the Possibility of "Progress" in Managing Biomedical Technologies: Markets, Lotteries, and Rational Moral Standards in Organ Transplantation' (2003) 31 *Capital University Law Review* 13 at 45 n 104. Shapiro notes that, in general, the use of lotteries in this context was discouraged. Other selection mechanisms such as queuing—a kind of first-come, first-served system—seem to be more popular (*ibid*, at 46).

But why stop here? Randomness is a valuable resource[66] and there is no reason why the law should not use random devices more extensively. Thus, for example, in the context of risk regulation, random selection mechanism can be used as a method for choosing those substances which will be subject to a more extensive regulatory scrutiny. This might be better than the regulatory arbitrariness which, as we saw earlier, characterises the application of the precautionary principle.[67] Random selection device can also be employed in planning decisions, such as in decisions over the location of hazardous facilities.

Random selection can also be used by the judiciary to resolve certain types of disputes. Thus, for example, random selection mechanism can be invoked to resolve disputes over the allocation of constitutional rights, replacing the standard procedure of constitutional balancing. An interesting example from the Israeli context is exemption from military service, an issue that has preoccupied Israeli society since the 1980s. The basic dilemma underlying this debate is the following: Israel feels it cannot survive without a strong army, which, to be viable, requires substantial manpower (soldiers). This need has forced Israel to establish compulsory military service. While it is possible to exempt a few people from military service, this exemption cannot be granted freely, as such action might undermine the ability of the army to fulfil its missions due to insufficient manpower. The question is how to allocate this limited number of 'exemption tickets' fairly. So far, Israeli law has granted these exemption rights exclusively to ultra-orthodox Jews who study at religious institutions (*Yeshivas*), recognising the deep cultural and ideological resistance of this community to military service.[68] This practice was challenged by repeated petitions to the Israeli Supreme Court; the petitions depicted this practice as discriminatory and unconstitutional.[69] It was argued that the law is discriminatory since it did not recognise the similar interest in exemption from military service of secular candidates, whether on grounds of conscience (eg, pacifism) or, alternatively, because they preferred to use the period of army service for studying at a university (which, according to the petitions, the courts should treat as equal to a *Yeshiva*). One possible solution to this dilemma, which would not have required the law to determine which of these conflicting world-views and interests—religious and secular—was more important, might have been to use a random selection device to allocate the limited 'exemption rights' among the competing communities and their members.[70]

---

[66] B Hayes, 'Randomness as a Resource' (2001) 89 *American Scientist* (July-August) 300.
[67] I assume here a scarcity of regulatory and industrial resources that does not allow society to consider every risk it is facing with the same degree of scrutiny.
[68] This refers to the male population. Different rules apply to women.
[69] See eg, Supreme Court Case 24/01 *Resler v Israeli Knesset* (20 February 2002).
[70] Of course, the random mechanism did not need to be applied directly by the court; the court could have directed the Ministry of Defence to do so (or give its approval to this practice).

Another interesting application can be found in the area of mass torts. The staggering size of these cases (in terms of the number of claimants and the financial cost involved) confronts the justice system with serious problems, first, because of the administrative burden these cases impose, but more importantly, because doing justice to each of the multiple claimants is very difficult. In response to these dual challenges, some courts (prominently in the context of asbestos-related litigation) have developed a procedure whereby samples of cases are tried and the resulting damages are then applied to the remaining population of cases.[71] Individual justice in these cases is preserved, arguably, through the application of random selection at the class level.

III. THE PARADOX RE-EMERGES

We have seen that randomness presents the law with a way to circumvent the discord between consistency and pluralistic sensitivity. The problem, however, is that the claim of randomness to provide a *perfectly neutral* mechanism for arbitrating among competing claims is in fact illusory. In that sense, randomness does not constitute a real solution to the paradox of regulating a pluralistic society in a 'fair' way. The paradox only shifts to a new hiding place from which it could re-emerge. Consider the following blind spots of random decision-making. The first concerns the initial decision to use a random-selection device. This requires one to show that the random rule is morally or legally preferable to any other decision rule (eg, by arguing that in those situations in which there are multiple, equally legitimate decision rules, randomness constitutes the best way for reaching a decision). But this decision requires substantive deliberation that cannot be randomised.[72]

A second problem is one of *classification*: of constructing a 'comparable class.' To enable the application of a random-selection mechanism, we need

---

[71] MJ Saks and PD Blanck, 'Justice Improved: The Unrecognized Benefits of Aggregation and Sampling in the Trial of Mass Torts' (1992) 44 *Stanford Law Review* 815.

[72] Thus, eg, in the case of using lottery to distribute some indivisible good one has to show why this method should be preferred to some (substantive) trait-linked criterion. 'Trait-linked rationality requires that distributional decisions be based on the individual traits—in the sense of personal characteristics of prospective recipients of a scarce resource. Thus, for any given criterion—say, 'social importance'—those who have it in greater strength are given more credit toward receiving the resource than those with lower measures', Shapiro, above n 65, at 33. An advocate of randomness must convince us, then, that it is both possible and justified, in the context of a certain legal dilemma, to suppress some of the differences between people through the application of random selection mechanism. A possible argument against the use of trait-linked rationality could focus, eg, on the problematic of devising a fair ranking scheme for different traits. For a discussion of this problematic (focusing on the question of how to distribute scarce medical resources) see Shapiro, above n 65, at 33–38.

to choose a criterion that will allow us to construct a set which consists of 'equivalent' members; this set will constitute the subject matter of the random-selection process. Thus, for example, in the context of chemical regulation, the law will have to create a list of substances—candidates for more stringent supervision—from which a more limited group of substances will be randomly picked out. In the context of exemption from military service, the law will need to construct a list of 'equal' claimants, representing 'equal' claims for exemption tickets, from which a smaller group could again be randomly selected. And in the context of transplantation decisions, the law will have to construct a list of candidates with 'equal' claims to the scarce organ or organs. Deciding on a principle which will guide the construction of such a set is not a mechanical matter; it requires a substantive argument that will demonstrate why this particular criterion was chosen. This decision necessarily involves an appeal to substantive principles.

Another blind spot concerns the perception of random selection as 'fair.' I noted above that random selection could be seen as fair, in the sense that it guarantees that every element of the set of potential claims has an equal chance of being chosen. However, the fact that random selection, in the pure sense, is an operation with no 'memory'—that is, the previous decision does not tell you anything about the next decision—can be regarded also as a reflection of intrinsic unfairness: 'In the sense that the [random] mechanism does not remember what happened previously and does not try to even the score, it is not entirely fair.'[73] The lack of memory means that a random device can generate a sequence of decisions which, in the short run, will clearly favour one side.[74] While it is true that this problem could be eliminated if you waited long enough (or, in other words, in the context of a very long sequence of decisions), society and people are usually not that patient. This may pressure the law to abandon the use of random mechanisms.

Resolving the foregoing dilemmas, without which one cannot employ random selection mechanisms, will require the law to invoke substantive reasoning, forcing it to choose from among competing conceptions of justice and fairness. Constructing a random decision-making scheme could thus generate the same paradoxical tension we tried to avoid by invoking the notion of randomness in the first place.[75]

---

[73] See J Binongo, 'Randomness, Statistics, and Pi' (2002) 95 *Mathematics Teacher* 224 at 225.

[74] Thus, eg, in the context of decisions over organ transplantation, lottery may be found to generate, in the short run, a preference for women over men, young people over elderly people, etc.

[75] In that sense, basing regulatory decisions on randomisation will not immunise them from judicial review, since it will always be possible, as was indicated above, to question the substantive reasoning that (necessarily) lies behind the use of randomness.

IV. CONCLUSION

Neither vagueness nor randomness provides a perfect solution to the paradoxical tension between coherence and pluralistic sensitivity. Another possible strategy could be to completely avoid the paradox. This could be achieved, for example, by allowing courts to refuse to give judgments in those cases presenting the law with the difficult choice of breaching either its claim for coherence or its commitment to pluralistic sensitivity. This strategy will avoid the paradox but at a price: it will undermine the claim of the law to serve as the ultimate social arbiter.[76]

What then, is left for the law? An alternative solution could be 'soft' deference or institutional diversification. While the law cannot refuse to give judgment, it can encourage and legitimise other forms of law-making, from private contracting to arbitration and alternative dispute resolution. This kind of institutional diversification (eg, self-regulation by polluting industries, mediation)[77] has become more common since the 1990s. But even here, there is no escape from the paradox. As long as the law *keeps* some residual authority to intervene in any social dispute in spite of any preliminary deference, the question will always be: to what extent has this power been used consistently and in a sensitive fashion? And this questioning might regenerate the paradox, necessitating once again the invocation of vague concepts.

It seems, then, that we would have to live with the paradox that is generated by the quest for fairness. But perhaps our problem does not lie in the paradox, but in a certain logical and anti-paradoxical state of mind which has become prevalent. Perhaps the dynamics that is generated by the mechanisms of deparadoxification unleashed by the paradox—in its varied and incessant dance between universal coherence and particularistic sensitivity—actually realises the ideal of fairness, maintaining in this way the structural integrity of the law.

---

[76] This strategy resembles the philosophical attempt to resolve the Liar Paradox by barring the use of statements involving pathological self-reference (eg, 'this sentence is false'). In both cases there is a problematic gap between social practice (of using the law or using language) and the solution.

[77] A prominent self-regulatory scheme of this type is the Responsible Care Program of the global chemical industry, see AA King and MJ Lenox, 'Industry Self-Regulation Without Sanctions: The Chemical Industry's Responsible Care Program' (2000) 43 *Academy of Management Journal* 698. For a discussion of the practice of mediation and its relation to law, see the contribution of Michal Alberstein in chapter 11.

7

Between Ritual and Theatre: Judicial Performance as Paradox

LIOR BARSHACK

> Final revelation is not logical nonsense; it is a concrete event which on the level of rationality must be expressed in contradictory terms, P Tillich, *Systematic Theology* (Chicago, University of Chicago Press, 1967, book I, 151)[1]

THAT LITIGATION CAN be viewed as a ritual process is an accepted idea which raises as many difficulties as it offers insights. One of these difficulties stems from the tension between the court's image as epitome of the rule of law and the characterisation of rituals—perhaps their most common characterisation—as interludes of lawless violence and normative void. Several schools of legal thought, including systems theory, have claimed that the determination and demarcation of legality in court are implicated in illegality.[2] Court proceedings suspend the rule of law and simultaneously stage its supreme realisation. The modest aim of this chapter is to look at the paradoxes which haunt authoritative statements of the law from the perspective of performance theory.

A central line of thought in performance theory evolved out of the anthropology of Victor Turner. The first section departs from Turner's theory of *social structure* and *communitas*, developing an account of structure and *communitas* as *corporate* and *communal* bodies respectively. According to the proposed account, during *communitas* the group forms a *communal body*: an immanent sacred fusion of all individual group members. The presence of the communal body generates the normative void that

---

[1] See also book III, 165. Tillich's text captures the structure of paradox which unfolds in institutional rituals such as court proceedings.
[2] See, eg, G Teubner, 'Economics of Gift—Positivity of Justice: The Mutual Paranoia of Jacques Derrida and Niklas Luhmann' (2001) 18(1) *Theory, Culture and Society* 29 at 31; N Luhmann, 'The Third Question: The Creative Use of Paradoxes in Law and Legal History' (1988) 15(2) *Journal of Law and Society* 153.

is often associated with *communitas* and which implicates court proceedings and other rituals in lawlessness. In the course of *social structure,* the communal body is projected outside of the group and transformed into an absent collective body, the corporate body. The presence of the sacred communal body gives way to the worship of an absent authority, communal fusion to individual autonomy. A discussion of the main features of social structures (corporate bodies), such as their dependence on the rule of law, is followed in the second section by an account of ritual (*communitas*) as a lawless moment in which the rule of law and the entire corporate order dissolve. In ritual, the group enacts its communal body in order to appease and exhaust anarchic communal forces which threaten to undermine its corporate structure. Developed social structures manage to appease anti-structural, communal forces with little resort to ritual, by employing instead the milder means of theatre. Advocates and adversaries of the 'bourgeois theatre' have considered it an outgrowth of ritual which tempered ritual lawlessness. Like ritual, theatre challenges the normative categories of social structure but without radically suspending them. It is a process of questioning and reaffirmation that is integrated into everyday life rather than interrupting routine.

In the third section, the ritual structure of court proceedings is outlined. The account of ritual in terms of presence of the communal body which suspends the rule of law sheds light on the tensions inherent in adjudication. The solemn enactment of the sacred in court threatens to suspend the law it seeks to uphold. For a court's decision to be valid and ritually efficacious, it has to involve at least a partial incarnation of founding sovereignty—of the collective body of the group, or 'constituent power'—which suspends the established definition of the court's own authority. The court at the same time occasions a moment of ritual immediacy and pretends merely to perform a repeated act of representation, to stage once more the same legal script. This tension between ritual and theatre, between presence and representation, seems to be particularly acute in the case of modern courts, since their sanctity—their solemnity and pomp—has been enhanced by the secularisation of political authority. Modern court proceedings repress their antinomic undercurrent by increasingly employing theatrical, as opposed to ritual, techniques, such as the sealed script, the distant stage and a growing number of professional, disinterested representatives. The horizontal, ritual enactment of conflict becomes ever more concealed by its staged representation.

I. SOCIAL STRUCTURE AS CORPORATION

Before considering the ritual process which unfolds in court, a few words on the concepts of social structure and ritual in general. One of the characteristic features of ritual is a relatively immediate experience of the sacred.[3] Whereas in ritual the sacred pervades the group, in social structure sacredness is projected outside the group, and transformed into an absent, transcendent authority. Stable social structures are premised on the relegation and confinement of sacredness to the group's absent, *corporate* body.[4] While social structures are organised as corporate bodies, during ritual the corporate structure of the group dissolves and the group is invaded and permeated by sanctity. A rough account of the idea of the corporate body would be instrumental for the elucidation of the concepts of social structure and ritual.

According to a theory of the corporation which we can consider today as classical—the theory of Maine, Maitland and Kantorowicz—the two defining features of the corporate personality are immortality and sovereignty. The family and the Crown served Maine and Maitland as the two paradigmatic, and intimately related, instances of immortal corporations. Families can preserve their identity across generations. Similarly, the Crown, or in Kantorowicz's terms, the public body of the king, is indifferent to the death of individual kings and retains its identity across generations. Kantorowicz's analysis of medieval kingship implies that sovereignty resides not in the private body of the king but in his corporate, public body. The king is obliged to defend and augment the inalienable possessions of the realm—they are not his own—an obligation that receives its clearest expression in the coronation oath. Maine makes this point in his discussion of the Roman family: The *pater familias* embodies the abstract legal personality of the family and is in charge of its affairs. He can only act in the name of its immortal interests, not out of his own passing interests and desires.

I would like to supplement the classical account of the corporate body with a few general suggestions, partly inspired by psycho-analytic theories of the group.

The separate corporate personality of the family and the state is associated with the mythical person of their founding ancestors. The examples of the family and state suggest that the corporation is identified with the person of the founding ancestor of the corporate group, such as the mythical, heroic founder of a Roman family, the founder of a royal dynasty or the founding fathers of modern nation states. The names and symbols of corporate descent groups refer, directly or indirectly, to their founding ancestors.

The corporate-ancestral personality of the group is an absent, transcendent object of worship. Through its corporate personality—its mythical ancestors and their multiple totemic representations—the group articulates itself for itself. According to Hegel and Durkheim, notwithstanding the differences between their theories of religion, society's self-representation is its

---

[3] See L Barshack, 'The Clerical Body of the Law' (2003) 24(3) *Cardozo Law Review*, 1151.
[4] *Ibid.*

object of worship. If the corporation is associated with ancestral figures, and ancestral law, and constitutes the self-representation of the group, it cannot fail to be sacred. Like the gods, corporations are transcendent; they are absent, invisible, external and superior to the group, and act through representatives. The religious dimension of political systems and families resides in their corporate structure. Civil and domestic religions worship the corporate bodies of states and families respectively, designated by national and domestic totemic symbols.

The corporate body originates in the projection of sacredness outside of the group. Corporations come into being through the projection of sacredness from the group onto a transcendent realm. Corporate formation secularises the social: once sacredness is projected outside the group, a temporal realm of pragmatic interaction can be established. In transitional and lawless states of *communitas*, the sacred is immanent to the social, and authority is often considered divine. The passage from divine kingship to rule-bound authority should be conceived in terms of projection: the private body of the king is deconsecrated and its sacredness projected onto the transcendent domain of the ancestral-corporate body. From this moment onwards, sovereignty vests in the corporate body of the King—in ancestral authority, the dynasty or the realm as a whole—not in his private body. Kingship becomes hereditary: the king is seen as an ordinary mortal, an organ of a sovereign corporate order, and his rights as grounded in categories of kinship rather than personal charisma.

It is the sacred communal body that is projected outside the group and transformed into its corporate body. By the concept of the *communal body*, I refer to the group as a simple, inarticulate, immanent unity that results from the dissolution of interpersonal boundaries. The communal body is the sacred fusion generated during rites of passage, carnivals, natural disasters, fascist regimes, wars, revolutions, referenda, elections, and many other instances of *communitas*. The projection of sacred communal fusion outside the social and its transformation into a transcendent corporate body allow for a heightened degree of interpersonal separation and individual autonomy within the social and for the emergence of secular spheres of interaction. It amounts to a social acceptance of division, absence and transcendence. Once projected and transformed into a corporate body, the group's collective body continues, in its new guise as ancestral authority and myth, to prescribe individual and social goals. It remains the ultimate source of law, will and motivation.

The corporate body and the communal body correspond to social structure and communitas respectively. In earlier work, I have proposed to read into Turner's distinction between structure and *communitas* two distinctions which Turner himself did not consider. The first is the psycho-analytic distinction between relations of mutual recognition among autonomous individuals and relations of violent fusion.[5] The second is the theological distinction between absence and presence. The combination of these two distinctions entails the characterisation of social structure as the absence of fusion and of *communitas* as presence of violent fusion. In light of the foregoing exposition of the corporate and communal bodies, Turner's concept of social structure seems to refer to a mode of social existence in which the collective body is external to the group, while his notion of *communitas* refers to a group invaded by its collective body. Thus, the proposed distinction between the corporate and communal bodies corresponds to Turner's distinction between social structure and *communitas*. During *communitas,* the group enacts its communal body by dissolving interpersonal boundaries, whereas in the course of social structure, the group's collective body is projected, transformed into a corporate body, and worshiped from afar by separate and autonomous individuals.

In *communitas,* the absence and promise which shape the human condition are replaced by presence, excess and immediacy. Every individual partakes of the communal body and is consecrated. No boundaries are recognised between self and other, life and death, sacred and profane, or between different spheres of interaction such as society and state. Social stratification and conflicts of status and interest, which in social structure enhance individual autonomy, are no more. The alienation of the subject from his own and other selves, which accompanies structural individuation and legally regulated interaction, is no longer tolerated. The personal self expands and coincides with the collective self. *Communitas* is an essentially lawless form of interaction: the normative system which structures everyday life is, in the course of *communitas,* suspended, challenged, and sometimes reformed. Fundamental interdictions are violated and traditional authority replaced by a charismatic leadership devoid of a genuine legal sanction.

In both structure and *communitas*, horizontal relations between individuals reproduce the vertical relations between individual and group or between group and leader. The horizontal and vertical axes mirror each other. In structure, there is a firm separation among individuals as well as between the group and its authorities. In *communitas*, by contrast, non-separation between the group as a whole and its charismatic-populist leader infects all interpersonal relations, (see figure 7.1).

---

[5] For Erich Fromm's account of authoritarianism as a state of violent communal fusion, see *Escape from Freedom* (New York, Farrar and Rinehart, 1941) 141; *Man for Himself* (New York, Holt, Rinehart and Winston, 1947) 151.

Figure 7.1 Structure and Communitas

Structure	Communitas
corporate body	communal body
(Rational-traditional authority)	(Charismatic-populist authority)
↑	↓
Individual a ←→ Individual b	Individual a →← Individual b
(relations of separation/transcendence)	(relations of fusion/immanence)

The corporate order is thoroughly legal In the passage from *communitas* to social structure, from an immanent communal body to a transcendent corporate body, the law comes into being. The law is always seen as prescribed by the ancestral-corporate authority of the group, and hence cannot be found in the course of *communitas* when the corporate body dissolves into a communal body. Law-giving is the predominant function of corporate ancestral authority: the more an authority is transcendent, the more its function is reduced to that of law-giving. Through the ideal of the rule of law, modern society articulates for itself the principle that the law is superimposed by a transcendent authority and is non-manipulable by human will, that the sacred omnipotence of the group's collective body is confined to the invisible realm of law. In the passage from *communitas* to structure, the magic of divine kingship is transformed into the magic of legal validity and ritual. Whereas the sacredness of the divine king is established through flagrant transgressions in which he is implicated, within the corporate order all individual organs are deconsecrated subjects of a sacred law. The savagery of presence under divine kingship and other forms of *communitas* may assume a contrived legal appearance, for example, in the spectacular rites and Kafkaesque formalism of fascist legal systems. Such extravagant legalism is essentially lawless, since a true rule of law is premised on the transcendence of the group's law-giving body.

The law keeps the corporate order intact by dividing society into alienated groups and individuals, to the effect that society can no longer contain its own unity, which finds refuge in the corporate realm. As the anchor of interpersonal separation and individual autonomy, the law allows for cooperation as well as competition among its alienated subjects. It equips its subjects with the power to advance legal claims in defence of their structural entitlements. It is of the essence of the rule of law that at least some of the rival bodies which law divides and empowers are able to address the law with complaints. In this way, the law sows the seeds of its inherent contestability, which simultaneously weakens and consolidates the rule of law, and which is played out in the legal ritual.

II. FROM STRUCTURE TO RITUAL

Normative Regeneration as the Purpose of Ritual

The corporate model of social structure entails an account of ritual as the collective enactment of the communal body. The dissolution of a corporate into a communal body in the course of ritual amounts to a return of the sacred into the group which suspends the law. This account is consistent with anthropological theory, which has often depicted ritual as a sequence of stages leading from the relaxation of social structure to its restoration. According to Van Gennep's theory, rites of passage proceed from the separation of initiands from an existing system of statuses, through the bestowal of new statuses, to an eventual reincorporation into structure. Similarly, Hubert and Mauss have identified three stages in sacrificial rites leading from the solemn interruption of routine affairs and purification of the participants, to the sacred moment of ritual killing, and finally to deconsecration and return to everyday life. Turner's version of the ritual sequence is unique in its attempt to encompass broad social processes rather than isolated events. According to Turner, ritual was originally devised to cope with social crises that resulted from breach of norms. Turner's theory of performance postulates a sequence of four stages: 'breach,' 'crisis,' 'redress,' and 'reintegration' or 'reaggregation' of structure.[6] Rituals occur in the third stage—they are society's means of redress—and consist of questioning and subversion of structural categories and hierarchies, which allow the reinstallation of order. Turner examines a variety of redressive rituals through which order is restored and consolidated, such as 'political processes (from deliberation to revolution and war),' 'legal-judicial process (from informal arbitration to formal courts)' and 'ritual processes (divination, affliction rituals, prophylactic rituals, embedded or independent sacrifice, etc).'[7]

Theorists of ritual have frequently pointed to a legal void through which normative structures revitalise and consolidate themselves.[8] During ritual, the rule of law is relaxed and replaced by an intense, immediate religious experience and moral licence. Since the sacred is not subject to society's norms, its presence suspends the law. Different accounts of ritual have

---

[6] V Turner, 'Are There Universals of Performance in Myth, Ritual and Drama?' in V Turner, *On the Edge of the Bush* (Tucson, Ariz, University of Arizona Press, 1985) 291–93.

[7] *Ibid*, at 293.

[8] See eg, EE Evans-Pritchard, 'Some Collective Expressions of Obscenity in Africa' in his *The Position of Women in Primitive Societies and Other Essays in Social Anthropology* (London, Faber and Faber, 1965) 76–101. G Balandier illustrated the dialectics of structure and transgression through elaborate examples taken from African societies. Balandier, *Le désordre: éloge du mouvement* (Paris, Fayard, 1988). Bakhtin described parallel phenomena in his account of the medieval and early-modern carnival. See M Bakhtin, *Rabelais and his World*, (1965 Iswolsky (trans), Bloomington, Ind, Indiana University Press, 1984). Already Freud's account of the totemic meal as re-enactment of a founding murder focused on the transgressive nature of ritual.

identified its essential mechanism with the controlled release and appeasement of anti-structural aspirations. Ritual introduces a contrived dynamism in order to exhaust dynamic forces and perpetuate existing structures. Several theorists of sacrifice, such as Frazer, Burkert and Heesterman, have specified that it is the call of death which is trumpeted in sacrifice in order to be eventually appeased and overcome by social structure as a life-asserting order.[9] Their claim can be applied to ritual in general: rituals accomplish a victory over death which proceeds through its temporary affirmation.

The checked ritual release and exhaustion of anarchic violence can be construed in terms of incarnation and projection of the communal body. However we break down the ritual sequence, it proceeds from incorporation of the communal body, through its collective enactment, to its eventual expulsion, ie, from the dissolution to the reconstruction of a corporate body. Society can overcome communal fusion and assume a normative structure only at the cost of occasional ritual surrender to the claims of the communal body. While unqualified presence is unattainable and near-complete presence is shunned by any life-affirming society, the central phase of all practised rituals is that of utmost presence of the communal body. Typical ritual phenomena described in anthropological literature—normative void, suspension of social roles, identities and statuses, eruption of violence and sexual license—can be explained in terms of dissolution of the corporate structure and enactment of the communal body.

Through ritual, the group can largely control the consequences of presence and guarantee an orderly reinstallation of a corporate structure. Society enacts its communal body periodically or in certain crucial moments in order to prevent its sudden, unbridled advent and to revitalise normative structures. However, rituals are devised not only to protect existing institutions, challenged by time and social change, from communal overthrow—to rejuvenate existing structures—but also to inaugurate new norms and statuses in private and collective rites of passage. The presence of the communal body relaxes law and structure, but is also their origin and source of vitality. The transformative power of ritual is employed both in founding new institutions and refounding existing ones.

Protective, as opposed to inaugural, rituals are either periodical or provoked by moments of crisis which threaten to unleash anarchic forces, such as orderly transformations of power, civil wars, deaths and natural disasters. These and similar moments tend to precipitate a descent of the communal body into the group, and are thus attended by a variety of rituals, adapted throughout history to the task of taming presence. The dangers of presence

---

[9] On the assertion of life through sacrifice, see W Burkert, *Homo Necans: The Anthropology of Ancient Greek Sacrificial Ritual and Myth* (Bing (trans), Berkeley, University of California Press, 1983) 38, 40, 45; JE Heesterman, 'Vedic Sacrifice and Transcendence' in Heesterman, *The Inner Conflict of Tradition* (Chicago, University of Chicago Press, 1985) 81.

cannot be fully averted by devising rituals in response to particular social crises. The group is inhabited by a longing for *communitas* that is permanent, rather than confined to critical moments which unveil the fragility of structure. Periodical rituals, such as seasonal festivals and athletic contests, are instituted in order to release in a regular manner the group's longing for presence. Ritual does not necessarily respond to a particular 'breach of norm' (Turner) but also to a founding—mythical or forgotten—conflict, indeed to the permanent threat of eruption of violence. Mythical representations of founding chaos and violence refer not only to historical events, but to the persistent threat of anarchic violence, which calls for a regular ritual appeasement. The cyclical alternation of structure and *communitas* is, as Turner suggested, the essential pattern of social life rather than the result of an accidental succession of crises.

Aspects of Presence

As spectres of the group's absent corporate authority, law and myth are stripped during *communitas* of their supreme and binding status, and resigned to the group to be ritually challenged, renegotiated and rejuvenated. When social structure is intact, ancestral law and myth are intertwined, validating each other as facets of a single normative order. Together, they construct individual and collective identities and provide the corporate group with its unity while dwelling outside of it as absent reservoirs of sacredness.[10] Descending from the skies, laws and mythical narratives and images are never treated as the products of a human legislator or artist. While in themselves sacred, law and myth command secularity and division and subject the human body to a regime of absence and representation: a regime of fiction and narrative. With the disintegration of law and mythology in *communitas* narrative gives way to action that is not grounded in reason and representation.

Engulfed in the communal body, participants in ritual no longer inhabit an ordered, domesticated space and time. As Canetti has pointed out in *Crowds and Power*, spatial boundaries amongst individuals, groups and spheres of life dissolve. The group is pervaded by the symbiotic violence that is ordinarily projected onto the corporate realm. The historical horizons of past and future blend and finally fuse in the permanent immediacy of *mythical time*, the time of primordial chaos and ultimate salvation. With the eventual return to linear history, some narrative account of the

[10] The law not only divides social structure into alienated groups and individuals but also gives it its unity. Ancestral law can divide and secularise society by becoming the repository of its sacred unity. Since corporate authority is manifested primarily through its laws, the unity of a corporate group is expressed through the unity of the ancestral law that defines and regulates it. Law constitutes the principal symbol of corporate identity and power. It performs the totemic function of denoting the unity of society and the transcendence of this unity to the group.

transitional moment will be projected onto the transcendent realm and will assume an exemplary mythical status. The suspension of ordinary temporality provides one among many indications that, through the incarnation of the communal body, death is made present within the group: temporality stands still because the march toward death has seemingly reached its goal.

Two Transformative Mechanisms: Theatre and Ritual

Utter presence of the communal body—a complete dissolution of law and representation—does not occur even in the most ecstatic rituals. Such presence, had it been conceivable, would have entailed death's final victory and the group's complete self-annihilation. The purpose of ritual, as already suggested, is to generate presence, and at the same time restrain and exhaust it, in order to re-establish transcendence and representation and make life emerge triumphant from the transitional celebration of death. The regeneration of social structure through the ritual mitigation of violence is often described as ritual's transformative power. In the following passage, Richard Schechner distinguishes between two transformative mechanisms or, in Turner's terms, two processes of redress, to which schechner refers as mechanisms of 'theatrical transformation':

> transformation is the heart of theater, and there appear to be only two fundamental kinds of theatrical transformation: (1) the displacement of anti-social, injurious, disruptive behaviour by ritualized gesture and display, and (2) the invention of characters who act out fictional events or real events fictionalized by virtue of their being acted out (as in documentary theater or Roman gladiatorial games). These two kinds of transformation occur together, but in the mix usually one is dominant. Western theater emphasizes characterization and the enactment of fictions; Melanesian, African, and Australian (aborigine) theatre emphasizes the displacement of hostile behaviour. Forms which balance the two tendencies—No, Kathakali, the Balinese Ketchak, medieval moralities, some contemporary avant-garde performances—offer, I think, the best models for the future of the theater.[11]

The first mechanism of 'theatrical transformation' Schechner describes— the enactment of violence—is hardly theatrical. It is a ritual process which takes place in *communitas*. Schechner's second type of 'theatrical transformation'—the staging of characters—is consistent with conventional notions of theatre. Compared to ritual, theatre is a process of redress which seems to be firmly integrated into social structure and which apparently does not

---

[11] See R Schechner, 'From Ritual to Theater and Back' in R Schechner and M Schuman (eds), *Ritual, Play and Performance* (New York, Continuum, 1976) 196–222 at 199.

require its temporary relaxation. By referring to both theatre and ritual as mechanisms of 'theatrical transformation,' Schechner rightly loosens the distinction between the two. However, the distinction between ritual and theatre remains helpful, schematic as it may be. In ritual, the enactment of conflict exhausts destabilising forces; in theatre, by contrast, structural categories and classifications are questioned—and then validated and reinstated—through their reflexive, dramatic articulation. To begin with ritual, liminal freedom is generated and violence acted out, tempered by means of magical channelling and substitution. The mitigation of utter presence leaves ritual violent enough: even war can often be seen as a contrived ritual release of violence designed to avert total destruction. During ritual, the divisions which underlie representation melt away to allow for an incarnation of the communal body. Participants not only passively contemplate the categories of social structure, but partake in a real process of destruction and reproduction of their social world. As Schechner noted, 'As in all rites of passage something has happened during the performance; *the performance both symbolizes and actualizes the change in status* ... This convergence of symbolic and actual event is missing from aesthetic theater.'[12]

In theatre, the separation between sacred and profane—the transcendence of the sacred—is observed. The horizontal and vertical divisions—between the self and the world, the self and other selves, the self and the other (the collective body)—that condition representation are accentuated. Every theatrical spectacle is an extension of the political spectacle of power through which society chains itself to the structural system of divisions and subdivisions. In the political and bourgeois spectacles, society beholds from a distance its own body and subjects itself to a regime of absence, and fiction. Every spectacle, whatever may be its particular subject, refers first and foremost to an ultimate and absent authority in whose name it separates itself from the group of spectators, that is, separates the group from itself.[13] The principal message of the political spectacle is encoded in the very distinction between spectators and stage, between the group and its body. The

---

[12] *Ibid*, at 205. Avant-garde performance art aims to transcend the limits of theatrical representation and revive ritual traditions with their enhanced transformative power. Avant-garde performances employ 'techniques of authentification' (Schechner) devised to collapse representation: to eliminate stage, fiction and narrative.

[13] 'The stage is theological for as long as it is dominated by speech, by a will to speech, by the layout of a primary logos which does not belong to the theatrical site and governs it from a distance. The stage is theological for as long as its structure, following the entirety of tradition, comports the following elements: an author-creator who, absent and from afar, is armed with a *text* and keeps watch over, assembles, regulates the time or the meaning of representation, letting this latter *represent* him as concerns what is called the content of his thoughts, his intentions, his ideas' (emphasis mine), J Derrida, 'The Theater of Cruelty and the Closure of Representation' in J Derrida, *Writing and Difference* (Bass (trans), Chicago, University of Chicago Press, 1978) 235. For Derrida, theatre is theological because it is premised on the fiction of an ultimate, transcendent script and author. Derrida's considerations are exclusively semiotic, failing to integrate anthropological arguments according to which theatre is theological because the ultimate object of any *mise-en-scène* is the group's own transcendent unity.

bare stage is not merely the setting but the final meaning of spectacle. The same message is repeated in every theatrical representation: The group contemplates itself—its corporate body—from a distance and affirms the human fate of living in alienation from God.

The bourgeois theatre does not subvert, then, the political order of representation, but reproduces and consolidates social structure. When hegemonic self-images are criticised on stage, the principle of separation between audience and stage as well as other axioms of representation are affirmed. Theatre replaces the enactment of anarchic violence by a questioning of the meaning of all that, addressed to the group's own body. In comparison with ritual, theatre hardly frees the group from the normative categories of social structure: it allows its spectators a brief reflective detachment from everyday existence and cannot radically challenge the norms of representation themselves.

Since Nietzsche's *Birth of Tragedy* and under the influence of Frazer's work, various theorists have suggested that theatre developed out of ritual, turning enactment into representation, collective participation in violence into collective contemplation of normative conflicts. Murray, Fergusson, Turner, Marin and Burkert, among others, have argued that theatre originated in the relegation of social friction and sacrificial violence to a distant stage, rendering harmless the indispensable repetition of the founding bloodshed.[14] According to Schechner, the passage from ritual to theatre is a passage from *efficacy* to *entertainment*, but every performance remains to a certain extent both efficacious and entertaining: 'there is a dialectical-dyadic continuum linking efficacy to entertainment—both are present in all performances, but in each performance one or the other is dominant.'[15] As Schechner rightly suggests, every social drama is placed somewhere along a continuum which stretches between pure ritual (efficacy) and pure theatre (entertainment), exhibiting a different amalgam of enactment and staging, presence and representation, immediate participation and contemplative distance. Pure ritual and pure theatre, the conceptual poles of that continuum, cannot be encountered in reality. As much as ritual cannot entirely dispose of representation, theatre enjoys ritual efficacy. The transformative effect of theatre, its capacity to rejuvenate structure by challenging it, is not produced exclusively by means of narrative. The setting of theatre, rule-bound as it may be, calls for a suspension of everyday identity

---

[14] G Murray, 'Excursus on the Ritual Forms Preserved in Greek Tragedy' in J Harrison, *Themis* (Cambridge, Cambridge University Press, 1912) 341–463; F Fergusson, *The Idea of a Theater* (Princeton, Princeton University Press, 1949); W Burkert, 'Greek Tragedy and Sacrificial Ritual' in Burkert, *Savage Energies: Lessons of Myth and Ritual in Ancient Greece* (Chicago, University of Chicago Press, 2001) 1–37; L Marin, 'The Utopic Stage' in Murray (ed), *Mimesis, Masochism and Mime: The Politics of Theatricality in Contemporary French Thought* (Ann Arbor, University of Michigan Press, 1997) 115–35. See, generally, V Turner, *From Ritual to Theatre* (New York, Performing Arts Journal Publications, 1982).

[15] R Schechner, 'From Ritual to Theater and Back' in R Schechner and M Schuman (eds), *Ritual, Play and Performance* (New York, Continuum, 1976) 196–222 at 210.

and a selfless examination of the normative categories of social structure. The self-forgetfulness demanded by theatre may signify an imaginary destruction of the existing structure on the way to its refounding. Even spectacles which approximate most to the conceptual pole of pure theatre/'entertainment' wield a tame ritual efficacy and produce a transformative effect. Paradox afflicts all forms of redress, whether predominantly ritual or theatrical, because their underlying, elementary mechanism consists in the simultaneous announcement of structure's death and immortality.

An Aside on Ritual, Death and Psychoanalytic Theory

While Freud places at the heart of ritual the Oedipal rebellion against the law of the father, ritual can be conceived as re-enactment of pre-Oedipal conflicts of separation from the maternal body. The proposed concept of the communal body is partly based on Klein's account of the maternal body at the beginning of life as an intensely violent fusion of mother and child. Like the maternal body with which it is identified by members of the group, the communal body is experienced during *communitas* as simultaneously nourishing and devouring, as the source of life and death. It threatens to dissolve individual autonomy, but at the same time it is the source of individual and collective vitality. Through its relegation to the transcendent corporate realm, the collective body continues to nourish the group from afar while the destructiveness provoked by its immediate presence is tamed.

Funerals provide a clear illustration of the simultaneous removal of the communal body and that body's preservation in the form of a distant benign power. In funerals, the corpse is separated from the community to avoid fusion with death. The deceased is distanced for fear that death/the communal body will pervade the group, and is elevated to an ancestral, transcendent position. Funerals assume the form of procession in order to accomplish the gradual transformation of the deceased into a distant ancestor, after death has for a time had the upper hand. The deceased is preserved by being transformed and represented in a new guise: as a transcendent, benign ancestor, a conqueror of death who secures from afar the vitality of the group.

Sacrifice provides another illustration of the ritual projection of death, or the communal body, onto a transcendent realm. According to a classic strain of anthropological interpretation, the sacrificial victim represents the group's own sacred collective body.[16] Through ritual killing, the group acts

---

[16] The ambivalence toward the communal body as simultaneously nourishing and devouring recalls the ambivalence of participants in sacrifice toward the sacrificial victim. According to Freud, the totemic animal is at once admired, loved and hated, as are parental figures in the Oedipal conflict. This ambivalence, ordinarily latent and concealed, surfaces in ritual. According to Burkert, the sacrificial victim is seen as the source of life because the victim was originally meant to be eaten. However, the victim also comes to embody violence and death for the group, once intrasocial aggression is channelled into it.

out and releases its own self-destructiveness: 'an important feature of sacrifice is that the people for whom it is made enact the death of a victim which in important respects represents themselves, in order to survive that death.'[17] Embodied by the sacrificial victim, death is first embraced and acted out by the group and then removed, deified and worshiped from afar. The disposal of the sacrifice symbolises the group's separation from its own sanctity and self-destructiveness, its renewed purity and return to life and structure. The sacrifice—the group's collective body—now resides in the corporate realm. Through the sacrificial process, the group incorporates and then projects sacred violence and refounds the secular corporate order. Thus, sacrifice has often been used to bring into existence various corporate associations and to re-establish existing ones.[18] Insofar as every ritual involves an exercise of (ultimately self-directed) violence, sacrifice can be, and often has been, seen as the elementary form of ritual.

III. THE COURT RITUAL

Transgression and Liminality in Court

The foregoing discussion suggests that in the courtroom, insofar as it is the site of a ritual, the law is suspended. The rule of law is undermined by the ritual acts which seek to uphold it, such as public allegations that a law has been violated and the subsequent, redressive interventions of the legal system. The meaningfulness of law persists as long as the gatekeeper hides it from view, as long as it can hover above the group in unchallenged passivity. When the law steps forward to speak, to dispel ambiguities and uncertainties, its meaning becomes increasingly vague. The heightened visibility of legal authority in court, indeed its presence, threatens to dissolve structure. Similarly, legal systems that are obsessed with the visualisation of legal authority do not in general excel in observing the rule of law.

Whether or not application involves an arbitrary leap from the general to the particular, it is tainted by lawlessness because the re-enactment of founding violence lies at the core of the ritual process. Hay has suggested that the

---

[17] G Lienhardt, 'The Control of Experience: Symbolic Action' in G Lienhardt, *Divinity and Experience: The Religion of the Dinka* (Oxford, Clarendon Press, 1961) 282–97. Various authors noted the equation of participation in sacrifice with communal membership. As M Fortes writes, 'Lineages and clans that celebrate the same festival are assumed to be kin of one another, in a broad sense, by virtue of the rule that people who sacrifice together must be kin.' M Fortes, *Religion, Morality and the Person: Essays on Tallensi Religion* (Cambridge, Cambridge University Press, 1987) 45. According to Burkert, 'Families and guilds organize themselves into sacrificial communities; so too cities at a festival, as well as gatherings of larger political groups.' W Burkert, above n 9, at 35.

[18] 'Whenever a new step is taken consciously and irrevocably, it is inevitably connected with sacrifice.' W Burkert, above n 9, at 40.

judge can choose between two postures: he can either enact a benign or enraged god, or serve as the passive, oracular medium of the deity's will.[19] In either case, adjudication involves a magical invocation of ultimate law-giving authority, namely, of constituent power. The exercise of legal authority undermines its own validity because pronouncing the law intimates the presence of the communal body.[20] For legal validity to be generated, the distinction between the legal and the illegal and the unity of the legal system have to be refounded in every proceeding out of the void of *communitas*.[21] In this, court proceedings resemble other social dramas, which always alternate between foundation and repetition/application. The magical, forbidden presence of the sacred turns the court into a site of transgression where sovereignty is appropriated. In procedures such as trial by battle and ordeal, this ritual aspect of court proceedings is predominant. The appeal for a direct intervention of the sacred, invisible, prelegal authority and source of the law is explicit. The enactment of conflict leaves little room for the theatrical staging of legal personae and of the normative categories of social structure.

The ease with which the court ritual lends itself to abuse by criminal associations and regimes, such as totalitarian states, mafias and sects, attests to the lawless, magical moment in court proceedings and to its capacity to overshadow other moments. In the fascist version of the cult of law, judicial magic and liturgy are no longer employed in the service of the rule of law, as mechanisms that celebrate and reproduce the absence of omnipotence. Instead, fascist systems aspire to enact sovereignty and actualise the bliss of union with God, which other systems reserve for an ever-postponed future.

---

[19] 'The judge might ... emulate the priest in his role of human agent, helpless but submissive before the demands of his deity. But the judge could play the role of deity as well, both the god of wrath and the merciful arbiter of men's fates. For the righteous accents of the death sentence were made even more impressive by the contrast with the treatment of the accused up to the moment of conviction. The judges' paternal concern for their prisoners was remarked upon by foreign visitors, and deepened the analogy with the Christian God of justice and mercy.' Hay, 'Property, Authority and the Criminal Law' in D Hay *et al, Albion's Fatal Tree: Crime and Society in Eighteenth-Century England* (Harmondsworth, Penguin, 1977) 17–65 at 30. Similar postures are assumed by other sacred figures including divine kings and their modern descendants, such as fascist and populist leaders.

[20] The suspension of the law and the experience of presence are far more intense in constitutional moments such as declarations of independence and constitutional crises than in ordinary legal proceedings.

[21] As J Clam writes, 'The system brings its boundaries forth in each of its own operations and only when it operates.' J Clam, 'The Specific Autopoiesis of Law: Between Derivative Autonomy and Generalised Paradox' in D Nelken and J Priban (eds) *Law's New Boundaries: The Consequences of Legal Autopoiesis* (Aldershot, Ashgate, 2001) 45 at 64. In N Luhmann's words, 'one has to apply [the distinction between legal and illegal] even though one can neither ask nor answer the question (because it would lead to a paradox) as to whether the distinction between legal and illegal itself is legal or illegal. The paradox itself turns unwittingly into a creative principle because one has to try so hard to avoid and to conceal it.' N Luhmann, *Law as a Social System* (trans Klaus A Ziegert (trans), Oxford University Press 2004, published in German 1993) 177. According to Luhmann (at 291), the paradox of the self-constitution of the legal system unfolds in court.

Sovereignty is appropriated and flaunted by a legal system wielding the unfettered blind powers which, according to fascist theology, dominate human lives.[22] The arbitrary, reified legal formality becomes, under fascism, the epitome of legality. It is divorced from procedural and substantial principles and revered as the embodiment of holy inevitability. Totalitarianism revels in form, turning it into black magic in the service of deep-seated lawlessness.[23] The ostensible invocation of law allows fascism to conceal its violence and disregard of boundaries. The fanciful resort to legal detail, which often decorates the most bellicose political oratory, is part of a political cult of unreason and arbitrary power and functions as a perverted aesthetisation of violence.[24]

The uncanny presence of the sacred in court places the parties to a legal case in a state of liminal bareness. Stripped of their social status while facing the social gaze and the instance of the law, their position resembles that of initiands in numerous rites of passage. The other's power over individual fates is dramatised in court as it is in other rituals. The parties are subjected to a decision which is experienced as the product of an unpredictable sovereign will. They are extracted from their position in social structure and placed in a liminal normative void, thrown into the centre of the public arena without the shield of their private sphere, a precarious refuge in moments of *communitas*. The procedural rights of the parties and the embrace of their family and friends do not alter the liminal, lawless nature of the event and the loneliness of the encounter with the law.

Scripture and its Modern Clerical Interpreters

The modern *Rechtsstaat* is premised on a strict transcendence of the law in relation to all branches of state and society. All state powers are more or less equally bound by a specified law which descends from the skies. This requires that the *theatrical* structure of the court proceeding be perfected: that the ritual moment of sovereign decision be concealed behind formalism, and the repugnant exercise of founding violence behind ostensible judicial impotence. Ritual enactment of conflict must be replaced by its staged representation,[25] the collective incarnation of sacredness by its judicial embodiment. A variety

---

[22] On authoritarian religion, see E Fromm, *Psychoanalysis and Religion* (New Haven, Yale University Press, 1950) 35.

[23] On the collapse of the autonomy of the legal system under totalitarian regimes, see J Clam, above n 23, at 62.

[24] On Hitler's affected innocence and dutifulness, see E Fromm, *The Anatomy of Human Destructiveness* (New York, Holt, 1973) 449. Begin shared with his mentor Jabotinsky a penchant for legal sophism. For a perceptive account of Begin's style of leadership, see J Shapiro, *The Road to Power* (Albany, NY, State University of New York Press, 1991).

[25] In 'Vedic Sacrifice and Transcendence', Heesterman traces a similar development in the history of sacrifice, transformed from a bilateral, horizontal re-enactment of conflict into an individual act strictly regulated by divinely ordained ritual imperatives. On the passage from ritual to theatre in general, see V Turner, *From Ritual to Theatre* (New York, Performing Arts Journal Publications, 1982).

of modern procedural developments reflect a single logic of deritualisation of court proceedings.

While prescribing the evacuation of sanctity from the courtroom, the ideal of the strict transcendence of the law inadvertently enhances the ritual sanctity of the modern court by depriving other branches of government of their religious aura. The court becomes the most sanctified branch of government because it enjoys a privileged access to the true meaning of the law and partakes in law's sovereignty. The legal system assumes functions which were traditionally performed by the clergy: the interpretation and enforcement of divine law. The clericalisation of the modern judiciary provides the keys to the understanding of the modern judicial spectacle. It suggests both the enhanced ritual sanctity of the modern court and the means by which sacred presence is tamed: the confinement of sanctity to an ostracised staged body.

Through the consecration of the judicial body, the sacred is prevented from infiltrating and polluting the entire group. Transgression is confined to an isolated clerical body which partakes in the lawlessness of the communal body—and to the lawbooks, treated in Kafka's *Trial* as interchangeable with obscene literature.[26] By means of the confinement of sanctity to the judicial body, the rule of law can largely remain intact in court. Clerical communities such as the judiciary play a crucial role in the social manipulation of the sacred. They facilitate the expulsion of the sacred outside of the group and the construction of a corporate, normative structure by absorbing and enacting the sacred on behalf of the group. The clerical body is placed in a permanent liminal position within structure and functions as a permanent, institutionalised container of sacredness.

Through the clerical body, the commands of the group's corporate, transcendent authority are revealed to the group. The clericalised judge utters an ancestral law which is impressed in legal scripture and in his body. Unlike King Solomon and other lay judges, the clericalised judge is not distinguished by practical wisdom or a sense of justice, but by omniscience of the law. As priest of the law,[27] the judge barely exercises the human capacities for thought and speech. In contrast to temporal authority, the judge does not function as a model of lawful, worldly existence. While embodying the law, the clerical body is implicated in permanent transgression. Through the privileges, interdictions and ritual observances which bind it, the clerical body is placed in a position of forbidden fusion with the communal body.[28]

---

[26] See the opening paragraphs of the third chapter of the novel.

[27] As Gaines Post noted, medieval lawyers viewed themselves as priests of the law. See G Post, X Giocarnis, and R Kay, 'The Medieval Heritage of a Humanistic Idea: "Scientia Donum Dei Est, Unde Vendi non Potest"'(1955 XI) *Traditio* 195 at 206.

[28] The judicial embodiment of sacred law and corporate sovereignty is produced through the subjection of the judge's body to violence and interdiction. It is through the sacrifice of its humanity out of a love for law that the clerical body can concentrate the sacred in itself and purify the group. According to Nietzsche, '[A] priest is and remains a human sacrifice,' *The Gay Science* (W Kaufmann (trans), New York, Random House Press, 1974) 294.

By facing temporal power, clerical authority at once precludes the dangers of an unfettered and irrational power—the dangers of divine kingship—and becomes the exclusive official container of the sacred and the non-human for human society.

There are several indications that during and around the eighteenth century, the clerical function was gradually transferred from the Church to the judiciary.[29] One clue comes from the increasing solemnisation of courtroom proceedings and ritualisation of judicial speech and conduct, which, according to several historians, took place during this era. Other aspects of clericalisation included the development of judicial independence and judicial review.[30] The judiciary came to embody a superimposed law and the legal limits of temporal power which under the old regime were represented by the Church. Traditional clerical privileges, such as legal immunity, fiscal independence and freedom from political intervention in appointment and decision-making, were bestowed on the judiciary in order to establish the modern cult of law and allow for the eventual rise of judicial review.

Court proceedings did not always possess the thick aura of sanctity that they have in modern civil religion. Douglas Hay has convincingly argued that only with the erosion of the legitimising power of royal and religious rituals were courts invested with heightened solemnity in order to command respect and obedience.[31] The court seems to have inherited the splendour of

---

[29] L Barshack, 'Notes on the Clerical Body of the Law' (2003) 24(3) *Cardozo Law Review* 1151 at 1164.

[30] On the development of judicial independence in eighteenth century England, see JM Baker, 'The Independence of the Judiciary' (1978) 94 *Selden Society* 137; S Shetreet, 'Historical Development of the Concept of Judicial Independence: Comparative Perspectives' in *Justice in Israel: A Study of the Israeli Judiciary* (Dordrecht, M Nijhoff, 1994) 19; A Lebigre, *La justice du roi: La vie judiciaire dans l'ancienne France* (Paris, Albin Michel, 1988) 98–115. On the history of judicial immunity, see EJH Schrage, 'The Judge's Liability for Professional Mistakes' (1996) 17(2) *Legal History* 101. Judicial privilege goes hand in hand with imposition of restrictions on the judiciary designed to minimise the worldly entanglements of the judicial body. On the rise in modernity of the image of the blindfolded judge, see DE Curtis and J Resnik, 'Images of Justice' (1987) 96 *Yale Law Journal* 1727 at 1757.

[31] 'The assizes were a formidable spectacle in a country town, the most visible and elaborate manifestation of state power to be seen in the countryside, apart from the presence of a regiment ... In the court room the judges' every action was governed by the importance of spectacle ... The powers of light and darkness were summoned into the court with the black cap which was donned to pronounce sentence of death, and the spotless white gloves worn at the end of a "maiden assize" when no prisoners were to be left for execution ... There was an acute consciousness that the courts were platforms for addressing the "multitude."' From D Hay, 'Property, Authority and the Criminal Law' in Hay *et al*, above n 21, at 27–28. While accepting some of the criticisms levelled at Hay's Marxist account, Lemmings affirms that 'there are reasons to believe that the administration of criminal law and its theatre became more significant in the overall context of governing eighteenth-century society' (at 48), and offers his own depiction of the new forms of judicial pomp, D Lemmings, 'Ritual, Majesty and Mystery: Collective Life and Culture Among English Barristers, Serjeants and Judges, c. 1500–c. 1830' in WW Pue and D Sugarman (eds), *Lawyers and Vampires: Cultural Histories of Legal Professions* (Oxford, Hart, 2003) 25–63. Hay's analysis suggests that the authority and rituals of law increasingly replaced traditional religion. 'In its ritual, its judgments and its channelling of emotion the criminal law echoed many of the most powerful psychic components of religion ... there

Between Ritual and Theatre: Judicial Performance as Paradox 163

both royal and church rituals with their gradual decline. Judicial pomp, Hay argued, was devised by the propertied elite in order to defend their hegemony and material interests. As Hay writes:

> The English ruling class entered the eighteenth century with some of its strongest ideological weapons greatly weakened. The Divine Right of Kings had been jettisoned in the interest of gentry power, but the monarchy lost as a consequence much of its potency as a source of authority, and so too did religion. At the same time control had flowed away from the executive in the extreme decentralization of government which characterized the century. With Stuarts plotting in Europe, Jacobitism suspected everywhere at home, and a lumpily unattractive German prince on the throne, English justice became a more important focus of beliefs about the nation and the social order. Perhaps some of the tension abated after the last Jacobite attempt in 1745, which may help to account for Blackstone's relatively favourable attitude to reform in mid-century. But within a few decades renewed assaults on the structure of authority—the riots of 1766 and 1780, Wilkes and the French Revolution—determined the English ruling class to repel any attacks on the mystery and the majesty of the law.[32]

Whether or not one is convinced by Hay's Marxist logic, judicial pomp and the clericalisation of the judiciary seem to form an integral part of the institutional configuration of the modern nation state. The symbolic and organising functions previously performed by the monarchy and the Church have been appropriated by the legal system, securing its standing within modern social structures. However, the infusion of the legal system with sanctity does not, as such, enhance reason and the rule of law in the courtroom. It elevates the status of justice but threatens to disrupt its administration. Sanctity has to be tamed by being set apart from society, confined to a clerical body and scripture.[33] The codification of law plays a central role in the

---

is some reason to believe that the secular sermons of the criminal law had become more important than those of the Church by the eighteenth century. Too many Englishmen had forgotten the smell of Brimstone, and the clergy—lazy, absentee and dominated by material ambition—were not the men to remind them ... Religion still had a place within the ritual of the law: a clergyman gave the assize sermon, and others attended the condemned men on the scaffold. But we suspect that the men of God derived more prestige from the occasion than they conferred upon it ... The secular mysteries of the courts had burned deep into the popular consciousness, and perhaps the labouring poor knew more of the terrors of the law than those of religion,' D Hay, 'Property, Authority and the Criminal Law' in D Hay *et al*, above n 21, at 29–30.

[32] D Hay, 'Property, Authority and the Criminal Law' in D Hay *et al*, above n 21, at 58–59.

[33] N Luhmann argues convincingly that the familiar conventions of judicial pomp are devised to conceal paradox. However, the inherent sanctity of legal proceedings is in the first place the *source* of paradox. The ritual embodiment of sovereignty releases lawless sanctity that the judicial *theatre* is designed to tame and contain. According to Luhmann, 'a decision is a paradox, which cannot make itself its own subject and which, at best, can only mystify itself. Authority, decorum, limitation of access to the mystery of law, texts to which one can refer, the pomp of entries and exits of judges—all this is a substitution at the moment at which one must prevent the paradox of decision-making from appearing as a paradox, so as not to disclose that the assumption that one could *decide legally about what is legal and what is*

processes of clericalisation and consolidation of the transcendence of sovereignty. Notwithstanding differences between the role of the text in the civil law and common law traditions, both traditions endevoured to compile an exhaustive legal scripture. Legal formalism is a rhetorical strategy of institutional self-grounding which prescribes that every detail derive directly or indirectly from legal scripture rather than from custom or decision. The lawbook reifies and authenticates the law and secures its facticity. It replaces the magic of decision by a 'magic of the book'. As the magical, tangible focal point of the court ritual, the lawbook concentrates in itself the sacredness ritual releases, and affirms the transcendence of the law-giver, its author.[34] Scripture transforms a text and the clerical voice which pronounces it into the exclusive media of revelation, excluding any possibility of immediate, popular embodiment of sovereignty.

Another aspect of the deritualisation of court proceedings alongside formalism and the confinement of sacredness to the judicial body, consists in the growing role of lawyers.[35] Access to the clerical, judicial body became over the last two centuries increasingly mediated by lawyers, which took the place of the parties, subsuming the concreteness of the event under general legal categories. Conflict is no longer enacted or illustrated by the parties, but staged in the form of an impersonal argumentation conducted by representatives. The judge himself is not one of the legal, human personae played on the courtroom's stage. He rather sets the stage on which human dramas unfold. All stages are premised on the fiction of a third, omniscient author/spectator who guarantees meaning, law and separation.[36] This fiction is verified by the body of the judge in a way which makes possible the ongoing spectacle in (and outside) the court. In the terms used by Rappaport, the taming of the court ritual proceeds by way of 'canonisation', namely, the substitution of self-referential personal gestures and utterances of real parties by a liturgy which announces an official, normative

---

illegal, is a paradox as well, and that *the unity of the system* can be observed only as a paradox,' *Law as a Social System* (KA Ziegert (trans), Oxford, Oxford University Press, 2004, published in German, 1993) 283–84.

[34] The structural correlation between the consolidation of textuality and transcendence can be illustrated through the example of the twelfth century as a period which saw the parallel development of corporate structures—and hence of transcendence—and expansion of literacy. On literacy in the twelfth century generally, see B Stock, *The Implications of Literacy* (Princeton, NJ Princeton University Press, 1983).

[35] On the increasing importance of lawyers in the eighteenth century, see JH Langbein, 'The Criminal Trial before the Lawyers' (1977) 45 *University of Chicago Law Review* 263 at 307; JH Langbein, 'Shaping the Eighteenth-Century Criminal Trial: A View from the Ryder Sources' (1983) 50 *University of Chicago Law Review* 1 at 123; JH Langbein, *The Origins of Adversary Criminal Trial* (Oxford, Oxford University Press, 2003).

[36] On the place of a transcendent author in theatre, see Derrida's essay on Artaud's theatre of cruelty (above).

view of the cosmos, a theatre which stages the existing order.[37] However, all social dramas, including the most contemplative ones, simultaneously employ representational and transformative means. As canonical as the court ritual may become, it repeats a prelegal, magical manoeuvre of normative refounding. The dramatisation of legal rights, duties and statuses in court, the staging of legally defined personae, is accompanied by a relaxation of law and identity and a repetition of a founding, lawless violence that is levelled at the parties as well as the judge.

---

[37] 'Whereas self-referential messages are concerned with the immediate, particular, and vital aspects of the current event ... invariant messages are concerned with the universal and enduring or even eternal aspects of the universe ... I refer to this class of messages as "canonical," or, in aggregate as the ritual's "canon," or "canonical order,"' RA Rappaport, 'Veracity, Verity and Verum' (1993) 23(1) *Studia Liturgica* 35 at 36. Courts overcome the dangers of presence and decision through the application of procedural canons: 'the formality, invariance, and solemnity of the courtroom ritual are placed in the service of getting the unique facts of the case out in systematic and orderly manner,' *ibid*, at 37.

8

The Paradoxes of Justice: The Ultimate Difference Between a Philosophical and a Sociological Observation of Law

FATIMA KASTNER

I. CONVERGENCES AND DIVERGENCES

THROUGHOUT HISTORY, ATTEMPTS to codify justice in law have been accompanied by a certain discomfort. Already with Plato, the central motive of this discomfort was carefully described in his famous *Politikos,* where law was compared with an 'egotistic and indocile human being.'[1] According to this understanding, law is fundamentally determined by violence and repression. Since it is organised by general rules, it is necessarily inadequate to the complexity of human life. Therefore, there is no licence for one binding rule for all parties involved and all situations. This, so the central argument goes, is because the formulation of binding rules for everybody involved can be achieved only by concealing a fundamental double difference: on the one hand, there is a difference between humans and their actions, because of their 'dissimilarities'. On the other hand, there is the difference in time, since 'there is no rest in human dimensions.'[2] Between the simple law and its permanently changing subject matter, Plato continues, lies an insurmountable abyss: for what is just for everybody is not doing justice to everyone.

It is well known that Plato's destructive lack of faith in the possibility of law's purification, or in any final epiphany of justice in law as such, led to his apologies for an absolute privilege granted to special skilled

---

[1] Platon, 'Politikos' in U Wolf (ed), *Platon. Sämtliche Werke* (FD Schleiermacher (trans), Hamburg, Rowohlt, 1994) vol 3, 294b.
[2] *Ibid.*

philosophers to rule beyond the legal sphere.[3] This is exactly the famous starting point of Popper's brutal attack against all so-called enemies of the open—that is to say, democratic—society.[4] The insight that the idea of justice beyond legal legitimation introduces masked or unmasked authoritarian anti-democratic consequences is as common as it is easy to have after the totalitarian experiences of the twentieth century. However, the challenge raised serves as a reminder that something is wrong, 'something rotten'[5] in law's rule and empire, as Benjamin put it. Indeed, this very 'something' marks at the same time the starting point of Derrida's[6] philosophical meditations and Luhmann's[7] sociological observation of law.

Both conceptions share a post-metaphysical, post-dialectical, post-structuralist and autological character.[8] They have equally abandoned the traditional conceptions of transcendental philosophy, ontology, hermeneutics, subject-centredness, binary logics, and so on, including the prohibition of circularity in theoretical argumentation. Therefore, it is hardly surprising that Luhmann's systems-theoretically-grounded sociology and Derrida's philosophical reflections offer a quite similar approach to Plato's objection. In so doing, their common subject matter is not a direct confrontation with law, but a questioning of the question of how to question the mode and shape of law after the failure of all utopian concepts, which were so strictly bounded with their theoretical designs, their political motives and their catastrophic consequences.

At first sight, Luhmann and Derrida present an obvious tautological answer to Plato's challenge: a questioning of the divide between law and justice is possible only as law's self-questioning. This leads to the further questions of who asks the question, and what are the conditions of asking this question? In other words, what are law's reference and foundation? As a result of their shared initial preferences for difference and against unity, for self-reference and against identity, for aporias and against synthesis, both conceptions expose the foundation of law, the origin and the evolution of its authority, to be ungrounded, invisible, absent and mystical. In substance, both Luhmann and Derrida stress the blind functioning of law's positivistic

---

[3] See Platon's critics, especially in 'Politia' in Wolf, above n 1, vol 2 at 561c–566d.

[4] KR Popper, *Die offene Gesellschaft und ihre Feinde* (Tübingen, Mohr Siebeck, 1980) vols 1 and 2.

[5] W Benjamin, *Critique of Violence* (London, Belknap Press of Harvard University Press, 1996) 286.

[6] See J Derrida, 'Force of Law: The Mystical Foundation of Authority' (1990) 11 *Cardozo Law Review* 919.

[7] On these aspects, see especially N Luhmann, *Archimedes und wir* (Berlin, Merve, 1998) 128. See, generally, N Luhmann, *Das Recht der Gesellschaft* (Frankfurt, Suhrkamp, 1993), English version: F Kastner, R Nobles, D Schiff and R Ziegert (eds), *Law as a Social System* (London, Oxford University Press, 2004).

[8] Compare papers in H de Berg and M Prangel (eds), *Systemtheorie zwischen Dekonstruktion und Konstruktivismus* (Tübingen and Basel, Franke, 1995).

kingdom, its autonomy, its structural determination and its reflexive identity as a result of a hidden underlying self-enforcing mechanism.

But in so doing, how does this extensive convergence correspond to the fact, as claimed by many critics, that both projects are considered to be radically divergent counter-concepts? Are they two sides of the same coin? And, if so, what is the coin? A two-sided reformulation of the same as a difference? The question arises, however, as to why deconstruction, characterised as an entertaining but obscure, narcissistic and irrational enterprise of criticism, simultaneously effective and ineffective, is permanently cited and argumentatively consulted by Luhmann, for instance, while contrariwise in Derrida's works Luhmann is not even mentioned in a single footnote?[9]

In what follows, I will try to elaborate upon these interrelated questions. A tentative answer to these questions might not only help us to understand Luhmann's fascinating asymmetrical communication with Derrida, but also the profound elective affinities between the two theoretical positions.[10] As a consequence, this could illuminate the ultimate difference between a philosophical and a sociological observation of law.

Let me start with a brief sketch of the outer profile of the two intellectual movements. The following antagonistic positions then arise: on the one hand, we have a highly methodologically disciplined and accurately elaborated autopoietic social theory. This theory makes explicit claims for a universal explanation of the order of the functionally differentiated modern society. It considers itself as a meta-theoretical 'super-theory,'[11] able to describe in a single vocabulary both the operations of the self-reproducing world society and the biochemical processes within a living cell. On the other hand, we have an unstable and dynamic open structure, presenting itself as a permanently changing, objectless, undirected 'theoretical jetty,'[12] without any claim for methodological or thematic finalisation.

---

[9] Luhmann's reference to Derrida is found in many articles and all monographs since his publication of *Soziale Systeme. Grundriß einer allgemeinen Theorie* (Frankfurt, Suhrkamp, 1984), English version: *Social Systems* (J Bednarz and D Baecker (trans), Stanford, Stanford University Press, 1995).

[10] My presentation refers to Gunther Teubner in Chapter 2. I am concentrating on the differences between Luhmann and Derrida in respect to their 'definition' of the paradox, rather than their treatment of the paradox. In a moderate discrepancy with Teubner, who defines the difference between the systems and deconstructive use of the paradox in 'sociologisation versus theologisation of paradox,' I prefer a theoretically immanent comparison of the theories by concentrating on their epistemological unifying notions, which I see in Luhmann's logico-formal conceptualisation of the paradox, in contrast to Derrida's experimental performance of the paradox. Compare G Teubner, 'The King's Many Bodies: The Self-Deconstruction of Law's Hierarchy' (1997) 31 *Law and Society Review* 765. See especially 'Economics of Gift—Positivity of Justice, The Mutual Paranoia of Jacques Derrida and Niklas Luhmann' (2001) 18 *Theory, Culture and Society* 29.

[11] N Luhmann, *Soziale Systeme, Grundriß einer allgemeinen Theorie* (Frankfurt, Suhrkamp, 1984) 5.

[12] J Derrida, *Einige Statements und Binsenweisheiten über Neologismen, New-Ismen, Post-Ismen, Parasiten und andere kleine Seismen* (Berlin, Merve, 1997) 9, 43.

While Luhmann's intention is to keep the complex theoretical design of his systemic autopoiesis accessible, by conceptual precision and permanent redefinitions of the central concepts and theorems in almost every published article, essay or book, Derrida, by contrast, is consciously expounding the problem of the unstable character of so-called deconstruction. He refuses to define a specific method or a guiding theoretical intention.

In fact, Derrida's cryptographic language at once performs and enacts a certain esoteric inaccessibility to its theoretical presuppositions by denying a theoretically external as well as an internal access. Therefore, Derrida is neither implementing fixed terminologies nor arranging a set of concepts according to a specific theoretical order. Even the artistic neologism deconstruction, or the other well-known deconstructive tools, such as *différance, trace, blanc, marges, sujectile* or *chora*, just to mention a few, are merely provisional instable infrastructural indicators. They were invented by Derrida's respective reading of a singular text, which could be a written text, a painting, an audio-visual presentation, a ruin, etc.[13] These infrastructural indicators constitute no definite understanding and they lack a solid function. For this reason, Derrida's a-theoretical movements emerge as artful single-point treatments, whose introductions are as artistic as the analysed source material.

II. PARADOXICAL EPISTEMOLOGIES

No two positions could be more divergent than those of the hypermodern scientific systems theoretician (who, in Habermas's words, represents today's 'perfection of technocratic awareness')[14] and the sophisticated, cryptic and 'dizzy'[15] ambassador of so-called post-modernity. In what way is a comparison possible between an elusive and inapprehensible performance and a clear concept of society as autopoietic, self-reproducing and operationally closed systems? The answer is: paradoxology. In fact, Derrida's intellectual movements and Luhmann's conceptual framework meet in their independently developed paradoxical epistemologies.

Luhmann's concern for the conceptualisation of the paradox is reflected in all of the systems-theoretical key tools: namely, the circular relationship among systemic evolution, systemic self-observation and systemic self-description. That is to say, systemic self-reference is not only taking place

---

[13] Compare HD Gondek and B Waldenfels (eds), *Einsätze des Denkens. Zur Philosophie von Jacques Derrida* (Frankfurt and Main, Suhrkamp, 1997). See also A Kern and C Menke (eds), *Philosophie der Dekonstruktion* (Frankfurt and Main, Suhrkamp, 2002).

[14] J Habermas with N Luhmann), *Theorie der Gesellschaft oder Sozialtechnologie* (Frankfurt and Main, Suhrkamp, 1971) 145.

[15] J Habermas, *Der philosophische Diskurs der Moderne* (Frankfurt and Main, Suhrkamp, 1989) 211.

on the basic level of the constitution and reproduction of the systemic elements, ie, autopoiesis, but at the same time as reflexive self-descriptions on the level of systemic processes. This involves the reference of a process to itself, or better, to a process of the same type. What is meant here is that the referring process and the referred process are structured by the same binary coding, for example, the regulating of norm-making[16] and the decisions over decisions,[17] etc. Luhmann has condensed this procedure into a trilogy of self-reference.[18] The trilogy of self-reference refers to the delicate situation in which the system shifts from the observation of its own operations to the observation of its own observations and, finally, to the observation of the system itself as a whole. All of this occurs only on the basis of an underlying distinction between system and environment. In other words, the self is the system to which the self-referential operation attributes itself and not only the systemic elements and processes. The problem then arises that, on every level, systemic operations essentially assume a paradoxical formation. Analogical to the circular reflections already recognised by the classical idealistic theory of cognition,[19] the main problem consists of the fact that paradoxes are necessarily caused when the signifying operation simultaneously belongs to what is signified. According to information theory, this tends to result in an endless, oscillating, negative self-reference formation. Applying this to the legal system, this would lead to the paralysing un-decidable question of whether the legal code's distinction between legal and illegal is itself legal or illegal, ad infinitum. In other words, these operations are not connectable, or better, they have no informational value for the system. However, they block the connectivity for further systemic operations. But, even so, de facto-empirically social systems are continuing their operations. The question, then, is how and why? Luhmann's answer is: through unfolding of the paradox and by its invisibilisation.

To fully understand these statements, it is necessary to take time into account. Operations, as defined by Luhmann, are single events without duration; they vanish as soon as they appear. Therefore, an observing operation is unable to observe its own observation—that is to say that the respective operation is not in the position to observe its own execution, and at the same time it is not even able to see that it is not able to see. As soon

---

[16] See N Luhmann, *Das Recht der Gesellschaft* (Frankfurt and Main, Suhrkamp, 1993) 165–213.
[17] See N Luhmann, *Die Politik der Gesellschaft* (Frankfurt and Main, Suhrkamp, 2000) 140–69. See also N Luhmann, *Organisation und Entscheidung* (Wiesbaden, Westdeutscher Verlag, 2000) 123–51.
[18] See N Luhmann, *Soziale Systeme. Grundriß einer allgemeinen Theorie* (Frankfurt, Suhrkamp, 1984) 599–607.
[19] See the critical debate in HB Schmid, 'Subjektivität ohne Interität. Zur systemtheoretischen, Überbietung der transzendentalphänomenologischen Subjekttheorie' in PU Merz-Benz and G Wagner (eds), *Die Logik der Systeme. Zur Kritik der systemtheoretischen Soziologie Niklas Luhmann* (Konstanz, Universitätsverlag Konstanz, 2000) 127–56.

as the system realises that the observed observation belongs to the system itself, it is already a temporally modified observation, which is as blind to its own conditions of reproduction as the prior observation. This punctual displacement from one operation to the other proceeds as long as the relevant autopoietic system exists.

To sum up, then, autopoietic systems displace their paradox, which is caused by coexistent affiliation and non-affiliation of the system's observation—punctually from event to event—that is, simultaneously and successively. Therefore, the system's paradox is not really solved in a classical sense of the word, but its blocking effects become invisible through the parallel and rotating execution of its operations. Consequently, such a concept of the paradox advances to a transformational-generative mechanism, which explains at the same time how systemic operations are connected—punctually, from event to event, in spite of the system's ongoing self-reference—and why: because otherwise, there would be no connectivity and accordingly no autopoietic system.

In this regard, the so-called 'blind spot,' Luhmann's preferred metaphor, gains its epistemological relevance: no observation is able to observe the unity of its own observation. Basically, these considerations lead to a paradoxical foundation of the systems-theoretical design as a whole. Luhmann's original sociological studies reflect the conditions of modern society's identity under the structural guideline of functional differentiation.[20] His later works reformulate this very question on the level of the elements of self-referential social subsystems.[21] The paradox as a constitutive form emerges on the level of the functionally differentiated society as well as on the singular communicational level of the elements of social subsystems. Luhmann's former idea of the impossibility of an all-over self-description of the modern society corresponds on the one hand to the impossibility of the identical self-observation of a single-function system and, on the other hand, to the impossibility of the identical self-observation of every communicational act.[22]

The centrality of the concept of the paradox in Luhmann's work and its undeniable radicality are under no circumstances a predicament; rather, they

---

[20] See N Luhmann, *Gesellschaftsstruktur und Semantik. Studien zur Wissenssoziologie der modernen Gesellschaft* (Frankfurt and Main, Suhrkamp, 1993) vols 1–4.

[21] See Luhmann's monographs: N Luhmann, *Die Wirtschaft der Gesellschaft* (Frankfurt and Main, Suhrkamp, 1988); *Die Wissenschaft der Gesellschaft* (Frankfurt and Main, Suhrkamp, 1990); *Das Recht der Gesellschaft* (Frankfurt and Main, Suhrkamp, 1993); *Die Kunst der Gesellschaft* (Frankfurt and Main, Suhrkamp, 1995); *Die Gesellschaft der Gesellschaft* (Frankfurt and Main, Suhrkamp, 1997). See also Luhmann's posthumously edited studies: *Organisation und Entscheidung* (Wiesbaden, Westdeutscher Verlag, 2000); *Die Politik der Gesellschaft* (Frankfurt and Main, Suhrkamp, 2000); *Die Religion der Gesellschaft* (Frankfurt and Main, Suhrkamp, 2000); *Das Erziehungssystem der Gesellschaft* (Frankfurt and Main, Suhrkamp, 2002).

[22] See eg, N Luhmann, *Die Gesellschaft der Gesellschaft* (Frankfurt and Main, Suhrkamp, 1997) 866.

constitute a 'transcendental necessity',[23] the very condition of possibility of knowledge, of culture and of society in general. From this point of view, social evolution is seen as a creative response to the underlying paradox. The appearance of social structures and their semantics is coextensive with the latency of the paradox. This also implies the impossibility of finding a universal formula that could represent a binding and entire social description. The problem then, to which Luhmann's key-concept of the paradox responds, is the cardinal problem of the impossibility of an entire identity or an all-over representation of the heterogeneous, polycon-structural, functionally differentiated world society. The paradox as the signum of modernity is at the same time the integrative brace and the central connector in all analytical systems theoretical levels. It is here that I perceive the radicality of Luhmann's sociology—that it is itself inherently paradoxical. The paradox of the paradox is, that it is temporally unfolded on the systems level and therefore always deparadoxified.[24]

A quite similar notion of a latent, constitutive and generative mode is in fact also framed as a central concern by Derrida's critical debate with the Western philosophical tradition.[25] Analogical to Luhmann's enterprise is Derrida's strategic focus upon a complex set of paradoxical conditions that serve to bring 'the ideality of a whole or a system simultaneously into reach and out of reach, and which articulates the limits—that is, that from which something begins but also where it ends—not only of words and concepts, but of just anything.'[26]

In contrast to Luhmann's precise definition of the paradox as a negative self-reference,[27] Derrida does not, to my knowledge, explicitly valorise, or

[23] N Luhmann, *Die Religion der Gesellschaft* (Frankfurt and Main, Suhrkamp, 2000) 132.
[24] See N Luhmann, 'Sthenographie und Euryalistik' in HU Gumbrecht and L Pfeiffer (eds), *Paradoxien, Dissonanzen, Zusammenbrüche: Situationen offener Epistemologie* (Frankfurt and Main, Suhrkamp, 1991) 58–82. See also the awesome reduced English version: 'Sthenography' (1990) 7 *Stanford Literature Review* 137. My presentation of Luhmann's concept of paradox refers to a much more detailed treatment I gave in former contributions, see especially, F Kastner, *Ohnmachtssemantiken. Systemtheorie und Dekonstruktion. Zum Primat der Paradoxie von Luhmanns Systemtheorie und Derridas Dekonstruktion am Beispiel ihrer autologischen Rechtskonstruktionen* (Frankfurt and Main, Fischer, 2002). I have tried to specify this in my recent work 'Luhmanns Souveränitätsparadox' in M Neves and R Voigt (eds), *Zur Staatstheorie von Niklas Luhmann* (Baden Baden, Nomos, 2005). See also F Kastner, 'Luhmanns Souveränitätsparadox: Zum generativen Mechanismus des politischen Systems der Weltgesellschaft' (2005) 13 *Mittelweg 36, Zeitschrift des Hamburger Instituts für Sozialforschung* 4–23.
[25] 'Derrida's concern' as emphasised particularly by Gasché 'is with a naivety unthought by philosophy in general, a blindness constitutive of philosophical thought.' See R Gasché, *The Tain of the Mirror* (Cambridge, Mass, Harvard University Press, 1986) 125.
[26] Gasché, *Inventions of Difference: On Jacques Derrida* (Cambridge, Mass, Harvard University Press, 1995) 7.
[27] Luhmann's precise conception of paradoxicality as a negative self-reference formation refers to the proto-logical works of George Spencer Brown. See the articles in the collective volume D Baecker (ed), *Kalkül der Form* (Frankfurt and Main, Suhrkamp, 1993); D Baecker (ed) *Probleme der Form* (Frankfurt and Main, Suhrkamp, 2001). See also N Luhmann, *Die Wissenschaft der Gesellschaft* (Frankfurt and Main, Suhrkamp, 1990). In contrast to my presentation and to Luhmann's treatment of the paradox as a general figure of negative self-reference, Clam's presentation discriminates between a so-called 'Urparadox' and several other 'partial paradoxes.'

even discuss, paradox: the word itself occurs only rarely in his writings. Nevertheless, his epistemological motivations culminate in a complementary diagnosis of a multiperspectival, poly-structural, organised, event-based performative force. However, this performativity articulated in Derrida's writings is, in a way, unlike the speech act defined by its opposition to the constative, which makes Derrida's works occasional responses, singular active engagements or event-orientated processes of negotiation. This explains Derrida's concern with questions of responsiveness and responsibility, of the other as the constitutive unarticulated, and of ethics in general.[28] Hence, Derrida's textual engagements become individual and singular in every case. Such singularity, of course, implies plurality on the other side and in particular the proliferation of genres, styles, voices, tonalities, formats, archives or even in non-categorisable ways—a plurality that no closed concept of so-called deconstruction could ever hope to totalise.

On the basis of such a self-image as an exercise in permanent motion, there is no way for a conceptual fixed arsenal or a stable significant profile. Therefore, by virtue of their event-character and singularity, Derrida's texts do not directly appoint the latent paradoxical logic, but they rather fulfil their paradoxical effects by inventing artistic place holders, which articulate nothing but the structural feature of being marked by this very latency and of relating to it. In other words, it is Derrida's texts themselves that become the articulation of the hidden paradoxical logic. For this reason, the provisional character of all deconstructive infrastructural indicators, such as *différance*, trace, iterability or supplementarity, for instance, is staging an asymmetrical structure of pointing away from these indicators. They mark and prepare the possible happening of a certain virtual openness to the incalculable, the unpredictable, the non-programmatisable, which can never be turned into a result or conclusion. Infrastructures stage an experimentation, and by performing, achieve a possible linkage between unlinkables, thus securing at once their minimal readability and their connection with the constitutive paradoxical law. In short, they elicit a possible intelligibility from the underlying structuring force through minimal contextualisation.[29]

In this sense, it should be comprehensible that Derrida's efforts lead equally to Luhmann's epistemological intentions as to a necessary 'quasi-transcendental'[30] paradoxical law, that allows the emergent use of distinctions

---

[28] See particularly, with regard to ethics, the recent publications: J Derrida, *Politik der Freundschaft* (Frankfurt and Main, Suhrkamp, 2000); *Von der Gastfreundschaft* (Wien, Passagen, 2001); *Schurken* (Frankfurt and Main, Suhrkamp, 2003); 'Autoimonisierungen, wirkliche und symbolische Selbstmorde. Ein Gespräch mit J Derrida' in J Habermas and J Derrida (eds), *Philosophie in Zeiten des Terrors* (Berlin, Philo-Verlag, 2004) 117–78.

[29] Therefore, it is not possible to draw with precision the boundaries between the invented infrastructures, but this impossibility makes a potential generativity 'possible,' though not necessary.

[30] R Gasché, *Inventions of Difference. On Jacques Derrida* (Cambridge, Mass, Harvard University Press, 1995) 162.

and betrays them at the same time. To quote Derrida, 'Things take place between *Versammlung* (gathering) (that is to say also the logos, ... and dissemination'.[31] As a consequence of this double movement of gathering and contingency, there is no specific genre of what are called infrastructural indicators. Not only is their number in principle infinite, but they are generically different and therefore out of reach of any mastering systemisation or totalisation. This fluid status of being in between prevents their synthetic and abusive generalisation. It prevents their becoming so-called elementary words, suitable unifying names or the articulation of an 'abyss of irrationality'[32] par excellence, as Habermas dreads so much.

So, if infrastructures are not simply tokens, words, names or concepts in the sense that is dominant throughout Western theoretical tradition, what are they?

They are interwoven undecidables with an indicating and an enabling function. Their indication function concerns the interrelationship between the conditions of possibilities and the conditions of limits under which any form of entity can be intelligible in the conventional sense of the word. Their enabling function concerns what Derrida calls the 'invention of the other'[33] or the advent of an inaugural event. For an invention to be an invention, or an inaugural event to be an inaugural event, it must be non-calculable, beyond established and legitimised social consensus. Therefore, Derrida's writings confront a conceptualisation of the closed texts with the open text; they prefer the plural pooling reading instead of the meaning-orientated interpretation. With that, Derrida's readings become a problem for their own reading. On this account, Derrida abandons each form of thematic reading in general. And it is for this reason that his works are subjected to the imperative of a constant change.

In an endless autological process of permanent auto-deconstruction, Derrida's enterprise consequently 'is' and performs the infrastructural paradox.

III. PARADOXES OF JUSTICE

This idea of a motivational and transformational power of the latent paradox, which establishes and enables the evolution of order in every sense, is indeed the unifying notion between Luhmann's logico-formal conceptualisation of the paradox and Derrida's dynamic and artful exhibition of the

---

[31] J Derrida, *Points de suspension* (Paris, Entretiens, 1992) 315.
[32] J Habermas, *Nachmetaphysisches Denken. Philosophische Aufsätze* (Frankfurt and Main, Suhrkamp, 1992) 159.
[33] J Derrida, 'Psyche: Invention of the Other' in L Waters and W Godzich (eds), *Reading de Man Reading* (Minneapolis, University of Minnesota Press, 1989) 29.

paradox. So, what kind of consequences do a systems-theoretical indication and a Derridian performance of the latency of paradoxical infrastructures have for the legal order?

From Luhmann's sociological point of view, all that matters is the highly improbable evolutionary achievement of the operative closure of the legal system within a communicational network that reproduces the society by recursively connecting communication with communication. The legal system only matters insofar as it is a social subsystem within the entire social system, one that reproduces society by communication. The core problem within this conceptual framework, then, is, 'How to define the operation that differentiates the system and organises the differences between system and environment while maintaining reciprocity between dependence and independence.'[34] In other words, how is the system organising its closure, its own social autonomy and its own immunity by fulfilling its social function, which is defined as 'producing and maintaining counter-factual expectations'?[35] According to Luhmann's conception, this bearing role of self-identifying, self-distinguishing and self-presenting belongs exclusively to the binary code. Defined as a strictly internal mechanical rule of attribution and connection, the code is a structural necessity that leads to legal decisions between legal right and wrong, without being itself a basic norm, a principle or guiding rule. Particularly at this point, the divergence between Luhmann's theory of positivity and accepted conceptions which relate law to values or morality becomes noticeable.[36] But furthermore, the effect of the radical bifurcation is not only the moral neutralisation of the legal system, but also the impossibility of immediate determinations of the legal system through, for instance, political interests or religious desires. The bifurcation necessitates decisions and thereby further legal operations, and decisions require the construction of normative rules (programmes) to connect them in a network for reproducing decisions. From this point of view, then, norms are purely internal creations, serving the self-generated needs of the system for decisional criteria without any corresponding items in its environment. It is this idea of normative closure, that is self-referential closure, that makes a theory of justice as exterior as well as superior criterion of the legal system obviously irrelevant. 'The guarantee of "justice,"' in Luhmann's words, 'is not the correspondence with external qualities or interests, but the consistency of internal operations recognizing and distinguishing them.'[37]

---

[34] N Luhmann, 'Operational Closure and Structural Coupling: the Differentiation of the Legal System' (1992) 13 *Cardozo Law Review* 1419 at 1426.
[35] N Luhmann, *Das Recht der Gesellschaft* (Frankfurt and Main, Suhrkamp, 1993) 134.
[36] Compare N Luhmann, 'Quod Omnes Tangit: Remarks on Jürgen Habermas's Legal Theory' (1996) 17 *Cardozo Law Review* 883. See also M Neves, 'From the Autopoiesis to the Allopoiesis of Law' (2001) 28 *Journal of Law and Society* 2.
[37] N Luhmann, 'Operational Closure and Structural Coupling: the Differentiation of the Legal System' (1992) 13 *Cardozo Law Review* 1431.

Consequently, justice can be only considered as a form of self-observation within the legal system. This does not mean, however, that Luhmann is abandoning the concept of justice as such, but that its position within the self-referential framework of the legal system is reorganised.

While 'validity', according to the systems-theoretical design, is a symbol which circulates in the system, links its operations to one another and recalls the results of operations for recursive further use, justice, however, has to do with self-observation and self-description of the legal system. The difference between self-observation and self-description is relatively clear: while self-observation concerns only 'the attribution of single operations to structures of the system', that means above all the implication or the explication that the relevant communication deals with legality or illegality, self-descriptions serve other imperatives. They reflect the just order of the legal system and represent, therefore, the unity of the system within the system. As explained above, this execution of describing the unity of the system through a part of the system, which has to differentiate itself and to identify itself at the same time, leads necessarily to paradoxical involvements. Therefore, Luhmann states explicitly that 'system's reflection is paradox's reflection.'[38] Consequently, these paradoxical reflections take the form of circular statements—and this circularity gives the so-called formulae for contingency their self-instating nativeness, which cannot be resolved any further. Equality, for instance, is a principle which legitimises itself—justice does not need to justify itself any further. Moreover, circular formulae for contingency, such as equality and justice, are not statements about the essence or nature of law, nor are they principles for substantiating the validity of law, nor are they values which could make law appear the preferred choice. In contrast to all these assumptions, circular formulae for contingency are abstract schemes for the search for reasons or values, which can become legally valid only in the form of programmes. They refer to the difference between indeterminacy and determinacy. Their function is to cross this boundary and claim historically given plausibilities for doing so. Seen from this perspective—that of the socio-structural relativity and according to the main systems-theoretical theorem of the relationship between social structures and semantics, segmental societies—feudal societies and today's functionally differentiated society provoke their own specified perception of the form of justice.[39] In short: according to Luhmann's sociological conception, justice can only mean a functionally adequate complexity of consistent decision-making. What is adequate follows from the relationship between the legal system and the social structure of the entire social system.

---

[38] N Luhmann, *Die Wissenschaft der Gesellschaft* (Frankfurt and Main, Suhrkamp, 1990) 484.
[39] See also N Luhmann, *Ausdifferenzierung des Rechts. Beiträge zur Rechtssoziologie und Rechtstheorie* (Frankfurt and Main, Suhrkamp, 1999). See, especially, N Luhmann, *Die Gesellschaft der Gesellschaft* (Frankfurt and Main, Suhrkamp, 1997) vol 2, 879–92.

According to this, justice is a self-reference in the scheme of a legal fiction but not as an operation, which means that it has not a factual selective function on the level of the code, but on the level of changing programmes. It is not a form of theory, but it is a form of a fictional self-referential norm. All this means that there are unjust, or more or less just, legal systems. As a consequence, neither the operative autopoiesis of the legal system nor the necessarily invariant legal code can be just.

So, what is really positively defined in such a sociological observation of the concept of justice, except its reduction to a fictional horizon? Is this simply a restatement of the Kantian insistence—that justice is an ideal of legal-historical reason, and as such, is irreducible to actual conventions of any existing legal system? How can this formula for contingency as a fictional self-referential quasi-norm be accurately described?

Derrida's possible contribution lies in this paradoxical understanding of the essential corelationship of a socio-structural historical divide between law as a positivistic legal system and the phenomenology of justice. To quote a central passage of Derrida's *Force of Law: The Mystical Foundation of Authority*, where all his decisive notions are summarised:

> The structure I am describing here is a structure in which law (droit) is essentially deconstructible, whether because it is founded, constructed on interpretable or transformable textual strata—(and that is the history of law (droit), its possible and necessary transformation, sometimes its amelioration)—or because its ultimate foundation is by definition unfounded. The fact that law is deconstructible is not bad news. We may even see in this a stroke of luck for politics, for all historical progress. But the paradox that I'd like to submit for discussion is the following: it is the deconstructible structure of law (droit), or if you prefer of justice as droit, that also insures the possibility of deconstruction. Justice in itself, if such a thing exists, outside or beyond law, is not deconstructible. No more than deconstruction itself, if such a thing exists. Deconstruction is justice.[40]

It seems evident that Derrida is addressing the question of justice in several interrelated discursive dimensions at once. So, first of all, Derrida's approach, as always in his writings, is not a direct confrontation with the specific genre of what is called the juridical issue as such, but rather is the recurring attempt to redefine and re-evaluate his own philosophical enterprise. Therefore, although the text is an homage, more precisely an explicit text in admiration of law and its positivistic apparatus, this text, rather than giving into proclaiming or acclaiming law's authority as such, proceeds in all detachment to an analysis of what makes law's empire possible. It is thus a text that, notwithstanding its respect for the legal affair, asks what it is that

---

[40] Derrida, above n 6, at 945.

'*forces*' the law. The answer, in Derrida's *Force of Law: The Mystical Foundation of Authority*, is that justice makes law possible and deconstruction is justice.

But 'Why is deconstruction justice?'[41] Derrida's answer is univocal: since the idea of justice is necessarily connected with the idea of infinity, it is not deducible from established criteria and rules of the legal machine. Therefore, Derrida is indeed stressing the unbridgeable divide between law and justice. To quote him, 'Law is not justice.'[42] While the law belongs to the element of calculation, justice demands for the incalculable. Still, according to Derrida's implementations, the ultimate experience of justice is possible in those exceptional moments where a decision between the just and the unjust is not secured by a specific legal criterion or rule. It is this situation of the undecidability, as an experience of the excessive unrepresentable situation of suspension, that Derrida calls the transcendent, which overreaches the definable.[43] That is why justice does not have a logical foundation, but a 'mystical' one. Its logic, therefore, is the transcendence of all discourses and the reinvention of their grounds.

Therewith, Derrida formulates his main notion: the permanent challenge, or better deconstructive confrontation with the legal order, is at the same time the possible, which means not the necessary articulation and the fictional performance of the infinite idea of justice. With this, a hidden infrastructural force of an underlying quasi-transcendental law becomes visible, 'the law itself, the law above other laws,' 'a law beyond legality,' a law of which the historical Western law is perhaps only an example.[44]

However, the question then arises if and how such an extreme experience of the 'mystical' could ever be realised, and correspondently, could it ever inspire or even guide legal factual activism? It seems that Derrida's meditation and simultaneous performance of the 'mystical,' which is just another name for the generic area of the infrastructural paradox, mean at the same time to reflect, to perform and so to invent the 'mystical.' But such invention, of course, serves merely to domesticate it. For an invention to be an invention, and hence to be a difference that makes a difference, its uniqueness must be wrenched from and negotiated within an established system of convention. Therefore, Derrida is neither pleading for a merely positivistic understanding of law without justice nor claiming a radical idealistic position that abolishes law for the sake of justice. Both viewpoints assume that the difference

---

[41] A crucial question, primarily formulated by D Cornell, 'Time, Deconstruction, and the Challenge of Legal Positivism: The Call for Juridical Responsibility' (1990) 2 *Yale Journal of Law and Humanities* 267.
[42] Derrida, above n 6, at 946.
[43] *Ibid*, at 993.
[44] J Derrida and M Tlili, *The Laws of Reflection: For Nelson Mandela* (New York, Seaver Books, 1987) 26.

between law and justice could be fixed and stabilized. But, according to Derrida, this is exactly the crucial point, since there is no clear-cut distinction, but an ambiguous and doubtful slide between law and justice. And this ambiguous and doubtful slide is precisely the very nature of deconstruction. Hence, only deconstruction is able to express the complex set of motions which bind justice with law even as they separate the one from the other. This is what Derrida means by saying deconstruction is justice.

To come to an end, what exactly is the difference, then, between a sociology of law that claims a fictional conception of justice as a contingent scheme of legal self-observation, and a philosophical experimental performance of the possible invention of a justice to come?

Part III

Local Paradoxes

9

Expectations and Legal Doctrine

ERIC TALLEY*

I. INTRODUCTION

A NUMBER OF important modern legal contexts are regulated by doctrines that turn, in large part, on a judicial assessment of either private or social 'expectations' rather than the imposition of hard-and-fast imperatives. Such expectation-grounded standards have long been pervasive in private law contexts, and they are becoming increasingly influential in both public and international legal contexts as well. Contract interpretation doctrine, for example, is nearly entirely devoted to the goal of implementing the parties' expectations at the time that they executed the agreement. But other important areas of law, including privacy rights, takings jurisprudence, personal jurisdiction, securities fraud and tax law, regulate behaviour through doctrines that hinge—at least in part—on assessing the reasonable expectations of the actors involved.

Often, in divining the precise nature of such expectations, courts look to evidence about context to make factual inferences. A particularly noteworthy example is the use of some form of capitalised market value—most commonly, price—to proxy for individual expectations. A contract claimant attempting to enforce an express warranty, for example, might attempt to demonstrate that the price she paid for the defective unit was substantially above the market price for a similar item not covered by a warranty. This pricing premium would plausibly represent evidence that the claimant had purchased something else in addition to the item itself—namely, insurance for product defects.

In many respects, the use of price as an informational proxy seems both prudent and sensible. A number of courts have apparently so concluded as well, and expectation-based theories appear to be gaining in popularity in a number of fields.[1] At the same time, however, this type of

---

* Many thanks to Bruce Chapman, Greg Keating, Dan Klerman, Lewis Kornhauser and Christophe Stone for helpful comments.

[1] See section II below (collecting examples).

doctrine introduces a self-referential circularity into the law that can prove mind-numbingly difficult to navigate. In the above warranty example, for instance, a buyer's genuine belief that she can recover on a warranty claim is likely to increase her willingness to pay for the item. If—as is likely—this enhanced willingness to pay is reflected in an increased price, then that premium will constitute the pivotal evidence required by a court to grant protection. But by granting protection, the court renders true the buyer's initial belief that the warranty was enforceable to begin with. On the other hand, if the buyer starts with a belief that the warranty is unenforceable, then she will pay no more than the competitive market price for the item. So doing, however, creates the evidence that will induce a court to refuse enforcement of the warranty, and once again the buyer's initial belief is ratified by a subsequent legal outcome. In what follows, I shall refer to this type of circularity—in which manifest expectations (often reflected in price) about future legal status in turn beget the very legal pronouncements that rationalise those expectations—as the *Pricing Paradox*.

Despite the ubiquity of the Pricing Paradox (and its recognition among at least some judges,[2]) only a few legal scholars (and virtually no economists) have squarely confronted it. While some in the legal academy (such as Frank Michelman) have defended expectation-based approaches by concentrating on their functional ability to provide a form of 'notice,'[3] such approaches do not delve sufficiently deeply into the difficulties created by the Pricing Paradox to provide a way out. Others (such as Richard Epstein) have strongly criticised doctrines that manifest the Pricing Paradox (at least those that have a strong subjective element), but these scholars have not been sufficiently attentive to the ubiquity of such doctrines in practice, nor do they appear to be interested in opining on when (if ever) such doctrines might be defensible on utilitarian grounds.[4]

This chapter attempts to provide such an analysis from an economic perspective. I argue that if there is a defence to the Pricing Paradox, it must come from its unique ability to enhance the flexibility of a legal system to deal with future unexpected contingencies. By providing this critical flexibility, expectation-centred doctrines afford individuals the opportunity to signal credible information to courts about fluctuations in their economic

---

[2] Kennedy J's concurrence in *Lucas v South Carolina Coastal Council*, for example, is typical: 'There is an inherent tendency towards circularity in this synthesis, of course; for if the owner's reasonable expectations are shaped by what courts allow as a proper exercise of governmental authority, property tends to become what courts say it is. Some circularity must be tolerated in these matters, however, as it is in other spheres.' *Lucas v South Carolina Coastal Council* [1992] 112 S Ct 2886, 2903 (Kennedy J concurring).

[3] FI Michelman, 'Property, Utility and Fairness: Comments on the Ethical Foundations of "Just Compensation" Law' (1967) 80 *Harvard Law Review* 1165.

[4] RA Epstein, 'A Tangled Web of Expectations: *Lucas v South Carolina Coastal Council*' (1993) 45 *Stanford Law Review* 1369.

environment. In such situations, the very circularity of the Pricing Paradox may constitute its critical strength rather than a fatal weakness (as many have alleged).

At the same time, however, the Pricing Paradox imposes tangible costs on at least three levels. First, it can increase the marginal returns to litigiousness, encouraging parties to contest the appropriate interpretation of a price (or other evidence of expectations), thereby exacerbating the overall costs of administering the legal system. Secondly, it can sharpen parties' incentives to make costly, non-productive prelitigation expenditures for the sole purpose of manipulating a court's subsequent interpretation. Finally, it can create a fundamental indeterminacy in the evolution of legal doctrine, which itself can be so severe as to undercut the expressive function of law as either a normative guidepost or an informative signal.

Given these costs, I argue that expectation-based doctrines are most defensible (and perhaps only defensible) from an economic perspective when: (i) the underlying environment is relatively unpredictable; (ii) the benefits of coordination are large; (iii) the stakes involved are largely zero-sum in nature (as measured ex post); and (iv) parties' expectations about their legal status are relatively important as compared to other economic considerations. While such conditions typify some settings, they need not be manifest uniformly (if at all) in others. Indeed, in applying these criteria, I argue, the pricing paradox is probably most justified when it is reflected in contractual rather than non-contractual (eg, tort, criminal, regulatory or some international) environments.

II. LEGAL EXPECTATIONS: SOME EXAMPLES

Before analysing the relative costs and benefits of the pricing paradox, it is probably prudent first to gain some purchase on how widespread it is in practice. Although an aggregated empirical assessment is probably not feasible (at least for my purposes), it is possible to explore how the Pricing Paradox manifests itself in numerous doctrinal areas of law. This section, therefore, presents a brief survey of applications, ranging from contracts to property to constitutional law to jurisdictional matters.

Contracts: Enforcing Non-credible Warranties

Many (if not most) contractual disputes concern disagreements about what interpretation of a contract is most consistent with parties' intent. Under many plausible jurisprudential accounts, courts endeavour to construe express terms so as to implement the parties' reasonable expectations—a concept that can (and frequently does) implicate expectations about subsequent legal entitlements. Consequently, it should not be surprising that contract law has spawned a wealth of case law that implicates the Pricing Paradox as described above. Though a number of doctrines in contract law (including conditions, material breach and foreseeability) arguably reflect the paradox, perhaps the most striking is in the doctrine regulating the interpretation and enforcement of express warranties.

Warranty law has come to play a far-reaching and important role in commercial and business law. To be sure, merchants have for a long time faced liability for breach of implied or express warranties concerning consumer goods. Yet warranty law long ago transcended this traditional role. A well-known example of this expansion is in products liability law, which is a product of a direct mutation of implied warranties during the last 50 years.[5] But warranty law is also increasingly playing a central role in the mergers and acquisitions ('M&A') context. For example, it is now commonplace for selling parties to make explicit warranties to buyers regarding the value of a company's goodwill, its intellectual property, its other tangible assets, the existence of adverse tax or wage consequences of a change in control, and the like. Such warranties are, in fact, particularly common in situations where an extensive due-diligence period is costly and/or time-consuming, either because of the secrecy of the acquisition, timing constraints or the lack of previous disclosures by the target (if, for example, it is privately held).[6] Indeed, such devices have become so prevalent within the M&A context in the last decade to have spawned an entire subindustry of liability insurance policies for sellers (and even buyers) who are later found to have breached express warranties in a control transaction or sale of assets.[7] Moreover, for disappointed buyers who purchase securities through privately negotiated transactions, state-based warranty law may be their most availing alternative.[8]

One quirky (but surprisingly oft-litigated) form of dispute involving warranties concerns representations that are disbelieved by the non-warranting party. At common law, a buyer's disbelief of an express representation is, for the most part, fatal. Under this approach, a buyer's disbelief is tantamount to a lack of reliance, rendering the alleged warranty wholly unenforceable (or at least that part that is disbelieved). Alternatively, defendants in such situations have frequently asserted that a buyer's lack of reliance on

---

[5] See, generally, KA Abraham, *Forms and Functions of Tort Law: An Analytical Primer on Cases and Concepts*, 2nd edn (Foundation Press, 2002).

[6] See JL Church, *Corporate Mergers and Acquisitions: Intellectual Property Aspects of Corporate Acquisitions* (American Law Institute, 1 September, 2000).

[7] JP Monteleone, Practising Law Institute PLI Order No. B0–00NV, 1199 PLI/Corp 479 (September, 2000).

[8] See eg, P Letsou, 'The Scope of Section 12(2) of the Securities Act of 1933: A Legal and Economic Analysis' [1996] 45 *Emory Law Journal* 95 (arguing that state warranty law is more availing than § 10b litigation for private purchasers after *Gustafson v Alloyd* 115 S. Ct. 1061 (1995).

the truthfulness of the representations constitutes evidence that the seller's statements were mere puffery, and did not constitute part of the bargain. In essence, this common law requirement of reliance puts express warranties on a par with that of misrepresentation and fraud doctrine, which has historically always required proof that the party claiming misrepresentation relied to her detriment on the truthfulness of the assertion. This common law rule is still in wide use and is routinely upheld by courts in a number of jurisdictions.[9]

An increasing number of courts, however, have begun to re-examine whether reliance is appropriately seen to be an element of a warranty claim.[10] In *CBS Inc v Ziff-Davis Publishing Co*,[11] the Court of Appeals of New York confronted this very issue in a dispute stemming from CBS's purchase of Ziff-Davis' consumer magazine business in the mid-1980s. In soliciting bids for the sale of the business, Ziff-Davis summarised portions of its annual financial statements in its offering prospectus, which was reproduced in a number of trade and business magazines and circulated among numerous possible buyers. CBS submitted a high bid of US$362.5 million based on this circular, and subsequently the parties entered into a binding purchase agreement in late 1984. In one express provision of the purchase agreement, Ziff-Davis warranted that the audited income and expense report for the magazine business for the year (which had appeared in the offering circular) had 'been prepared in accordance with generally accepted accounting principles' (GAAP) and that the report 'presented fairly the items set forth.'[12]

Nevertheless, during the course of its own due diligence investigation, CBS came to believe that the financial statements did not fairly and accurately reflect the fiscal health of the magazine segment. This suspicion led to a series of correspondences between the parties and a disagreement that had not been settled even at the time of closing. The sale, nonetheless,

---

[9] See eg, *Royal Business Machines, Inc v Lorraine Corp* 7th Cir 633 F 2d 34 (1980) (holding that reliance on the underlying truthfulness of a representation is necessary for enforcement of a warranty, and that increasing familiarity of buyer with seller's product can, over time, nullify this reliance element).

[10] This relaxation of the reliance requirement in warranty law actually predated a similar relaxation of the element in fraud doctrines. See eg, *Basic v Levinson* 485 US 224 (1988) (holding that the reliance requirement in a Rule 10b–5 action could be predicated on one's reliance on the integrity of market price alone—the so-called 'fraud on the market' theory); *Virginia Bankshares v Sandberg* 501 US 1083 (1991) (holding that the elements of a Rule 14a–9 private right of action for fraud in connection with a proxy solicitation are met, notwithstanding the lack of belief by the plaintiff in the truthfulness of management's representations).

[11] *CBS, Inc v Ziff-Davis Publishing Co* 75 NY 2d 496, (1990).

[12] In a later interim expense report required in the purchase agreement, Ziff-Davis warranted that there had not been any material adverse change in the company's health, and that all warranties and representations were true and correct at the time of closing. *Ibid.*

closed on its intended date of 4 February, 1985, and immediately thereupon CBS brought suit in New York state court claiming that Ziff-Davis had (inter alia) breached express warranties made as to the division's profitability. Ziff-Davis moved to dismiss the claim on the basis that CBS's allegations included the admission that 'it did not believe the representations set forth in the ... contract for sale were true,' and asserting that New York law on express warranties required reliance by the claiming party. The trial court granted the motion, a decision that was subsequently affirmed by the Appellate Division.

On CBS's ensuing appeal, the Court of Appeals of New York reversed. In so doing, the court distinguished warranty claims from more conventional fraud claims—where reliance is traditionally a required element. Like fraud, wrote Justice Hancock, a successful warranty claim in New York would still require a showing of reliance; however, the buyer's reliance on the underlying *factual* truthfulness of the claim was no longer the linchpin of the analysis. Rather, the court held, the touchstone test for enforceability of a warranty was whether the representation and its anticipated legal consequences had become part of the bargained-for exchange between the parties. The court quoted a (relatively neglected) opinion by Learned Hand, who wrote:

> A warranty is an assurance by one party to a contract of the existence of a fact upon which the other party may rely. It is intended precisely to relieve the promisee of any duty to ascertain the fact for himself; it amounts to a promise to indemnify the promisee for any loss if the fact warranted proves untrue, for obviously the promisor cannot control what is already in the past.[13]

Thus, Hancock continued, it is not necessary that the buyer actually believe the facts represented in order for the warranty to become part of that bargain; all she must believe is that she will be able to recover in the event that the warranted facts fail to materialise. Consequently, the trial court's dismissal of CBS's action was premature, and should have considered evidence of whether the warranty had become part of the bargain. While the plaintiff must still bear the burden of proof here, among the evidence that the trial court can consider was whether CBS had paid a premium for the purchase over what it would have paid had no such warranty been made. Such a premium would constitute objective evidence that CBS had reasonably expected recovery on the basis of the warranty.

Ziff-Davis provides an excellent example of the self-referential nature of the Pricing Paradox. Suppose there were a roughly competitive population of buyers for Ziff-Davis, including CBS, which happened to be the highest

---

[13] *Metropolitan Coal Co v Howard* 2nd Cir. 155 F.2d 780 (1946).

valuer. Assume further that if the representations made by Ziff-Davis were true, then CBS would value the company at US$362.5 million. Finally, suppose that if the Ziff-Davis' representations were untrue *and* not actionable, the magazine unit would have fetched a US$300 million bid from CBS. How much would CBS be willing to bid to purchase the magazine? The answer to this question depends crucially on whether CBS thinks it will be able to recover the value of the warranty from Ziff-Davis. If it believed that the answer to this question was 'yes,' then CBS would be willing to pay US$362.5 million. In contrast, if CBS believed that it could not recover, then it would be willing to bid at most US$300 million.

This dependence of its purchase price on its expectations about enforceability of the warranty is what spawns the Pricing Paradox. Explicitly, a belief in the enforceability of the warranty would cause CBS to capitalise the value of the warranty into a higher bid. In turn, the capitalisation of that value into the bid would create the evidentiary preconditions for which the court will enforce the warranty: ie, the warranty would clearly be part of the basis of the bargain. In contrast, if CBS did not believe the warranty was enforceable, it would not capitalise the value of the warranty into its bid, and the lack of such capitalisation provides the evidentiary preconditions for a court to withhold a remedy from CBS: ie, the warranty was never made part of the basis of the bargain.

To be sure, the Pricing Paradox illustrated by *Ziff-Davis* spawns a type of logical circularity: initial beliefs about subsequent court actions, under this approach, become a form of self-fulfilling prophecy. Circularity itself, however, need not always constitute a principled basis for criticism of the doctrine. It is perfectly plausible that, in some situations and under certain criteria, circularity can provide much needed doctrinal flexibility. Although I shall defer my assessment of this normative point until the next section of this chapter, I should note at this point that insofar as the Pricing Paradox implicates two-party contractual settings (such as that considered above), the windfall, if any, realised by one party will be directly visited on the other party. The internalised consequences of the Pricing Paradox in contractual settings will prove important for the analysis to follow.

Property: Regulatory Takings and *Penn Central*

Property law, as well, has not been free from the Pricing Paradox. Among many examples, the current state of the takings jurisprudence represents a notable example of how legal expectations—capitalised in market prices—are accounted for explicitly by legal doctrine. While takings doctrine did not historically utilise this approach, a more modern set of cases dealing with regulatory (as opposed to physical) takings have become both a battleground for litigation generally and for the Pricing Paradox in particular.

Although it was recognised nearly a century ago that under certain conditions, an invasive regulation proscribing certain uses of one's property might constitute a regulatory taking,[14] it was not until 1978 that the US Supreme Court clarified precisely what those conditions were. In *Penn Central Transportation Co v New York City*,[15] plaintiff landowners challenged a 1965 historic preservation Act enacted by the City of New York which, inter alia, created a Preservation Commission charged with evaluating the historical and aesthetic character and restricting alterations (particularly those to the exterior of the building) of so-designated properties. Penn Central owned Grand Central Station, which had been designated a landmark, and sought the Commission's approval to add a 55 storey addition to the building through one of two alternative plans. (Under the less invasive of these plans, the facade of the station would not be altered, though the office building would be cantilevered above the exterior facade and would rest on the roof of the terminal itself.) The Commission rejected Penn Central's application, largely on aesthetic grounds, and refused to allow the plan to go forward. Penn Central (and its developer) then brought suit against the city, alleging that the application of the ordinance constituted a regulatory taking without compensation in violation of the Fifth and Fourteenth Amendments to the US Constitution.

In a seven to two decision, the Supreme Court upheld the ordinance and its application. Justice Brennan's opinion began by stating the confused state of the doctrine as it then existed (which may not be far from the truth today):

> [T]his Court, quite simply, has been unable to develop any 'set formula' for determining when 'justice and fairness' require that economic injuries caused by public action be compensated by the government, rather than remain disproportionately concentrated on a few persons. Indeed, we have frequently observed that whether a particular restriction will be rendered invalid by the government's failure to pay for any losses proximately caused by it depends largely 'upon the particular circumstances [in that] case.'[16]

The Court then offered such a test. While preserving the casuistic nature of the inquiry, Brennan's opinion then spelled out three factors for determining whether a regulation restricting one's use of property rose to the level of a taking: (1) the economic impact of the regulation on the claimant; (2) the extent to which the regulation had interfered with distinct investment-backed expectations; and (3) the character of the governmental action. In analysing the third of these factors, the Court found that, unlike

---

[14] See *Pennsylvania Coal v Mahon* 260 US 393 (1922).
[15] *Penn Central. Transp Co v New York City* 438 U.S. 104, 98 (1978).
[16] *Ibid*, at 123–4.

other situations where a regulatory taking had been found,[17] the government in this instance was not acting with the purpose of enhancing its own welfare as an enterprise. Rather, the aim was solely to provide a set of prohibitions that served the public interest more generally. As such, the nature of the regulation was deemed permissible.

As to factors (1) and (2), the Court's analysis viewed them as intertwined with one another (as they frequently are).[18] For at least two reasons, the Court was unpersuaded by Penn Central's allegation that the restriction dramatically reduced the market value of the property, and should therefore be considered a taking. First, it was not disputed that the restriction imposed by the Landmark Commission did not revoke any theretofore-existing use of the property in which Penn Central had engaged. It was at the time (just as it had always been) used exclusively as a train station. Secondly, it was similarly uncontroverted that the building could continue to be operated profitably as a train station, yielding a reasonable return for its owner. The confluence of these observations, Brennan concluded, was sufficient to support the legal determination that Penn Central's principal expectation for the building—that of operating a profitable train station—was still met under the application of the ordinance.

The test expressed in Penn Central invokes the Pricing Paradox insofar as it turns on the regulated party's expectations about the property's future legal status. In many ways, the facts of Penn Central proved enormously convenient by allowing the Court to avoid engaging the paradox directly: indeed, Grand Central Station was historically a single-purpose building and had been purchased years before high-rise office buildings were perceived as feasible. Consequently, it was relatively easy for the state to demonstrate that Penn Central could make a reasonable return on its investment by continuing the homogenous use of the property.

In more common cases, however, ownership of commercial real estate can transition and vary much more frequently, and such transactions can be expected to capitalise heterogeneous future options into the price. Suppose, for example, that the property at issue were an ordinary office building built with a similarly flamboyant Beaux-Arts facade, and had been sold to a developer, just before the passage of the Landmarks Preservation Act, for an amount triple the square footage price for transportation buildings in midtown Manhattan. It would seem that this developer could convincingly argue that the price she paid reflected the option value of altering the space

---

[17] Eg, *United States v Causby* 328 US 256 (1946) (holding as a taking a federal regulation that allowed military overflights above the claimant's land destroying the present use of the land as a chicken farm, and emphasising that the government had not 'merely destroyed property [but was] using a part of it for the flight of its planes').

[18] Indeed, from the text of *Penn Central*, it is difficult to know whether these factors were ever intended to be distinct.

so as to add significant square footage to the building. In such an instance, this premium would certainly go a long way towards establishing not only that the regulation visits a disproportionate harm on the developer, but also that it significantly upends her investment-backed expectations of future value. Assuming (plausibly) that such a showing would satisfy the multifactor test in Penn Central, then the price premium would constitute the linchpin piece of evidence for establishing a right to just compensation. This is nothing more than the Pricing Paradox identified above.

In the quarter-century since *Penn Central*, a number of subsequent Supreme Court takings cases have altered and constrained the factual universe in which the doctrine applies. Perhaps most noteworthy in this regard is the series of decisions beginning in 1992 with *Lucas v South Carolina Coastal Council*.[19] *Lucas* created an exception to the multifactor test announced in Penn Central, for situations where the regulatory encumbrance is so severe as to constitute a 'total' taking of the plaintiff's property, in that it 'deprives land of all economically beneficial use.'[20] In such circumstances, the *Lucas* Court held, there is a per se conclusion that a taking exists, unless the state can demonstrate that the nature of the owner's estate was such that it precluded the proscribed use (under, say, a pre-existing easement, nuisance doctrine, or the like) to begin with.

The *Lucas* 'total takings' exception substitutes a type of categorical rule in place of the fact-specific standard announced in *Penn Central*, and as such does not run the same risk of inducing the Pricing Paradox.[21] Many of the opinions issued since are symptomatic of an ongoing doctrinal debate about what precisely constitutes a 'total taking', thereby triggering *Lucas*. This debate is perhaps inescapable, insofar as the *Lucas* test is only meaningful once one has specified the cognisable universe of uses outside of the regulation. Takings claimants have an incentive to characterise this universe as a small one (by, for instance, severing from the whole only certain strands of the property in space or time), so as to make the regulatory proscription appear total (or nearly so). If such efforts were routinely successful, then the *Penn Central* standard would likely be on its way to complete erosion, whittled away one case at a time.

---

[19] *Lucas v SC Coastal Council* 505 US 1003 (1992).
[20] Ibid, at 1027–28.
[21] Note that the 'rule' in *Lucas* could easily devolve into a standard, particularly if the state attempts to demonstrate that the regulation does nothing more than codify a pre-existing proscription under nuisance law. Indeed, in such a situation, the Court noted, one would have to analyse a number of factors, including 'the degree of harm to public lands and resources, or adjacent private property, posed by the claimant's proposed activities, the social value of the claimant's activities and their suitability to the locality in question, and the relative ease with which the alleged harm can be avoided through measures taken by the claimant and the government (or adjacent private landowners) alike'. Ibid, at 1031. This type of inquiry, however, is unlikely to invoke the Pricing Paradox identified above.

In a recent holding, however, the Supreme Court appears to have largely resuscitated the *Penn Central* test by expressly limiting a claimant's ability to conceptually manipulate the relevant 'denominator' for establishing a total taking. In *Tahoe-Sierra Preservation Council, Inc v Tahoe Regional Planning Agency*,[22] the Supreme Court confronted the question of whether a total development ban on plots adjoining Lake Tahoe constituted a regulatory taking when the ban was explicitly temporary in nature, pending the formulation of a regional development plan. In essence, the question raised in *Tahoe-Sierra* was whether a claimant could conceptually sever the short-term use of her property so as to render the temporary ban on development 'total' as to that specific use, thereby triggering the *Lucas* doctrine. In affirming the Ninth Circuit, a six-person majority of the Supreme Court held that Lucas was not applicable for such temporary takings, and that as such, the ban should be analysed under *Penn Central*. Because the regulation had been provisionally upheld below under the *Penn Central* standard, and never appealed, the Court concluded that no taking had occurred.

Consequently, after *Tahoe-Sierra*, it appears that *Penn Central* will continue to govern a significant portion of regulatory takings cases, and that the encroachment of various categorical exceptions (such as *Lucas* and its progeny) has likely subsided. In the main, then, evidence of one's investment-backed expectations (usually capitalised into price) remains relevant for determining whether a governmental regulation as to the use of one's property must be compensated under the takings doctrine.

Note that, unlike in the contractual setting, in a takings context, the effect of Pricing Paradox is not necessarily internalised by the parties. Indeed, if one's investment-backed expectations are partially (or wholly) reflected in a purchase price, then it is one that is set without direct state involvement. But it is the state that is a principal player (and payer) in any subsequent takings dispute. I shall consider the implications of this observation below.

Other Examples

Although it is beyond the scope of this chapter to canvass all doctrinal areas where the Pricing Paradox exists, it is not difficult to highlight numerous others in which the paradox can be seen either directly or indirectly through courts' embracing of standards that hinge, at least in part, on the parties' objectively measured expectations about the eventual legal status of an act or pattern of behaviour. In civil procedure, for example, there is a

---

[22] *Tahoe-Sierra Preservation Council v Tahoe Regulation Planning Agency* 122 S. Ct 1465 (2002).

large and well-established body of case law governing the conditions under which a court can exercise personal jurisdiction over a defendant who is domiciled in another state or country. While physical presence in the jurisdiction had historically been perceived as the requirement of the due process clause in the US Constitution, the so-called *Pennoyer* doctrine[23] subsequently was relaxed, almost certainly in response to increasing interstate and international commerce that significantly complicated jurisdictional disputes. Under the standard enunciated by *International Shoe Co v Washington*,[24] the due process clause was read to require not that the defendant actually be present within forum jurisdiction, but rather merely that she 'have certain minimum contacts with it such that the maintenance of the suit does not offend "traditional notions of fair play and substantial justice."'[25]

What, precisely, the minimum-contacts test entails has proven elusive in the years since *International Shoe*. In some circumstances, the Court has specified categories of cases in which the test is presumptively satisfied, such as when the defendant's contact with the forum state over time has been continuous and systematic.[26] In addition, single or sporadic contact may be sufficient under the doctrine if such contact is directly related to the wrong complained of.[27] In those cases that fall within the interstices, however, the minimum contacts test devolves into a question of expectations. Indeed, in just such a case, the Supreme Court in *World Wide Volkswagen Corp v Woodson*[28] measured the extent of the defendant's contacts through the lens of how foreseeable it was that the defendant would be sued in the forum state. The foreseeability of such litigation was an indicator of whether the defendant 'should have reasonably expected being haled into court there,' given the nature and substance of his contacts.

As with the examples given above, the reasonable expectation test announced in World Wide Volkswagen has a markedly self-referential nature, very much akin to the Pricing Paradox. This self-referential feature did not go unnoticed by Justice Brennan, who wrote in his dissent that the majority created this circularity by focusing foreseeability on legal status rather than on the likely destination of the product being produced:

> The Court suggests that this is the critical foreseeability rather than the likelihood that the product will go to the forum State. But the reasoning begs the

---

[23] See *Pennoyer v Neff* 95 US 714 (1877).
[24] *International Shoe Co v Washington* 326 US 310 (1945).
[25] *Ibid*, at 315, quoting *Milliken v Meyer* 311 US 457, 463 (1940). Under most accepted readings, the minimum contacts portion of the test must be satisfied before any inquiry into fair play and substantial justice occurs. *World-Wide Volkswagen Corp v Woodson* 444 US 286, 293, (1980).
[26] *Perkins v Benguet Consol Mining Co* 342 US 437 (1952).
[27] *McGee v International Life Ins Co* 355 US 220 (1957).
[28] 444 US 286, (1940).

question. A defendant cannot know if his actions will subject him to jurisdiction in another State until we have declared what the law of jurisdiction is.[29]

Indeed, if one presupposes that the Court would deny personal jurisdiction in a given forum, then it is reasonable for a potential defendant to expect that she will not be haled into court within that forum. Conversely, if one presupposes that *in personam* jurisdiction will be upheld, then one would reasonably expect to be subject to suit. As before, the presupposition creates the very conditions that control the doctrine, thereby fulfilling the prophecy of that proposition.[30]

Legal tests that circuitously turn on parties' expectations about the eventual outcome of the same legal test can be found in a number of other areas of law not considered above. The issue of retroactivity upon a change in law or new precedent, for instance, often centres around whether the risk of the change was reasonably foreseeable to the affected parties.[31] In tax law, penalties for evasion can often turn on whether a tax preparer acted with a good faith belief that there was a 'realistic possibility of success' for a particular type of avoidance strategy.[32] In criminal law, the Fourth Amendment right to privacy is governed by whether a suspect has 'a reasonable expectation of privacy.'[33] While these legal standards certainly vary in the degree to which they turn on expectations about future legal status (and one can easily find other doctrines that do not share this characteristic at all)[34] it is surprising just how large is the set of doctrines that do. Legal expectations appear to be a significant factor in many real-world situations. In what follows, I shall turn to consider the relative merits of such an approach.

---

[29] *Ibid* at 311 note 18. It is, of course, mildly surprising that Brennan was the one to notice this circularity when it was he himself who authored the pivotal majority in *Penn Central*. Multiple personality disorder among Supreme Court justices, however, is beyond the scope of this chapter.
[30] Similarly, in claim preclusion jurisprudence, there is a relatively self-referential standard for whether a counterclaim is compulsory or permissive (a determination that often determines the appropriateness of such a claim for federal court). See eg, *Plant v Blazer Finan Servs* 598 F 2d 1357 (5th Cir 1979) (articulating a multifactor test for counterclaims that can be interpreted as an inquiry into whether one could reasonably expect the two claims to be related as a matter of legal procedure).
[31] See eg, L Kaplow, 'An Economic Analysis of Legal Transitions' (1986) 99 *Harvard Law Review* 509.
[32] See § 6662 of the IRC. See also § 6664(c), under which penalties are avoided if there was a 'reasonable cause' for the taxpayer's position and the taxpayer acted in good faith.
[33] See *Katz v United States*, 389 US 347 (1967). See also RS Julie, 'High-Tech Surveillance Tools and the Fourth Amendment: Reasonable Expectations of Privacy in the Technological Age' (2000) 37 *American Criminal Law Review* 127.
[34] For example, at-will employees can be fired for any reason whatsoever short of discrimination, even though most at-will employees expect that they will be dismissed only if it is for cause. See eg, Epstein, above n 4.

III. EVALUATING THE PARADOX

As the previous section reveals, it is not particularly challenging to find a wealth of legal doctrines that share a particular self-referential characteristic. Under each of those doctrines analysed above, a party's expectations about her own legal rights or obligations play a pivotal role in determining whether those rights or obligations eventually materialise to begin with. Often, the link between expectation and outcome is indirect, mediated by an ostensibly objective measure, such as the pricing mechanism. Here, if the price clearly capitalises expectations about legal rights, then that premium can perpetuate a self-fulfilling prophecy.

At first blush, doctrines that induce the Pricing Paradox seem highly suspect. Indeed, as a number of authors have argued, the Pricing Paradox (and its conceptual cousins) exemplify a jurisprudential approach that spawns uncertainty, unpredictability and analytical mush. To be sure, some of these criticisms seem well-founded. But at the same time, if such self-referential doctrines were as unwieldy and imprudent as commentators suggest, one might predict that they would have been abandoned long ago. Indeed, much of the cost from the confusion inherent in such approaches is visited directly on the presiding judge herself: for it is she that is charged with the duty to navigate the doctrine in order to divine a parsimonious outcome. If these precedents were so unwieldy as to render the game unworthy of the candle (at least from the judge's perspective), then one would predict that they would die out over time, slowly distinguished and then extinguished by encroaching alternative rules that are held to govern most 'nearby' similarly situated cases. Moreover, even if judges did not bear a significant burden from such precedents themselves, one would conjecture that litigants would have incentives to challenge such precedents with greater frequency, a selection effect that can lead to similar types of jurisprudential erosion.

Interestingly, however, the predicted erosion does not appear to have enveloped the Pricing Paradox (at least in the areas described in the previous section). To the contrary, the recent *Tahoe-Sierra* case actually worked to limit *Lucas*, thereby protecting, preserving and arguably expanding the applicability of the expectation-based *Penn Central* doctrine in the takings context. The *Ziff-Davis* doctrine did even more, actually reversing what had at the time been a relatively homogenous historical practice in warranty law to explicitly introduce an expectation-based scheme for enforcement.[35] The ongoing attraction of self-referential law, notwithstanding its obvious shortcomings, is therefore curious and something that deserves further

---

[35] Similarly, *International Shoe* introduced expectations into a jurisdictional (Pennoyer) doctrine, that theretofore had been highly objective in nature.

investigation. In this section, I offer a few preliminary thoughts as to why (and under what circumstances) the Pricing Paradox may not only be defensible, but also may constitute a form of second-best legal policy.

As an aside, the metric by which I shall measure the relative merits of the Pricing Paradox centres principally on utilitarian efficiency considerations, leaving aside more deontological considerations that cannot be tied to rankable consequences. To be sure, this is not the only means for analysing these doctrines, though I will have little to say about those alternative approaches. As such, the thoughts expressed below at best provide a single perspective on what is certainly a much larger policy picture.

Because they tend in practice to be the most salient, it is perhaps prudent to begin enumerating the various costs that are frequently perceived to attend the Pricing Paradox. Three articulated costs appear to be the most prevalent. First, the Pricing Paradox can give rise to significant amounts of strategic behaviour because it provides parties with perverse incentives. In particular, a doctrine that turns on parties' respective expectations about their future legal status can significantly sharpen their incentives to engage in non-productive efforts solely to manipulate a court's subsequent inferences. In the context of the Pricing Paradox, this argument goes, buyers would have a strategic incentive to overpay for the property they purchase. Indeed, only by surrendering a premium could buyers ensure that the price reflected an expectation for future compensation (even one that is, ultimately, somewhat disingenuous). Such contrivances could arguably undermine the virtue of using competitive market prices to allocate goods and services, since price would no longer reflect the individual efforts of profit-maximising buyers and sellers to bargain for the best possible terms.

Secondly, the pricing paradox is thought to increase litigiousness, since it centres judicial attention on the appropriate interpretation of a price premium. Indeed, premia could occur for many reasons, and it is likely that a judicial attempt to decode the source of a premium will invite litigiousness among those making claims for compensation and those resisting them. For example, the state, in resisting a takings claim, might well argue that the price paid by a claimant does not reflect investment-backed expectations about regulatory status, but instead embodies some assessment of a distinct quality dimension unrelated to regulatory status. The net effect of this additional litigation contest, the argument goes, is to elevate the administrative costs of adjudication without significant enhancement of judicial accuracy.[36]

Finally, the pricing paradox is often said to spawn a fundamental indeterminacy in the evolution of legal rules. Should an unanticipated shock to parties' expectations occur, the argument goes, legal doctrine can suddenly

---

[36] See eg, A Bernardo, E Talley and I Welch, 'A Theory of Legal Presumptions' (2000) 16 *Journal of Law Economics and Organization* 1 (analysing litigation contests and how they are affected by evidentiary presumptions and burdens of proof).

and precipitously change to respond to those changed expectations. Consequently, there would be little certainty that today's precedent will remain stable tomorrow, thereby undercutting the integrity of the legal system and dampening investments that turn on a secure, predictable environment. Moreover, such unpredictable and non-representative evolutionary shifts can cause the expressive function of law to lose much of its force as either a normative guidepost or an informative signal.[37]

Notwithstanding the costs noted above, the Pricing Paradox may have a number of unappreciated benefits as well as compared with more rule-like counterparts. First, it is important to realise that most legal rules are promulgated in an atmosphere of significant complexity. The future is often costly, if not impossible, to predict, not only for parties writing contracts but also for courts in formulating case law. In such a complex environment, doctrinal flexibility may be just as important (if not more so) than reliability and stability of a particular doctrinal standard. A system made up of inflexible legal rules is likely to be one that falls into considerable disuse and disrepair, and is eventually abandoned by those it is meant to serve, at which point is serves no one.[38] Viewed in this sense, self-referential doctrines may play a valuable transitional role, not in spite of their unpredictability, but rather because of it. The introduction of the Pricing Paradox, for example, to a staid and encrusted legal doctrine, may provide a mechanism by which courts can switch to one that is more responsive to social circumstance. At the very least, such an introduction may invite litigants to come forward, providing courts with a new influx of information about whether the status quo ante is worth preserving.

This last point suggests a second important role that the Pricing Paradox can play: that of filtering information from the litigants to the court. In contracting environments, for example, the principal efficiency role of courts is to facilitate coordination among the contracting parties. In the case of risk allocation, for example, courts should attempt to interpret contracts in a way that systematically channels risk towards the party or parties that are (1) most able to bear it and (2) most able to avoid it. The identification of an implicit insurance premium in price can be enormously helpful in divining which of the two parties is the most efficient risk-bearer. But even beyond a contractual environment, price can conceivably signal information. In the takings context, for instance, a court may wish to collect information about the effects of a regulatory change. Because plausible uses of

---

[37] R McAdams, 'A Focal Point Theory of Expressive Law' (2000) 86 *Virginia Law Review* 1649. Also see R Scott, 'The Limits of Behavioral Theories of Law and Social Norms' (2000) 86 *Virginia Law Review* 1603.
[38] L Bernstein, 'Opting Out of the Legal System: Extralegal Contractual Relations in the Diamond Industry' (1992) 21 *Journal of Legal Studies* 115; L Bernstein, 'Private Commercial Law' in *New Palgrave Dictionary of Law and Economics* (1998).

Expectations and Legal Doctrine 199

property evolve over time (in *Penn Central*, for example, the technology for constructing high-rise office buildings was only around 15 years old at the time of passage of the Landmarks Preservation Act), it may not be well known to the court how costly a use restriction is on property owners. Here again, permitting litigation over property owners' expectations may be a way to collect information about the relative costs of a zoning restriction.

It is difficult to know, on a priori grounds, whether the costs of expectation-based doctrines are justified by their benefits. This is a difficult question for which I cannot offer a complete analysis here. However, it may be possible to identify circumstances in which the pricing paradox is more or less likely to be defensible on utilitarian grounds. This task will consume the balance of this chapter.

A Crude Example

In order to focus the discussion, consider for illustrative purposes a hypothetical negotiation (and subsequent transaction) between a seller S and a buyer B over a building that is currently zoned for either commercial or residential use. Assume (for simplicity) that S places no intrinsic value on owning the land (eg, he does not live in the town or operate a business), and that B is clearly the highest valuer of the property regardless of its use. Nevertheless, the value that B places on the land depends critically on two contingencies. First, she is most interested in using the property as a piano showroom, which would require high-quality, commercial-grade construction in the building's support structure—a characteristic that is difficult to observe directly. If the building is commercial grade, B can earn US$500,000 in profits from operating the building (in present-value terms). If, however, the building is only residential grade, B would choose instead to occupy it solely as a residence, which she values only at US$200,000 (again in present-value terms).

Suppose that S explicitly warrants that the building is of commercial grade. In addition, B is concerned that the local zoning board may later decide to rezone the property for residential use only, since there are currently no operating businesses within the multi-use district. Should this regulatory change occur, then she could only occupy the building as a residence, in which case she would only capture her US$200,000 value as described above. In tabular form, then, B's value of the building is as shown in Table 9.1.

Table 9.1 Value of the building

	Not rezoned	*Rezoned residential*
Commercial grade construction	US$500,000	US$200,000
Residential grade construction	US$200,000	US$200,000

After inspecting the building, B learns information leading her to conclude that (with high probability) the building is not of commercial grade, but S continues to warrant that it is. In the midst of this uncertainty, the parties must negotiate a price term for the building (which, for simplicity, I shall assume is equal to B's willingness to pay). Under the above scenario, consider how the *Ziff-Davis* and *Penn Central* doctrines would affect both negotiations and the final adjudication as to outcome. In other words, suppose that courts would examine the price paid by B as indirect evidence of whether the transaction manifested an expectation about quality or the future use of the property. If the price clearly reflected such expectations, then the court would afford B a remedy (either from a breached warranty or a regulatory taking, as the case may be).

Consider first the asserted costs associated with the Pricing Paradox, and in particular the incentive to overpay strategically for property so as to capitalise expectations into price. Inspection of this example reveals immediately that B would have an incentive to pay more than US$200,000 for the property. Indeed, paying only US$200,000 would signal to a court that B expected that either (a) the warranty would be unenforceable; (b) that residential rezoning was certain to occur; or (c) both. If, for example, it were possible for B to alter her rights by paying a single dollar over US$200,000 for the property, this type of insurance would be cheap to purchase indeed. But even if the underlying doctrine required that the premium paid satisfy some measure of materiality (say, US$1,000), it seems quite plausible that B would still willingly bid above US$200,000, so as to secure her rights. This type of behaviour could easily lead the market price to divorce itself from the true expected value of the property, particularly if either of the necessary contingencies for high value were unlikely to obtain.

To be sure, the Pricing Paradox may lead buyers to engage in a form of strategic overbidding, which can trigger the attendant inefficiencies noted above. However, the likelihood of such behaviour occurring would be mitigated by at least two factors. First, when attempting to divine B's expectations, courts would likely have to measure the 'premium' paid against some benchmark market price, which probably would be the sale price of similarly situated properties in similarly zoned areas. If all (or even many) such buyers were analogously affected by the incentive to overbid strategically, then one would expect each buyer to attempt to bid a premium similar to B's. However, when buyers do so, the benchmark price of comparable real estate will rise sharply, thereby ratcheting up the premium that B will be forced to offer. Once the benchmark price rises sufficiently, B may actually have an incentive to bid significantly less than the benchmark, thereby sacrificing her future legal claims for a possibly steep discount.

Moreover, the strategic incentive to overbid is, at least in some contexts, countered by an equally strong strategic incentive on the other side of the transaction. The seller, S, may be worried about the enforceability of his warranty, aware of the fact that a material premium paid by B would cause a court to put S in the place of an insurer. If S's intent was merely to 'puff' about the value of the property rather than to warrant its value, then he will have a strong incentive to retreat from his representations at the time that B offers a premium on the price. Thus, it is far from clear that B's incentive to overpay will necessarily culminate in a premium actually being paid.

Note, however, that S's incentive to check overbidding turns centrally on his realisation that the risk will be imposed on him personally. In the takings context, the risk of a rezoning restriction is not one that S would generally have to insure; moreover, S would still benefit by having a higher sales price. Thus, when regulatory status rather than contractual obligations are at stake, both B and S may have an incentive to edge the price above that which would prevail in a non-strategic world.

Another potential cost of the Pricing Paradox (noted above) is the assertion that it will engender greater litigiousness among the relevant parties later on. Here, however, the case seems far from clear. On the one hand, the example above is one where there are two possible contingencies that might cause B's value to be low, and this fact may cause an increase in litigation. Suppose, for example, that B pays US$300,000 for the property, and subsequent to the purchase, it is rezoned residential and B also discovers that it is not of commercial grade. In defending against B's warranty claim, S may attempt to escape liability by arguing that the overriding aspect of B's expectations hinged on the property's commercial zoning status rather than that of its quality. As such, S will assert, B cannot prove causation in the warranty suit unless she first can recover on the basis of a takings claim. Because the city can essentially raise the same argument, B might be forced to become maximally litigious in order to recover anything.

Again, it is plausible that the Pricing Paradox can induce the type of litigiousness described above. At the same time, however, this argument turns on a number of assumptions about how courts handle causation matters; nothing in the Pricing Paradox preordains the outcome asserted above. Courts could, for example, require something other than but-for causation in either or both of the above actions, and the conclusion would be changed considerably. Moreover, the above argument ignores the fact that if courts did not use price to proxy for expectations, the litigation process might be exacerbated through other means. Imagine, for example, how S might go about proving B's disbelief of the warranty in the absence of using readily available indicia like the price B paid. Clearly, while self-referential doctrines may cause certain parts of litigation to become more expensive, they can (and do) often economise elsewhere.

Finally, consider the assertion that an expectations-based doctrine may lead to unpredictable and capricious evolution of the underlying legal standard. While the example above is not capable of directly evaluating that claim (at least as currently constructed), one might at least posit that a Pricing

Paradox doctrine may be capable of certain types of undesirable cycling. For instance, suppose, as noted above, that courts measure price premia relative to a benchmark market price, and suppose that all buyers initially believe they will not recover for either a breached warranty or a taking. Consequently, all sales would be at a price of US$200,000, and it seems likely that a handful of buyers may have an incentive to offer premia. Once such a practice catches on, however, market price would likely increase and the strategy of offering a premium would become prohibitively expensive, at which point buyers would start defecting back to the strategy of offering US$200,000 again. This process of switching strategies may never settle down to a single equilibrium, and along with it, the underlying legal status of B's claim would likely oscillate as well.

While the prospects for cycling of this sort seem relevant, they must be offset against the advantages of flexibility and signalling (noted above) that the Pricing Paradox provides. These advantages are particularly salient when the underlying values at risk are in a constant state of flux. For example, suppose that the relative value of commercial real estate could vary for B between US$200,000 (ie, his residential-use valuation) and US$1 million. The justifiability both of not enforcing the warranty and of an uncompensated taking would likely vary as well. Indeed, when the relative value of commercial real estate is high, B has much more at stake—a fact that both the warranting party S and the city should take into account when acting themselves (at least from an economic efficiency perspective). A doctrine that reflects the Pricing Paradox may be a way of measuring whether such a shock to underlying values has occurred, and if so, whether doctrine should be altered to match it.

Moreover, the Pricing Paradox may be a particularly good mechanism to encourage coordination between B and S about who should bear market risk (particularly in the case of the warranty). Indeed, it is the parties themselves that are best able to gauge whether the underlying contingencies affecting contracting have occurred. If, for some reason, the parties have resolved that S is the best insurer, they can attempt to signal that to a court by including a premium in the price.

Synthesis

Although the analysis above has been relatively brief, it suggests a few helpful intuitions that permit at least some speculation on the conditions under which a Pricing Paradox doctrine (or other expectation-referencing doctrine) is most justifiable. Based on the discussion above, such a doctrine is most likely to be prudent when:

(1) *The underlying economic environment is relatively unpredictable.* As noted above, a volatile environment (in the sense of fluctuating

economic valuations) enhances the virtues of doctrinal flexibility—a fact that turns the indeterminacy of the Pricing Paradox into what is conceivably a significant benefit.
(2) *The value of coordination is large.* Unpredictability is not sufficient alone to justify the Pricing Paradox. Indeed, the parties themselves have to be in a good position relative to the court to realise and assess how the environment has changed. It is this informational advantage that can be incorporated into price, which in turn can serve as a form of reliable signal. If courts were better informed than the parties about unpredictable swings in value, such a signal would serve no real purpose.
(3) *The stakes are largely internalised.* Recall that in the warranty context above, the seller would not be willing to allow the buyer to bid up the price unless the seller was the more efficient insurer. In contrast, the seller's incentives in the takings context are likely consistent with the buyer's—for the seller does not bear any downside risk from a price premium. Rather, it is the state that would be held responsible in some subsequent takings case if the price premium were held to reflect the buyer's investment-backed expectations.
(4) *Expectations about legal status predominate.* Finally, the analysis above has presumed throughout that expectations about future legal status 'mattered' to the parties in a material way, and were not overshadowed by other considerations having little or nothing to do with the underlying legal question. This is probably a strong assumption in many contexts, particularly those in which the parties are relatively confident about the future state of the world, thereby rendering other contingencies remote. Because of their remoteness, legal contingencies in these contexts are unlikely to affect the pricing process, and thus the premium (if any) constitutes a relatively impoverished and unreliable signal. In such situations, the Pricing Paradox is probably also tautological.

These considerations suggest that at least *ceteris paribus,* contractual settings are probably more promising than regulatory settings for the utilisation of the Pricing Paradox by courts. In regulatory settings, the parties setting price may have a strong incentive to collude in order to manipulate the underlying legal rule. In contrast, contractual settings (where no outside insurer is involved) provide a natural check on the incentive to manipulate price, since it is the seller who will be held responsible if such manipulation succeeds.

At the same time, of course, it is not impossible for the Pricing Paradox to be of value in regulatory contexts as well. Particularly in volatile environments where coordination is important, the threat of collusion between the parties may be a small price to pay for the flexibility that is required of the doctrine. In such situations, however, the case must be made on that basis alone, and it therefore is likely to represent a relatively modest set of circumstances.

IV. CONCLUSION

This chapter has focused on a particular type of self-referential paradox that transcends both private and public law. I have argued that the Pricing Paradox, while somewhat circular, may also play a critical role in facilitating legal transitions within a volatile economic environment. At the same time, however, courts should be judicious about the contexts in which they promulgate and enforce such expectation-based doctrines. Particularly when the parties to the transaction that establishes price do not collectively bear the legal risk at issue, the dangers of strategic abuse of the rule are significant. For this reason, courts might do well to limit such doctrines largely (though perhaps not exclusively) to contractual and quasi-contractual environments where this collective risk-bearing requirement is met.

10

Equality as a Paradoxical Ideal or Respectful Treatment versus Equal Treatment

YITZHAK BENBAJI*

I. INTRODUCTION: THREE CONCEPTS OF EQUALITY

EQUALITY IS PERHAPS one of the most fundamental ideas in legal, political and philosophical discourses. Egalitarians believe that equality is an ideal under the banner of which people fight against racism, sexism and other wrongful discriminatory practices. In somewhat different contexts, they believe that the same egalitarian ideals command a reduction of social and economic differences.

It has long been noticed, however, that the word 'equality' is used in many different senses. In some sense, it expresses a formal ideal.[1] To be formally just or fair, a state or an institution should apply its guiding principles universally. For example, an office should not be inaccessible to one just because of one's race. This is true, unless it is a matter of law, principle or declared policy that the office in question is *equally* inaccessible to *all* people of that race. As this example makes clear, some policies are utterly unjust and radically anti-egalitarian, however universal they are.[2]

A second and more substantive notion of equality was developed within the Aristotelian tradition. The famous formula, drawn from Aristotle, is

---

* I would like to thank Michal Alberstein, Hagit Benbaji, Harry Frankfurt, Shai Lavi, Shahar Lifshitz, Ron Shapira, Daniel Statman, Saul Smilansky, Oren Perez, Michael Walzer and (especially) Yoram Egozi, for helpful comments and discussions.

[1] I use Larry Temkin's categorisation. See LS Temkin, 'Inequality: A Complex, Individualistic and Comparative Notion' (2001) 11 *Philosophical Issues* 327 pt I, s A. For the full discussion, see LS Temkin, *Inequality* (Oxford, Oxford University Press, 1993).

[2] Sometimes formal equality concerns more specific issues. For instance, formal equality means that each party is seen as having equal freedom to negotiate a contract, irrespective of the economic stress they are under, because it is conceived as irrelevant to signing a contract (unless it falls under the formal exceptions, such as duress). This is not the notion I use here.

'similar treatment for those who are similarly situated.' The key notion is relevancy: the Aristotelian imperative prohibits disadvantaging a person based on irrelevant criteria. True, under some readings, this slogan too has no specific instructive power. Kantianism, utilitarianism and, at least according to Sen,[3] every other moral theory, respect it, while debating which criteria are morally relevant.[4] Yet, in both the legal literature and in practice, the slogan is commonly conceived as a kind of rational ideal: it allows unequal treatment, as far as such a treatment can be rationalised by some *valid* objective. This reading of the slogan assumes,[5] as we do in real-life situations, that we have a true substantive conception of what is reasonable. It also assumes that maximising utility is a reasonable objective. The Aristotelian ideal, as it is commonly understood, can thus permit any substantively reasonable unequal treatment.

Can this notion of equality explain, for example, the fight against gender discrimination? Indeed, gender seems irrelevant, at least in most cases. But is the irrelevance of gender what *triggers* egalitarians' objections to gender-based inequalities? Is irrelevancy *what defines the scope* of egalitarian objections to gender-based inequalities? It is fairly obvious, though their views may be somewhat controversial, that at least some egalitarians believe that gender-based inequalities are wrong, even where differences between men and women can fully rationalise the inequalities in question. I wish to focus on this form of 'egalitarianism.'

Here is a recent example of such an egalitarian position. In his attack on egalitarianism, Professor Christopher J Peters argues that gender discrimination, as well as every other instance of wrongful inequality, is prohibited just because of the right not to be disadvantaged based on 'irrelevant' criterion.[6] He adopts the Aristotelian formula, but *refuses* classifying it as a formulation of an egalitarian ideal. It has nothing to do with equality, he claims. Professor Kenneth W Simons[7] disagrees with respect to the normative question. There are, he believes, wrongful inequalities that the Aristotelian formula permits. He observes that 'gender is often at least minimally "rational" or relevant to permissible ends of government,' and furthermore, that 'even racial classifications are sometimes relevant to legitimate government ends; their invalidity does not depend on their being "irrelevant."'[8] Equality, Simons claims, is a moral ideal that the Aristotelian formula does not capture. Interestingly

---

[3] A Sen, *Inequality Reexamined* (Cambridge, Mass, Harvard University Press, 1993) ix.

[4] See eg, B Barry, 'Equality,' *Encyclopedia of Ethics*, vol 1, 323. As Western notes, the requirement for 'equal treatment' is usually based on a factual claim that we 'are' equal. See P Western, 'The Empty Idea of Equality' (1982) 95 *Harvard Law Review* 263 at 266–67.

[5] See TM Scanlon, *What We Owe to Each Other* (Cambridge, Mass, Harvard University Press, 1998) 17.

[6] CJ Peters, 'Equality Revisited' (1997) 110 *Harvard Law Review* 1210 at 1220, 1254–55, 1259-62.

[7] KW Simons, 'The Logic of Egalitarian Norms' (1999) 80 *Boston University Law Review* 693.

[8] *Ibid*, at 738.

enough, both theorists *agree* with regard to a conceptual issue: equality cannot be construed as a *merely* rational ideal, the Aristotelian policy is not 'egalitarian' in the sense that both Simons and Peters have in mind.

Thus, a third notion of equality is clearly needed. Let me present it by pointing to the limits of the Aristotelian formula. Suppose that, due to a fair competition, a certain person became badly off, as he had lost a well-paid office position to a much more talented competitor. Clearly, talent-based inequality is Aristotelian-permitted. Yet, according to comparative egalitarians, this very fact—namely, that there is a good reason to generate inequality—is undesirable. More specifically, egalitarians believe that it is inherently bad, or unfair, for some to be worse off than others through no fault or choice of their own. As John Rawls famously puts it, the natural endowment is arbitrarily distributed.[9] Hence, in most cases, the loser whose condition is worse off than his competitor is not worse off due to his own fault.[10] Following Larry Temkin,[11] I shall call this principle 'equality as comparability.'[12]

In this chapter, I would like to ask the following question: what are the guiding principles for egalitarians which lead them to judge gender-based inequalities as being wrong? Of course, egalitarians do not constitute a homogeneous group; hence, in the next section (section II), I shall clarify the

---

[9] True, Rawls says that 'the natural distribution is neither just not unjust. ... These are simply natural facts.' But then he continues, 'caste societies are unjust because ... the basic structure of these societies incorporates the arbitrariness found in nature. But there is no necessity for men to resign themselves to these contingencies' (J Rawls, *A Theory of Justice* (Cambridge, Mass, Harvard University Press, 1971) 102). The belief that natural distribution is morally arbitrary constitutes one of the more powerful arguments for justice as fairness. For a clear presentation, see W Kymlicka, *Contemporary Political Philosophy* (Oxford, Clarendon Press, 1990) 55–58.

[10] We have to assume, of course, that the agent is to be blamed for his laziness. In trying to spell out this moral intuition, GA Cohen and Richard Arneson elaborated the so-called 'luck egalitarianism'. See GA Cohen, 'On the Currency of Egalitarian Justice' (1989) 99 *Ethics* 906 and R Arneson, 'Equality and Equality of Opportunity for Welfare' (1989) 55 *Philosophical Studies* 77. Arneson modifies his view in his 'Luck Egalitarianism and Prioritarianism' (2000) 110 *Ethics* 339. For Dworkin's attack on equality of welfare, see R Dworkin, 'What is Equality, Part 1: Equality of Welfare' (1981) 10 *Philosophy and Public Affairs* 185.

[11] See Temkin, 'Inequality,' above n 1, at 331.

[12] Note the non-instrumental character of comparative egalitarianism; it is not that inequality is bad because it has bad consequences, such as humiliation or partiality, nor is equality good because it has good consequences, like respectful treatment and well-being. Distinguishing between instrumental and non-instrumental egalitarian ideals is tricky. For a statement of the distinction, see Temkin, 'Inequality' above n 1, at pt I, s B. In essence, Parfit has this distinction in mind when he distinguishes between teleological and deontological egalitarianism. See D Parfit, 'Equality or Priority?' *The Lindley Lecture*, (University of Kansas, 1995) 4–10. Due to the principle of diminishing marginal utility, utilitarianism often recommends equal distribution. This does make utilitarianism a version of instrumental egalitarianism. Among instrumental egalitarians, there are some who believe that equal distribution *necessarily* maximises utility. These philosophers are closer to comparative egalitarianism. Yet, their belief is clearly false. See Harry Frankfurt, 'Equality as Moral Ideal,' reprinted in his *The Importance of What We Care About* (Cambridge, Cambridge University Press, 1988) 138–44; see also Parfit, 'Equality or Priority?' at 27.

scope of my discussion. I will show that some gender-based inequalities are conceived by some egalitarians to be wrong *and yet* fully rational. In section III, I shall ask whether the comparative ideal can explain the beliefs of *these* egalitarians. My answer is no. Following Temkin, I claim that comparative equality is at best an indeterminate, or maybe a paradoxical, ideal. Embarrassingly enough, comparative equality will often show that in *some* cases *all* possible choices are unfair, without telling us *how* unfair these choices are compared to one another. Thus, equality as comparability may explain some of the egalitarians' moral judgments, but in many disturbing and central cases, it can also *lead* them nowhere. Bearing in mind this character of comparative equality, in section IV, I sketch an overlooked ethics of distribution (I name it 'the respectful treatment theory'), which I believe best explains many egalitarian convictions. The doctrine is distinctive in being weaker than comparative egalitarianism but stronger than the Aristotelian imperative.

Before getting down to business, however, I would like to make a methodological remark. I am interested in a descriptive rather than normative question; I ask, what *actually explains* egalitarians' convictions, rather than which principles *should* guide them. Yet, I am committed to the charity principle in interpretation. That is, I assume that if a model or principle is inherently problematic, then, other things being equal, it is a less attractive candidate for *explaining* any given policy. Thus, I reject some explanations of the egalitarian convictions when they lead nowhere, or at least not decisively so. My rejection therefore is contingent; it is contingent upon the plausibility of the alternative I propose in the closing section. That is to say that my thesis cannot fall under either side of the classical distinction: it is neither purely descriptive, nor is it purely prescriptive.

II. SPECIFYING THE EXPLANANDUM

Until the mid-1990s, women had no opportunity to be pilots in the Israel Defense Forces (IDF); they were not admitted to the preliminary tests held by the Air Force. By appealing to 'the equality principle,' an Israeli woman named Alice Miller challenged this policy. After describing the advantages of being a pilot in Israeli society, Miller claimed that her right to equal treatment was violated: she was discriminated against for being a woman.[13]

For the sake of simplicity, I stipulate a response by the IDF spokesman—freeing myself from any commitment to the historical facts. According to this response, Miller might be right in claiming that she could be a successful

---

[13] Supreme Court Case 4541/94 *Alice Miller v Minster of Security and three others*, 48(4) ('*Miller*').

pilot. It is, however, too costly to check whether or not this is the case. Selecting and training one skilled pilot from a group of 500 men with the highest health profile is 50 percent less expensive than selecting and training a skilled pilot from a mixed group of men and women (who enjoy the same health profile) The same is true, according to the IDF spokesman, of a group composed of perfectly healthy and minimally near-sighted men. Indeed, Alvin (Alice's brother) might also be a skilful pilot; yet, he is minimally near-sighted, and hence, according to the IDF spokesman, Alvin's potential for being a good pilot would be too expensive to examine.

To return to the historical facts for a moment, the court's decision was in Alice's favour. Interestingly, the judges did not doubt the complex factual system of utilitarian considerations put forward by the IDF. Also, it was taken for granted that the alleged considerations proved that, from a utilitarian standpoint, allowing Alice to enter the competitive process would be unjustified. The unequal treatment was based on a relevant difference, hence it would be permitted from a utilitarian standpoint. Why, then, did Miller win the case? Which egalitarian principle best explains the Court's decision?

First, consider two radical responses to this question, which undermine the Aristotelian framework itself, as well as its underlying notions of relevancy and rationality. In one radical view, the existing power relations within society determine what is called 'rational' and 'relevant' in this society. Unequal treatment is not based on *natural inequalities*, since there are no natural inequalities; there are only *neutral differences* that are exploited by the more powerful group in its own favour. Accordingly, the 'relevant criteria' test has no moral basis. To put it in Iris Young's words, 'since impartial, value neutral, scientific measures of merit do not exist, I argue that a major issue of justice must be who decides what are the appropriate qualifications for a given position.'[14] I can ignore this view here, since I am interested in explaining how judges, philosophers and legal theorists who take it that the Aristotelian imperative is a self-evident rational ideal deal with gender-based inequalities.

Young's text, however, can be read in a less radical way. According to the alternative reading, Young does not deny that many specific instances of gender-based inequalities are reasonable, nor does she debate the moral significance of such reasons. She does insist, however, that there are reasons only for micro-level inequalities, and that these reasons consist mostly of other micro-level inequalities. In fact, gender-based inequalities support each other, so that together they constitute a system whose oppressive character is to be explained by manmade historical causes, causes that involve

---

[14] IM Young, *Justice and the Politics of Difference* (Princeton, NJ, Princeton University Press, 1990) 193.

discriminatory practices and offensive world-views. Young envisages a system in which there are fewer gender-based inequalities and claims that it is morally preferable to the current one.

As far as it goes, the view attributed here to Young might be true. Yet, thus understood, Young's view does not have the immediate practical implications that can justify the egalitarian responses to gender-based inequalities. Indeed, a more egalitarian sociological structure, in which it would be reasonable to give Alice Miller an opportunity to be an IDF pilot, can be imagined. We might suppose that this structure is morally preferable to ours. Even so, this is not a reason to disqualify the IDF's unequal treatment, given the assumption that it is reasonable *within* the system in which we live. The struggle against a specific instance of inequality is to be justified only if there is a reason to believe that abolishing that non-egalitarian policy is a first step towards a comprehensive change of the system. It is doubtful, however, that judges see themselves as long-term reformers of policy, given positivist views of jurisprudence and the constitutional separation of powers. But even leaving theoretical considerations aside, judges simply lack any measure to make sure that any given policy is the necessary first step to social change. Given my commitment to charitable interpretation, I reject this explanation of the Court's decision: it attributes to the Court a position that is as theoretically problematic as it is practically improvable.

So much for the radical responses to our story. Let us turn now to views that suggest that the complaint against the IDF policy can be made within the Aristotelian framework. First, it might be conceded that gender differences are relevant. Still, the amount of inequality generated by the challenged policy is not proportional to the differences that are supposed to justify it. If this were the case, Aristotelians would oppose the IDF policy. Alternatively, and much more interestingly, Aristotelians might claim that the gender differences to which the IDF appealed are only 'accidentally' relevant. That is, they overlie other, more basic properties that are the 'truly' relevant features for the issue at hand.

Let me elaborate the second point first. Suppose that many more men than women view service as a pilot in the IDF as being challenging and prestigious. Call this assumption 'the supervening fact.' Recall the statistical fact that supposedly justifies the challenged policy: selecting and training one skilled pilot from a group of 500 men is 50 percent less expensive than selecting and training a skilled pilot from a mixed group of men and women. Let us call this 'the supervened fact.' Finally, assume that the supervening fact fully explains the supervened fact. Suppose, that is, that the reason many fewer women than men are qualified pilots is fully explained by differences in their motivational states and beliefs. In this case, the truly relevant differences have nothing to do with gender. If so, and if unequal treatment is justified from the utilitarian standpoint, egalitarians would demand that the selecting criterion be based on the truly relevant difference—which is a difference in motivation rather than in gender. To be sure, Alice Miller would pass the alternative test.

It seems plausible that gender differences are never truly relevant; they are always to be elucidated by more basic supervening facts. It should also be noted that gender differences are visible and thus very easily recognised. Thus, on the one hand, the visibility of gender should make us suspicious of any gender-based unequal treatment. For, possibly, basing the needed criterion on the truly relevant might be doable at relatively low cost, in which case, if the inequality in question is based on gender, it is a wrongful discrimination by the Aristotelian lights. Yet, on the other hand, there might be cases in which this is not so. After all, the truly relevant features are, by their nature, more basic, and hence tracking them might be very expensive. Thus, at least conceptually, it is possible that, despite being only accidentally relevant, gender is the best (economically) relevant criterion for unequal treatment.

Some egalitarians accept that, in reality, there are cases of the second type: cases in which, from the Aristotelian standpoint, gender is the most utilitarian, most efficient and hence most rational criterion for a necessary unequal treatment. The truly relevant is hidden, and the utilitarian consideration against exposing it is sufficiently weighty. These egalitarians object to gender-based unequal treatment even in such cases. Simons is a clear example. He acknowledges that 'even racial classifications are sometimes relevant to legitimate government ends; their invalidity does not depend on their being "irrelevant."' He would approve the court's ruling in Miller's case even if the statistical facts alluded to by the IDF spokesman fully rationalised disadvantaging Alice; 'the relevance of relevance is much less than [Aristotelians like] Peters believes.'[15] Similarly, in discussing the notion of equality, Rohd observes that the American equal-protection analysis has been developed largely within the Aristotelian tradition, and that 'the focus on whether challenged classifications track some existing differences between the sexes has obscured the disadvantages that follow from such differences ... We must insist not just on equal treatment but on Woman's treatment as equal.'[16]

These quotes clearly suggest that some egalitarians believe that their ideal would rule out certain cases of unequal treatment, which would not be excluded by the Aristotelian standards mentioned above. Indeed, such an unequal treatment is wrong, even when it is proportional and the truly relevant would be an impractical criterion. It is wrong even when it is Aristotelian permitted. Reading closely the main verdict in *Miller* gives the same impression: Dalia Dorner J has in mind a moral ideal that *defeats* the Aristotelian ideal.

---

[15] Simons, above n 7, at 739.
[16] Quoted by Dorner J in *Miller*, above n 13, at s 6.

In conclusion, it is inescapably clear that at least some egalitarians—and upon these I wish to focus—view some cases of unequal treatment as wrong, even where such treatment is rational. Equalising Alice's condition seems desirable, despite the fact that she has been disadvantaged for cogent reasons. Should we conclude that the decision in the reconstructed *Miller* case is based on comparative egalitarianism? In the next section, I will argue for a negative answer.

III. COMPARATIVE EQUALITY AS AN INDETERMINATE OR EVEN PARADOXICAL IDEAL[17]

If not the Aristotelian formula, what does explain these egalitarians' responses to *Miller*-like cases? The belief in the comparative egalitarian ideal, whose defenders appeal to the Rawlsian critique regarding the arbitrariness of natural distribution, seems to be the most promising candidate.[18] I argue in this section that this interpretive route is, ultimately, a dead end. Note, however, that my argument is not intended to be a refutation of the comparative model of equality. Rather, it aims at proving that it does not prescribe anything specific in some of the central cases, and hence, that interpreting the egalitarians' struggles as based in the ideal of comparative equality is problematic.

For the purposes of this section, I shall take it that egalitarians have come to an agreement regarding the 'equality of what?' question.[19] They believe, say, that opportunities should be equalised, at least in some of the cases where a utilitarian strategy would recommend unequal distribution of them. Additionally, I shall suppose that a person who has more opportunities is 'better off' than is a person who has fewer. Now imagine a community composed of a hundred individuals, and imagine two levels of well-being A and B, where A is much higher than B in terms of welfare. Next, consider the following three cases:

---

[17] This section roughly sketches the main argument in Temkin, 'Inequality,' above n 1, at pt II. For the full discussion, see Temkin, *Inequality*, above n 1.

[18] It is not, however, the only candidate for explaining the egalitarian response, nor is it the only Rawlsian response to our question. Rawlsians might find another natural candidate. Parfit names the doctrine I have in mind 'The Priority View,' and in Temkin's book, it is named 'extended humanitarianism.' According to this doctrine, benefiting people matters more, the worse off these people are. Like comparative egalitarianism, the priority view has a built-in bias towards equality. Yet, I believe that this view cannot help us to understand the egalitarian response to gender-based inequalities. Even if we assume (as I shall do in the text shortly) that Alice is worse off than she might have been because of the IDF's unequal treatment, it is certainly possible that equalising her condition would worsen the condition of others who are worse off than her. If this is the case, the prioritarians would be reluctant to benefit her. This is enough to show that the priority view is no better than comparative equality.

[19] The 'equality of what?' debate starts with A Sen, 'Equality of What' in S McMurrin (ed), *Tanner Lectures on Human Values* (Cambridge, Cambridge University Press, 1980). For the two very well-known answers, see Dworkin, above n 10, and R Dworkin 'What is Equality, Part 2: Equality of Resources' (1981) 10 *Philosophy and Public Affairs* 283.

(a) Case I: 95 individuals are at level A and five are at B;
(b) Case II (the 'Middle Case'): half at A and half at B;
(c) Case III: Five at A and 95 at B.

I treat these cases as theoretical 'stations' in a continuous process that begins with Case I, passes through the Middle Case, and ends with Case III. How would the inequality in one situation be compared to the inequality in the others? As Temkin shows, comparative egalitarianism seems to have various cogent readings that imply three *incompatible* answers to this question.

Consider the egalitarian formula, 'it is inherently bad that some are worse off than others,' from which it follows that, as far as equality is concerned, the best state of affairs consists of absolute equality. If so, then from the *pure* egalitarian standpoint, it does not really matter whether all individuals are at A or at B. Hence, Cases I and III are equally preferable to the Middle Case, since they symmetrically deviate from absolute equality, while the Middle Case is the maximal deviation from it. In other words, in the transition from I to III, matters first get worse, and then, after arriving at Case II, improve again. Call this ranking R1. To put this in a numbered form:

R1, first things get worse and then better, since
(R1-1) Case 0, where all are at A, and Case IV, where all are at B, are perfect (from the egalitarian standpoint).
(R1-2) The deviation of Case I from Case 0 = the deviation of Case III from Case IV.
(R1-3) In the transition from Case I to Case III, the deviation of the Middle Case from absolute equality is maximal.

A different line of argument would also support R1: in Case I, only a relatively insignificant number of people can complain, but their complaint is significant—they are worse off than the many others who are well off. In Case III, though a significant number of people can complain, their complaint is relatively insignificant: after all, they are no worse off than the vast majority. Again, Case II, in which a significant number of people, half, have a *significant* complaint, seems to be the worst.

However, the egalitarian formula could equally imply another way of conceptualising the issue. Note that in Case I, it would be very easy for the majority to elevate such a tiny number of worse-off. Hence, the worse-off in Case I are especially victimised, as they could have become much better-off at almost no cost for the majority. Every inequality is bad, but an inequality that can be remedied so easily is particularly bad. According to this line of thought, in the transition from Case I to Case III, matters get better. Temkin supports this intuition by observing that we are more sensitive to a situation where a particular person or a small number of people is singled out for discriminatory treatment. In fact, this seems to be 'the paradigmatic case of where we judge a harmful discrimination to be grossly unfair'.[20] To put it more formally, when moving from Case I to Case III, the second possible ranking would be R2:

R2, things get better, since
(R2-1) Inequality is worse, the easier it is to abolish it.
(R2-2) It is easier to elevate the Bs in Case I than it is in Case II, while doing so in Case II is easier than it is in Case III.

Finally, here is another way of ranking these cases: think why, from the egalitarian standpoint, it is at least intuitively bad that more and more people become poor, while the number of the well-off is in constant decline. Surely, one of the reasons is the very fact that the worse-off are so numerous, relative to the fortunate few who are well-off. This line of thought would directly lead to ranking Case I as the best state of affairs. Accordingly, in the transition from Case I to Case III, matters get worse:

R3, matters get worse, since
(R3-1) Inequality is worse if more people suffer from it.
(R3-2) In the transition from Case I to Case III, the number of well-off is in constant decline.

Let me briefly analyse the *Miller* case in light of R1, R2 and R3. Suppose that, thanks to the court's decision, Alice has an opportunity to serve as a pilot. Do matters get worse or better as a result of this decision, insofar as comparative equality is concerned? By letting Alice in, all women can now benefit from the new opportunity. Therefore, near-sighted Alvin finds himself sharing the fate of lacking the opportunity of being an IDF pilot with a much *smaller* group of people. Hence, after the court's decision, things improved according to R3; alas, they worsened, according to R2. Consider the R2 perspective in more detail. It says, in effect, that attending to Alice's complaint makes Alvin's stronger than it was before, such that, as far as equality is concerned, the benefit for Alice makes things worse overall rather than better. Hence, the court is justified in its ruling only if not merely women but also near-sighted men are given the opportunity to be IDF pilots.

Finally, in accordance with R1, determining whether matters got better or worse consists of determining whether or not the court's decision moves Israeli society closer to a Middle Case situation. Matters become worse if it does; otherwise, they become better. In fact, the puzzle of measuring inequality in light of R1 is even more perplexing, since it is utterly unclear

---

[20] Temkin, 'Inequality,' above n 1, at 342.

what the comparative egalitarians' frame of reference should be. The difficulty is this: the Millers belong to many subsocieties, and, interpreted in accordance with R1, the legal system has the goal of absolute equality of opportunities in one of these subsocieties. Now, the attempt to determine whether or not we get closer to a Middle Case situation is pointless, before determining who 'we' are. Note that, on reflection, the natural tendency to take the general Israeli population as the immediate frame of reference might seem misplaced, given the fact that there are some sectors that are not at all interested in joining the army, and other sectors that are not allowed to do so. *Comparison among whom* thus becomes the central question. Presumably, exclusion from the 'comparison group' is itself an unfair disadvantage when compared to others. But who are the 'others'? Since the 'others' is essentially a 'precomparison comparison group', the R1 solution collapses into an endless riddle of 'the chicken and the egg' variety.[21]

A reader of Temkin's book might infer that his discussion 'marks the end of egalitarianism as a coherent political doctrine.'[22] This is not Temkin's own conclusion; he believes that comparative inequality is unfair, despite the grave difficulties in measuring it. Nonetheless, even in his view, comparative equality is not only a *vague* ideal, in the sense that there are cases where there seems to be *no* clear ruling, but it is also a *complex* ideal, in the sense that in some of the most central cases, there seem be *too many* possible rulings. When comparing the underlying, yet conflicting, valuations of R1, R2 and R3, we might hope to find some implicit ranking that motivates the egalitarian, but I cannot see one. On the contrary, somehow the valuations R1, R2 and R3 all seem equally, yet paradoxically, appealing. All three seem rooted in the same intuition of justice, yet branch off into opposite directions. This intuitive confusion, coupled with the chicken-and-the-egg riddle regarding the 'comparison group,' provide ample reason to turn to an alternate moral ideal that might explain the egalitarian convictions under discussion.

To conclude the last two sections: some egalitarians do not use the Aristotelian relevance formula for explaining what is 'wrong' with wrongful

---

[21] I thank Yoram Egozi for this formulation.
[22] Quoted in Temkin, above n 1, at 352. The ideal of equality was attacked by philosophers and legal theorists alike. Harry Frankfurt (above n 12, at 134–37) claimed that the desire to be equal to others is undesirable, alienating and prompts people to be comparative and envious. Parfit (above n 12 at 18–28) shows that what is usually conceived to be egalitarian practices is justified by the non-comparative ethics of distribution that Parfit calls 'the priority view.' Similar arguments were developed by Westen in the 1980s. See eg, P Westen, 'The Empty Idea of Equality,' (1982) 95 *Harvard Law Review* 537; for a more recent discussion, see Peters, above n 6. The egalitarian literature that tries to deal with these challenges is vast. (See a good survey in Simons, above n 7, nn 1–3.) I think, though, that Temkin's paradox is the most profound challenge faced by egalitarians—since it is based on a thoughtful observation regarding the egalitarian convictions themselves.

gender-based inequalities. We have also seen that their reaction to gender-based inequalities probably does not have very much to do with comparative egalitarianism. A clearer and less indeterminate guiding principle would be preferable.

IV. RESPECTFUL TREATMENT VERSUS EQUAL TREATMENT

In light of the complexity/vagueness/incoherence of the comparative egalitarian ideal, it is worth trying to find another model that explains the egalitarians' shared moral intuitions with regard to gender-based unequal treatment. That is the objective of this section. I shall formulate a theory—I call it the respectful treatment theory—that distinguishes between morally permissible and morally wrong gender-based inequalities. The respectful treatment theory implies that some unequal treatments are wrong even if they track *relevant* differences. And I shall argue that, compared to comparative egalitarianism, this theory better interprets the egalitarian convictions according to which Aristotelian-permitted inequalities are wrongful.

But note that I shall *not* claim that, contrary to comparative egalitarianism, the respectful treatment theory is perfectly precise. Nor shall I claim that there will always be agreement regarding its correct application. I would only maintain that the respectful treatment theory is preferable since it is a more charitable interpretation of the egalitarian fight against gender discrimination even when that discrimination is fully rational. I intend to show first that there are paradigmatic cases of rational, well-motivated inequalities that are *nonetheless* considered *wrong* by the respectful treatment theory; secondly, that egalitarians are all in agreement with regard to these cases, and thirdly, that disagreement among them can only be found with regard to borderline cases. In light of the complexity/paradoxicality of comparative egalitarianism, an alternate theory that can fulfil even these modest requisites would still seem more charitable than its rivals.

Another advantage of the alternative ideal for which I shall argue is that it is local rather than holistic. It focuses on micro-level injustices or wrongs from which individual people suffer. In contrast, comparative egalitarianism (in all its various readings) is about how good or just a certain society is *as a whole*. The badness of inequality cannot be reduced to the micro-level injustices from which individuals suffer. From the comparative egalitarian standpoint, benefiting individuals is only important insofar as it reduces the inequalities of society.

Respectful Treatment Theory Displayed

Once again, the starting point is the Aristotelian relevance formula: a person should be treated on the basis of those aspects of his/her particular character or circumstances that are actually relevant to the issue at hand. As noted, this formula is commonly conceived as expressing a rational ideal. However, Harry Frankfurt justly emphasises that the Aristotelian formula should be read as a *moral,* not merely rational, imperative.[23] Its moral content stems from a psychological fact: a person whose relevant features are not taken into account would be offended, since he or she is ignored, and his or her voice, virtues, merits or talents are disregarded. My thesis is, then, that gender discrimination is prohibited, under the imperative 'treat people respectfully,' and that the respectful treatment theory constitutes a distinctive ethics of distribution. For, normatively speaking, this theory is generally weaker than comparative egalitarianism, but stronger than the Aristotelian imperative.

Before arguing to this effect, I would like to clarify two points, since, as it stands, the respectful treatment theory might seem ambiguous.

First, I would point out that, although the respectful treatment theory might naturally be interpreted as employing the Kantian notion of respect, it in fact does not. Drawing on a distinction made by Daniel Statman and others, I shall claim that the notion of respect, which makes the respectful treatment theory distinctive, is *psychological* rather than *moral.*[24] Let me explain.

Usually, the moral notion of respect is presented by the third version of the Kantian categorical imperative, which roughly says, 'Treat human beings as ends, and not merely as means.' Lying to a person, stealing from her, breaking a promise and, according to Kant, any disrespectful treatment are, by definition, immoral deeds. The opposite is true as well: there are no moral actions that involve disrespectful treatment. Indeed, in this framework the very combination 'moral though disrespectful treatment' is self-contradictory. It follows that, within Kant's system, the philosophical and epistemological role of the notion of respect is secondary. Philosophically, 'treating someone merely as a means' is to be defined through the system of moral imperatives, whose fundamentals are determined *independently* of the Kantian notion of respect. Epistemologically, respect does not constitute an independent mark of immoral behaviour—we identify disrespectful treatment on the basis of prior moral knowledge.[25] In sum, respecting people (in the normative sense) is treating them in accordance with moral rules.

---

[23] H Frankfurt, 'Equality and Respect,' reprinted in his *Necessity, Volition, and Love* (Cambridge, Cambridge University Press, 1999) 152–54.

[24] D Statman, 'Humiliation, Dignity and Self-Respect' (2000) 13 *Philosophical Psychology* 523; D Statman, 'Two Concepts of Dignity' (2000–1) 24 *Tel-Aviv University Law Review* 541, SJ Massey, 'Is Self-Respect a Moral or Psychological Concept?' (1983) 93 *Ethics* 246. cf S Darwell, 'Two Kinds of Respect' (1977) 88 *Ethics* 36.

[25] See Statman, 'Humiliation, Dignity and Self-Respect,' above n 24, at 544–53, for a full and illuminating discussion of this distinction.

This Kantian notion of respect is *not* the notion employed by the respectful treatment theory as it is constructed here.

The sense in which breaking the Aristotelian imperative would involve 'disrespectful treatment' is psychological. As Frankfurt would put it, violating the Aristotelian imperative is sinning against the individual's true self, rather than sinning against her humanity. Hence, in many contexts, even deeds that would be immoral in the Kantian sense, like lying or breaking a promise, would nonetheless not be disrespectful. Quite to the contrary, one may lie or break a promise in order to avoid humiliating people. The conceptual possibility of *immoral* deeds whose rationale is preventing *disrespectful* treatment proves that, aside from the Kantian conception, in real-life situations we also employ a psychological notion of respect.

My second point is that the respectful treatment theory as constructed here is *not* subjectivist.[26] It is essential for feelings and emotions to have (good or bad) reasons: a person who sincerely claims, 'I am humiliated just because today is Tuesday' does not really understand what humiliation is. I assume, thus, that there is an objective standard for legitimate feelings of humiliation, which is implicitly understood when we speak of 'humiliation.'[27]

The respectful treatment theory fights humiliating policies—that is, policies that generate *good reasons* for feeling disrespected—rather than feelings of humiliation per se. And it is this notion that makes the respectful treatment theory distinctive and substantive: gender-based disrespectful treatment— treatment that constitutes a *good* reason for people to feel disrespected—is an instance of gender discrimination, even if it is guided by what is relevant and results in morally desirable consequences.[28]

Thus construed, the respectful treatment theory faces obvious difficulty. Why is it morally wrong to offend someone? The answer is to be given in

---

[26] This point is controversial. Statman, for example, denies that an exploited brainwashed housekeeper is humiliated; after all, he claims, she enjoys her poor condition. The housekeeper does not *actually* feel disrespected (see Statman, 'Two Concepts of Dignity,' above n 24, at 558). Yet, I will argue that the fact that she does not feel disrespected is compatible with the assertion that she has good *reasons* for feeling so. And this means that she is humiliated. In the same article, Statman seems to make another invalid step: he says, 'It is possible to humiliate live people, who, as a result of the humiliating deed, would feel that their dignity was hurt. Not only that killing is not humiliating, it ends the possibility to humiliate (the dead person)' (*ibid*, at 565). I argue that hanging an embarrassing picture of a person on the wall of a crowded museum *involves* humiliation, even if the person does not exist. After all, had she been alive, she would have had reasons to feel offended, and this might be enough for asserting that she was humiliated. I do not argue for my intuition here, I just note that adopting it does not commit me to abandoning the psychological notion of disrespect.

[27] Compare Margalit's definition: humiliation is 'any sort of behaviour or condition that constitutes a sound reason for a person to consider his or her self-respect injured' (A Margalit, *The Decent Society* (Cambridge, Mass, Harvard University Press, 1996) 9).

[28] Suppose, for instance, that Alice is oversensitive to gender profiling, or suppose that women in general are oversensitive to gender-based inequalities. They feel humiliated by any gender-based inequalities, whatever their reasons. In such circumstances, denying that she has good reasons for her feelings is counterintuitive.

terms of welfare: it makes the victim badly off. Alas, if this is the answer, so the objection goes, the distinction that constitutes the respectful treatment theory vanishes. It becomes utterly unclear why it is of special importance to abolish the facts that *justify* one's feeling of disrespect, rather than to prevent one's *feeling* that he is disrespected. After all, the external offence, and the psychological response (justified or not) equally contribute to making the victim badly off.[29]

A famous story by Ronald Dworkin might be helpful in addressing this question. Louis requires ancient claret and plover's eggs in order to reach an ordinary level of welfare.[30] Intuitively, we would deny Louis's requirement for a special allowance, claiming that financing it demands more than his fair share.[31] According to the respectful treatment theory, as I understand it, the same intuition is operative in cases where people feel disrespected for no good reason. Hence, I have to explain what makes expensive tastes morally irrelevant in a way that the respectful treatment theory can embrace.

The explanation for our reluctance to assign a special allowance in order to satisfy Louis's desire has to do with the moral status of what might be called 'constrained volitional needs.' Clearly, in some cases the agent might be better off if he frees himself from some desires, despite the difficulty of doing so. We deny Louis's requirement, I suggest, since we believe that what Louis really needs is to free himself, through his own effort, of his desire for plover's eggs. People would become better off, not by our fulfilling their unreasonable desires, but by helping those people to be reasonable. Similarly, if one feels disrespected for no good reason, her true need is to understand why there is no reason for her to feel humiliated.

Paradigmatic Cases of Disrespectful Treatment: The Respectful Treatment Theory is Stronger than the Aristotelian Ideal of Equality

I am now in a position to argue for the disparity between the respectful treatment theory and the Aristotelian formula. Respectful treatment is, I am about to argue, an external restriction on the Aristotelian permissiveness with regard to unequal treatment.

---

[29] H Frankfurt, 'Necessity and Desire,' reprinted in his *The Importance of What We Care About*, above n 12, at 106.
[30] Dworkin, above n 10, 229.
[31] According to Dworkin, there are expensive tastes (in the sense defined above) and their very existence proves that *welfare*-based theories of distribution are all faulty. Dworkin is quick to infer that the 'fair share' is determined independently of Louis's level of well-being. Hence Dworkin's conclusion: a theory of justice is after equality of resources. See J Rawls, 'Social Unity and Primary Goods' in A Sen and B Williams (eds), *Utilitarianism and Beyond* (Cambridge, Cambridge University Press, 1982). Rawls attacks utilitarianism with the help of the expensive taste objection. Dworkin shows that welfare egalitarianism is as problematic.

As mentioned, following the rational imperative means to be guided by what is relevant. Now, Frankfurt claims that rational treatment is *identical* to respectful treatment, while I claim that one direction of Frankfurt's equation is not valid: though respectful treatment would certainly be rational, you might still be rational without being respectful.[32] This means that the moral requirement for respectful treatment goes quite beyond the Aristotelian formula.

The most apparent cases of disrespectful but rational treatment are the gender- or race-based inequalities that accurate stereotypes justify. So-called 'racial profiling' would offer a clear example. Suppose that, in high-crime areas, making it easier to arrest people reduces crime. The local law enforcement agency's use of the eased rules increases the probability that (completely) innocent and obviously unsuspicious people of a certain race will be arrested. The reason is obvious: although they are a minority, most crimes are allegedly committed by people of a certain race. I take it that, generally speaking, being under arrest necessarily triggers feelings of humiliation, and also that the humiliation of a person who is arrested is significantly intensified if he is not even remotely connected to any criminal activity. Even so, the law-enforcement agent cannot be blamed for violating the Aristotelian imperative: the statistical fact that arresting people of a certain race reduces crime makes race relevant in these circumstances. We can even assume that the officer himself is not a racist and is acting in good faith, to protect and to serve. Still, this has nothing to do with the fact that being arrested when innocent is humiliating.[33]

Why is this so? Let us stipulate that the unequal treatment is necessary for reducing crime, and the 'truly' relevant features, whatever they are, are only expensively traceable. Still, it seems intuitively true that the victim might feel humiliated, and for good reason. Taking this into account should bring the officer to *ignore* the cogent reasons he has for exercising the eased rules. In order to treat people respectfully, he has to become intentionally colour-blind, despite the fact that colour is crucial for elaborating an efficient strategy for fighting crime. That is to say, that the respectful treatment theory provides 'second-order reasons' or 'exclusionary reasons' for not being guided by what is relevant.

---

[32] This is implied by the following statement made by Frankfurt: 'There must be something else about deviations from respect, *besides the fact that they are breaches of rationality*, that has a more immediate and more specific moral import' (above n 23, at 152).

[33] As noted above, I use the notion of relevancy in the broadest sense. In some legal contexts, the notion of relevancy is precisely meant to reduce the scope of things that may seem relevant substantively, but formally are irrelevant, eg, the prior record of a criminal which, in some sense, is relevant (for instance, statistically) but formally is irrelevant to the crime performed. Now, limiting the scope of what is relevant has to be justified somehow. And it is precisely one of the primary goals of the respectful treatment theory to provide reasons for limiting the scope of what is *formally* relevant.

The notion of exclusionary reasons was first introduced by Joseph Raz, who pointed out that one might have reasons for not acting in accordance with otherwise good reasons. Raz's example is as follows: Ann's friend, Bob, offers her a deal, which involves investing some of her money. The conditions of the proposal are such that Ann has only two hours to decide whether she takes it or leaves it, for during the third hour, the investment opportunity will expire. Being too tired for a relaxed and thoughtful deliberation, Ann refuses to consider the deal. Bob complains that her refusal comes down to rejecting the offer, so he accuses Ann of rejecting a wonderful proposal without checking its profitability. Bob is right: the reasons Ann has for rejecting the deal are exclusionary; she has second-order reasons not to be concerned with the reasons for or against making the investment. Similarly, the respectful treatment theory restricts the Aristotelian ideal of equality from the 'outside'; it does not deny that some instances of unequal treatment might be reasonable according to the Aristotelian standard. Rather, it provides overriding exclusionary reasons for not being guided by what might otherwise be good reasons.

In summation, the respectful treatment theory is normatively stronger than the Aristotelian imperative. It says that we should avoid taking into account accurate stereotypes, even if they are cogent reasons for disrespectful practices. This is one of the essential aspects of the ethos of decent societies.[34]

Clear Cases of Respectful, Unequal Treatment: Comparative Egalitarianism is Incompatible with the Respectful Treatment Theory

The respectful treatment theory is generally weaker than comparative egalitarianism. The difference is simple: comparative egalitarians will try to fight any undeserved inequality, while the respectful treatment theory is directed against policies that generate good reasons for feeling humiliated. According to the respectful treatment theory, equality per se does not have any intrinsic value.

To illustrate the difference between these theories, suppose first that the government decided to require security checks only of people under the age of 75, on the grounds that there have never been terrorists above that age. Would those younger than 75 resent this, or be humiliated by being profiled in this way? In my opinion, the obvious answer is 'no' In Western societies, the significance of being young is positive, despite the fact that it carries with it a capacity to do wrong.

The same is true of cases in which undeserved inequality is really striking. Assume that a scarce medicine is to be allocated to those who have the

---

[34] See Margalit, *The Decent Society*, above n 27.

best chance to benefit from it. Finding these people by appealing to statistical information regarding gender and race seems not only permissible but also obligatory. Likewise, if resources are limited, a distributor should encourage people at risk of being HIV positive to be tested by, say, reducing the test's price only for them. Again, it is at least permissible to use statistical information about gender or race to find out who is at risk. In both cases, gender-based and race-based inequalities are anticipated (only people of a certain race will get the medicine or the affordable test) and in both cases the inequality is tragic: people might die because they are not of a certain race.[35] Even so, I do not find any reason for the disadvantaged person to feel humiliated.

It should be asked, of course, why these assertions ring true—and I shall address this question below, where I analyse *Miller*'s case from the standpoint of the respectful treatment theory. Before doing so, let me note that, in some cases, the respectful treatment theory might be more restrictive than comparative egalitarianism. Respectarians would plausibly argue that the respectful treatment theory is, in some cases, stronger than comparative egalitarianism. Recall that, according to this version of egalitarianism, if a person is worse-off because of being untalented, he is entitled to compensation, since being untalented is a matter of bad luck. Hence, 'luck-egalitarians' would force the untalented person who needs the special allowance to reveal his incompetence and to prove that his being worse-off than others is not his fault. That is, the untalented person must indicate some facts about himself, whose very revelation would cause him to feel shame. Many philosophers would agree with Jonathan Wolff that 'the only thing to do is to stop asking the humiliating questions: Stop collecting the data on why the unemployed is unemployed.'[36] Wolff would concede that the fact that people are badly off through their own fault is a cogent reason for *not* attending to their needs. He just claims that, even so, if identifying these people involves humiliation, collecting the relevant data should be stopped. Respectarians believe that humiliation constitutes an exclusionary reason even if what is at stake is justice—that is, equalising the condition of people who suffer from undeserved inequality.[37]

---

[35] For a trickier case, think of the common wisdom according to which, other things being equal, a physician's son or daughter is more likely to be a good doctor. I would say that since physicians' training is very expensive, this statistical fact should not be ignored.

[36] See J Wolff, 'Fairness, Respect, and the Egalitarian Ethos' (1998) 27 *Philosophy and Public Affairs* 97 at 117. But see T Hinton, 'Must Egalitarians Choose between Fairness and Respect' (2001) 30 *Philosophy and Public Affairs* 72.

[37] The respectful treatment theory bears resemblance to the doctrine of sufficiency proposed by H Frankfurt in his 'Equality as a Moral Ideal,' above n 12, at 23; E Anderson, 'What is the Point of Equality' (1999) 109 *Ethics* 287. Anderson's notion of equality draws on the notion of complex equality, elaborated in M Walzer, *Spheres of Justice* (New York, Basic Books, 1983) ch 1.

To conclude: the respectful treatment theory is generally weaker—though, in some cases, stronger—than comparative egalitarianism.

Alice Miller as a Borderline Case

As noted above, Alice complains that she does not have an opportunity that healthy men have. She is right. And, according to comparative egalitarians who seek to equalise opportunities, the fact that she has less than others suffices to justify her complaint. What would a 'respectarian' court (a court that would adopt the respectful treatment theory) decide in her case? The question comes down to this: does Miller have a *good* reason to feel humiliated because she was denied the opportunity to become a pilot? (Remember that this is not a purely psychological question.) Unfortunately, there seems to be no intuitively compelling answer to it. Hence, in order to answer this question, I shall try to offer objective criteria for humiliation in the context of gender- or race-based unequal treatment. My strategy will be to speculate about what in the paradigmatic cases make the feelings of humiliation justified.

My suggestion, in short, is as follows. Disrespectful treatment satisfies two conditions: first, it makes an *accidental* characteristic of a person crucial to the fact that this person's life is significantly worse than it would have been, absent the treatment. Secondly, due to its significant impact on one's life, this characteristic becomes a *label* by which one is identified by oneself and by others. The arrest case is the simplest illustration. By arresting an innocent person, the law enforcement officer temporarily excludes this person from society and, for a certain period, the arrest causes this person's life (while incarcerated) to be controlled by a faceless authority whose sensitivity to one's autonomy is extremely limited. Now, being arrested because of one's race would make the victim's race a label through which he and others conceive him. Since, in most cases, one's race is completely external to one's personality, being arrested on the basis of race further demeans one's life, by making an accidental feature of his life absolutely crucial to how it is led. (Hence, people of colour might take pride in being arrested because of their colour. Usually, this happens when they conceive their arrest as part of a long struggle against racism, during which their race becomes an essential part of their *volitional* nature.)[38]

Similar considerations are relevant in less extreme cases. In selecting eligible candidates for higher education, modern Western societies should resist the temptation to appeal to statistical facts about gender, race and other 'suspect' classifications. For, in such societies, higher education provides the subject with status-opportunity that only rarely can be acquired in other ways.

---

[38] See Statman, 'Humiliation, Dignity and Self-Respect,' above n 24, at 532–35.

Hence, whatever utilitarian reasons a government has for generating race-based inequalities in the sphere of higher education, the meaning of such inequalities will inevitably be to exclude—at least in part—certain ethnic groups from society. And this would cause members of this group to be labelled through their ethnic origin. This labelling is humiliating because it makes the life of the members of the group controlled by what they rightly conceive as an accidental feature—and, as a consequence, this label becomes essential to their self- and other- conception.

Compare these humiliating practices to the practice of preferring individuals at risk of being HIV positive on basis of their gender or race. Some people are disadvantaged because of their race as a result of this preference. Yet, these people are not *labelled* in the society by the features that explain the disadvantage; hence, they do not have to be humiliated by the practice in question.

Obviously enough, the IDF policy did not make Miller's life *controlled* and *labelled* by what she perceives as an external, accidental feature. Indeed, her desire to be an IDF pilot might be very strong and its frustration might colour her life. But perhaps she should rid herself of this desire, just as Louis must resist his appetite for ancient claret and plover's eggs; she can still lead a rich life, a life in which the fact that she is a woman need not play any undesirable role.

Our question was: if this policy is permitted by the Aristotelian imperative, why did the court force the IDF to let Miller in? My analysis of the legal response to the Aristotelian permitted unequal treatment is as follows: according to the most charitable interpretation, the court tried, but failed, to correctly apply the respectful treatment imperative. I have claimed that this analysis is better than the comparative egalitarian explanation, as the ideal of comparative equality is not concerned with individual injustices and (at best) is too complex. It cannot really explain why the Supreme Court Justices thought that letting Miller in would make society more equal than it was before.

V. CONCLUSION

When gender-based inequality is taken by (some) egalitarians to be wrongful discrimination, it is not necessarily because the Aristotelian relevance imperative was violated (as Peters and Frankfurt seem to hold); nor is it wrong for being a non-egalitarian policy (contra Simons, among many others.) It is wrong because it is disrespectful. The respectful treatment theory's basic concern is preventing disrespectful practices—that is, practices that generate good reasons for feeling disrespected or humiliated.

11

Mediating Paradoxically: Complementing the Paradox of 'Relational Autonomy' with the 'Paradox of Rights' in Thinking Mediation

MICHAL ALBERSTEIN

I. INTRODUCTION

THIS ARTICLE DEVELOPS a paradox-based model of mediation, emerging out of the existing discourse on conflict resolution.[1] At first, the argument follows the intellectual history of the idea of 'relational autonomy,' which characterises the contemporary notion of consent in mediation, through three stages: antecedent; the first stage; and the contemporary stage. Then, the paradox of rights and the self-referential quality of disputes, as described by the social scientists of law, are discussed, referring to the 'Naming, Blaming, Claiming'[2] (NBC) model of dispute analysis. An interpretive model of mediation is offered later as answering these two paradoxes, and as being capable of guiding the work with those paradoxes. This interpretive model is inspired by the theoretical legal discourse emphasis on 'hard cases,' and on interpretation, as in Ronald Dworkin's account of law.[3]

---

[1] The words mediation, negotiation, dispute settlement, dispute resolution and alternative dispute resolution (ADR) are used interchangeably throughout the chapter, and refer to the emerging and developing discourse on alternatives to courts, together with other movements and theoretical developments, which since the 1970s have promoted ideas of mediation and social harmony. Even though the range of processes with which the ADR movement deals includes adjudication and arbitration, I refer to mediation as the paradigm of an ADR process due to the radical alternative it offers to adjudication, as representing a counter-image and a new ideal of justice.

[2] WL Felstiner, RL Abel and A Sarat, 'The Emergence and Transformation of Disputes: Naming, Blaming, Claiming ...' (1980–1) 15 *Law and Society Review* 631.

[3] See R Dworkin, *Taking Rights Seriously* (Cambridge, Mass, Harvard University Press, 1977).

The paradox focus, therefore, will have two levels. The first level is the analysis of the conceptual paradox of 'relational autonomy,' which is central to the discourse of mediation, followed by the analysis of the self-referential quality of the NBC model of dispute analysis, which is central to the social studies of law. The second level is the constructive effort to build a paradox-based interpretive model of mediation that will work with these two paradoxes. This search assumes that sensitivities to paradoxes are important and enriching as a humanist endeavour within the discourse of conflict management and negotiation.

A basic assumption underlying this sequence is that exposing paradoxes and drawing their contours can enlarge our sensitivities and challenge our modes of engagement in reality by enriching the practical models with new questions and sensitivities.[4] The paradoxes I discuss are dealt with in metaphorical terms, not through formal logic or analytical presentation, and the 'answer' to them is offered in paradoxical terms as well, through interpretive perspective. Thus, in contrast to a long philosophical tradition that perceives paradoxes as the exception, or as problems to be solved and rationalised, the assumption here is that paradoxes represent a mode of rationality typical of our era, and that pursuing them is both cognitively enriching and basically demanded in order to advance to the next stage.[5]

II. THE ADR MOVEMENT: A BRIEF HISTORY

The alternative dispute resolution movement in the USA (the 'ADR movement') emerged during the late 1970s, has been institutionalised and has spread around the country, transforming the judicial system to include various mechanisms and alternatives to adjudication as part of its routine services. The call for mediation as replacing litigation was promoted by numerous players representing diverse interests and claims.[6] Among them were rights proponents, interested in increasing 'access to justice'[7]; community

---

[4] The argument follows, in that sense, the ideas expressed in Gunther Teubner in chapter 2: 'For ultimately it is not their undeniable critical and destructive potential that drives the interest in paradoxes. The really fascinating thing is the productive possibilities of working with them ... What role they play today as a ubiquitous and central aspect of social dynamics becomes clear from the following extreme formulation: paradoxes take the place of the transcendental subject; typical structures are historically contingent phenomena.'

[5] For a perspective which emphasises the fertility of paradoxes in thinking about conflicts, see JP Lederach, *Preparing for Peace: Conflict Transformation Across Cultures* (New York, Syracuse University Press, 1995).

[6] See eg, A Sarat and S Silbey, 'Dispute Processing in Law and Legal Scholarship: From Institutional Critique to the Reconstruction of the Juridical Subject' (1989) 66 *Denver University Law Review* 433 at 440–58. The authors describe the teams and players within the ADR movement, as well as the main track of reform and institutional transformation, which responds to the 'litigation explosion' problem within the court system.

[7] See A Sarat, 'Access to Justice: Citizen Participation and the American Legal Order' in L Lipson and S Wheeler (eds), *The Handbook of Law and Society* (New York, Russell Sage Foundation, 1987) 519.

empowerment movements; and quality proponents. The mainstream dominant sequence, however, that the movement promoted was responsive to a pragmatic search for the resolution of what was defined during the 1970s as 'the litigation explosion.'[8] Within this search, the actual need for settlement and to 'fit the forum to the fuss'[9] constitute the predominant concern of the ADR scholars. Effective conflict management and dispute resolution are perceived by these scholars as their goal, and the professional pragmatic allocation of disputes is supposed to promote efficiency and functionality. The epistemology of this ADR discourse and its private-public perception is equivalent to the 1950s optimistic jurisprudence of 'the legal process school' in American legal jurisprudence, which assumed that the role of law was to be a navigator between the market and the legal system, aspiring toward 'institutional settlement.'[10] These aspirations, being by nature both scientific and optimistic, assume that the roles of the judge and the mediator are managerial and that conflict is an anomaly needing to be settled. This functional perception naturally collides with the 'public law scholarship' which flourished during the 1980s in the American legal theoretical realm.[11] The idea of settlement as the direction of social progress contrasts with the fundamental progressive idea of law of that time, which depicted law as progressing through conflict and destabilisation—not through 'solving problems,' as in the 1950s, but through handling 'hard cases', which are monitored from an Herculean point of view.[12] This 1970s idea of law was inspired by *Brown* (1954)[13] and was related to the post-war 'interpretive turn' in law.[14]

The above clash between the predominant jurisprudential perception of law during the 1970s and 1980s and the pragmatism of ADR reforms, which emerged and flourished during this period, has resulted in an explicit resistance to and critique of ADR at the first stage of the development of

---

[8] For a critical evaluation of the actual 'reality' of 'explosion' see M Galanter, 'Reading the Landscape of Disputes: What We Know and Don't Know (and Think We Know) about our Allegedly Contentious and Litigious Society' (1983) 31 *UCLA Law Review* 4; M Galanter, 'The Day After the Litigation Explosion' (1986) 46 *Maryland Law Review* 1 at 37.

[9] The phrase is quoted from F Sander and S Goldberg, *A User-Friendly Guide to Selecting an ADR Procedure*, supp (1995) to S Goldberg *et al*, *Dispute Resolution: Negotiation, Mediation and Other Processes*, (2nd edn) (Baltimore, Aspen Publishers, 1992) 81–96.

[10] For a discussion of the relation between the ADR movement and the legal process school and other streams in American pragmatic legal thought, see M Alberstein, *Pragmatism and Law: From Philosophy to Dispute Resolution* (Hampshire, Ashgate Publishers, 2002).

[11] See WN Eskridge, Jr and G Peller, 'The New Public Law Movement: Moderation as a Postmodern Cultural Form' (1990) 89 *Michigan Law Review* 707.

[12] The reference here is to R Dworkin, *Law's Empire* (Cambridge, Mass, Harvard University Press, 1986) ch 7.

[13] *Brown v Board of Education* 347 US.483 (1954). In this famous case, the US Supreme Court announced the doctrine of 'separate but equal' as unconstitutional and, as a result, in a series of rulings the educational system in the South underwent a structural reform in which racial segregation was abolished.

[14] See MS Moore, 'The Interpretive Turn in Modern Theory: A Turn for the Worse?' (1989) 41 *Stanford Law Review* 871.

the movement.[15] Legal scholars viewed the call to settle and to mediate as an effort to subvert and resist the progressive rulings of the Supreme Court in favour of minority groups.[16] The pragmatic, efficiency-oriented search for problem-solving and 'win-win' solutions to legal disputes was perceived as undermining the progressive humanist aspiration to protect rights and encourage consciousness-raising through legal decision-making. This clash is characteristic of the first stage in the development of the discourse of mediation.[17]

III. THE 'RELATIONAL AUTONOMY' NOTION OF CONTEMPORARY MEDIATION: THREE STAGES

The 1970s and 1980s were marked as a formative period of the ADR movement and were characterised by a clash between the ADR scholars and the mainstream progressive legal intellectuals. By 1994, a new stage in mediation had emerged, presenting itself as both answering the rights critique and offering a new notion for the work of mediation. This stage aimed to escape the private-public dichotomy of the 1980s ADR pragmatists and to overcome the efficiency orientation of the discourse, by moving mediation to its next, 'relational' stage, manifested in the idea of 'transformative mediation.' This section explores the intellectual development of this relational notion within

---

[15] See eg, PE Bryan, 'Killing Us Softly: Divorce Mediation and the Politics of Power' (1992) 40 *Buffalo Law Review* 441; K Dayton, 'The Myth of Alternative Dispute Resolution in the Federal Courts' (1991) 76 *Iowa Law Review* 889; R Delgado, 'ADR and the Dispossessed: Recent Books about the Deformalization Movement' (1988) 13 *Law and Social Inquiry* 45; R Delgado et al, 'Fairness and Formality: Minimizing the Risk of Prejudice in Alternative Dispute Resolution' (1985) *Wisconsin Law Review* 1359; HT Edwards, 'Alternative Dispute Resolution: Panacea or Anathema?' (1986) 99 *Harvard Law Review* 668; OM Fiss, 'Against Settlement' (1984) 93 *Yale Law Journal* 1073; T Grillo, 'The Mediation Alternative: Process Dangers for Women' (1991) 100 *Yale Law Journal* 1545; MG Hermann, 'The Dangers of ADR: A Three-Tiered System of Justice' (1989–90) 3 *Journal of Contemporary Legal Issues* 117; D Luban, 'Bargaining and Compromise: Recent Work on Negotiation and Informal Justice' (1985) 14 *Philosophy and Public Affairs* 397; C Menkel-Meadow, 'Pursuing Settlement in an Adversary Culture: A Tale of Innovation Co-opted or 'The Law of ADR'' (1991) 19 *Florida State University Law Review* 1; MA Silver, 'The Uses and Abuses of Informal Procedures in Federal Civil Rights Enforcement' (1987) 55 *George Washington Law Review* 482; JB Singer, 'The Privatization of Family Law' (1992) *Wisconsin Law Review* 1443.

[16] See JS Auerbach, *Justice Without Law* (Oxford, Oxford University Press, 1983); also see O Fiss, 'Against Settlement' (1984) 93 *Yale Law Journal* 1073.

[17] For a description of the critique of ADR as constituting a separate second stage or ripple within the effects of the Pound conference, see DJ Della Noce, 'Mediation Theory and Policy: The Legacy of the Pound Conference' (2002) 17 *Ohio State Journal on Dispute Resolution* 545. See also J Resnik, 'Many Doors? Closing Doors? Alternative Dispute Resolution and Adjudication' (2003) 10 *Ohio State Journal on Dispute Resolution* 211. Resnik speaks about the transition from questions of whether ADR programmes are justified at all, to questions of how to operate the system and implement the critique, while taking the spread and existence of the programmes for granted. These questions are characteristic of our era. See also EK Yamamoto, 'ADR: Where Have the Critics Gone?' (1996) 36 *Santa Clara Law Review* 1055.

the discourse of mediation, starting with an antecedent, continuing with a legal scholar who worked at the same time as the emergence of the ADR movement but has not addressed it directly, moving to the insertion of the idea into the discourse by the 'transformative model,' and concluding with a contemporary formalisation of that model within the ADR scholarship.

The first signs of this unique perception of mediation arose during the 1920s in the writing of Mary Parker Follet, one of those considered an antecedent, or 'mother,' of the ADR movement.[18] Follet, an exceptionally brilliant scholar and a social activist, was interested in integrative negotiation long before the subject became a popular 'do-it-yourself' best seller or a major academic interest. Expressing herself in 'simple, fairly commonplace terms,'[19] she claims that:

> The conception of circular behaviour throws much light on conflict, for I now realize I can never fight you, I am always fighting you plus me. I have put it this way: that response is always to a relation. I respond, not only to you, but to the relation between you and me.[20]
> I never react to you, but to you-plus-me; or to be more accurate, it is I-plus-you reacting to you-plus-me ... That is in the very process of meeting we become something different ... Through circular response we are creating each other all the time.[21]

If I never react to you, but to you-plus-me, and the same holds true with you-plus-me, who reacts always to me-plus-you, then Follet's notion of mediation supposes a diffusion of the self long before Carol Gilligan and many other feminists spoke of the unique feminine epistemology of care and relations. Follet's ideas of the merging of desires through the mode of integration emphasise this relational perception of hers, which assumes that the parties will 'let the problem solve them' if they will only recognise their diffused situation. This is a notion of heteronomy:

> There is a way beginning now to be recognized at least, and even occasionally followed: when two desires are *integrated*, that means that a solution has been found in which both desires have found a place, that neither side has had to sacrifice anything.[22]

---

[18] See C Menkel-Meadow, 'Mothers and Fathers of Invention: The Intellectual Founders of ADR' (2000) 16 *Ohio State Journal on Dispute Resolution* 1 at 11–16.
[19] See AM Davis, 'An Interview with Mary Parker Follet' in M Wheeler (ed), *Teaching Negotiation: Ideas and Innovations* (Cambridge, Mass, PON Books, 2000) 63: 'Why did Follet fade from our view? One reason, given by an admirer of hers ... she almost always expressed herself in simple, fairly commonplace terms. Perhaps she would be more carefully studied if she had developed a jargon that invited periodic efforts at interpretation.'
[20] *Ibid*, at 71.
[21] DM Kolb, 'The Love for Three Oranges, or: What Did We Miss about Ms. Follet in the Library?', *ibid*, at 85.
[22] *Ibid*, at 65.

When two desires are integrated, it is the reconstitution of the parties which has enabled them not to clash anymore. Since they experience themselves as different subjects, now they can accept new solutions and reevaluate their needs and desires. A second indication for this different epistemology, which mediation might suggest, appears in Fuller,[23] one of the famous legal process scholars, who was occupied with finding the logic, function and morality of a variety of dispute resolution mechanisms.[24] The central quality of mediation, according to his view, is the focus it has on process without a fixed structure, a process in which parties establish new perceptions of their relationship.[25]

Fuller suggests that a serious study of mediation can serve to offset 'the tendency of modern thought to assume that all social order must be imposed by some kind of authority':

> When we perceive how a mediator, claiming no 'authority,' can help the parties give order and coherence to their relationship, we may in the process come to realize that there are circumstances in which the parties can dispense with this aid, and that social order can often arise directly out of the interactions it seems to govern and direct.[26]

The idea that social order can arise out of the interaction it seems to govern is typical of the legal process scholarship, and is based on the prominence of 'private ordering' as the foundational institution in society within this approach. The belief in a bottom-to-top growth based on private interactions, which only occasionally demand legal intervention, is common to Fuller and the ADR pragmatist. The uniqueness of Fuller's emphasis on mediation, though, is his depiction of the 'ideal type' of mediation as being based on relationship, which becomes the primary concern of the parties and cannot be regulated by rules. The central quality of mediation is thus:

> Its capacity to reorient the parties toward each other, not by imposing rules on them, but by helping them to achieve a new and shared perception of their relationship, a perception that will redirect their attitudes and dispositions toward one another.[27]

---

[23] LL Fuller, 'Mediation: Its Forms and Functions' (1971) 44 *Southern California Law Review* 305 at 309.

[24] Regarding the prominence of Fuller's scholarship and his uniqueness as a legal theorist, see WJ Witteveen and W van der Burg (eds), *Rediscovering Fuller: Essays on Implicit Law and Institutional Design* (Amsterdam, Amsterdam University Press, 1999); LL Fuller in K Winston (ed), *The Principles of Social Order* (Oxford, Hart Publishing, 2001).

[25] LL Fuller, 'Mediation: Its Forms and Functions' (1971) 44 *Southern California Law Review* 305 at 309.

[26] *Ibid*, at 315.

[27] *Ibid*, at 325.

Within the dispute resolution realm, the next elaboration of this idea comes in a less academic fashion, through a book considered to have established a new school of mediation practice: 'the transformative mediation.' This new notion of mediation was presented by Bush and Folger in their 1994 book, *The Promise of Mediation*.[28] At the beginning of their book, the authors try to present their account of the historical development of the mediation discourse up to that time. As part of their discourse, they present a few stories, two of which are noteworthy here. The first is 'the satisfaction story,' essentially claiming that 'the mediation process is a powerful tool for satisfying the genuine human needs of parties to individual disputes.'[29] In contrast, haunting the optimism and constructive attitude of pragmatic mediators, stands the familiar, critical legal scholar presenting the oppression story, which claims that 'mediation has turned out to be a dangerous instrument for increasing the power of the strong to take advantage of the weak.'[30]

In order to avoid the dichotomy between satisfaction and oppression noted above, and in order to push mediation up to 'the next step,'[31] Bush and Folger suggested, at their crossroads point in 1994, a new notion of dispute and mediation—a notion which, for the first time, explicitly introduced the critique of the individual liberal subject into the mediation discourse. This move, though, was executed not as a direct challenge, but through the incorporation of the counter-image of the individual liberal subject— Gilligan's relational caring feminine subject or the communitarian one of Sandel and MacIntyre.[32] Bush and Folger present their model as representing the shift to 'a new, relational, paradigm,'[33] which has the ability to transform society as a whole.[34] Their initiative is reminiscent of other professional spheres and is 'part of a larger trend away from the dominant

---

[28] RAB Bush and JP Folger, *The Promise of Mediation* (San Francisco, Jossey-Bass Publishers, 1994).
[29] *Ibid*, at 16.
[30] *Ibid*, at 22.
[31] This expression is, of course, inspired by 'Realistic Jurisprudence: the Next Step' of Karl Llewellyn, which sets with its own declaration the new epistemology of pragmatic legal thought. See KN Llewellyn, 'A Realistic Jurisprudence: The Next Step' in WW Fisher III, MJ Horwitz and TA Reed (eds), *American Legal Realism* (Oxford, Oxford University Press, 1993) 53. For a discussion of 'the next step' as the epistemological new stage of the jurisprudential discourse of the time, see Alberstein, above n 10, at 70–91.
[32] Bush and Folger, above n 28, at 255. The reference is made to Gilligan only in their writing.
[33] *Ibid*, at 253.
[34] 'The conscious choice to employ certain social processes can itself help enact and reinforce an emerging paradigm. Because transformative mediation is a relational institution, choosing a transformative approach, and practicing it, support and reinforce the emergence of the Relational outlook in a very concrete way... Conscious adoption of a transformative approach to mediation is thus a way of strengthening the movement toward the new paradigm, by enacting it in concrete form.' *Ibid*, at 259.

Western "individualist" worldview, which holds at its highest values individual autonomy and fulfilment, toward a "Relational" worldview, which holds as its highest value the integration of individual autonomy and concern for others.'[35]

The transformative model's move toward the 'social' emphasis, together with this initial challenge to the essentialist private perception of mediation, is at this stage portrayed in a somewhat paradoxical way, that is, in the name of super-individualisation and psychologisation of the mediation subjects. Bush and Folger claim that a dispute is not a problem but rather constitutes an opportunity for growth and learning, while they assume the 'original' condition is a feminine or a communitarian one. When holding that the basic assumption spells connectedness and self in a relationship, the dispute ceases to be a threat, instead becoming an opportunity to experience individuality and self-determination in a world which is basically a mosaic of connections and relations, unable to be differentiated into old liberal individual agents. The dispute subjects experience 'empowerment' and 'recognition'; it is this process orientation which should guide the mediators, instead of their earlier pragmatic and paternalistic search for efficient solutions. Five years after the transformative notion was presented by Bush and Folger, Nolan-Haley refers to this discrepancy by offering mediation the paradoxical explicit notion of 'relational autonomy'[36]:

> The idealized vision of autonomy in mediation, 'mediation autonomy,' is grounded in relational and communal values. As a governing principle, it is concerned not just with one's self but with the other party ... Thus, unlike the way that autonomy is expressed and understood in traditional liberal theory with its emphasis on privacy and self, mediation autonomy is connected to other human beings; it requires cooperation and collaboration with other persons whose values may differ.[37]

Nolan-Haley draws her notion of autonomy both from Fuller (who is also considered one of the 'fathers' of the ADR movement,[38] at least in some historiographies) and from Bush and Folger. She is the first to endorse this stamp not only as a vision of an antecedent, as a hearsay of a legal scholar, or as a fresh practical trend challenging the mainstream of mediation. Her writing is that of an ADR scholar describing the conditions for 'informed consent.'[39]

---

[35] PL Franz, 'Habits of a Highly Effective Transformative Mediation Program' (1998) 13 *Ohio State Journal on Dispute Resolution* 1039.
[36] JM Nolan-Haley, 'Informed Consent in Mediation: A Guiding Principle for Truly Educated Decision Making' (1999) 74 *Notre Dame Law Review* 775.
[37] Ibid, at 790.
[38] See Menkel-Meadow, above n 18, at 11–16.
[39] The article addresses the conditions for informed consent through reference to the elaboration of this notion in the medical domain, and by exploring its various philosophical and practical dimensions.

Yet, a closer examination of the notion of 'relational autonomy,' as developing through the four stages described above, reveals a paradox and an impossibility. As Gilligan (1988) says:

> The values of justice and autonomy, presupposed in current theories of human growth and incorporated into definitions of morality and self, imply a view of the individual as separate and of relationship as either hierarchical or contractual, bound by the alternatives of constraint and cooperation. In contrast, the values of care and connection, salient in women's thinking, imply a view of self and other as interdependent and of relationships as networks created and sustained by attention and response. The two moral voices that articulate these visions, thus, denote different ways of viewing the world.[40]

A relational world-view denies autonomy, at least in a traditional sense, and it emerges as challenging the possibility of such a mode of acting.[41] If parties rebuild their relationship and reconstitute themselves through the mediation process, with a relational world-view as the underlying assumption, there are no epistemological grounds for experiencing 'empowerment' before, or together with, recognition. The basic condition of the parties' perception is heteronomy. In terms of paradoxes, writing this situation conceptually entails an antinomy or an aporia:

> Paradoxes thus arise when we have a plurality of theses, each individually plausible in the circumstances, but nevertheless in the aggregate constituting an inconsistent group. In this way, logical paradoxes always constituted aporetic situation, an *apory* being a group of acceptable-seeming propositions that are collectively inconsistent. Viewed separately, every member of such a group stakes a claim that we would be minded to accept if such acceptance were unproblematic. But when all these claims are conjoined a logical contradiction ensues.[42]

The individualistic proposition and the relational-communitarian one cannot conjoin without exposing the tensions and contradictions produced by

---

[40] C Gilligan, 'Remapping the Moral Domain: New Images of Self in Relationship' in C Gilligan *et al* (eds), *Mapping the Moral Domain* (Cambridge, Mass, Harvard University Press, 1988) 8.

[41] 'The definition of the self and morality in terms of individual autonomy and social responsibility—I of an internalized conscience enacted by will and guided by duty or obligation—presupposes a notion of reciprocity, expressed as a "categorical imperative" or a "golden rule"... A different way of describing self, generally confused with a failure of self definition, has been clarified in recent years by attention to the experience of women. In this alternative construction, self is known in the experience of connection and defined not by reflection but by interaction, the responsiveness of human engagement.' *Ibid*, at 6–7.

[42] N Rescher, *Paradoxes: Their Roots, Range, and Resolution* (Chicago and La Salle, Illinois, Open Court, 2001) 7. See also WV Quine, *The Ways of Paradox* (Cambridge, Mass, Harvard University Press, 1976) 5: 'An antinomy produces a self contradiction by accepted ways of reasoning. It establishes that some tacit and trusted pattern of reasoning must be made explicit and henceforward be avoided or revised.'

their engagement. A genuine experience of autonomy cannot live in peace with a relational perception of the human subject. There is always, of course, the possibility to view these two claims as living together in tension, or to present the mediation discourse as incorporating both assumptions; but the claim here is that, as long as the contradiction is not even acknowledged and is denied within the discourse, there is no possibility of overcoming it. Bush and Folger, as well as Nolan-Haley, who draws from Bush and Folger's writing, do not present any difficulty in assuming simultaneous perceptions which are juxtaposed reflections of each other. Nevertheless, my claim is that these four stages of development of the decision-making notion of mediation expose a paradox fundamental to the discourse. The interpretive model that will be offered here will strive for an explicit acknowledgement of the paradox[43] suggested by this development, and only then can a conceptual possibility to either overcome or to work with the paradox be described.[44]

IV. THE PARADOX OF RIGHTS AND THE 'NAMING, BLAMING, CLAIMING' MODEL OF DISPUTE ANALYSIS

The legal social scientists of the 1980s introduced the notion of 'legal consciousness,' suggesting that the perception of reality is itself conditioned by a code or a script, which limits the horizons of experience. Their model of dispute analysis was introduced at the same time as the ADR movement was spreading around the USA, carrying the pragmatic managerial message of conflict management. The social scientists of law, inspired by neo-Marxism, bear a subversive critical and political tradition of challenging the mainstream scientific claim, and their model deconstructs the focus on disputes as a valid unit of analysis.[45] Their ideas appear in a famous 1980s article, which describes the 'transformation of disputes' through the phases of 'naming, blaming, claiming' (NBC):

> We provide a framework for studying the process by which unperceived injurious experiences are—or are not—perceived (naming), do or do not become

---

[43] I perceive this combination as a paradox and not a mere inconsistency. See Rescher, *Paradoxes*, above n 42, at 7: 'When claims involve a conflict or tension that stop short of actual legal conflict—of strict inconsistency—this is generally indicative of irony rather than paradox.'
[44] See section V below.
[45] Regarding the ADR superficial pragmatic call to minimise the costs of litigation or to encourage less adversarial approaches, informality and reconciliation, they say: 'Dispute processing research has thus acquired its own ideology which, apart from its intrinsic merits, further obscures the social context of disputing. It denies, implicitly, that disputes and disputing are normal components of human association.' RE Miller and A Sarat, 'Grievances, Claims, and Disputes: Assessing the Adversary Culture' (1980) 15 *Law and Society Review* 525 at 526–27.

grievances (blaming) and ultimately disputes (claiming), as well as for subsequent transformations. We view each of these stages as subjective, unstable, reactive, complicated, and incomplete.[46]

Disputes, in the authors' view, are 'social constructs,'[47] and thus studying the emergence and transformation of disputes means 'studying the conditions under which injuries are perceived or go unnoticed and how people respond to the experience of injustice and conflict.'[48] The perceptions of people are dictated by a norm or a code within the specific dispute culture in which they operate. People are influenced by social status, emotional experiences and cultural acquired responses, and they screen and absorb disputes solely through these prisms. Yet the prisms themselves could switch and change, evolve or regress, throughout the dispute process. Their only viable detected movement might be the play of difference between the consciousnesses, enacted by a code, which is perceived as given and inherent, and by the new experience which encounters the code. The experience itself does not exist without the legal consciousness that absorbs and interprets it, but the structures themselves can transform following the experience when 'hard cases' and 'difficult conversations'[49] are at stake. This way, conflict exists between ontology and epistemology as a self-referential entity. Disputes, within this perception, exist as circular, scratching the edge of consciousness and discourse in order to realise at the next stage of consciousness they were not 'real'—or, in other words, how they were conditioned by a previous ideology which is not the current epistemological framework. In contrast to the external positivistic view of conflicts as presented above, followed by a prescription to handle the conflicts, this approach focuses on a descriptive account of the relation between perceptions of disputes and the social context.

Legal consciousness, according to this view, is an internalised rule of law, which enables a glimpse of the limitations of our socially constructed reality. Furthermore, its development is less linear and straightforward than the progressive agenda regarding law and society might suggest.[50]

---

[46] See Felstiner *et al*, above n 2.
[47] *Ibid*.
[48] *Ibid*, at 632.
[49] The reference here is to 'hard cases' in law, as discussed by Dworkin, above n 3, and to 'difficult conversations' as discussed by the Harvard Negotiation Project in D Stone, B Patton and S Heen, Difficult Conversations: How to Discuss What Matters Most (New York, Viking Press, 1999). On the relationship between these two perceptions of disputes and their public-private demarcation, see M Alberstein, 'Getting to Where? On Peace Making and Law Teaching at Harvard Law School' (1999) 10 Law and Critique 323.
[50] For a delicate account of the relations between 'rights discourse and the life stories of individuals,' see DM Engel and FW Munger, Rights of Inclusion: Law and Identity in the Life Stories of Americans with Disabilities (Chicago, University of Chicago Press, 2003).

This self-referential quality of disputes, as it emerges from the NBC model and the legal consciousness idea, posits mediation as searching for a reality principle, one that balances between the perceived internal and external, fusing into a contemporary formula. Self-reference occurs in this scene, due to the fact that dispute perception is conditioned by consciousness, and the said consciousness is basically a legal one. The elasticity of both the perception and the legal code which conditions it makes it impossible to delineate the 'real' core of the dispute.[51] Disputes exist mostly in the eyes of their beholders, and the 'third party' intervention of the mediator should strive to provide an intersubjective experience which will enact their existence in the outside world. Mediation work, according to this stance, plays an intermediate role of stabilising the external and internal by providing a current law for discourses which organise the parties within the dispute. The study of disputes should begin by examining the gap that exists between their perception and their reality, and continue by challenging that 'reality,' referring to its social construction. The play between the construction of the internal and external will determine the substance of the dispute process. In contrast to the transformative model, this one gives a lot of emphasis on law and context and does not focus on the psychological and the internal room of the dispute.

When some elements of justice are misperceived by the dispute parties, with this distortion sometimes inherent in their social-structural relations, one of the roles of the mediator is to expose hidden conflicts, helping them advance and change through the 'naming, blaming, claiming' matrix. Whether the UnPIE (unperceived injurious experience)[52] derives from lack of knowledge or from false consciousness, the mediator who internalised the legal social scientists' critique has to be aware of her/his role as reflecting the law or, in a broader sense, reflecting the symbolic order.

In some sense, the NBC model, though arising before the transformative model, can be perceived as containing the critique of liberalism which the transformative model offers and as offering a 'next step' for the understanding of disputes. If subjectivity is indeed conditioned by a script or a social code, as Felstiner *et al* suggest, then it can be either relational or individualist, without necessarily assuming hierarchy and a concrete temporality between them. If consciousness is constructed by legal and cultural norms, then attention to the gap between consciousness and perceived reality is the business of dispute thinking. Furthermore, the transformation and evolution of society, and of the parties within mediation, is neither as linear or as straightforward as the progressive agenda regarding law and society might suggest.

---

[51] See also Rescher, above n 42, at 204: 'The cycle never closes. The question of a referent is never fully resolved. Self involving identification is effectively toothless: it has no identifactory bite.'

[52] See Felstiner *et al*, above n 2, at 633.

Their movement is dependent upon 'the paradox of rights,' and is very subtle and complex.

The 'paradox of rights' is actually a reframing of the self-referential quality of disputes as discussed above: 'rights talk' is aimed at individuals, and is supposed to protect them and promote their well-being. Yet, as the 'legal consciousness' notion discussed above suggests, the 'owner' of the right is always an individual, conditioned by consciousness, which is itself constructed by society. Thus, there is no way to promote rights and enhance major social processes without working on consciousness raising and internalisation by individuals of the rule of law. The NBC model shows that social reality, by definition, causes less disputes to materialise than there actually are beneath the apparent surface, and that rights penetrate the reality of social interaction only in a limited manner. 'The transformation of disputes,' in this context, is the articulation of rights, determined by a certain community, into an individual consciousness. This phenomenon can be named 'the paradox of rights' since the abstract advanced liberal individual is given a 'right,' but the actual constructed person of the dispute is given an opportunity which he/she cannot enjoy without having the proper internal code of perception to realise it. Disputes, therefore, are transformed through the realisation of rights.

This paradox, which conditions the NBC model, emphasises the role of dispute-handling as being primarily to develop conflicts and help more rights to materialise. Society suffers from a deficit in disputes, according to this view, and what comes to the surface is not representative of the real social struggles at stake. The disputes expert's job within this context might be to encourage conflict, to emphasise its positive aspect and to support individual education to self-assertion and rights acknowledgment. This is not a mediating role but rather a challenging, combative one of claiming, deriving from the self-referential need to reconstitute the dispute subject and to develop its 'right consciousness.' The next stage will try to answer both paradoxes within a contemporary interpretive model of mediation.

V. THE INTERPRETIVE ANSWERS TO THE PARADOXES

An Interpretive Account of the Transformative Model

What kind of autonomy remains in the realm of mediation when we assume an interpretive paradigm of analysis? What level of progression in terms of rights and legal consciousness can be achieved through the transformative process?

From the autonomy aspect, if the dispute is denied in the name of relational values, the exercise of dispute resolution skills during mediation becomes a means to experience only *secondary* autonomy, a performative[53] one, within the diffusion of identities that characterises that dispute. As Bush and Folger say:

> According to this conception, the mediator's role is neither to promote agreement nor to protect rights per se. Instead, the mediator's role is to encourage the parties' exercise of their autonomy and independent choice in deciding whether and how to resolve their dispute, and to promote their mutual recognition of each other as fellow human beings despite their conflict.[54]

Encouraging the parties to 'exercise autonomy' and independent choice cannot produce an 'original' liberal autonomy, as Bush and Folger might assume. Parties that conceptually bear no genuine autonomy, as the relational critique suggests, 'exercise' autonomy as a performative discursive activity. I title it 'secondary' autonomy, as it is not the old liberal notion of the autonomous subject but rather the post-post-modern experiencing entity,[55] which was introduced into mediation in order to let the 'problem solve the parties.'[56] The parties to the dispute, in a way, are 'solved' and reconstituted as the residue of the mediation process.

Bush and Folger's gesture, through interpretive lenses, thus transforms mediation into an encounter in which the need to 'solve the problem' is denied, while emphasising the sustaining of the conflict, making use of its potential to produce growth. In accordance with the relational world-view, Bush and Folger propose to view conflict as a chance for growth rather than as a problem.[57] They deny the teleological and pragmatic efforts, maintaining that the primary role of the mediator is to develop the conflict by responding to it, providing room for the parties to experience empowerment and recognition and to perform their drama without aspiring toward

---

[53] The term 'performative' is used here to indicate the fact that mediation can be described as constituted of 'speech acts' as functioning within an interpretive framework having a performative power as a language game and as a form of speech. See JL Austin, How to Do Things with Words, (2nd edn) (Cambridge, Mass, Harvard University Press, 1975).

[54] RAB Bush, 'Efficiency and Protection, or Empowerment and Recognition?: The Mediator's Role and Ethical Standards in Mediation' (1989) 41 Florida Law Review 252 at 258.

[55] The reference here is to the 'subject position' of the individuals within the mediation context. For a discussion of the genealogy of the subject according to historical phases, see E Balibar, 'Citizen Subject' in E Cadava, P Connor and J Luc-Nancy (eds), Who Comes After the Subject? (New York and London, Routledge, 1991) 33–57.

[56] The expression is taken from JR Seul, 'How Transformative is Transformative Mediation?: A Constructive-Developmental Assessment' (1999) 15 *Journal of Dispute Resolution* 135 at 154. The author assesses the transformative model from a constructive developmental approach and points to the limited applicability of the search for empowerment and recognition.

[57] For an overview of earlier voices within the mediation discourse which have already emphasised the constructive side of a conflict and the opportunities it provides for learning and growth, see Menkel-Meadow, above n 38, at 6–10.

any closure. Mediation, according to them, becomes for the first time an opportunity to experience conflict within the collectivist orientation of process handling,[58] and in a counterintuitive and perhaps psychoanalytic mode, they construct it as a denial of the threatening, irresolvable elements of the conflict. This sequence parallels in an interesting way a public transformative approach in law: just like Robert Cover in law, who emphasises the transformative aspect of the law,[59] Bush and Folger emphasise the counter-private image via the transformative dimension of mediation. In the same way, society is transformed as a result of the 'interpretive act or the structural reform,' which will aspire to link 'a concept of reality to an imagined alternative,'[60] the small societal unit in the conflict will change and transform as a result of the mediating act. Numerous small transformations will result from the relational ideal of transformative mediation operating within disputes, and society as a whole will move to a new paradigm.[61] The preliminary stage suggested by this transformative notion does not acknowledge the interpretive, violent character of the mediation activity and claims its ability to defer any 'social' judgment:

> This does not (and cannot) mean that mediators somehow do away with personal values or viewpoints. Rather, the mediators develop the ability both to recognize their own judgmental feelings when they arise and then to pull back and suspend judgment instead of exercising it ... Awareness, control, and suspension of judgment thus constitute a clear hallmark of transformative practice.[62]

Bush and Folger thus consider their model as able to overcome 'the oppression story,' that being the mainstream critique of the ADR movement from the late 1970s up to their time in the 1990s. They do not maintain that there is any oppression when the parties are empowered—or at least the parties experience empowerment—and the mediator does not assume the

---

[58] For the collectivist orientation of the transformative mediation and its influence on mediators in the US Postal Service mediation programme, see D Pitts *et al*, 'Individualism, Collectivism, and Transformative Mediation,' prepared for submission to the 15th Annual Conference of the International Association for Conflict Management, 9–12 June 2002, Salt Lake City, Utah, available at http://papers.ssrn.com/sol3/papers.cfm?abstract_id=305165
[59] See R Cover, 'Nomos and Narrative' in M Minow, M Ryan and A Sarat (eds), *Narrative, Violence and the Word* (Ann Arbor, University of Michigan Press, 1992) 95 at 101: 'Law may be viewed as a system of tension or a bridge linking a concept of reality to an imagined alternative—that is, as a connective between two states of affairs, both of which can be represented in their normative significance only through the devices of narrative.'
[60] *Ibid*.
[61] Bush and Folger, above n 28, at 259.
[62] JP Folger and RAB Bush, 'Transformative Mediation and Third-Party Intervention: Ten Hallmarks of a Transformative Approach to Practice' (1996) 13 *Mediation Quarterly* 263 at 268.

paternalistic role of balancing power relations between them and setting down the law. The extreme privatisation of the dispute they promote ignores the social context, which provides the materials from which transformation can be achieved and, in their opinion, mediation is not the method to preserve legal rights and to balance power relations:

> One important test of a mediator's commitment to this hallmark of practice is the way the mediator responds when there seems to be a clear power advantage on one side. In this situation, it is easy for a third party to feel a need to defend and assist an apparently weaker party. However, this feeling involves judgments and assumptions on several levels: that the power balance is in fact what it seems to be, though power relations are often complex and multilayered; that the 'powerful' party is being strategic or conniving, though he or she may actually be uncertain of how to act and relying on power patterns that he or she would prefer to change; or that the 'weaker' party wants a shift in the power balance, though he or she may prefer the current situation for reasons unknown to the intervenor. Any or all of these judgments, and the power balancing strategies that they justify, lead to third party moves that quickly negate empowerment in the transformative sense.[63]

Mediators, according to Bush and Folger, have to steer clear of the temptation to provide the social text underlying the parties' dispute, or to try and capture it in terms of rights and outcomes. They should defer judgment in cases of imbalance or social wrongs, and not assume they can see the whole picture of the dispute. The underlying story might be much more complex and the case much more indeterminate than it appears at first glance. In fact, if we acknowledge the social aspect and the judgmental inevitable quality of the mediating act, the transformative model calls for moving forward, letting the parties enact their relationship within this self-referential dispute system:

> The mediators understand that shifts in power can certainly occur within a transformative approach, but they do not presume to prompt such shifts. Instead of exercising independent judgment about the power balance, the mediators are guided by the parties' judgments. The mediator looks for and inquires about signals from a disputant that he or she is troubled by an imbalance or is unable to sustain a viable position without some change in the power balance. If and when such dissatisfaction is expressed, the mediator helps the disputant to clarify exactly what he or she wants, to convey what he or she wants to express to the other party, and to make the decisions that are then called for. However, if a seemingly weaker party gives no signals of need when he or she appears to be overrun by a stronger disputant, then the mediator who pushes the imbalance issue substitutes his or her own judgment for the party's and moves toward a highly directive intervenor role that is inconsistent with the transformative approach.[64]

[63] *Ibid*, at 268–69.
[64] *Ibid*, at 269.

According to this concept, the mediation drama involves 'the transformation of disputes' only to the extent that the parties deliberately choose to experience it. A party whom the mediator believes has not reached the dispute-related 'naming' stage, or is stuck on a different level of the social order, in acknowledging and claiming her or his rights, should clearly not be encouraged to go through transformations unless he/she chooses to do so. The transformative mediator should defer judgment regarding the transformative stage of the dispute, assuming the parties re-enact their social order in the utopian internal room of the relational dialogue. When mediators stop overtly acting as pragmatic lawyers, Bush and Folger believe the parties can learn much more about themselves and feel empowered to handle their own dispute:

> 'The parties have what it takes ...' To frame the point differently, the mediator does not base his or her view of the disputants on immediate appearances. The mediator sees the disputants, even in their worst moments, as being only *temporarily* disabled, weakened, defensive or self-absorbed. The mediator is convinced that while the conflict may be causing the parties to be alienated from themselves and each other, it has not destroyed their fundamental ability to move—with assistance, but of their own volition—from weakness to strength or from self absorption to recognition of others.[65]

The relational underlying perception and ideology of the transformative mediator generates a maternal optimistic gaze at the parties, which denies the 'immediate appearance' of escalation and depicts it as 'temporary' and 'worst moments.' But herein lie the problem and the insufficiency of the relational account of mediation altogether, and here the need for combining 'right sensitivities' is exposed: is not the 'temporality' of disputes their main quality—their being conditioned by legal consciousness and social construction, a product of a specific time and place which clash with one another? Entering the internal room of transformative mediation assumes that the return to the relational interaction in denial of the actual dispute will eventually trivialise the latter to a non-'real problem' in the outside world; but, in some cases (and actually in most cases), a social context exists, and without a reference to the law governing it, the mediation process might look detached or even oppressive.

It is suggested that, from an interpretive point of view, the relational call promotes, for the first time, the paradoxical nature of disputes and their existence between the private and the public, between the fantastic and the real. If social construction is indeed the surface on which disputes emerge, as the first-stage critics and the oppression story suggest, then internalising the idea deconstructs the experience of dispute altogether. Looking from the outside, what we experience as dispute is nothing but a social construct

---

[65] *Ibid*, at 269–70.

imposed upon us, used as a script to process external events. If that is indeed the case, the mediator should not try to 'solve the problem,' which is never the 'real' problem. Instead, the parties should put the false, legal-consciousness experience of disputes aside and focus on transforming the conflict by working on their communication skills on the intersubjective level. This is a deferral of the urge to settle in favour of improving relationships and promoting harmony. In the internal room allocated to the parties for their communication, perceptions will automatically change and the dispute will be resolved; otherwise, the time has probably not come yet for settling.

According to Bush and Folger's utopian vision of transformative mediation, people can indeed detach themselves from the problem, becoming transparent to themselves, realising the 'no-real-dispute' (or: the fact that there is no real dispute) in the outside world. This is the Hegelian story, wherein the spirit is 'coming back to itself' and the dispute is a 'false consciousness,' since in a post-transformation stage the 'problem' it represents could be easily resolved. Once the emotional underlying motives are treated, the hard core of the encounter is transformed into cooperation.

The problem this model poses is in its concept of utopia as the horizon of mediation, which is, in effect, a situation of 'no life.' When the inside is transformed, the ideologies realised, then the dispute disappears and the parties reach 'nirvana' or become transparent to themselves; the driving force of conflict disappears, leaving the parties in a 'no life' experience. If a dispute is an opportunity and not a problem, and the aim of mediation is to emphasise the conflict by working in the internal room of denial, then the therapeutic task of the transformative mediator seems endless and aimless.[66] It is left in an autistic framework of a relational dialogue, producing

[66] There is some equivalency between the critique of the transformative notion of mediation and the attack of radical feminism, as manifested by Catherine Mackinnon's writings on the relational feminism of Carol Gilligan. According to Mackinnon, 'ethics of care' is nothing but a false consciousness and an oppressive ideology that women have been told for hundreds of years in order to keep them out of the public sphere and to subordinate them to men's control. The relational world-view is the counter-reflection of the real world: caring, sharing, not competing, focusing on feelings and acknowledging diffused identities. Leaving women to experience only this world, or at least as having primary access to it, reinforces the power imbalances in society and enhances a masculine hegemony. As Williams puts the difference between Gilligan and Mackinnon in her 1989 article 'Deconstructing Gender,' referring to Gilligan's famous 'Amy and Jack,' who exemplify typical relational and individualistic attitudes: 'Gilligan argued that her goal was to assimilate Amy's voice into the mainstream of society. Mackinnon responded that her goal was more to have Amy develop a new voice, one that 'would articulate what she cannot now, because his foot is on her throat.' Gilligan's Amy,' said Mackinnon, 'is articulating the feminine. And you are calling it hers. That's what I find infuriating.' JC Williams, 'Deconstructing Gender' in KT Bartlett and R Kennedy (eds), *Feminist Legal Theory: Readings in Law and Gender* (Tucson, Arizona, West Press 1991) 95, 100. See also C Gilligan, *In a Different Voice: Psychological Theory and Women's Development* (Cambridge, Mass, Harvard University Press, 1982); CA Mackinnon, Toward a Feminist Theory of the State (Cambridge, Mass, Harvard University Press, 1989). By the same token, it can be claimed that depicting mediation as a relational and maternal process, one which does not aim to reach solutions to problems, reinforces its place as marginal, and as an other of the masculine legal discourse.

meagre signs of change, which bear no results in the real world.[67] From another perspective, as a utopian, messianic horizon, the transformative notion is important as providing the ideal of internalisation of law through choice and empowerment.[68] This horizon will be preserved within the interpretive model.

An Interpretive Account of the NBC Model

A person experiences a dispute when his/her legal consciousness detects a gap between a perceived reality and her/his internalised rule of law. 'The paradox of rights' suggests an examination of the dialectic between the 'social law' and the 'law of the dispute.' In a progressive society, the gap between them might invite an activist mediation style, which emphasises the conflict aspect in the unexplored dimensions of the dispute, those that are not yet named or transformed. However, a more conservative style of mediation might suit many other cases, following the transformative, more therapeutic lesson, since it is not for each private party to experience the transformation of society to a next step of legal consciousness.

If, as the social scientist of law suggests, 'the transformation of disputes' proceeds along the lines of cultural and social norms, which are somehow arbitrary and can themselves be transformed, then the only comprehensive method to overcome the context-based perception of disputes is to aspire to simultaneously draw the legal lines between perception and context, internal and external, private and public, while settling them. The interpretive model of mediation, according to this view, will not only try to answer the paradox of 'relational autonomy' by suggesting that attention is needed upon a law which will differentiate the 'I-plus-you' from 'you-plus-me' from the outside. It will also answer the self-referential quality of disputes as social constructs, which exist, transform and settle only in the eyes of their beholders. The effort to determine the law of perception, the culture of dispute processing, and the actual script with which the parties will reach reconciliation constitute the interpretive model's answer to this quality. Although, as discussed above, the tendency to promote disputes along

---

[67] For further critical accounts of the transformative model, see C Menkel-Meadow, 'The Many Ways of Mediation: The Transformation of Traditions, Ideologies, Paradigms and Practices' (1995) 11 *Negotiation Journal* 217; N Milner, 'Mediation and Political Theory: A Critique of Bush and Folger' (1996) Law and Social Inquiry 737. JA Seul, 'How Transformative is Transformative Mediation?: A Constructive-Developmental Assessment' (1999) 15(1) Ohio State Journal on Dispute Resolution 135; M Williams, 'Can't I Get No Satisfaction? Thoughts on the Promise of Mediation' (1997) 15(2) *Mediation Quarterly* 143.

[68] For a more contemporary practical model which incorporates this sensitivity through using the 'social constructionist' approach, see J Winslade and G Monk, *Narrative Mediation: A New Approach to Conflict Resolution* (San Fransisco, Jossey-Bass Publishers, 2001).

social norms in principle parallels the tendency to settle and deny disputes in order to achieve peace and stability without going through rights consciousness, the model suggested here will be progressive and will aspire to promote disputes to the level that the concrete context of the conflict allows.

The Interpretive Answer

The interpretive paradox-based model offered here tries to overcome the problematique of the 'relational autonomy' notion by supplementing the intersubjective internal encounter it offers with 'rights sensitivities' that incorporate 'the paradox of rights,' as discussed above. Regarding both paradoxes, this model offers an interpretive framework which tries to incorporate the contradicting sensitivities they entail.

The interpretive model envisions mediation as executing double commitments: the first is the familiar mediation effort to settle the dispute between the two parties, promoting it to a level of mutual realisation and transformation, which enables an exploration of hidden dimensions of justice; the second is the search for a genuine expression of will and a value judgment, which involves inquiry into the social law of the dispute and its determination. The first commitment is represented by the existing pragmatic and the transformative models[69] and represents the construction of dispute settlement as a realisation and rationalisation of chaotic worlds of desires, needs and emotions. The pragmatic problem-solving mediator aspires to achieve this rationalisation through emphasising mediation as settlement and problem solving, while the transformative mediator wishes to do so through the opportunity offered by conflict for relational internal dialogue. This relational growth is the utopian horizon of mediation as aspiring to peace and harmony. The second commitment constitutes the legal aspiration to resist the settlement as well as the conflict drive per se, considering each dispute an opportunity to set new law through a pragmatic violent intervention in a world based on eternal and structural conflicts that can never be fully resolved or rationalised. This drive internalises 'the paradox of rights,' and causes a constant reality search for actual settlements, settlements between non-contemporaneous scripts and narratives, within the existing singular materialisation of reality and fiction, public and private.

According to this model, the seemingly tranquil effort to negotiate for distributive justice that will organise interests and needs or, alternatively, the striving for procedural justice that will transform the relationship

---

[69] For a discussion of these models, see sections II and III above.

between the parties until such organisation will be trivial,[70] is accompanied by a determined will to fight for law—namely, to determine actual boundaries between reality and fiction, public and private, through what Cover calls the 'violence of the word.'[71] The first drive corresponds to the classic liberal mode and modernism, while the second responds to the liberalism and modernism critique carrying a post-modern note. The call to reconcile these drives and to use them as a paradox-based model of mediation is the interpretive model's answer both to the 'relational autonomy' paradox and to the rights paradox of the NBC model. Only awareness of the double bind and of the complexity of the calls of mediation will promote due process, which will be both peaceful and just.

VI. SUMMARY

The sequence above reveals the paradoxical qualities of mediation, as manifested first by the theoretical accounts of mediation within the discourse of ADR. The autonomy notion of mediation, which is depicted as 'relational,' suggests an endless internal quest without manifest consequences in reality. The notion of 'relational autonomy,' central to the discourse of mediation, carries both a contradiction and a paradox. The relational worldview denies autonomy in the classic liberal sense, thus exercising autonomy within a 'self in relation' epistemology, and suggesting a paradoxical performance that assumes a transformation of identities within the defused atmosphere of the mediation context. This perception reinforces the therapeutic and psychoanalytic poles of mediation, and constructs this process as extremely private, secluded from the outside world.

Further on, the argument exposes a paradoxical quality of disputes as depicted by the social scientists of law in their NBC model, and as reflected in the 'paradox of rights' notion. When 'legal consciousness' is assumed as the surface on which disputes emerge, conflict can be understood not as an external objective event, but as the gap between the internalised code that enables perception and the perceived reality. The NBC model emphasises this self-referential quality of disputes as existing mostly in their beholders'

---

[70] For an examination of dispute settlement through the dichotomy of distributive and procedural justice as paralleling the pragmatic and transformative dichotomy, see T Nabatchi and LB Bingham, 'Expanding our Models of Justice in Dispute Resolution: A Field Test of the Contribution of Interactional Justice,' working paper, available at ttp://papers.ssrn.com/sol3/apers.cfm?abstract_ d=305205

[71] For a further discussion of the relation between the legal discourse and the conflict resolution one, and for more elaborations of the interpretive model, see M Alberstein, 'Negotiating for Justice, Fighting for Law: The Dialectic of Promoting and Settling Disputes in the Current Global Era' in A Sarat and P Ewick (eds), *Studies in Law, Politics and Society* (New York, JAI Elsevier Science, 2003) vol 29.

eyes, and draws attention to the possibility of influencing the codes and scripts as a way to change the dispute perception.

In order to overcome the paradoxes and to combine the sensitivities they call for, an interpretive model of mediation is suggested. This model first offers an interpretive account of both paradoxes, and then incorporates both a legal sensitivity of conflict as manifested by an NBC framework of analysis, and a settlement sensitivity as suggested by the pragmatic and transformative current models of mediation. In response to the 'relational autonomy' paradox, the interpretive model suggests a performative perception of autonomy, and a pragmatic legal drive to set the law and to end the dispute. In response to the 'paradox of rights,' the model pays attention to the contextual and legalized background of the dispute, and to the need to exercise choice between promoting the conflict or aspiring for settlement without giving rise to 'rights consciousness.' The double commitments the model suggests, in a way, offer a 'new paradox'—one more aware of those the model has been trying to answer, and providing a fertile tension for working within 'real-world' conflicts.

Paradox sensitivities in thinking mediation seem, to me, like promising tools to handle the conflicts which surround us, the conflicts that constitute us. The paradoxification of conflict, through reading the current perceptions of disputes, and its reparadoxification, through the interpretive model formula emphasised in this chapter, reveal the constructive movement of discourse, which can be described as the movement of a mediation process as well. The promise of mediation in this context lies in its deconstructive-reconstructive quality of transforming paradoxes of rights and relationships into their next discursive stage, aiming for a more tranquil reality in the meantime.

12

Autopoiesis, Nihilism and Technique: On Death and the Origins of Legal Paradoxes

SHAI LAVI*

I. INTRODUCTION

IN HIS BOOK on *Law as an Autopoietic System*,[1] Professor Gunther Teubner illustrates the fundamental paradox of law by referring to two classic texts, one from Greek tragedy, the other from the Jewish Babylonian Talmud. The first text tells of the famous dispute between Antigone and Creon regarding the unlawful burial of Polynices. The second text, perhaps less well known, tells of a dispute between Rabbi Eliezer and the other rabbis on a halakhic question. After failing to convince his fellow Rabbis with reason, Rabbi Eliezer turned to the help of miracles, making a tree move, a stream of water flow backwards and the walls of the synagogue to bend. Even after a voice from heaven confirmed Rabbi Eliezer's view, the other rabbis remained unconvinced. They maintained their position, claiming that the law is not in Heaven, but as God himself said on Mount Sinai, 'One must bend to the will of the majority.' The Talmud concludes by describing God's response. He laughed and said, 'My sons have defeated me, my sons have defeated me'.[2]

Both tragedy and Talmud teach how the self-referential character of law gives rise to the fundamental paradox of law—specifically, that law's attempt to distinguish legal from illegal can itself be illegal. According to Teubner, one should neither attempt to resolve this paradox nor think of it as paralysing. Rather, a careful study of law may carry on, not despite the

---

* For insightful comments and helpful suggestions, the author would like to thank Gunther Teubner, Oren Perez, Michal Alberstein, Roei Amit, Lior Barshack, Yitzhak Benbaji, Jean Clam, Fatima Kastner, Nir Kedar, Roy Kreitner and Philippe Nonet.

[1] G Teubner, *Law as an Autopoietic System* (Oxford and Cambridge, Mass, Blackwell Publishers, 1993).

[2] Talmud, Baba Mezia 59b, quoted in *ibid*, at 1.

paradox, but through it.[3] Teubner recommends neither shying away from the paradox nor moving quickly to resolve it but rather, perhaps like God Himself, to remain amused.[4]

This chapter is concerned not with the ancient paradox of law, but rather with its reincarnation and renewed significance in modern times. According to autopoietic theory, modern law can be characterised by two fundamental and interrelated paradoxes.[5] The first is the radicalisation of the ancient paradox of self-reference as it appears in the form of positive law. Positive law brings the notion of self-reference to its extreme by seeking the validity of law within law itself and by rejecting all extra-legal sources of authority.[6] But how can positive law, which claims no ground, ground itself?—The first paradox.

Secondly, a new, yet related, paradox emerges, the paradox of self-regulation. Modern law is often characterised as regulatory law, due to its growing involvement in the ordering of different spheres of human existence, from domestic partnerships to international markets. This paradox emerges from the fact that it is precisely the self-referentiality of law (ie, law's normative closure), which enables the modern legal system to regulate other social spheres (ie, law's cognitive openness).[7] But how can law, which claims autonomy, regulate that which is external to it?—the second paradox.

The following inquiry takes as its departing point the autopoietic theory of law and its formulation of these two paradoxes, but proceeds to criticise autopoiesis for offering a merely descriptive account of modern law. The critique is based on the notion that truth entails more than an accurate account of reality by providing a sense of significance as well.[8] We may agree that, in our times, law has become an autopoietic system and still wonder what is the significance of this fact. Can the autopoietic existence of law be accounted for, not merely described, by autopoietic theory itself?

One immediate objection to this mode of questioning may arise: how can one search for the significance of autopoietic systems outside of any

---

[3] For a similar view, see N Luhmann, 'The Third Question: The Creative Use of Paradoxes in Law and Legal History' (1988) 15 *Journal of Law and Society* 153.

[4] Teubner, above n 1, at 12.

[5] *Ibid*. See also N Luhmann, *Law as a Social System* (Oxford, Oxford University Press, 2004).

[6] N Luhmann, above n 3. See also H Kelsen, *Pure Theory of Law* (Berkeley, University of California Press, 1967).

[7] N Luhmann, 'The Coding of the Legal System' in A Febbrajo and G Teubner (eds), *State, Law, Economy as Autopoietic Systems: Regulation and Autonomy in a New Perspective* (Milan, Giuffre, 1992).

[8] Within the autopoietic analysis of developed systems, specifically the psychic and social systems, one may find the concept of significance or meaning as well. N Luhmann, *Social Systems, Writing Science* (Stanford, Stanford University Press, 1995) 59–102. Yet, it is essential that autopoiesis does not draw a stark distinction between description and meaning, precisely because for autopoiesis, in the final analysis, there is no meaning outside of description.

particular autopoietic system? After all, is it not the central claim of systems theory that description is nothing but another operation of systems and consequently that there is no truth outside of the system?[9] Is the search for the 'essence' of the system as distinguished from its operation and the correlative adoption of a 'totalising' standpoint from which the phenomenon of systems can be viewed not a relic of metaphysical thinking? And if so, is the attempt to search for the significance of autopoiesis not neglectful of system theory's endeavour to free us from the oppressing heritage of metaphysics?

To this, one may reply that autopoietic theory is indeed driven by the desire to overcome metaphysics in the study of law. Yet, here as elsewhere, willing does not guarantee success. After all, autopoietic theory offers its own metaphysics by assuming first, that the essence of law is 'system,' and secondly, that this essence is characteristic, not only of law, but of the totality of sociological, psychological and biological phenomena. The force of the critique is thus turned against autopoietic theory itself. To think through and beyond metaphysics, one must view 'system,' not as the essence of law but only as one possible way in which law is.[10]

In order to avoid an overly abstract discussion of theoretical concepts, this inquiry will explore the history of euthanasia as a case study of the emerging paradoxes of self-reference and self-regulation.[11] These modern paradoxes of autopoiesis emerge when law regulates (or becomes able to regulate) the practice of euthanasia. The paradox of self-reference lies in the fact that euthanasia, which would otherwise be judged as murder, becomes justified merely because the law says this is so. Modern euthanasia is distinguishable from other forms of lawful killing, such as self-defence[12], the death penalty and killing in war. The former is an inherently modern problem, which bears intimate connections to positive law, while the latter have long been recognised and justified within natural law. Euthanasia as a modern practice seeks its justification in positive law. The medical hastening of death, an otherwise unlawful act, becomes legal only because the law posits so. With euthanasia, the ancient paradox seems to re-emerge: can law's attempt to distinguish the legal (euthanasia) from the illegal (murder) itself be illegal? Hence, euthanasia can serve as a paradigm for what systems theory calls law's self-referential character.

---

[9] See, eg, *ibid*, at 36–37.
[10] For a similar argument, see F Ewald, 'The Law of Law' in G Teubner (ed), *Autopoietic Law: A New Approach to Law and Society* (Berlin, Walter de Gruyter, 1988).
[11] A more elaborate account of the history of euthanasia can be found in S Lavi, *The Modern Art of Dying: A History of Euthanasia in the United States* (Princeton, Princeton University Press, 2005). While relying on my previous work, this chapter is concerned with a new and more narrowly defined question of the relation between the history of euthanasia, systems theory and metaphysics. This discussion is presented here for the first time.
[12] GP Fletcher, 'Paradoxes in Legal Thought' (1985) 85 *Columbia Law Review* 601.

The attempts to legalise euthanasia bring to the fore the paradox of self-regulation as well. Positive law not only legalises the practice of euthanasia, but also regulates it. For euthanasia to be lawful, it is not enough for law to decree that it is no longer a crime. As we shall see, the regulation of euthanasia does not (or does not merely) determine for patients or doctors whether euthanasia should be practised, but rather prescribes the conditions and procedures under which euthanasia may take place.[13] It is self-regulation, ie the creation of transparent legal procedures, which allows for the external regulation of euthanasia, thus manifesting the paradox of self-regulation.

In autopoietic terms, the emergence of the two paradoxes can be described in the following stages. The first is the undifferentiated character of law and society as a total normative system and its decline (section II). Second is the emergence of medicine (section III) and law (section IV) as subsystems of autonomous rationality. And finally, there is the emergence of law as an autopoietic system of self-regulation, through which the regulation of medical euthanasia takes place (section V).[14] While this chapter is organised along this line of development, the development itself cannot be understood from within the logic of systems theory.

Thus, before proceeding, another layer should be added to our understanding of autopoietic paradoxes. What is the phenomenon of self-reference in law? Understood from within systems theory, it means little more than the closure of the legal system. But if law is not understood in advance as a system, what does self-reference imply? Self-reference points, first, both to the decline of natural law and the rise of positive law. It invokes the loss of a world order that had been grounded in the unity of God or Reason. Secondly, it signifies the attempt by modern man, now facing the groundlessness of existence, to overcome metaphysics by seeking the ground of law within the law (or the legal system) itself. Rather than a playful autopoietic paradox, we are facing that which Nietzsche has called nihilism.

Similarly, one may ask what is the significance of the phenomenon of self-regulation? Again, from the point of view of systems theory, it primarily means the cognitive openness of the legal system, which exists side by side with its normative closure. And yet, law as self-regulation signifies much more than that. Though all normative orders strive to regulate, most aim to order human conduct with the purpose of achieving a further good

---

[13] The legal regulation of euthanasia marks the practice as a specifically modern form of legalised killing. It is in this sense that contemporary euthanasia proposals are distinguishable from previous euthanasia proposals in the history of the West. While both Thomas More and Francis Bacon had advocated euthanasia in the sixteenth and seventeenth century, the earlier proposals emerged in the philosophical and imaginary genre of utopias. Not so with the late nineteenth-century euthanasia proposals, which offer the practice as public policy and positive law. The new proposals share the concreteness of a regulatory regime, rather than the abstractness of a thought experiment.

[14] Ewald, above n 10.

(eg, religious ethics seeking salvation, medical ethics seeking health, etc). Law as an autopoietic system operates differently. The term *self*-regulation itself hints at the character of autopoiesis as a unique way in which law is. For autopoietic law, regulation is not merely a means but rather an end in itself (eg, regulatory law in public health seeking transparency and accountability, which are themselves regulatory ideals).

This insight into the way regulatory law operates leads to a deeper understanding of the conditions of its possibility. For regulation to take place, the phenomenon to be regulated—dying, in our case—must undergo a transformation through which it severs its connections with anything that cannot itself be regulated. Thus, we shall see how dying, traditionally a liminal moment between this world and the world to come, gradually became a 'this-worldly' problem and a question of life proper. This change in dying, its coming under the sway of technique, is fundamental for understanding the significance of autopoiesis. Again, what we are facing is not the innocent evolution of a social system but rather the phenomenon to which Heidegger refers as the rise of technique. The underlying movements of nihilism and technique give autopoiesis its significance, but remain a (deliberate) blind spot for the theory itself.

II. DYING AND RELIGION: THE COLLAPSE OF A UNIFIED WORLD

Two explanations are commonly offered for the rise of euthanasia as an end-of-life treatment. One explanation points to advances in medical technology, which include the growing medical capacity to prolong life and significant changes in the causes of death.[15] Throughout the course of the twentieth century, antibiotics, dialysis machines and respirators have changed the way we die, and patients are more likely to die from slow and painful killers, such as heart disease and cancer, than from the swift and comparatively painless ailments of the nineteenth century, such as influenza, cholera and pneumonia. Under these new circumstances of death and dying, so the argument goes, there is an ever-growing need for new solutions to the problem of painful death.[16]

The second explanation ties euthanasia proposals with the development of patient rights and the emerging struggle for patient autonomy and control over end-of-life decision-making. Indeed, since the 1960s, alongside the development of civil rights movements, patients have claimed a right to be fully informed about their medical condition and to be treated only on the basis of informed consent. Gradually, patients' demands to withhold and withdraw

---

[15] S Nuland, *How We Die* (London, Chatto and Windus, 1996).
[16] *Ibid.*

medical treatment have been recognised, culminating in the legal recognition of a 'right to die' short of taking life.[17]

Both explanations, convincing as they may seem, relate the rise of euthanasia to developments characteristic of the second half of the twentieth century. And yet, the modern problem of dying, along with euthanasia proposals, predate the advances that are so commonly associated with it. Moreover, both explanations assume that dying gives rise to medical and legal concerns, without reflecting on the historical conditions that have brought the deathbed under the supervision of medicine and law. These questions are closely related to the rise of medicine and law as autopoietic systems.

The first euthanasia proposal in the English-speaking world dates back to 1870.[18] It is a piece entitled 'Euthanasia,' written by Samuel D Williams, an otherwise unknown businessman.[19] Its author proposes a solution to the problem of dying patients suffering from unbearable pain. He writes that:

> in all cases of hopeless and painful illness it should be the recognized duty of the medical attendant, whenever so desired by the patient, to administer chloroform—or such other anaesthetic as may by and by supersede chloroform—so as to destroy consciousness at once, and put the sufferer to a quick and painless death; all needful precautions being adopted to prevent any possible abuse of such duty; and means being taken to establish beyond the possibility of doubt or question, that the remedy was applied at the express wish of the patient.[20]

Soon after, Williams's proposal stirred a hot debate in the USA, leading to the first attempts to legalise euthanasia in 1906. Several years later, in 1938, the first American association for euthanasia was established.[21]

Thus, while there is little doubt that the experience of dying has indeed been revolutionised by medical and legal advances, the problem of dying—and euthanasia as one possible solution—predates these developments and cannot be explained by them. What, then, are the historical conditions that had to be met in order for euthanasia to emerge as a possible solution to the problem of dying? Most notably, dying had first to emerge as a medical problem. But what allowed for this transition? For this we must first learn how Americans died prior to the medicalisation of death. What were the

---

[17] See eg, N Cantor, 'Twenty-Five Years after Quinlan: A Review of the Jurisprudence of Death and Dying' (2001) 29 *Law, Medicine and Ethics* 182.

[18] See EJ Emanuel, 'The History of Euthanasia in the United States and Britain' (2004) 121 *Annals of Internal Medicine* 793.

[19] SD Williams, *Euthanasia* (London, Williams and Norgate, 1872). For a more general discussion of the history of euthanasia and Williams's proposal, see Emanuel, above n 18.

[20] Quoted in CB Williams, 'Euthanasia' (1894) *Medical Record* 70.

[21] Lavi, above n 11.

laws governing the deathbed before medicine and law emerged as autopoietic systems?

It is commonly said that, prior to the nineteenth century, dying was ordered by religion. Such a saying is true but, as we shall see, somewhat misleading. During the time, especially in the context of death and dying, religion was not a separate sphere of human existence but rather signified the totality of the human world. For centuries, in the Catholic world dying was a highly ritualised and structured event. The rituals of the deathbed were led not by the dying patient herself, but by the help of the Catholic priest, who would offer guidance to the dying in her final hours. There was much at stake in the death of the Catholic believer. On the one hand, the deathbed presented the dying with the hope of eternal salvation, through repentance for sins and their forgiveness. On the other hand, the last article of life was a test and a final temptation. The dying man will see his entire life passing before his eyes, and he will be tempted by despair over his sins, by the 'vainglory' of his good deeds, or by the passionate love for things and persons. His attitude during this fleeting moment will erase at once all the sins of his life if he wards off temptation or, on the contrary, will cancel out his good deeds if he gives way.[22]

There were clear ways of overcoming the fear and danger of the hour of death, ways to secure a good death. The dying was not expected to face death on his own, and the responsibility to die a good death did not lie, at least not entirely, on his shoulders. The presence of the priest at the deathbed, and the power vested in him to administer the Eucharist and the Extreme Unction, structured the deathbed scene and assisted the dying in achieving a good death. These rituals could be practised even if the dying patient was not in her full senses, emphasising the fact that not all depended on her will. Moreover, the Catholic believed in Purgatory, where sinners could still be saved from the fires of hell.[23]

The ritualised death of the Catholic correlated with an understanding of dying as a passage between this world and the world to come. The rituals at the deathbed were in this sense a *rite de passage*, preparing the dying person for his final journey into a better world. With the intervening role of the priest, mediating between this world and the world to come, the dying Catholic could maintain the hope that through the love of God and the power invested in the Church, he would achieve eternal salvation.

Yet, the deathbed in early America was much more likely to be ordered through Protestant or, more accurately, Puritan beliefs and practices than by Catholic dogma. And it is in the Puritan way of dying that we may find

---

[22] P Ariès, *Western Attitudes Toward Death: From the Middle Ages to the Present* (Baltimore, Johns Hopkins University Press, 1974).

[23] Ariès, however, argues that the sixteenth-century transitions in the deathbed were not directly related to the Reformation, *ibid*.

the first seeds of the rise of the self-reference and self-regulation paradoxes of euthanasia. Indeed, the Protestant ethic of dying, characteristic of pre-nineteenth-century America, was quite at odds with the traditional Catholic death. For the Protestant, dying belonged to this world and thus lost the unique transformative power it had had. Accordingly, there was no place at the deathbed either for the traditional rituals, which were considered a superstitious belief, or for the priest as mediator between this world and the world beyond. In comparison to the Catholic death, the Protestant way of dying put the believer in an intense uncertainty as to how to confront his death.

It is in this context that the emergence of the *ars moriendi* tradition should be understood. The *ars moriendi* consists of manuals detailing exactly how dying should take place. The first printed manuals on the art of dying were published in the late fifteenth century, and though the tradition was revised and revitalised by the Humanists, the Reformers and Counter-Reformers, by far the majority of works in the English *ars moriendi* are Protestant.[24]

Books on the craft of dying were a compilation of guidelines concerning the proper way of passing the final test of the deathbed. Focusing on the last hours of the dying person, they gave rules for appropriate conduct to be practised and beliefs to be held before death approached. In addition, such books would occasionally include suggestions on how to overcome bodily and spiritual pain, as well as rites that should be practised on the corpse of the dead.

In essence, these were practical manuals designed to assist the dying in preparing for the deathbed and its temptations. In some cases, additional advice was given to bystanders on how to assist the dying patient, and in other cases recommendations were made regarding prayers that were especially appropriate at the hour of death.

One highly influential book of this kind was Jeremy Taylor's seventeenth-century *Holy Living and Holy Dying*.[25] Taylor writes within and yet against the tradition of *ars moriendi*. Unlike the tradition, his advice does not address *the dying* but rather *the living*, long before the first signs of their approaching death appear. The practice of *ars moriendi*, according to Taylor, cannot wait for the last moment and must be exercised throughout one's life.[26] This is the case, not only because a long preparation is needed but also because death is no longer seen primarily as a passage from this

---

[24] For a more elaborate discussion of the *ars moriendi* tradition, see DW Atkinson, *The English Ars Moriendi, Renaissance and Baroque Studies and Texts* (New York, P Lang, 1992).
[25] J Taylor, *Holy Living and Holy Dying* (Oxford, Oxford University Press, 1989).
[26] Ariès makes this point more generally about a new variety of *ars moriendi*, which he names 'The New Arts of Dying,' arguing that already by the sixteenth century, 'the art of dying was replaced by an art of living.' For Ariès, the emergence of these new 'arts of dying' is a manifestation of the devaluation of the hour of death, which will ultimately lead to the modern denial of death, see Ariès, above n 22.

life to a world to come. Rather, death for Taylor becomes another way of approaching life and facing death changes from an otherworldly into a this-worldly experience.

For Taylor, death is transformed from an event taking place at the outer limit of life to the condition under which life itself takes place. This understanding of death shares, no doubt, the old Christian notion that man after Original Sin is afflicted by death. And yet, Taylor diverges from tradition in his application of this insight to the practice of *ars moriendi*. Death is not merely a metaphor for the condition of man in a corrupted world but an actual practice of living—living towards death.

Taylor's great innovation in rethinking the relationship between living and dying marks a transformation in the Anglo-American way of death. For Taylor and for many who followed, living and dying were no longer two distinct temporalities of human life. Rather, living and dying became different aspects of one continuum and thus became equally amenable to the desire of humanity to master its destiny.

The doubt, hope and fear that characterised the pre-Reformation *ars moriendi*, for which dying was still a bridge between this world and the world to come, were no longer acceptable for early Americans, who were influenced by Taylor and his followers. The latter wished to secure the experience of dying with a this-worldly assurance of salvation, a way of dying that was accompanied by a disposition of certainty in the power to master death. It is here, at the turn-of-the-nineteenth-century deathbed, that one may find the first signs of law (here, Protestant ethics) attempting to escape metaphysics (here, Catholic ethics) through self-referentiality (this-worldly salvation), an attempt driven by the desire for self-regulation, regulation for the sake of regulation alone. It is on the basis of this transition that euthanasia, soon understood as the this-worldly *medical* treatment of dying, became possible.

III. DYING AND MEDICINE: MEDICINE AS A SELF-REFERENTIAL SYSTEM

The decline of the art of holy dying was captured in an 1861 edition of *The Sick Man's Passing Bell*, an *ars moriendi* book first published early in the seventeenth century. The edition had a melancholy tone, especially lamenting the fact that the physician and the lawyer are sent for when a man is dying, but the 'physician of the soul stands outside the door.'[27]

A new way of dying was emerging and its most visible sign was the increasingly dominating presence of the physician at the bedside. Whereas

---

[27] CW Bodemer, 'Physicians and the Dying: A Historical Sketch' (1979) 9 *Journal of Family Practice* 827. The book referred to is T Adams, *The Sick Man's Passing Bell* (Edinburgh), vol 1.

in past centuries, the medical doctor would commonly leave the bedside when it was clear that the patient was hopelessly ill, a new ethic developed in which the physician was expected to remain at the deathbed. While the content of the duty was still unclear, its name was quickly spreading among physicians of the nineteenth century; it was called 'euthanasia.'

But the appearance of the physician at the deathbed signified a deeper change, namely, the medicalisation of dying and its ordering within the now-autonomous sphere of medical action (or communication). Only in the nineteenth century did the treatment of the dying, as such, become a medical concern and thus medically governed. The law of the deathbed shifted from the unified world of religion to the specialised sphere of medicine—a shift that, in its turn, gave rise to a paradox of medical self-referentiality.

The new competence of the medical profession proceeded neither from new scientific knowledge nor from innovations in medical technique. On the contrary, the physician's role at the deathbed was secured long before he had any medical treatment to offer the dying patient. It is precisely this paradox—that physicians did *not* have the means to cure dying patients, but nevertheless became the new governors of the process of dying—that characterises the rise of dying as a medical problem. And it is precisely out of this paradox that the final shift in euthanasia takes place: from the benign duty of easing death to the troubling practice of hastening death.

Despite the hopelessness and the inevitable decline associated with the dying condition, and perhaps precisely because of it, the medical profession followed a deeper calling to attend the deathbed. The physician's new duty was to remain with the dying patient to the very end, despite the fact that nothing of the *materia medica* in his possession was of any avail. What the physician had to offer the dying patient was a new kind of treatment in the face of imminent despair: hope.

Thomas Percival, the first to institute a modern code of medical ethics, identified this new role:

> For, the physician should be the minister of hope and comfort to the sick. ... The life of a sick person can be shortened not only by the acts, but also by the words or the manner of a physician. It is therefore, a sacred duty to guard himself carefully in this respect, and to avoid all things which have a tendency to discourage the patient and to depress his spirits.[28]

It is hope, but more accurately a specific kind of hope, which characterises the medical treatment of the dying and the medicalisation of the deathbed in mid-nineteenth-century America. To clarify this new identity of the medical

---

[28] CFH Marx, 'Medical Euthanasia: Thesis' (1952) 7 *Journal of the History of Medicine and Allied Sciences* 410.

profession as a hopeful profession, we can contrast it with two alternatives: first, with the role of the clergy at the deathbed and secondly, with the role assumed by alterative practitioners of medicine, or 'quacks', as they were more commonly referred to by the emerging medical establishment.

As mentioned, physicians tended to relinquish their responsibilities at the deathbed, leaving the treatment of the dying in the hands of the clergy. Early in the nineteenth century, however, young physicians were reproved for such behaviour, and were reminded that not only were they capable of caring for the dying but also that they might be even more suitable for the task than the clergy. Marx, a nineteenth-century German physician, warns his colleagues:

> Whoever refuses his part in this duty [administering some kind of higher comfort] and assigns it solely to priests deprives himself of the most noble and rewarding aspect of his work. Where the priest, administering the sacraments, comes to the bedside to soothe the longing soul with the last solace of religion and comfort, who will not see the patient's deep shock when he faces this quasi-harbinger of death?[29]

Not so with the physician. The physician will not raise such terror, for he is associated with hope for a cure not with the inevitability of death. Of the two, the minister of hope rather than the minister of fate should accompany the sick in his last hour. From the medical viewpoint, the presence of the priest at the deathbed could offer nothing but fear and terror. The possibility of saving the soul that was so intimately related to the *ars moriendi* deathbed was no longer acceptable in principle to the medical profession. Regardless of one's religious belief, the only hope that the clergy could offer was a hope in a world to come. In this world, the presence of the minister at the deathbed could mean only one thing—imminent death. Therefore, only medicine could offer real hope—ie, this-worldly hope—grounded in the powers available to medical science and technique.

But what were these powers? What possible content could there be to the hope ministered to the dying patient? And how could the medical physician become the minister of hope, when it was medicine itself that announced that the dying patient was incurable? The answer that mid-nineteenth century physicians came up with was in the form of a new breed of hope—one that did not deny the dying patient's incurable condition in the name of the all-powerful capacities of medicine, but that would at the same time refrain from undermining the new role of the physician at the deathbed as the minister of hope.

The hope that the physician was to inspire in the patient should neither be a groundless optimism nor, as it had been in the past, a manipulative

---

[29] *Ibid.*

effort to deceive the patient. Precisely in this way, the hope ministered by the physician differed from that exerted by the quack. This distinction was particularly important at a time when medical orthodoxy was trying to establish its professional boundaries. Physicians of the mid-nineteenth century were forming professional organisations to secure public recognition in their professional capacities. The American Medical Association, which was established in 1847, launched a war against quackery and excluded from its ranks homeopaths and other non-orthodox practitioners. Similar distinctions were drawn in day-to-day practice. Specifically with respect to the treatment of the dying, the medical profession sought to offer a scientifically grounded hope that would win the confidence of the dying patient and counter the deceitful practices of non-orthodox sectarian groups.[30] Hooker explains:

> The quack always gives assurances of a cure to those whom he undertakes to dupe; for, besides being incompetent to estimate the degree of danger in any case, he is unable to inspire confidence in his measures except by a strong appeal to the hopes of the patient. And some physicians imitate the quack in this particular.[31]

One of the many deceitful strategies of the quack doctor was to first give a disparaging diagnosis of the patient's condition, and then match it with an excessive confidence in the powers of the drugs that he could offer. For the quack this seemed to be a win-win situation. Either his dire prediction would come true or, if it did not, he could take credit for the recovery.[32]

The physician, like the quack, had to minister hope. And though the physician might benefit from raising false hopes, and at times a deceived patient might enjoy temporary comfort, such practice was highly criticised. This was not only because of the moral objection that the end (ie, a hopeful

---

[30] Some medical historians have ignored the importance of this distinction, and hence have undermined the central place of the administration of hope in modern medicine. Most explicitly, Rothstein writes, 'The therapeutic value of hope and confidence exists solely because of the patient's faith in the physician. Therefore, any practitioner who inspires faith in his patients is the physician's equal in this regard. Indeed, lay healers, faith healers, Indian doctors, nostrum vendors, and the whole range of practitioners who relied largely on their charismatic qualities for their success were probably more successful than most physicians in inspiring hope and confidence in their patients.' WG Rothstein, *American Physicians in the Nineteenth Century: From Sects to Science* (Baltimore, Johns Hopkins University Press, 1972) 10.

[31] W Hooker, *Physician and Patient* (New York, Baker and Scribner, 1849) 348.

[32] Early in the century, Rush criticises this practice in medicine: 'I know that the practice of predicting danger and death, upon every occasion, is sometimes made use of by physicians, in order to enhance the credit of their prescriptions, if their patient recover, and to save a retreat from blame, if they should die.' B Rush, *Selected Writings of Benjamin Rush* (Philosophical Library, 1947). For a general discussion of orthodox medicine and its relation to the different varieties of sectarian medicine, see HL Coulter, *Divided Legacy: A History of the Schism in Medical Thought* (Washington, Wehawken Book Co, 1973).

patient) could not justify the means (ie, deceit). Nor could the physician's duty to express scientific hope be explained solely as an attempt to distinguish the honourable medical profession from the unprofessional quacks. More importantly, the *kind* of hope that the physician was expected to minister to the dying patient was essentially different from that provided by the quack. The task of the physician was not merely to create a feeling of hope, but to secure that feeling based on the scientific healing powers of medicine.

Hope was much more than an emotion characterising the personality of the medical doctor or the dying patient. Hope, and specifically the incremental hope offered at the deathbed, coloured the entire deathbed scene and ordered its interactions. Hope was to be seen as the most articulate mark of dying coming under the control of a closed medical system. As opposed to other-worldly salvation or even to complete recovery in this world, both of which depend on external measures of success, 'intelligent hope' offered a promise of self-referential medical treatment of the dying.

Carrying the logic of self-reference to its logical ends would entail a further change in the sense of euthanasia. From this benign sense ascribed by mid-nineteenth century physicians to euthanasia, that of a hopeful death, a more radical form of euthanasia as the medical hastening of death would soon emerge. Death itself could become a medical operation bearing a medical logic.

In the age of medical therapeutics and technique, hope became a call for action. It was no longer possible to wait passively for death; something must be done. Awaiting death was no longer fitting for the modern science of dying, which demanded action. Not only was waiting a state of uncertainty, but it was a state of indifference. Oliver W Holmes, arguably the most notable American physician of the mid-nineteenth century, expressed this notion when he declared, 'No human being can rest for any time in a state of equilibrium where the desire to live and that to depart just balance each other.'[33] As long as the patient is in good mind and hopeful, he will not be bothered by inconveniences. But when hope of cure or improvement are gone, 'every incommodity stares out at him, each one of them packing up his little bundle of circumstances and calling him to move to his new home, even before the apartment is ready to receive the new bodily tenant.'[34]

Though Holmes was by no means advocating euthanasia, his telling metaphor demonstrates how the modern impatience toward awaiting death gave rise not only to euthanasia as the medical treatment of the dying patient, but also to euthanasia as the medical hastening of death. The overambitious desire to profess hope at the deathbed, despite the incurable condition of the dying patient, was the origin of the medical hastening of death

---

[33] OW Holmes, cited by EP Buffet, 'Pleasures of Dying' (1891) 55 *New Englander and Yale Review* 240.
[34] *Ibid.*

as a last resort to the problem of dying. It is simultaneously the moment when all hope is lost, but also the moment in which a final effort is made to overcome the helplessness of the deathbed by hastening death.

At times, the dying could be comforted with the promise of partial or temporary recovery. At other times, or for other people, this was not sufficient and a new call for action was made despite the apparent hopelessness of the situation. In the same way that dying was defined as a problem of medical mastery (as the apparent incapacity to cure), so the solution to the problem became a task of mastery, ie, the ability of medicine to prolong life or, when such an attempt fails, to provide a good death. Medical technique was summoned to save the patient from dying, not by curing him but by hastening death.

Thus, we find the same logic behind the prolonging of life and the hastening of death. In both, the treatment of the dying becomes a duty; in both, the determination of the time of death shifts from the providence of nature to the intercession of technique. Both share a belief in the power of medicine to secure a good death by technical means; and for both, euthanasia is seen as medical treatment in aid of dying. Finally, both share the same disposition of hope, ie, the possibility of technique to become the modern art of dying.

Modern medicine could no longer guarantee the great promise of salvation. Thus, physicians opted for a more tangible and limited promise of hope. This hope was not the promise of a world to come, but a this-worldly guarantee that, as long as life persisted, hope could be renewed indefinitely. It is this modest megalomania that characterised the medical practitioner of the latter half of the nineteenth century, and it is the paradoxical nature of his duty that eventually led some physicians to offer euthanasia of a very different kind, ie, medically hastened death. Euthanasia, from this perspective, can be seen as the attempt of physicians to 'do something' when really nothing more could be done. This desire demonstrates how close late-nineteenth-century medicine came to will the mastery of death for the sake of mastery alone. The movement toward regulation would become complete, once dying turned from a limited medical problem to a problem of public policy and positive law.

IV. DYING AND LAW: LAW AS A SELF-REFERENTIAL SYSTEM

Early on, it became clear to both advocates and opponents of euthanasia that the law was the main obstacle standing in the way of institutionalising medical euthanasia. By 'law,' both sides meant the traditional norms of criminal law, which in principle prohibited the taking of life. There were very few exceptions to this rule and euthanasia did not seem to fall under any of the traditional defences.

For centuries, criminal law was unequivocal. The common law made no distinction between the life of a dying patient and any other human life. Shortening life by a few minutes or by a few years was equally considered murder. Moreover, the fact that the patient was suffering from intolerable pain could serve as no justification for the action, since motivation under common law could only affect the severity of punishment not culpability itself. The medical responsibility to seek the relief of pain could not legally justify shortening the life of a dying patient.[35]

The simple solution to this problem that proponents of euthanasia were advocating was changing the law. And though to contemporary readers, this may seem an obvious solution to the problem, it was not as obvious to jurists at the turn of the twentieth century. The prohibition on euthanasia was not only a legal one but also moral. For euthanasia to become a regular practice, either the moral evaluation of the practice had to change, to the extent that the general public would view euthanasia as a positive act or, more likely, the strong connection between law and morality would have to dissolve and, specifically, the moral judgment of euthanasia would become irrelevant to the question of its legal validity. If euthanasia were to be considered as anything other than murder, law would have to change from a common law tradition based on ancient custom and morality to a modern instrument for regulating medical practice. Law, in other words, would have to become a normatively closed, autopoietic system.

Early attempts to justify the practice of euthanasia were based on the argument that euthanasia is a specific case of the more general problem of suicide. And it is through the legal developments in suicide that one can see clearly the transition of law into a closed system. Supporters of euthanasia emphasised the patient's wish to die and the physician was construed as merely assisting the patient in the fulfilment of his wish. Euthanasia, accordingly, would not be murder but a particular way of committing suicide. The legitimacy of the first would then depend on that of the latter.

The linking of euthanasia to suicide was especially important, since the legal status of suicide underwent gradual change throughout the nineteenth century.[36] Suicide, which was considered a crime for many centuries, was

---

[35] Such a medical duty could be legally justified on the basis of the necessity defence. This hypothetical justification of euthanasia was not raised at the time. Compare, however, with more recent discussions, eg, G Williams, *The Sanctity of Life and the Criminal Law* (New York, Alfred A Knopf, 1957).

[36] For some turn-of-the-twentieth-century discussions, see W Larremore, 'Suicide and the Law' (1904) 17 *Harvard Law Review* 331; W Mikell, 'Is Suicide Murder?' (1903) 3 *Columbia Law Review* 379. For a general overview of the legal history of suicide, see K Burgess-Jackson, 'The Legal Status of Suicide in Early America: A Comparison with the English Experience' (1982) 29 *Wayne Law Review* 57; T Marzen *et al*, 'Suicide: A Constitutional Right? ,' (1985) 24(1) *Duquesne Law Review* 1. For a general history of suicide, see G Minois, *History of Suicide: Voluntary Death in Western Culture, Medicine & Culture* (Baltimore, Johns Hopkins University Press, 1999).

slowly losing its criminal character. Thus, suicide seemed to be a particularly appealing venue for grounding the legality of euthanasia. The decriminalisation of suicide suggested that not every taking of human life would be considered murder.

While Williams' original proposal did not mention suicide, one of the very early reviews of the essay by Dr Lionel Tollemache praised the proposal by describing it as an attempt to 'legalise suicide by proxy.' Moreover, Tollemache believed that Williams' proposal could have been stronger if he had advocated the more general 'legalisability of suicide.'[37] Therefore, the move to legalise euthanasia was tied up from its very inception with the legality of suicide.

Juxtaposing euthanasia to suicide was more than a scholastic exercise. It raised a fundamental question regarding the grounds of the legal objection to euthanasia. The prohibition on euthanasia could no longer be stated in the simple terms of the sanctity of life, because that principle no longer governed the legal status of suicide. Even if euthanasia and suicide were not precisely the same, on what basis could the law continue to object to euthanasia while removing its ban from suicide?

A close examination of the history of suicide will demonstrate not only that the legal status of suicide had changed but also, and more importantly for our concerns, that the relation between law and morality had shifted and that law was emerging as an autonomous normative system. This latter shift had direct implications on the possible regulation of euthanasia.

Suicide was a crime under common law up to the nineteenth century. It was treated like any other crime and was punishable even when successfully performed. Bracton, one of the earlier common law scholars who wrote in the thirteenth century, mentions two such punishments. First, there was the financial sanction of forfeiture to the king of possessions held by the person who had committed suicide. In applying fiscal sanctions to suicide, the law treated suicide like many other crimes against the Crown. However, a second punishment uniquely applied to the case of suicide. This punishment was to mutilate the body by driving a stake through it and then burying it at a crossroad. These sanctions were practised throughout the eighteenth century and were still on the books during the first part of the nineteenth century.

The original prohibition against suicide was grounded on the presupposition that suicide was an act of self-murder. The same logic that prohibited the taking of another's life applied to the taking of one's own. Suicide was known as the act of *felo de se*, a felony against oneself.

Gradually, however, the punishments inflicted were changed. In 1701, Pennsylvania became the first colony to depart clearly from the common

---

[37] LA Tollemache, 'The Cure of Incurables' (1873) 225 *Fortnightly Review* 218.

law tradition by abolishing forfeiture as punishment for suicide. This position spread throughout most of the colonies by the end of the century.[38] Suicide, however, was still a crime in most states at the end of the eighteenth century. Blackstone admitted that the laws of suicide may be too extreme, but still mentioned them as valid law. On the other hand, Zephaniah Swift, later the Chief Justice of Connecticut, was much more critical. Speaking of the more modern approach to suicide, he wrote:

> There can be no act more contemptible, than to attempt to punish an offender for a crime, by exercising a mean act of revenge upon his lifeless clay, that is insensible of the punishment. There can be no greater cruelty, than the inflicting a punishment, as the forfeiture of goods, which must fall solely on the innocent offspring of the offender.[39]

And yet, Swift admitted that suicide was immoral:

> Indeed, this crime is so abhorrent to the feelings of mankind, and that strong love of life which is implanted in the human heart, that it cannot be so frequently committed, as to become dangerous to society.[40]

In the course of the nineteenth century, ignominious burial was also abolished. But although suicide was no longer punishable, for a while it was still considered a crime. This anomalous condition did not persist for long and soon after, the crime as well as the punishment were entirely dropped out of the lawbooks.[41]

The gradual decriminalisation of suicide does not imply that suicide became morally more acceptable. It points, rather, to a widening separation between legal norms, on the one hand, and moral and religious norms on the other. Law could not punish the deceased after his death, neither by degrading his honour nor by confiscating his property. Law could only be concerned with the this-worldly being of the criminal, not with his 'afterlife.' Moreover, modern law, unlike morality, was concerned only with

---

[38] See discussion in Marzen *et al*, above n 36. The latter have found interesting variations among the different colonies.

[39] Z Swift, *A System of the Laws of the State of Connecticut* (New York, Arno Press, 1972) vol 2, 304.

[40] *Ibid*.

[41] In 1877 in Massachusetts, a woman accidentally killed her lover in an attempt to commit suicide. The legal question was whether her attempt to commit suicide would be considered a felony, in which case killing her lover—since it was performed in the course of committing a felony—would be considered murder. The defence lawyer argued that, since suicide was no longer a crime, neither was the attempt to commit suicide. The trial judge, however, ruled that suicide had not ceased to be criminal even if it was no longer punishable by statute and the prisoner was convicted of manslaughter. In reviewing the case, the Supreme Court did not challenge the notion that suicide was still a crime, but only doubted whether the act of the defendant, in attempting to take her own life, was malicious enough to make the killing of another person, in the attempt, murder. See discussion in Marzen *et al*, above n 36.

harms caused by individuals to others and wrongs committed against oneself could no longer be considered crimes, without showing the price society would have to pay. The decline of the strong ties between law and morality is precisely what allowed law to transform into a vehicle of social regulation through self-regulation.

Indeed, that the law no longer understood suicide to be a crime did not mean that suicide became socially legitimate.[42] To the contrary, as the criminality of suicide was subsiding, the deviant nature of the act persisted. While it was no longer prohibited under the law, it became suspect in the eyes of the human sciences. For example, suicide was often considered an act of insanity and those who attempted suicide were treated as insane and were often locked up in asylums to cure them of their destructive impulses.[43]

Consequently, the legal status of suicide re-emerged as a problem. Did the law merely decriminalise suicide, ie, remove the negative prohibition on suicide? Or did the law positively protect the right to perform suicide? Very tellingly, the question of the positive legitimacy of suicide was now tied to the question of whether suicide could ever be a rational act.

In 1895, an article, appropriately titled, 'The Right to Commit Suicide,' argued that:

> Suicide is frequently a consequence of a species of insanity, particularly melancholia, but it is not necessarily a positive proof of a diseased mind. It is, therefore, unjust in many cases to declare the suicide a lunatic, and while it may greatly benefit the relatives of the unfortunate as far as provisions through life insurance policies are concerned, to insist on this view and bless the law for it, it is certainly not proper for the thinker to admit it.[44]

The right to commit suicide became dependent on the rationality of suicide. The prevailing view was that not all suicides should be seen as illegitimate, only those that stemmed from irrational motivations. This new approach to the problem of suicide was, in an important way, diametrically opposed to the older legal tradition expressed by Blackstone. The latter, discussing the conditions for suicide to be a crime, wrote:

> The party must be of years of discretion and in his senses, else it is no crime. But this excuse ought not to be strained to that length to which our coroner's juries are apt to carry it, viz.: that the very act of suicide is an evidence of insanity; as if every man who acts contrary to reason, had no reason at all; for

---

[42] In fact, there is evidence that in some lawbooks, suicide was still considered a crime, at least nominally. Boehm, for instance, mentions that in 1895, suicide was still present in the Penal Code of New York. G Boehm, 'The Right to Commit Suicide' (1895) *Bulletin of the Medico-Legal Congress* 462.

[43] Minois, above n 36.

[44] Boehm, above n 42 at 462.

the same argument would prove every other criminal *non compos*, as well as the self-murderer. The law very rationally judges, that every melancholy or hypochondriac fit does not deprive a man of the capacity of discovering right from wrong, which is necessary to form a legal excuse. And therefore, if a real lunatic kills himself in a lucid interval he is a *felo de se* as much as another man.[45]

While for Boehm, suicide is socially legitimate only if it is rational, for Blackstone, almost to the contrary, it is illegal and illegitimate only if it is rational. This historical reversal makes sense only if we understand the different kinds of problems that suicide posed.

Under the old legal regime, suicide that was committed while the person was of sound mind was viewed as a threat to sovereignty both temporal and divine, since it was performed in defiance of the Crown. The suicide of the insane, on the other hand, could be treated with forgiveness.[46] However, with the decline of sovereignty—not only as a political form but, more importantly, as a way of perceiving the legal order and threats to it—suicide posed a new challenge to the social order. But this time, the challenge was not to sovereignty but rather to the rational organisation of society. It was therefore irrational suicide that now posed the greater threat.[47]

The shift in the conceptualisation of suicide from a challenge to the sovereign's right over death to a problem of rational and scientific governance of life has been explored by one of the most insightful thinkers of modern times, Michel Foucault:

> It is not surprising that suicide—once a crime, since it was a way to usurp the power of death which the sovereign alone, whether the one here below or the Lord above, had the right to exercise—became, in the course of the nineteenth century, one of the first conducts to enter into the sphere of sociological analysis. ... This determination to die, strange and yet so persistent and constant in its manifestations, and consequently so difficult to explain as being due to particular circumstances or individual accidents, was one of the first astonishments of a society in which political power has assigned itself the task of administering life.[48]

---

[45] W Blackstone, *Commentaries on the Laws of England* (Chicago, University of Chicago Press, 1979) vol 4, 7190.

[46] The question of what, precisely, makes a suicide rational was highly debated in the literature. It is interesting to note that the wish of the dying patient, one who is suffering from great pain, to commit suicide was interpreted both as rational and irrational. This is a problem that to this day is at the centre of the physician-assisted suicide and euthanasia debate.

[47] From a strictly legal point of view, only rational suicide counted as suicide proper. Thus, for instance, when the question of life insurance came up, it was clear that the benefits of the policy could be contractually deprived only from a person who committed suicide while being in sound mind.

[48] M Foucault, *The History of Sexuality*, 1st American edn (New York, Pantheon Books, 1978) 138–39. See also M Foucault *et al*, *Society Must Be Defended: Lectures at the Collège De France, 1975–76* (New York, Picador, 2003).

The new concern with suicide had little to do with its offence against sovereignty and much more to do with its offence against the rational order of society. The new legal and social question that the practice posed was not so much how to punish rational suicide but how to prevent irrational suicide. Suicide that could be rationally explained was less threatening and therefore more easily acceptable than suicide that had no rational or possible explanation. The more rational the suicide, the more likely for it to be socially and legally acceptable. The possibility of euthanasia becoming legal was dependent, therefore, on proving its rational grounds.

V. EUTHANASIA AND AUTOPOIESIS: COUPLING LAW AND MEDICINE

The legalisation of the medical hastening of death entailed first the operative closure of both the legal and the medical systems. Operative closure had different significance in medicine and in law. For medicine, operative closure referred first to the monopoly of the physician over the deathbed as master of ceremony, and second to the rise of a this-worldly hope that coloured the treatment of the dying. More radically, operative closure meant that even death could become part of the medical arsenal in the treatment of the dying patient. The external expectation of recovery was replaced by the internal goal of medical control.

For the legal system, operative closure implied normative closure in its most radical sense. In theory at least, any deed could become legal simply because positive law declared it as such. Thus, suicide, previously considered an illegal and immoral act of self-murder, lost its inherently criminal character. Not even the sanctity of life remained outside the scope of positive law.

Operative closure, however, was a necessary but insufficient condition for the emergence of the legal regulation of euthanasia. Each system considered on its own, as we shall now see, could not achieve this result. It was only through the coupling of law and medicine that the legal regulation of medical euthanasia became possible. Thus, a further development of law and medicine into a cognitively open autopoietic system had to take place.

Legal self-closure in itself was insufficient for the regulation of medical euthanasia. The legal system was required to distinguish between legitimate and illegitimate suicide and, more importantly, between the legitimate act of euthanasia and the illegitimate act of murder, but lacked the internal resources to ground such a distinction. The internal distinction had to be grounded on external input from the medical environment, which determined to what extent the taking of life served a medically rational ordering of society. It was the incorporation of medical cognition within the legal system (rational/irrational suicide) that allowed normative selection (legitimate/illegitimate suicide).

Similarly, the self-closure of the medical system could not suffice for the regulation of euthanasia. While for the medical system, euthanasia could be a legitimate practice, it was not clear when it should be applied. The medical ban on euthanasia could not simply be removed. After all, removing the ban could mean opening a door to unjustified killing. True, the physician could easily put an end to his patient's suffering by hastening death. Yet medical ethics gave no guidelines for how the physician should choose between prolonging life and hastening death. There was always the danger that the physician might abuse his power of discretion by illicitly bringing life to an end.

For this reason, even advocates of euthanasia believed that the treatment of the dying should not simply be decriminalised, but regulated. Whereas *decriminalisation* is a removal of the legal sanction, *regulation* brings the practice under the domain of law. Proponents of legalised euthanasia viewed the law as an instrument to shape the conditions and safeguards under which euthanasia could be performed. Law was to play a central role in institutionalising euthanasia, turning it from a discreet medical practice into an established public policy. The power of the law was, in other words, constitutive and formative, not only preventive and nay-saying.[49]

The first wave of attempts to legalise euthanasia took place during the early decades of the twentieth century. In 1906, an attempt to legalise euthanasia took place in Ohio and Iowa, where the Euthanasia Society of America was founded in 1938, setting as its main objective the legalisation of medically hastened death. Its agenda was based on an odd combination of humanitarian and eugenic concerns.

The second wave of attempts to legalise euthanasia began in the aftermath of the Second World War. It may seem, at first, that the new advocates broke from previous attempts to legalise the practice. From the 1960s onward, supporters of euthanasia were more likely to base their claims on patient autonomy and rights than on social Darwinism and eugenics. A closer examination, however, shows an affinity between the two movements. What characterises both is their reliance on legal process, not merely to mark the conditions under which euthanasia would be illegal but, more importantly, to devise the process and procedure under which euthanasia would be legitimate. The formal and procedural regulation of euthanasia was more important for advocates of euthanasia than its moral and legal content, both before and after the Second World War. In autopoietic terms,

---

[49] The constitutive power of law has often been neglected in the analysis of juridical power. The constitutive role of law is especially important with respect to legalisation at the turn of the twentieth century, in the context of emerging welfare and public health legislation. A Hunt and G Wickham, *Foucault and Law: Toward a Sociology of Law as Governance, Law and Social Theory* (London, Boulder and Colo, Pluto, 1994).

internal legal regulation became the means for external medical and social regulation. In terms of technique, the regulation of dying through euthanasia became not merely a means but, an end in itself.

Euthanasia Society of America

On 16 January, 1938, the National Society for the Legalization of Euthanasia was incorporated in New York City. With its establishment, the efforts to legalise euthanasia entered a new phase. The Society set as its goal to 'create public demand for the legalization of voluntary euthanasia, and to secure the enactment of state laws permitting voluntary euthanasia with procedure as simple as is consistent with security against abuse in the state of New York.'[50] A year later, the society changed its name, but not its goal, and became known as the Euthanasia Society of America (ESA).

The founding of the ESA entailed more than just a change in organisational tactics. It manifested a more radical shift in the understanding of euthanasia and its goals. Both the problem of dying and its solution— euthanasia, which had initially been understood as confined to medical concerns—were now understood more broadly as social concerns. Dying became one among a broad array of public health issues, such as birth rates and mental health. Similarly, euthanasia became one among several new practices regulating the biological processes of birth and death, such as birth control, abortion and sterilisation. All reflected a belief that human beings could use their knowledge to control events and better their lives.[51]

In addition, for the ESA, euthanasia no longer meant merely hastening the death of patients who were already dying. Rather, by the early twentieth century, euthanasia was advocated as a solution to a broader range of cases, which included the 'physically handicapped.' For both its supporters and its opponents, euthanasia was no longer confined to the dying patient.

What is most striking about the ESA's agenda is not that a small group of individuals believed that mentally retarded patients should be killed. The debate showed a much broader and more troubling phenomenon. At no point along the way, as far as the documents can reveal, was the question raised whether the killing of mentally retarded and physically handicapped people was justified independently of social benefits. Most concretely, the question whether law itself posed a challenge to such a practice, one that could not be overcome by legislation, was never seriously debated. The only obstacle that seemed to stand in the way of legalising non-voluntary

---

[50] Founding statement of the National Society for the Legalization of Euthanasia, 16 January 1938 (from the archives of the Society).
[51] See also SL Kuepper, *Euthanasia in America, 1890–1960: The Controversy, the Movement, and the Law* (Rutgers University, 1981) 112–13.

euthanasia was public opinion. It was in the court of public opinion that law in its regulatory capacity (rather than normative capacity) played a central role as a justificatory mechanism.

During the first meeting of the ESA's Executive Committee on 30 March, 1938, the Committee discussed whether the Society should support euthanasia for incurable idiots. The discussion ended with the decision that, while the ultimate aim of the Society did include such cases, it would be well not to raise the issue in the first bill to be introduced. The Committee decided that, at first, its goal would be limited to securing the legalisation of voluntary euthanasia.

The standard ESA Bill stated that a person of sound mind over 21 years of age who suffered from a painful and incurable disease could petition any court of record or judge thereof (except appellate courts) for euthanasia. The court was to appoint a committee of three persons, at least one of whom was a physician, to determine the merits of the request. If two or more of the committee members agreed that merciful death was warranted, and if the court approved, then the patient's life could be terminated. Death would be administered by a physician or any other person under a physician's direction, in the presence of two witnesses.

The emphasis on regulation as grounds for justification reached a peak after the Second World War, after the Nazi atrocities and, specifically, the Nazi euthanasia project were revealed. The Society, continuing its activities, tried to fend off any attempt to compare its euthanasia proposals with those of the Third Reich. One strategy that the ESA chose was to clarify the voluntary character of the American proposals; another and much more striking strategy was to emphasise the fact that American euthanasia, unlike Nazi euthanasia, would be regulated by law:

> Misunderstandings of our aim still exist. Some people think we're in favour of the government secretly killing off defectives, as in Nazi Germany; others believe that even now, before the law is amended, the Society can somehow arrange to have euthanasia administered, as we receive piteous appeals from hopeless sufferers.
> So during the past year we have taken every opportunity to explain that we are opposed to illegal, surreptitious, compulsory, 'mercy killings,' that what we are working for is to legalize medically supervised euthanasia for incurable sufferers who ask for it.[52]

The problem with Nazi euthanasia, according to the ESA, was not so much its non-voluntary character as its arbitrariness manifested by its 'illegal, surreptitious' and 'compulsory' character. In a single word, the problem of the Nazi euthanasia was its *unlawfulness*, while the moral superiority of the ESA proposal was its lawfulness.

---

[52] Taken from notes from the annual meeting of the ESA in 1943.

The 'law' was seen as a means of controlling the dangers of an unfettered application of euthanasia. The Nazi euthanasia had allowed medical technology to run amok, while euthanasia, according to the ESA, would be restrained by the law. Law was therefore praised for its capacity to implement public policy and medical technique, and not for its independent moral judgment, independent of both public opinion and technical concern.

VI. CONCLUSION: DEATH AND THE LAW

From the first euthanasia debate in late nineteenth-century America, to its most recent application in early twenty-first-century Oregon in the USA, the problem of dying and its solution have been framed in medico-legal terms. Though the involvement of medicine and law in the way we die has become natural for us, it is by, or more precisely through, autopoietic theory that we can begin to unpack the significance of this transformation.

In the beginning, opens the autopoietic book of Genesis, there was the undifferentiated social system. It is through a historical process of (self-)differentiation that law, medicine, economics, aesthetics and other operatively closed subsystems developed. Since the operation of a closed system can only take place according to the system's own terms, self-reference is a necessary characteristic of autopoietic systems.

In the history of euthanasia, the paradox of medical self-reference became manifest once the physician took responsibility over the care of the dying patient. Health proper was no longer the criterion for medical care. Rather than health, the medical profession offered the dying patient this-worldly hope, which now signified the exclusive power of the proficient doctor to control the condition of the dying patient, either by temporary relief or by accurate diagnosis and short-term prognosis. The paradox of self-reference achieved a climactic peak, once death in the form of the medical hastening of death became one more way to inspire the new hope of medical control.

In the legal field, the paradox of self-reference became apparent once law was divorced from morality, akin to the way in which medical treatment became separate from health proper. The decriminalisation of suicide in the course of the nineteenth century signified the rise of a new form of legality, positive law. It is this transformation that allowed law to declare lawful the unlawful practice of taking life.

Decriminalisation of suicide was the first step toward the regulation of euthanasia. The latter included the creation of a bureaucratic mechanism under which the taking of life would become possible. What is important to notice is that in the case of euthanasia, as in many similar instances of bureaucratic regulation, the setting of formal procedures becomes the primary source of legitimization, regardless of the content of the act. This at least was the line of defence suggested by the ESA in the years before and after the Second World War.

The rise of law and medicine as autopoietic systems is only one way to characterise the historical transformations of the treatment of the dying patient. This story captures quite accurately the facts but leaves unveiled their deeper significance. We are now able to lay out the deeper layers of the history of euthanasia, first, as the rise of nihilism and secondly, as the coming of death and law under the sway of technique.

Nihilism as the attempt to overcome metaphysics, or in Nietzsche's words 'the devaluing all values,' unfolds as a tale of three subsequent deaths. First came the death of God. Dying, which in the traditional Catholic world was a *rite de passage* between this world and the next, became, in the *ars moriendi* tradition, a way of living. The other-worldly nature of dying gradually disappeared.

Secondly came the death of death, as the question of dying became a question of living, and the physician, the caretaker of life par excellence, became the master of death. The desire to master the hour of death gradually expanded: dying was medicalised and the treatment of the dying patient became regulated by medical technique. Mastery over death, in other words, was not the consequence of the growing power of medicine but rather the reverse. The new disposition toward dying gave rise to a constant search for treatment and to impatience toward what was perceived as a merely passive waiting for death.

Finally came the death of law, as law became nothing more than an instrument of regulation. While law always entails an ordering of human action, the history of euthanasia suggests that for some normative forms, mastery is only a means for achieving a further goal. This was the case with the Protestant art of dying. Likewise with medical ethics, which initially directed the physician to ease the pangs of death and support the dying in his final hours.

The narrative of three subsequent deaths captures only the nihilistic and depraved character of this historic movement. The movement can also be captured in positive terms under the name of technique.

Far from a mere instrument or device, technique stands for a radical transformation in the way different phenomena, such as death, become amenable to regulation. Though death in all known cultures is subject to regulation, it is only under the modern conditions of medicine as health management that regulation becomes a purpose in itself, no longer answerable to religious faith in other-worldly salvation or to the secularised desire for this-worldly salvation. It is this basic transformation of dying which allows for its regulation to take place.

Similarly, what is unique about modern law as regulatory law is that the ultimate end of the law *is* further mastery. The history of euthanasia suggests precisely this development. At first, the ethics of the deathbed were religious belief and *ars moriendi* practice. Gradually, however, the deathbed became governed by legal measures aimed at the regulation of the treatment of the dying. Under the rule of technique, humans were dominated by the desire to master their world for the sake of mastery alone.

Though foreign to the language of systems theory, the notions of nihilism and technique are, in the final analysis, quite close to self-reference and self-regulation. Is not self-reference precisely the attempt to overcome metaphysics and the grounding of the system in itself, and does not self-regulation signify the regulation of the system for the sake of its own regulation and production? But even if one may argue that the notions of nihilism and technique lie dormant in self-reference and self-regulation, the former carry with them a further truth.

It is at this point that we should return to the stories with which we opened, to Greek tragedy and Talmud—not in order to reflect further on the competing sides of the paradox, but rather to bring to life a third voice, that of the divine witness, which gives the paradox its sense and significance. It is precisely the absence of the divine voice which characterises the modern condition and it is an account of this absence which should be present in our account of historic transformations.[53]

First, as we turn to Sophocles' tragedy, we should listen to the Dionysian choir, which sings, in the wondrous Ode to Man, of the powers of humans to conquer the earth, the skies and the seas:

> Manyfold the *deinon*[54] and nothing towers more *deinon* than man. He who even across the grey sea by wintery south-wind advances, amidst engulfing waves traversing. Of gods the highest, Earth, imperishable untiring, he wears-out with ploughs moved-back-and-forth year upon year, with horses turning-over.

A name is given to these powers, *techne*. And it is this acquired wisdom that allows man to reign (*mēchnoen texnas*) over nature beyond expectation. The power of mortals to control their destiny seems boundless. Nothing appears to stand in the way of Man blocking his future (*aporia*). Nothing but these two: *thanatos* and *dikē*.

First, appears death: though Man is known for 'overcoming-all-obstacles'— 'from the one that approaches, *Hades*, flight he cannot find.' Secondly, comes the law: 'joining together the laws of the earth, and the sworn *dike* of the gods' he is 'towering-high-over-the-*polis*' but 'he loses the *polis*, he with whom the not-shining always is, for the sake of bold-venture'[55] (*apolis hotōi to mē kalon exunesti tolmas charin*).

---

[53] For a different discussion of the 'absent third,' see L Barshack, 'Notes on the Clerical Body of the Law' (2003) 24 *Cardozo Law Review* 1151.

[54] The translation cited is by Philippe Nonet (unpublished). Nonet writes, 'The Greek word *deinos* is a key word of tragic poetry. It will be left untranslated. It signifies at once all the following, with various emphases: 'terrifying,' 'awesome,' 'powerful,' and 'wonderful.'

[55] I owe this close translation of the Greek text to Philippe Nonet.

Though at first it may seem that law and death are still present today as limits to the power of medical technique, in truth a radical transformation has taken place. As we have seen, both death and law have succumbed to the reigning powers of modern technique and have thus been fundamentally transformed.

Similarly, when we think of the Talmudic text, it is not the dispute between the rabbis, nor the overruling voice from heaven that should concern us, but rather God's response. Again, while it may seem that our modern law is no different than that of the Jewish Talmud—both committed to the paradox of self-reference—the differences are more striking than the similarities.

The key here is to see the way in which the voice from heaven differs from the word of God. While the former partakes in the dispute, the latter observes not merely from outside but from above. While the former attempts to ground the law, the latter transcends it. Thus, the voice from heaven is captured within the legal system, whereas the divine standpoint is free for reflection.

The unique character of the Dionysian choir and the Divine gaze is not accounted for by autopoietic theory. The problem, to be sure, is not that transcendence is missing from the autopoietic description of the modern world but rather that transcendence is missing from the modern world itself and that autopoietic theory fails to see this, and attempts to overcome this fundamental lack by the notion of system. Turning to the ancient texts thus allows us precisely what the history of euthanasia has provided—namely, a moment of reflection from which we can think of ourselves as different from who we are. Far from providing amusement or laughter, this moment of reflection may more properly lead to anxious hope.

13

The Paradox of the Law: Between Generality and Particularity—Prohibiting Torture and Practising it in Israel

ROEI AMIT*

THE QUESTION, 'WHAT does the *law mean?*' opens up a long series of new questions, such as: what it *means* to whom, where and by what *means* it does so, and so on. Even just by posing the question of meaning, we dare a paradox. Asking about the meaning of the law, in a way, is suggesting that this meaning is not evident, and that this meaning is not contained in the words of the law; it means that some other means are required in order for the law to *mean*. Posing the question also suggests that the general aspect, considered one of the characteristics of the law, is actually a matter of particular context and of further interpretation and means.

Trying to comprehend the relationship between a law and an event may suggest that no event is a law unless specifically pronounced—by an act of judgment in its largest sense, ie, attribution of meaning—and hence, it is no longer a general law but rather a particular 'application' of it. This also applies in the reverse—namely, that no specific event is the law, unless several such events share the same character, and then it is a particular event no longer but an abstract deduction of their 'resemblance.'

We are dealing here with a complex relation, wherein there is a major gap between what we conceive to be the meaning of the law, which by definition is general and abstract, and its concrete signification, which realises over particular and singular cases. The law acquires meaning, then, where it is no longer general as it pretends to be, but rather is a unique case, which in its turn can never be the law.

---

* It is my pleasure to thank the participants of the Conference for their enriching and stimulating remarks, to Oren Perez, Gunther Teubner, Peer Zumbansen for their organisation and hospitality, and to the precious remarks of my dear friends Michal Alberstein and David Shammai.

The act of judgment (judgment about the meaning), on the one hand, announces the law of the case and hence makes it general, a case that is subsumed and becomes 'conform' with the law. On the other hand, it announces the law of a case in a particular event; the law exists in some way only by this case, by its singularity.[1]

A paradoxical logic is taking place between these elements, between rules and events, law and the case, code and exception—when simultaneously they exclude and depend upon each other in order to have a meaning. Most of the time, this problem does not attract attention, since the systems of judgment and of meaning are functioning 'as if' the relationship between the general and particular were present and transparent. This means that either the law is conceived to be directly and clearly applicable on events, or that it is a set of casuistic events from which the law is deduced. It presupposes that the meaning of the law resides in its words that need only to be applied or explained in a direct way. Daring the question of meaning is necessary in order to have a more ample comprehension of the law phenomena: what does it mean to prohibit torture? And in order not merely to discuss it in a *general* way, this chapter will analyse a *concrete* case.

The Israeli legal system's treatment of torture is an 'example' of a discursive mechanism, which manipulates (in the sense of 'putting into work') the paradox of the law—from a 'non-existing' phenomenon, through denial and then implied authorisation, to an explicit interdiction; but still accompanied by current practices and indifference; the meanings produced by the Israeli legal system are constantly being changed, as part of a general sociocultural context.

This chapter will study several aspects of this question of meaning, mainly in its legal context: starting in section I with the general meaning/meaninglessness of the words of the law and the discursive taboo that ruled the *question of torture*[2] in Israel. The concrete meaning of the law will be discussed in section II through the judicial approval of torture, and of several performative contradictions involved. The expressed prohibition of torture will be examined between abstract and concrete meaning of the law and its contingencies in section III, in order to evoke other sources of its meaning,

---

[1] Or by accident, as explains Jean-Luc Nancy, who speaks about the necessity of the accident: 'The law must be the universal code, which even the definition itself implies the omission or the absorption of any accidentally. The case must be predicted. As a matter of fact (but this fact is constitutive in the law, it's the fact of the juri-diction), the case must be assigned and legitimated case by case. ... The order of law is this order that is instituted by the formal consideration (*prise en compte*)—in all the sense of this word—of the accident itself, however without conceiving its necessity'; it is the *Lapsus Judicii*, as he calls it. JL Nancy, *L'impératif catégorique* (Paris, Flammarion, 1983) 39.

[2] For some etymologic-historical relations between posing a 'question' and practising 'torture,' see J Derrida, *Voyous* (Paris, Galilée, 2003) 27.

involving a permanent rule of exception in section IV. This will lead to the conclusion, section V, by suggesting some theoretical considerations of the law's paradox as one of meaning on the one hand, and the meaning of this paradox on the other, specially as viewed by the torture example.

I. GENERAL MEANING/MEANINGLESSNESS OF THE LAW AND THE DISCURSIVE TABOO

The positive law as a general standard seems to have no concrete sense; its words need pragmatic context in order to acquire meaning: if one looks at some of the relative sources of the positive law in Israel, one may think that torture is forbidden. The Declaration of Independence, without a consensual legal status but as an interpretative guideline, announces that the 'State of Israel shall take care of the development of the country for the benefice of all its habitants, and will be founded on liberty, justice and peace.' The Basic Law of Human Dignity and Liberty, from 1992, known as Israel's 'Bill of Human Rights' and the cornerstone of its 'Constitutional Revolution,' declares in article 2 that 'There shall be no violation of the life, body or dignity of any person as such.' A simple inspection of these sources reveals no authorisation for torture or its like—not under any circumstances. Following these general declarations, a series of more concrete and detailed dispositions can be found, for example, in the Penal Code or in the Penal Procedure Law (Authorization of Coercion and Detention) 1996,[3] addressing all public agents, which condemn any use of force or violence against any person during police work.[4]

At the same time, Israel signed up to several International Conventions, which forbid in the clearest way any kind of torture. The prohibition of torture is one of the more disciplined subjects in international law, utilising high-precision instruments:[5] from the Universal Human Rights Declaration of 1948, through to the Declaration against Torture of 1975, followed by the treaties upgrading the normative standard, such as the UN Covenant on Civil and Political Rights from 1966 and the UN Convention Against Torture and Other Cruel, Inhuman and Degrading Treatment or Punishment from 1984. Both of these Conventions were signed by Israel close to the time of their adoption by the United Nations, but ratified only

---

[3] Article 1.2 of the Penal Procedure Law (Authorization of Coercion and Detention) 1996; article 277.1 of the Penal Code. This disposition also details the detention conditions, etc.

[4] All these sources merit a careful look and close reading, which will place them in a context where many other paradoxes might be involved; they serve here as a provisional starting point.

[5] See M Nowak, 'Civil and Political Rights: Prohibition of Torture' in J Symonides (ed), *Human Rights: Concept and Standards* (Cornwall, Unesco and Ashgate Publishers, 2000) 78.

toward the end of 1991.[6] Since their ratification, they have obliged Israel, not only from an international aspect but also from an internal, positive law perspective.

These general sources say nothing by themselves; they need to be interpreted, to have their sense in concrete contexts, ie, to have a pragmatic use.[7] So, though in plain reading these texts prohibit torture, they must be placed in a context, must be reread, and need to be understood as such, which is not always the case.

Furthermore, all these normative texts presuppose a 'regular time' that the special case of Israel excludes. Many jurisdictions and legal systems acknowledge a 'state of emergency' legal regime, when separation of power is suspended and the executive authority takes the lead for a while, whenever particular conditions have occurred. Israel, since its creation, has existed under a legal state of emergency, where the government can revoke legal and basic legislation and initiate state-of-emergency ordinances. This situation is reinforced by the existing Defence (Emergency) Regulations, issued in 1945 by the British-mandated regime in Palestine, regulations still valid (through their adoption by the state of Israel) and authorising, among other things, administrative detention, deportations and house demolitions. The proclamation of an 'exceptional' and 'provisional' legal state of emergency has been renewed regularly since 1948,[8] and hence has become a sort of regular, basic norm.[9]

---

[6] The Convention was adopted on 16 December, 1966, signed by Israel on 19 December 1966 and ratified 25 years later on 18 August 1991. It indicates what was afterward specified by the Convention Against Torture, adopted 10 December 1984, signed by Israel on 22 October 1986, and ratified 3 October 1991: 'For the purposes of this Convention, the term "torture" means any act by which severe pain or suffering, whether physical or mental, is intentionally inflicted on a person for such purposes as obtaining from him or a third person information or a confession, punishing him for an act he or a third person has committed or is suspected of having committed, or intimidating or coercing him or a third person, or for any reason based on discrimination of any kind, when such pain or suffering is inflicted by or at the instigation of or with the consent or acquiescence of a public official or other person acting in an official capacity. It does not include pain or suffering arising only from, inherent in or incidental to lawful sanctions': Article 1.

The beginning of the 1990s in Israel was a time of important human rights legislative work; see the legislation of the Basic Law and the declaration of the Constitutional Revolution. David Kretzmer, 'The New Basic Laws on Human Rights: A Mini Revolution is Israeli Constitutional Law?' (1992) 26 *Israel Law Review* 239.

[7] The pragmatic use in these cases is mostly the work of courts, which are considered to be in charge of the law's interpretation (but not only them, see below); see O Cayla, *La notion de signification en droit. Contribution à une théorie du droit naturel de la communication* (Thèse, Paris II, 1992). More than this, these 'general sources' are also particular cases; each one of them cannot be understood without a proper context implying other paradoxes. Here, they will be considered only from one aspect, ie, in relation to the context and meaning of torture.

[8] The first declaration took place on 19 May 1948, and since then it has been renewed every year by the Knesset; its rules are in the Basic Law of the Government, articles 49–50, and its amendment from 1992 and 2001.

[9] 'State of emergency' should also be contextualised. Although there have been several periods since it was first declared and applied in 1948, and even sometimes a public debate calling to abrogate it (in 2000, for example), still, from the positive law perspective, it has been constantly in force; see below.

The Paradox of the Law: Between Generality and Particularity 279

Another inversion of the general and the exceptional occurs when the Israeli regime presents itself as—and is supposed to be—democratic, human-rights oriented, a regime which shares 'rule of law' convictions and practices, at the same time being constantly involved in an 'ongoing occupation system.' This situation brings with it a multitude of antinomies, such as the use both of an argument and its opposite to treat the occupied territories in one way and its population in another: introducing different treatment to different people on the basis of their ethnicity (ie, discrimination); refusing a stable, civil, egalitarian status for over a million and a half Palestinians; and inventing a contradictory legal apparatus that at once acknowledges and rejects legal dispositions, including Basic Laws and international law (especially the Fourth Geneva Convention). We will not be able in this chapter to address all the paradoxical nuances of this state[10]; but we can notice that nowhere, neither in the Defence (Emergency) Regulations nor in the published Military Regulations governing the occupied territories, can a formal authorisation for torture be found.

Israeli positive and published law, although containing anomalies and structural paradoxes, does not contain permission to torture, at least if we stop here, at the words of the law and at its abstract meaning. Throughout the first few decades of the occupation, no one spoke (in a public or recorded way) about torture; it is as if it did not exist. A discursive taboo is thereby exercised[11]; the word torture is not authorised. This lack of signifier does not indicate, however, that some concrete means do not exist, but rather, that their meaning for the moment is not publicly pronounced.

---

[10] See D Kretzmer, *The Occupation of Justice: The Supreme Court of Israel and the Occupied Territories* (Albany, State University of New York Press, 2002). The period studied by Kretzmer is the one following the June 1967 war; other perspectives regarding the periods and terminology do exist.

'In Israel, the term "Occupation" is used in a similar way to the phrase "exception to the rule", except that its target audience is different. "Exception to the rule" is the sop used by the nationalist camp and the larger segment of the population that constitutes the "middle ground"—those who are not politically aware. The term "Occupation," however, is a sop used by the left-wing Zionist camp. The evils that we witness and create are supposedly the result of the Occupation. The Occupation is presented as a mystical law, inevitability; everything is the fault of the Occupation. If only the Occupation were done away with, all others evils, brutality, folly and malice would disappear. This line of thinking is prevalent in, and strongly adhered to by, the respectable liberal segment of Israeli society. It prevents one from seeing the wider deeper context of our life here in Israel. The "exception to the rule" and the "Occupation" each in its way and with its specific audience, enable many well-meaning Israelis to exempt themselves from the responsibility of maintaining human rights'. R Marton (ed), *Torture: Human Rights, Medical Ethics and the Case of Israel* (New Jersey, Zed Books, 1995) 2.

[11] The lack of materials (for the moment) prior to the mid-1980s makes it difficult to study the situation before the first public manifestations of this question between 1948 and 1967 and afterwards; this research still needs to be done.

II. SOME CONCRETE MEANINGS OF THE LAW, THE JUDICIAL APPROVAL OF TORTURE AND SOME PERFORMATIVE CONTRADICTIONS

Only after some serious accidents occurred was this silence about torture broken. One event in particular affronted public opinion and provoked the High Court of Justice to address the first element of this problem. After liberating the passengers of a hijacked bus, two General Security Service (GSS) agents executed the terrorist perpetrators of the hijacking, terrorists who had already been surrounded and captured alive. The daily newspaper, *Hadshot*, published the story, along with photographs of the terrorists being taken alive after the incident ended. As a result of the article, the Minister of Interior shut the newspaper down for several days for breaching censorship law.[12] The High Court of Justice confirmed the legality of this decision, saying: 'Between the secrecy required to assure the national security and of public order, and the non-written right of being informed, it's the secrecy that should prevail.'[13] In an exceptional occurrence, a Presidential pardon was granted to the GSS agents before any criminal proceedings against them even commenced. The High Court also validating this decision, the judges agreed that:

> There are cases where those who are the shield of the country and bear the responsibility for its survival and of its security, consider that certain deviation from the law is inevitably a necessity in order to protect its security.[14]

The judges themselves recognised in a legal text (ie, in a judgment) that certain deviation from the legal domain was authorised. Secrecy and exception dominated the emergence of the issue, where the logic of secrecy ran like a light-motif through these affairs: in order to have a secret, the knowledge that it exists must circulate; if it does not, then the secret does not 'excite.' In 1987, the *Nafsu* case[15] came to light, wherein several GSS agents, retired from service, acknowledged the systematic use of physical force during interrogations of suspects in order to obtain confessions. Consequently, the government decided to appoint an Inquiry Commission to look into these allegations.

Once the phenomena became a matter of discourse, three aspects of outspoken treatment were shared by several agencies: (a) there are no cases of torture in Israel; (b) if there were any, they are not 'torture' but 'interrogation means' and 'moderate physical pressure'; and (c) even if there is torture,

---

[12] Dating as well to the days of the British Mandate.
[13] *Hadashot Inc v Minister of Interior*, 1984, PDI 38(2) 477.
[14] *Barzilai v State of Israel*, 1986, PDI 40(3) 505.
[15] *Isath Nafsu v Military Attorney*, 1987, PDI 41(2) 361.

it is justifiable in the war against terrorism. It is a well-known, paradoxical mixture of an ontological refutation, a semantic treatment and a justifying approach,[16] mixed in a performative contradiction.

The Landau Commission, chaired by the President of the Supreme Court at the time, published a report[17] containing both public and confidential sections. This report denied the existence of torture practices, using the term 'moderate physical pressure.' Furthermore, it introduced 'a code,' a normative text for their conduct, which was not publicly published. In their Report, the Commission determined that (a) agents of the GSS frequently used physical force during investigations, and (b) that they lied regularly and systematically in court. Hence, the normative conclusions of the Commission were: (a) it is legal to use 'moderate physical pressure' during interrogations, but (b) it is completely forbidden to lie in court. The article of 'necessity defence,' from the Penal Code, was the decisive source for this authorisation.

The Commission declared that 'We regard our principal function as being to guide the essential process of rehabilitation and healing with regard to the GSS activity[18] ... by integrating this vital activity into the framework of the values of the rule of law, which the state of Israel espouses,'[19] and this only a couple of years after the High Court of Justice acknowledged that 'certain deviations from the law are necessary,' going on to say: 'The effective interrogation of terrorist suspects is impossible without the use of means of pressure, in order to overcome an obdurate will, not to disclose information and to overcome the fear of the person under interrogation that harm will befall him from his own organization, if he does reveal information ... and we think that a confession thus obtained is admissible in a criminal trial.' And it is by 'the exertion of a moderate measure of physical pressure ... guided by setting clear boundaries ... as is set out in detail in the second part of this report.'[20] We can remark that the Commission mixed several functions of the

---

[16] See Plato, *Gorgias' Dialogue*, Plato, *Œuvre complète III* and the J Lyotrad analysis, *Le Différend* (Paris, Editions de Minuit, 1983) 31; see also S Cohen, 'The Social Response to Torture in Israel' in R Marton (ed), *Torture, Human Rights, Medical Ethics and the Case of Israel* (London, Zed Books, 1995) 20: 'Nothing is happening ... What is happening is really something else ... What is happening is completely justified.'

[17] 'Commission of Inquiry into the Methods of Investigation of the General Security Service Regarding Hostile Terrorist Activity' (1989) 23 *Israel Law Review* 146.

[18] 'Members [of the GSS], and in particular members of the Investigation Unit, may be able to overcome the feelings of distress and anxiety due to the burden of the past that weighs on them': *Landau Commission Report*, at 184.

[19] *Landau Commission Report*, at 149: 'The first way is to recognize that because of crucial interests of State security, the activity of the GSS in their war against terrorism occurs in a "twilight zone" which is outside the realm of the law, and therefore these services should be freed from the boundaries of the law and must be permitted deviations from the law. This way must be rejected': *ibid*, at 182–83.

[20] *Ibid*.

'physical pressure.' It can be used, not just for the purpose of finding crucial information in order to prevent forthcoming terrorist attacks; it is also used in order to find information in general, to get confessions and to help the interrogated person overcome his own fears (a kind of a 'self-salvation' or expiation aspect).[21] And, in an exceptional manner that differentiates from usual proof-admissible rules, information hence obtained can also be used in court.

The Commission transformed the 'necessity defence,' which is used as a reply in a criminal trial after liability had been proved, an ex post factum defence, to a general, a priori excuse. From a concrete and contextual response to criminal liability, it becomes the source for a general normative code of conduct.[22] This transformation from the extraordinary, exceptional case to a general abstraction can be found also in the use of the 'ticking bomb' criterion. The Commission tried to suggest this exception as the standard model in order to authorise the use of 'physical pressure.' Even before they studied the way this exception is used and the manner in which it is formulated, ie, as a general justification model, they proposed that it would become the norm[23]—as it did.

The Commission, toward the end of its Report, proposed a general normative code of conduct,[24] expect that this code was confidential, which is another exception for the principles of 'the rule of law.' This code became, for a while, a positive law of the State of Israel. No particular measures were recommended against any person involved in the disorder, torture and disinformation that the Commission denounced in a general way.

Over the years, in spite of attempts to challenge the interrogation methods and the Landau Commission's Report that became their code, a judicial approval[25] of these methods has been evolving. In the actual framework, we will demonstrate just one of the many aspects of the ruling series implicated,

---

[21] See GR Scott, *The History of Torture* (Middlesex, Senate, 1995) 6 .

[22] SZ Feller, 'Not Actual "Necessity" but Possible "Justification"; Not "Moderate" Pressure, but Either "Unlimited" or "None at All"' (1989) 23 *Israel Law Review* 201.

[23] On the relativity and the sequentiality of the terminology regarding terror as exception and as justification for moving the borders of the 'rule of law,' see S Zizek, *Welcome to the Desert of the Real* (New York, Wooster Press, 2001), and see below: terror and torture can be understood as activities defined and defining borders, in an incessant definition struggle.

[24] 'We have therefore formulated a code of guidelines for GSS interrogators which define, on the basis of past experience, and with as much precision as possible, the boundaries of what is permitted to the interrogator and mainly what is prohibited': *Landau Commission Report*, at 185.

[25] It is the dialectical aspects of the discourse which reveal and mask; see J Butler analysing Foucault: 'The shift from the subject of power to a set of practices in which power is actualized in its effects signals a departure from the conceptual model of sovereignty that dominates thinking on politics, law and the question of right ... among others is the creation of the subject itself,' J Butler, 'Sovereign Performatives' in *Excitable Speech: A Politics of the Performative* (New York, Routledge, 1997) 78. In our case, it is the possibility of accessing the tribunal that frames the subject as a speaking one, but the system does not hear him.

mainly the subtle manipulation of the general and the particular. In 1991, the Court delivered a decision to a petition asking them to forbid the use of violent pressure that had been permitted by the Landau Commission.[26] The Court affirmed that questions regarding the legality of interrogation measures could only be examined within the context of a concrete case. Such a case arises if the validity of a confession extracted by means of the 'special' interrogation is challenged in court, or if a member of the GSS is charged with acting illegally. The Court therefore refused to rule on the questions of principle raised by the petitioners. It also refused to order publication of the secret part of the Report.

This decision was paradoxical.[27] On the one hand, the Landau Commission tried to explain that the use of pressure was not meant to obtain general information or confessions, but to extract preventive information. The authorities were unlikely to charge a person if the evidence against him or her consisted of a confession extracted by use of force. Furthermore, the authorities held that, as in the Code, the use of these methods was permitted; so, on the other hand, an interrogator using those methods was acting legally and would not be prosecuted—as indeed followed. This means that the Landau Commission Report cannot be attacked, in the way the Court stated. And although, in this specific case, one of the petitioners was formerly an interrogated person, the petition was rejected as being general.[28]

Some elements of general context must be kept in mind: the first Intifada broke out a couple of months after the publication of the Landau Commission Report; those were days of an unsteady national-union coalition. At the same time, toward the end of the Twelth Knesset in 1992, two Basic Laws concerning Human Rights were being voted on, and a 'Constitutional Revolution' was being proclaimed.[29]

In most of the cases concerning that affair, the Court was content with a short, laconic decision, not signed in a nominative way, contrary to the Supreme Court's habits of long, explicative and signed decisions.[30] Most of

---

[26] *MA Salachat v State of Israel*, 2581/1991 TKDIN 93(3) 592.

[27] Kretzmer, above n 10, at 137.

[28] The Court terminated its decision, saying 'The most that I can say in this matter is that I am not seeing myself obliged to one doctrine or another concerning the legality of GSS activities; and if in a concrete future case, the question of this legality will be raised, I am reserving myself the right to uphold or to reject all or part of the Landau Commission recommendations, according to the different circumstances': *Morad Adnan Salachat v State of Israel*, 2581/1991 TKDIN 93(3) 592.

[29] *Ibid*.

[30] See Y Shakar and R Harisse, 'The References of the Supreme Court: Quantitative Analysis' (1996) 27 *Mishpatim* 119. Such cases are treated as non-important, with no symbolic or educational value; they are considered to belong to the series of 'technical decisions' the Supreme Court is giving in short, laconic style; the decision about the 'importance' or the 'technicality' aspect of a case is in itself a normative decision.

the time, the official printer did not publish these decisions. We can find expedited decisions, such as: 'We have heard the investigators, they gave us the general outline of the information and the particular aspects concerning the applicant. After having heard them, we are content to see the conditions are fulfilled.'[31] Judicial reasoning, fact-based analysis or general human rights discourse were absent; the petition was rejected after a closed-door hearing. Inside the courtroom stay only the judges, the state attorney, and the GSS agents. The applicant, who was always missing (and is held by the GSS, being interrogated) was represented by a lawyer who faced a 'Catch 22' decision when asked to agreed on a closed-door hearing. If he agrees to the hearing, he was sent out of the room and the Court received classified information, rejecting the application as a *specific case* that satisfied the conditions.[32] If he refused, the judges asserted that they did not have specific information and the case was rejected as being *general*[33] (and the lawyer was reproached for interfering with the Court's work). Whatever the decision of the lawyer, the petition was doomed to be rejected.

The Court renounced its role of interpreting an abstract law in order to explain the singularity of a case, or to mitigate between the general and the particular aspects by a judicial decision. It did so in favour of the GSS, which became the entity which decides. It was the GSS that the normative general code addressed; it held all the information concerning the specific cases, and there was no other procedure, no other forum that either could or was willing to control its activities. The Court rejected the case, saying: 'The petitions are of theoretical aspects, and in consequence they cannot be judged; the Court is not dealing with theoretical questions.'[34] The Court took the word of the GSS (behind closed doors) for granted, not verifying or collaborating its version: 'At this stage, physical pressure is not being used against the applicant, and at this actual stage, such measures are not being considered.'[35] Whether a general or a particular case, the Court was content to say, 'As a result of the Attorney General's announcement, the petition is not actual any longer.'[36] The case was dismissed.

---

[31] 4045/95, 5584/95 *Human Rights League v Prime Minister* (not published).

[32] Professor Y Zamir, before being nominated to the Supreme Court, wrote: 'The applicant does not know the reason and the evidence which support the decision. He has no opportunity to refute them. ... Justice is not seen, it is concealed in the judges' chamber,' Zamir, 'Human Rights and National Security' (1989) 23 *Israel Law Review* 377 at 399; two months later, he was appointed to the Supreme Court and began to practice the same working methods.

[33] 'We have not been informed about the investigations methods that the respondent [GSS] is going to use; hence we will not give our opinion about it': 8049/96 *Mohamed Abdel Aziz Hadan v GSS* 4.

[34] *Salachat*, above n 28, at 837.

[35] 3802/87 *Camel v Minister of Defence*.

[36] 3029/95 *Arkan v GSS*.

The Paradox of the Law: Between Generality and Particularity 285

The Court did not say what the law is; neither did it interpret the Basic Law, which was constantly missing from the Court's discourse in this matter. They simply used the formula: 'The decision does not imply an authorisation to use illegal measures during the interrogation, or measures that donnot correspond to the limitation required in order to evoke the necessity defence.'[37] This defence reinforces its position as an ex ante general justification and source of law. Nevertheless, the unwillingness of the Court to decide is a decision after all.[38]

When the Court was obliged to refer in a detailed way to concrete allegations, we can find other paradoxical aspects. In one case, *Mobarak*,[39] the Court agreed that 'hard chaining' of detainees on an inclining low chair is needed to 'protect the interrogation room and the interrogators, and to prevent the detainee from attacking them. Nonetheless, it had been declared that the chaining is not serving the interrogation.'[40] This was a supplementary means to the interrogation and hence was authorised. In another case, the Court affirmed: 'After hearing behind closed doors the explanation of the GSS and having the agreement of the State Attorney, we have decided to publish the following information: the conditions in which the interrogation are being held change according to different circumstances that sometimes require making the interrogated sit on a low chair as part of the interrogation.'[41] So now, the chaining and the low chair were essential elements of the interrogation methods and hence were also authorised. This confusion between supplementary and direct interrogation means was maintained, not only here, but also concerning other practices, such as use of the opaque headsack, of 24-hour loud music, and especially of the 'shaking method,' all tolerated by the Court.[42]

The meaning of the law, of the Basic Law of Human Dignity and Liberty, is established by the way it is performed, in each event wherein it is put into use, and even when it is not.[43] There is no a priori knowledge of the Basic Law's exact meaning—for example, in determining whether pressure is moderate, extensive[44] or torture. As the Court in a way has renounced its

---

[37] 8049/96 *Hamdan v GSS*.
[38] As might happen in other cases less 'politically loaded' when the Court decides on a single matter; but then again appears the tension, a particular decision that makes a general law at least until the next case.
[39] 3124/96 *Mobarak v GSS*.
[40] *Ibid*.
[41] 8714/96 *Al Rahman v Israel Police*.
[42] 7964/95 *Balbisi v GSS*.
[43] In certain contexts, where the requirements for its use have been set up, abstention, silence, etc are also a kind of performance, and not just a lack of it.
[44] See Yitzhak Rabin's remark authorising the GSS to use extensive pressure during investigation: the Israeli Information Centre for Human Rights in the Occupied Territories, Betzelem, 1/1997.

performative role in these affairs, the only place in Israel where these meanings are defined is in the interrogation rooms. This situation has been maintained throughout the 1990s. However, for reasons such as the Oslo Agreements, transformation of public opinion and increasing numbers of internal and external critics, the Court cannot persevere with this status quo. So it prefers to defer its decision: 'We have not yet had the time to hear all the parties' arguments. We would like to hear more about the judicial basis for these activities [and also about the necessity defence]... We therefore ask the clerk of the Court to schedule another hearing.'[45] But since a 'delay' also acquires meaning by specific actualisation—performance[46]—it takes the court five years to have its audiences and to reach a decision. During this time period, as before it, the GSS is left to continue its practices.

III. SPECIFIC MEANING OF THE LAW AND ITS CONTINGENCIES: PROHIBITING TORTURE

A decisive moment was the High Court of Justice's important decision of September 1999, which *categorically prohibited physical means of interrogation*. This decision handled in a different way the above-mentioned paradox between general signification and particular agencies' performances. The meaning of the law can be understood as an ongoing work of contradictions, supposed to be general and inclusive, though it can only be at once contextual and exclusive, and hence not a law.[47]

One of the main characteristics of the decision in the matter of the Public Committee Against Torture in Israel (PCATII decision) was an absolute disregard of the past. Chief Justice Barak, who signed an especially long decision, ignored the series of precedents and judicial tradition existing at the time. He wrote:

> Until now, the Court did not actually decide the issue of whether the GSS is permitted to employ physical means for interrogation purposes in circumstances outlined by the defence of 'necessity.' Essentially, we did not do so due to the fact that it was not possible for the Court to hear the sort of arguments that would provide a complete normative picture, in all its complexity.[48]

Then, towards the end, he added: 'From the legal perspective, the road before us is smooth.'[49] Barak first gave the impression that it was not the

---

[45] 7563/97 *Abed El Rhaman Janimat v Minister of Defence and the GSS*.
[46] See, for analogy, the paradox of limits: when adding one straw to another, at which point is it a heap? N Falletta, *Le livre de paradoxes* (Paris, Diderot Multimedia, 1998) 73.
[47] The law is bounded in time and place, within a context, while denying it; see also Gunther Teubner in chapter 2.
[48] PCATII decision, para 17.
[49] 'Our apprehension that this decision will hamper the ability to properly deal with terrorists and terrorism, disturbs us. We are, however, judges. Our brethren require us to act according to the law. This is equally the standard that we set for ourselves': PCATII decision, para 40.

Court which was in charge of its own proper hearing agenda,[50] and then he treated the legal situation as if it always was and had been clear. The radical inversion of the current position was ignored. As a matter of fact, no legal change had occurred that could explain the turnover at that particular moment—unless, of course, we consider the legal discourse as open-ended, as part of a bigger socio-political system. Then we could suggest, for example, the election of Ehud Barak to the post of Prime Minister a few months earlier, along with the 'hope' this injected into the peace process, as a possible reason for this judicial turn. However, the Court's disregard for its past shows the contingency and the precarious status of judicial decision and the fluid meaning of law, based on nothing but a local performance that needs to be iterated.

This inversion of past decisions without a word is remarkable in all its aspects. For instance, in spite of the fact that the detained persons had already been released, condemned or, as in one case, dead, the Court was now willing to judge cases which were general and theoretical. As Barak wrote, the Court 'has elected to continue hearing their case, in light of the importance of the issues they raise in principle.'[51] The Court had no problem judging general cases as they once had, and as they would again have in the near future, while rapidly changing both their minds and the categorisations.

One of the important aspects of this decision was the formal recognition by the state of the physical means it used. No more an ontological refutation,[52]

---

[50] While answering questions at Bar-Ilan University, Barak made the following remark: 'You have brought as example the Torture case. I do not like to call it torture, because it was not torture as is meant in International Conventions. But that is not the point. You cannot imagine the discussion we had. Asking if it was unanimous, so why did it take so long? It took so long because we needed to convince each other, hours and hours. We have set and talked from judge to judge, trying to convince. Because I saw to myself a superior importance, that in cases like this that tear apart the people, that the Court will speak unanimously. ... There are cases where, as in the Torture case, that it is of vital importance that the Court will express one opinion. ... It does not mean that there was a dicta to join the same version, because every Judge seeks for coherence with what he thinks and is already written.' Bar-Ilan intervention, 21 March 2001, at 4. We should notice the slip of the tongue, when first Barak denied it was about torture, and then he treated it as such. We should also note his vision about 'coherence' and the reason he gave for the delay (five years to convince?).

[51] PCATII decision, para 3.

[52] 'Among the investigation methods outlined in the GSS' interrogation regulations, shaking is considered the harshest. The method is defined as the forceful shaking of the suspect's upper torso, back and forth, repeatedly, in a manner, which causes the neck and head to dangle and vacillate rapidly. According to an expert opinion submitted in one of the applications (HC (motion) 5584/95 and HC 5100/95), the shaking method is likely to cause serious brain damage, harm the spinal cord, cause the suspect to lose consciousness, vomit and urinate uncontrollably and suffer serious headaches', PCATII decision, para 9; 'A suspect investigated under the "Shabach" position has his hands tied behind his back. He is seated on a small and low chair, whose seat is tilted forward, towards the ground. One hand is tied behind the suspect, and placed inside the gap between the chair's seat and back support. His second hand is tied behind the chair, against its back support. The suspect's head is covered by an opaque sack, falling down to his shoulders. Powerfully loud music is played in the room. According to the affidavits submitted, suspects are detained in this position for a prolonged period of time, awaiting interrogation at consecutive intervals,' *ibid*, at para 10.

and so the interrogations means were named: the shaking, the 'shabah' waiting position, the 'frog crouch,' the excessive tightening of handcuffs and sleep deprivation. The consequences of these means were also detailed, as, for example, the death of Al Samed Charizat, though his name, along with the names of other tortured individuals, was missing from the text of the judgment. In a general manner, but one which nevertheless refers to the specific means, the Court upheld that the practice used is 'not part of a fair interrogation. It harms the suspect and his (human) image. It degrades him'[53] (ie, torture) and so it is forbidden.

The legal argument to condemn these methods consisted in the absence of a specific law, authorising the function of the GSS and especially its interrogation means. Until recently, in 2002, the mere existence of the GSS was a *permanent exception* to the 'rule of law' state, as it was a public organ which did not appear in positive legislation. Annexed to the Prime Minister's office, this body did not exist from a legal point of view (ie, in its structure, activities, budget, nomination, control, etc). The court hence looked at the authority of the GSS as part of the executive power in general, and specifically as the police.[54] It is important to note that Justice Barak, in his legal argument, insisted upon not referring to the Basic Law of Human Rights when he gave a general perspective about the principles involved. The Basic Law of Human Dignity and Liberty was mentioned twice in the judgment, not regarding its normative content, but only referring to its article 8,[55] which concerns normative hierarchy. Regarding the torture prohibition, Barak prefered to refer to a series of international conventions, academic articles, and precedents from other domains,[56] in order to conclude by saying: 'At times, the price of truth is so high that a democratic society is not prepared to pay it. These prohibitions are "absolute." There are no exceptions to them and there is no room for balancing.'[57]

The Court tried to regain its power as the 'decider': 'We declare that the "necessity" defence, found in the Penal Law, cannot serve as a basis of authority for the use of these interrogation practices, ... allowing them to employ interrogation practices of this kind. Our decision does not negate the possibility that the "necessity" defence be available to GSS investigators, be

---

[53] PCATII decision, para 28.

[54] 'The GSS constitutes an integral part of the executive branch. ... A so-called administrative vacuum of this nature does not appear in the case at bar, as the relevant field is entirely occupied by the principle of individual freedom,' PCATII decision, para 19.

[55] Section 8: Violation of rights: 'There shall be no violation of rights under this Basic Law except by a Law fitting the values of the State of Israel, designed for a proper purpose, and to an extent no greater than required or by such a law enacted with explicit authorisation therein.'

[56] PCATII decision, paras 22–23.

[57] Ibid.

within the discretion of the Attorney General,[58] if he decides to prosecute, or if criminal charges are brought against them, as per the Court's discretion.'[59] The Court's decision in this matter might have more interest in institutional power reorganisation than in effectively changing the situation: the missing positive law is the basis of the argumentation, and it is only in reference to it that the Basic Law is mentioned. The Court is trying to impose on the GSS another line of conduct, but as it lies mainly on a general and abstract level, the chances for success are dubious.

No particular measures are being decided—that is, there is no suggestion to change the method of control over the GSS; no one was prosecuted although the actions in question were found illegal, and no compensation was given to the victims. The Court was content making general announcements, creating an *abstract* interdiction to torture, accompanied by some details concerning certain methods, but the *particular* cases and concretes aspects were not directly treated.[60]

This decision in itself, from an actual perspective, is an *exception*, an attempt perhaps to change the situation, but which is caught in its own contradictions and in wider political-normative systems. Toward the end of the decision, the Court was trying to distinguish itself explicitly from the political dimension, but at the same time, it reinforced its dependence:

> Deciding these applications weighed heavy on this Court. True, from the legal perspective, the road before us is smooth. We are, however, part of the Israeli society. Its problems are known to us and we live its history. We are not isolated in an ivory tower. We live the life of this country. We are aware of the harsh reality of terrorism in which we are, at times, immersed. Our apprehension that this decision will hamper the ability to properly deal with terrorists and terrorism, disturbs us. We are, however, judges. Our brethren require us to act according to the law. This is equally the standard that we set for ourselves. When we sit to judge, we are being judged. Therefore, we must act according to our purest conscience when we decide the law.[61]

The Court affirmed its only attachment to the law and detachment from political context while also saying the *contrary*; the Court was also aware

---

[58] The State Attorney General published soon afterwards: 'GSS Interrogations and the Necessity Defence—Framework for State Attorney's Discretion,' 44 *Hapraklit* (October) 1999: 'In urgent cases where an interrogator would use means required to obtain information in order to prevent a tangible threat, and there was no other reasonable alternative ... State Attorney will decide not to engage criminal procedure against him', s 7.1.

[59] PCATII decision, para 40.

[60] In this specific kind of writing, the particular cases and disputes are insignificant. In that sense, the paradox of the particular and the general is even sharper: The Court avoided its particular function of dispute resolution and focused only on the transformative one. See SD Smith, 'Reductionism in Legal Thought' (1991) 91 *Columbia Law Review* 68.

[61] *Ibid.*

of the political dimension of its act of judgment, but pretended not to be a political agent, though it acted as one.

In order that the general interdiction of torture will have concrete meaning, it must be followed, concretized in the particular contexts, which in return could give this abstract rule its future sense. Over two years later, we can say that this interdiction does not have the sense we might have thought it would—manipulating once more the delicate paradox of the law between general and particular meanings.

This important decision is an act of reading—reading of the normative situation which it signifies. It is simultaneously a moment of writing, especially when it formulates the 'torture interdiction.' The decision identified this general rule as having permanent value, while referring to several cases that have become somewhat abstract due to such long delay. From a particular point of view, the decision changed the normative situation, prohibiting 'moderate physical pressure,' particularly concerning some interrogation means that were being analysed. Those aspects worked together in order to create the general meaning of the decision. Its concrete signification is yet to come, in particular cases and in the iteration of the general signification as well—ie, the interdiction of torture must be repeated in order to be stabilised, as must the practices of interrogations and of the discourse that gives this interdiction its actual meaning.

IV. OTHER MEANINGS OF THE LAW AND SOME PERMANENT RULES OF EXCEPTION

Before examining some more recent cases, other events that followed that judgment should be highlighted. The first is the publication of the State Comptroller Report[62] concerning *General Security Service Interrogations System, 1988–1992*. The report dealt with the implementation of the Landau Commission recommendations during the first five years after they were published. The report was not delivered until 1995, due to the time needed for its preparation and due to some 'delays caused by the reviewed body', ie, the GSS. The content and even the existence of this report were classified immediately as confidential. Only in February 2000, after a recommendation made by the Supreme Court, the subcommittee for intelligence matters of the State Control Committee of the Knesset, decided to publish a short résumé of the report, which essentially remains confidential. Nonetheless, the part that was disclosed is an edifying text. The State Comptroller wrote:

> The control shows that all the hierarchy of command and staff are implicated at the situation, where a series of deficiencies, consisting in that those who

---

[62] *State Comptroller Report* (Jerusalem, 2000) no 1.

The Paradox of the Law: Between Generality and Particularity 291

are responsible for the Organization have severely failed in their duty to keep the GSS actions within the limits of law.[63]

The report goes on:

> The deviations were not ignorantly made, but willingly. Expert interrogators, including high-ranked ones at the Gaza branch, have acted in systemic grievous anomalies. During this time commanding officers at the GSS did not prevent that from happening, authorizing these anomalies. ... Even after the publication of the Landau Commission Report, the misinformation phenomena did not disappear. Among the interrogators, there were those who lied in court and to other judicial and control authorities, inside and outside the GSS. The assertion of the GSS directors to the Landau Commission, as if inside the Service the rigour of truth-telling was strictly enforced, is unfounded in reality.[64]

Several important aspects of this Report should be mentioned. First, it is an official source that attests to the existing gap between what is being said and what is being done, between an abstract account and its formulas on the one hand, and the interrogation praxis on the other. It shows that confidence in and dependence upon the GSS discourse fabricate another reality, one which is unfounded in the reality of their actions. As a reminder, the report is referring to the time when the Supreme Court prefered to rely exclusively on GSS discourse, and hence participated in manipulating reality and the normative consequences denounced by the report. It attests also to the constant deviation of torture praxis and the inherent breach between the code of conduct (of the Landau Commission) and general normative discourse, and the infinite richness of practices, exceptions and deviations—ie, the actual meaning—in each particular case.

The report also shows the recurrent problem of this kind of discourse as part of larger socio-political systems, condemning lying in court more severely than torturing detained persons: 'Lying is the mother of all evil, and it should be strictly removed from GSS work methods.'[65] But perhaps one of the more important aspects to which this report attests is the lack of knowledge and the partiality of any source concerning these matters, including, of course, the investigation commissions and the legal system. Information is not accessible; we do not know how many other reports or similar sources of such information might exist. We can only suspect that

---

[63] *Ibid*, at 3. 'Limit of law' means within the framework of the Landau Commission recommendations, which is treated as law, *ibid*, at 2.
[64] *Ibid*, at 6.
[65] *Ibid*, at 9: 'From this report, we can learn about the double standard, concerning the deviation from authorization and the deviation from truth-telling as a obligatory rule. We can find examples of ignoring authorization and manipulations'. Chief Justice Landau, once he learned about this report, said that he 'feels betrayed by the GSS', Haaretz, 15 March 2000.

the Court or some of its members knew about this one over the ensuing years (as it was the Court's decision that recommended its publication),[66] but they preferred to ignore it.

The question of meaning is imposed in all its seriousness: to whom, where, and by what means the law has meaning. Only by corroborating the definition of 'torture' by other sources, a more comprehensive understanding of the meaning of law in this case could be obtained. One cannot have any certitude concerning the sense of the law and its signification unless a much broader spectrum of sources is considered.[67]

GSS Law, 2002 The Court's decision of 1999, and the echoes aroused by it, attracted attention to this major deficiency: the lack of positive law, legalising the form and content of GSS existence and activity. Some drafts had been studied, among others explicitly authorising the 'physical pressure means' in order to bypass the Court's decision. The parliamentarian compromise that had been found was to vote on a law without mentioning this problem. We will not be able to analyse here all the aspects of this problematic law that defined in very broad and vague ways the authority and competence of the GSS.[68] However, some aspects should be explored: this new law does not establish real external control mechanisms on the GSS activities, but rather covers it all by strict rules of confidentiality, ordering severe punishment to non-conforming behaviour (mostly regarding the media). Current efforts to amend this law, and to introduce some articles that, for instance, authorise 'special means in extreme cases, relaying on the necessity defence,'[69] are at different stages of consideration by the Knesset. But perhaps bypassing the courts will not be necessary, because the Supreme Court sitting as the High Court of Justice itself does not seem eager to reiterate and work within the framework it tried to set up via the PCATII decision.

Some recent cases perform yet another meaning of the torture interdiction. A year after the publication of the PCATII decision, the El-Aktsa Intifada broke out. Although some indicators showed decreasing numbers of cases of torture[70] during the first year following the decision, the political

---

[66] We can find only its reference, probably because it is classified: HCJ proceeding 607/98 given 11 November 11, 1999; referred to in *State Controller Report*, at 1.

[67] See 'collage of evil,' A Ofir, *The Present Work, Essays on Israeli Contemporary Culture* (Tel Aviv, Kibbutz Meohad, 2001) 165.

[68] Critics of the new law begin to be outspoken: M Kremnitzer, *Marive*, 11 February 2002.

[69] M Goraly, 'Torture Could be Authorized by a Special Law', *Haaretz*, 24 March 2002; see Law Project: Penal Code (Competence and Methods of Special Interrogations Cases of Security Needs, S1999, 15th Knesset, no 878; and others no 743, no 29.

[70] UN Report in the framework of the Convention Against Torture's committee in Geneva, 23 November 2001; see also Gidon Levi, 'A Year Without Torture,' *Haaretz*, 3 September 2000.

situation and the practices of different state agencies announced that they were subsiding. Torture still seems to be a recurring praxis structured and tolerated by different bodies, including the courts.

Soon after the 1999 decision, the High Court of Justice was confronted with the consequences of its own ruling. When the Court did not rule upon the particular aspects in its decision, the family members of the late Charizat petitioned that the GSS interrogators causing his death should be brought to justice in penal proceedings. At that time, only one of the interrogators involved had been brought before an internal disciplinary committee of the GSS, which exonerated him of five of the six charges against him (the sixth being a technical charge that was sanctioned with warning).[71] For the time being, the High Court of Justice did not pronounce; but at the hearing, the state's attorney renewed and repeated the old arguments, as if the PCATII case had never been decided. Suggesting that the 'necessity defence' should be considered as an a priori exonerating source, suggesting also that since the causal link between the interrogation and the death was not proven, a criminal proceeding should not take place. In the courtroom, no one protested this reverse order of things, ie, preventing the possibility of proving (in a criminal proceeding) by arguing that it had not been proven.[72]

In other cases that followed, the court did not refer to the PCATII ruling. In the *Amana Muna* case, the Court returned to its previous stylistic form of brief decision:

> Interrogation is not a friendly talk and sometimes it is obliged to prevent sleep. This is legal, as long as it is a proportional means ... directly needed to advance the interrogation, and as immediate consequence of it; and not an objective by itself, meant to break the detained's spirit.[73]

The Court renewed the obscure distinctions between direct and supplementary means of interrogation, not considering the fact that the detainee was interrogated after the crime in which she was accused had been committed; and so no preventive reason was argued.[74] Furthermore, the Court reiterated its unconditioned belief, without verification, in the GSS reports and announcements: 'We have been informed that the GSS is paying attention that even during long interrogation, "a reasonable time will be given to eat, to personal needs, and even to rest, as long as it is possible considering the

---

[71] That person was not even expelled from the service; M Reinfeld, 'Shaking is Back in Front of the High Court of Justice,' *Haaretz*, 12 December 2000.
[72] Ibid.
[73] 970/2001 *Amana Mona v GSS*, 15 February 2001.
[74] The detained was accused of setting a trap through the Internet for an Israeli man, who was murdered after coming to the meeting.

interrogation needs." We have been convinced that these measures were applied in this case. Petition rejected.'[75]

In the *Ahamar Haman* case, the preferences of the Court were even more significant:

> We heard behind closed door the interrogators, and especially the person who declared before us that the chair which the detained has been placed on is a normal chair. The handcuffs were presented to us, and one interrogator demonstrated on his colleague all we have asked him ... We come to the conclusion that the petitioners did not support their allegations and the measures taken are not forbidden as in Court's 5100/94 ruling. Hence the petition is rejected.[76]

The remarkable element is how the Court prefered to believe the GSS agents, and to construct the normative reality based on their discourse, even though time and time again it had been stated that GSS agents systematically lie in court. This fact is according to retired GSS agents themselves, the Landau Commission, the State Comptroller and even in court findings.[77]

These and other performances give the 1999 decision its exceptional dimension of meaning. The High Court of Justice renewed the distinction between general and particular cases in order to reject petitions, even those that detail allegations concerning breaking fingers, mud dragging and other degrading and torturous activities allegedly committed in the mass incarceration camps[78] built to accommodate Palestinian detainees:

> In these petitions there is no individual claim, but rather a public one [made by several human rights organizations]; ... the main argument is that the respondent [the Military Commander] must authorize meetings between the detainees and their lawyers, as it is not yet clear if they are suspect persons or terrorists ... We think it inconceivable that during combat time and soon afterwards, meetings with lawyers will take place, by persons that put at risk or might put at risk the security, before attaining the conditions that permit us to consider each individual case. ... As for the allegations regarding torture, the respondent rightly noticed that it is a general allegation that cannot be discussed. Bodily harm is forbidden and the presumption is that the respondent will inquire into any claim if submitted'.[79]

The Court 'shall not deal with general affairs' (although detailed), and it will do whatever it takes to prevent the affairs from becoming particular, ie, giving the opportunity to the detainees to meet a lawyer and to formulate a

---

[75] *Amana Mona*, above n 73.
[76] 4592/2001 *El Abed Ahamar Haman v Minister of Defense and the GSS*, 6 December 2001.
[77] See the *Nafsu* case, above n 15.
[78] A Yosef, 'During Combat, Judicial Control and Effective Injunction are Not Possible,' *Haaretz*, 15 March 2002.
[79] 2901/2002 *Centre for Human Protection v Military Commander*, 4 July 2002.

The Paradox of the Law: Between Generality and Particularity 295

claim. The Court adheres to the military position, by a presumption without allowing any possibility either to verify or to control its activities, leaving once again the security services to decide by themselves and to determine the meaning of these concepts: 'physical measures of interrogation,' 'torture' and the 'application of human rights.'

We can observe that concepts such as 'torture,' 'human rights' etc, are 'floating' signs. They acquire meaning when they stop at different places by occurring performances, giving them meaning where their sense is being 'judged', (1) in a context, (2) by someone, and (3) in a particular way; this meaning must then be iterated and disseminated in order to have somewhat of a stable, recurrent sense.

One principal question that follows this inquiry is the question of sources: from where can we apprehend the meaning of law, in our case, that 'prohibits torture'? From general sources or from particular ones? Can this distinction be maintained, or is it but another aspect of the same paradox between general order and its micro-arrangements, between different sources of meaning?

Multiple sources seem necessary in order to have an ample idea about the meaning of the law. It is hard to have any certitude concerning the 'real' state of torture; it is even harder to know what concrete meaning its interdiction gains through the perspective and work of different agencies. This is because most of them are not as well documented as, for example, the Court's work. But even by reading only 'official sources' up to this stage, we have been able to observe their internal contradictions, their paradoxical argumentation and the multiple meaning and treatment they give to these concepts and rules. These sources, even when they pretend to be objective, judicial, etc, are always within a context: political, ideological, social, and hence, discursive and preconditioned. The construction of the normative discourse goes well beyond the players we have mentioned and the meaning which 'torture' and 'human rights' have acquired in Israel over the last decades are part of a larger discursive order, one in which many actors with various points of view and abilities participate. So, in order to learn more about what the interdiction of torture means, to whom and in what circumstances, studying only positive law or its legal interpretation cannot be satisfying.

In this framework, we will not be able to thoroughly analyse other discursive agencies participating in and conditioning the normative construction and resolutions by different means. But we will introduce them briefly in order to expose their variety.

The *testimonies of the tortured*, for example, are absent completely from the legal proceedings, for the simple reason that most of the time, the tortured are not even present at the hearing of their petitions. Nevertheless, a petition is already a kind of 'success story,' even though the result is predictable; it is a way of leaving a trace and having a public voice, because most of the cases remain completely ignored, silenced by a variety of 'physical means' that only practice can invent. In this respect, the *humanitarian organisations* and civil society actors[80] who try to collect these neglected testimonies expose another meaning of 'physical interrogations' and play a crucial role.[81] Another important source is the *discourse of the torturers*, whether professional or occasional torturers, giving a glimpse of the way these individuals understand and practise the law.[82] The *mediation discourse of lawyers* is also an important factor: the discourse of attorneys from the Attorney General's office, representatives of the state in courts or in different international forums, etc—it is this discourse that translates into legal and normative formulated phrases, the reality that the GSS promotes. The *media and political* discourse plays a major role in fabricating consensus and 'common knowledge,' giving the spectrum of discursive possibilities in which specific meanings can be formulated.[83] More agencies, each of them playing a role, contribute in one way or another to the 'general construction' of meaning[84] by their 'particular performances.'

All of these discursive agencies take part in a heterogeneous, complex mechanism that creates meaning; they contribute to the creation and circulation of that meaning; they provide the conditions for the possibilities of meaning to occur, and in our case, eventually allow the possibility of each particular act of torture.[85]

---

[80] See eg, the following reports: PCATII *Racism, Violence and Degrading Treatments, Force of Order Attitudes toward Detained Persons, during September–October 2000 Events* (Jerusalem, April 2001); PCATII B*reached in the Defence, Torture and Molestation during Interrogation of the GSS after HCJ Ruling* (Jerusalem, September 2001); other Israeli NGOs, such as BETZELEM, Human Right League, Physicians for Human Rights; international organisations such as Amnesty, Human Rights Watch, Medicine Without Frontiers, etc, which publish regular reports.

[81] See A Ofir n 67 above, in the postscripts for his article about Betzelems Report.

[82] This can be obtained from various sources, eg, direct interviews and depositions, indirect interview and depositions, depositions before different organisations, in different legal proceedings and protocols. The GSS agents are not just opaque tools of the occupation's administration; they are subject-constituted and operating in a larger social field that must be analysed. Consequently, a clearer understanding of the functioning and the change possibilities—through education, instruction, etc and not just banning, enforcing/not enforcing 'the law'—might then be gained.

For a sophisticated analysis of the functions and meanings of the law and its discursive system within a multisources perspective, see M Alberstein, *Pragmatism and Law: From Philosophy to Dispute Resolution* (Hampshire, Ashgate, 2002).

[83] See eg, the statistics about reporting these affairs: Amnesty International, *Broken Lives: A Year of Intifada*, ch 4; *Arrests, Torture and Unfair Trail by Israel*, (2001) 50; and Butler, above n 25.

[84] For example, the academic discourse about torture and its legitimisation: during these years, two special editions were published, one in English and one in Hebrew, see (1989) 23 *Israel Law Review*; (1998) 4 *Mishpat v Mimshal*. Besides these, the subject is not considered a main priority in the academic sphere.

[85] See Butler, above n 25, at 37, who suggests that a 'speaker assumes responsibility precisely through the citational character of speech.'

V. THE PARADOX OF MEANING, THE MEANING OF PARADOX: TORTURE, SOURCES AND THE TEXTS

The paradox of law can actually be a very wide one. It includes relations that at first sight seem to be direct, simple, univalent relations of application or of deduction; but upon further study, they appear to be complex, ambivalent, contingent, manipulated constructions of meaning. Forbidden torture as a general rule, based on positive law, on court precedents and other sources, is put constantly into *use*, ie, is being *performed* in various ways giving it concrete meanings.

Relations between the international norms and the normative situation within the states' parties; relations between the Basic Law and other legal dispositions within Israel's legal system; the continued, regular exceptional situation of a 'state of emergency'; the retroactive and punctual 'necessity defence' that becomes an omnipresent authorising source; the particular case of the 'ticking bomb' that turns out to be the case of everyone. These are just some examples we have seen of these complex relations between general and particular.

The act of meaning is always already situated, marked within a process, within a discursive system, as it is also an original act of meaning, a new affirmation, an additional performance of sense. The paradox here is not just the ontological phenomena of the world, nor just a contradictory construction of the way we grasp it; it is also a way of reading in search of broader meaning. Paradoxalising the construction of meaning might be useful as a critical reading of 'evident situation,' of the 'becoming evidence' and of what 'is' the 'meaning' of law.

The paradox in this case belongs to the logic of discourse, wherein the meaning of law is at once general and particular, excluding each other and forever binding. The argument of this article, then, is about the ways the meaning—especially the legal meaning—of these events is being made a vehicle, how the sense becomes possible within a discursive order throughout various performances, where some of them are of a grievously violent nature, ie, the effective torture and the pain it causes, and about the ways of reading it with paradox.

The Paradox of Meaning

The event of meaning can be found in the place of the particular case, where every event is singular and unique, participating in the becoming of sense; but it can also be found in the place of the general, since it is a source of meaning and of information, indicating its proper becoming. Hence, the paradox of law is intimately related to the paradox of meaning itself, where on the one hand meaning is always already prefigured in signs, in a representational system, making an abstraction of the event it is supposed to signify.

On the other hand, it is also a performance, participating in a particular way in the creation of the concrete event of meaning; and the two are relating in an ongoing complex process without end.

The object of a 'text,' as the event of 'torture,' can be accessed only through meaning, which does not exclude other aspects of its 'being'; but in order to be comprehended in one way or another, meaning is involved; bringing with it its paradoxes. The encounter with the law is always singular, occurring in permanent oscillation between general and particular, as Kafka's countryside man discovers, forever in front of his own personal door to the law. What does the law mean? To whom, where and by what means? And we are back at the beginning of the chapter.

After reading Israel's discursive culture of torture, which negates, forbids, tolerates and justifies it, we can see that in order to grasp a more complete meaning of the law, a hermeneutic study should be undertaken, one which accentuates the mechanism of paradox. Analysing the different practices in order to gain a fuller meaning of law is required, so as not to presuppose some former knowledge about its meaning as the right answer. The paradox of law, exposing the incommensurable differences between the general and particular aspects of the law that are nevertheless bound together, is suggested as an interpretive grid that can be practised as a way of critical reading.[86]

The Meaning of Paradox

After analysing how meaning is being implied between general and particular aspects of law, between signification and performance, I cannot ignore the way this chapter (current performance) uses the term of *paradox*, relating it to the notions and practices of *texts*, *sources* and *torture*, of which none is 'completely accidental.' Paradox here is understood in its larger, etymological sense, ie, one contrary to the 'commune,' to what 'is believed to be the rule,' the *doxa*, etc. It functions on several levels: in the way meaning is constructed/deconstructed, in the way law is put into work, and about how different Israeli discursive agencies treat the question of torture (noting that the Israeli case is a particular case, but not a singular or special one, as any other case might be).[87]

This chapter is caught in the same logic between the general and particular. Torture is, on the one hand, an 'example' or a 'particular case,' demonstrating the general rule of paradox, but also only a singular, non-representative ele-

---

[86] See R Amit, *Les paradoxes constitutionnels, le cas de la Constitution Israélienne* (Thèse, Paris, Ecole des Hautes Etudes en Sciences Sociales, 2002).

[87] For a recent update and example of the situation of torture and its discourse around the world, see the cover page article 'Is Torture Ever Justified?,' *The Economist*, 1 November 2003.

The Paradox of the Law: Between Generality and Particularity 299

ment; in this respect, any other 'example' could have been used. On the other hand, torture could also be *the* example. Torturing a detained person to extract information from him—using his body as a surface on which to engrave the signs of sovereignty, of power—has perhaps a signifying, general role, not as in the death penalty, where the subject dies at the ultimate moment, whilst becoming a 'complete subject.' In the case of torture, the subject lasts, but from that moment on, he is signed, marked forever by the power, and hence attesting to it.[88] The 'radical' 'exception' characteristic of torture, which haunts the history of order and sovereignty, attests to its logic, which is in our case the manipulation of law between general and particular, between order and exception—combining together the de/construction of the biological, the political, the judicial and the semantic.

This combination includes the aspect of 'source' which becomes apparent. Torturing and interpreting have some resemblance, related to the performance that 'makes sources.' But when torture is thought to forget paradox, to ignore it, the current interpretation which this chapter has engaged seeks the contrary. The Israeli *differentia specifica* regarding all other current practices of torture, if such a 'difference' exists, resides in the explicity of the discourse, in its outspoken manners, and in the tradition now developed of the judicial work on the matter. It helps to explore the subject, where torture becomes also a kind of an exemplary phenomenon, as much as exemplary can be one thing, linking sovereign powers, normative judgments and the logic of meaning.

And so 'torture,' 'meaning' and 'paradox' have their sense only in a complex relation, oscillating with no end and with no synthesis, between their general and particular aspects, between signification and performances, as the one we are about to finish for the time being here.

---

[88] See G Agamben, *Homo Sacer, Le pouvoir souverain et la vie nu* (Paris, Seuil, 1997), especially when he speaks about 'Human Rights and Bio-power' (at 137) and about the 'Camps as Nomos of Modernity' (at 179), where the utmost exception reviles the logic of the system itself.

Index

Alternative dispute resolution (ADR)
see also **Disputes**
critique, of, 227–8, 239
development, of, 226–228
integrated desires, 229–30
integrative negotiation, 229
jurisprudential perception, 227
legal intervention, 230
private-public dichotomy, 228
resistance, to, 227
Aristotelian formula
equality, and, 33, 205–207, 209–10, 215–17
and see **Equality**
respectful treatment theory, and, 216, 219–21
and see **Respectful treatment theory**
Authority
see also **Legal authority**
clerical authority, 160–164
court proceedings, and, 145–7, 158–9
and see **Court proceedings**
legislative authority, 112–3
political authority, 146
transcendent authority
law, and, 102, 116–7
legal authority, and, 104
natural law, and, 105
rejection, of, 106, 111
ritual, and, 147
self-reference, and, 112, 114
social history, and, 106, 111
Autopoiesis
autopoietical closure, 88
autopoietic systematicity, 90
autopoietic system, 35–6, 101–103, 171–2

autopoietic theory, 35–6, 248–250
critique, 248
divine witness, and, 272–3
euthanasia, and, 252–3
and see **Euthanasia**
meaning, 15
metaphysics, and, 249–50
nihilism, and, 25–1
self-reference, and, 248–50
and see **Self-reference**
self-regulation, and, 248–50

Bounded rationality
see also **Tort law**
decision costs, and, 24
decision-making, and, 24
deliberation costs, 24
legal agents, and, 24–5
levels of care, 24
optimisation, and, 25
and see **Optimisation**
regress problem, 25–6

Coherence
see also **Paradoxes of coherence**
law, and, 29–30
legal paradoxes, 29–30
and see **Legal paradoxes**
randomness, and, 136, 143
and see **Randomness**
vagueness, and, 127–131, 143
and see **Vagueness**
Communal bodies
communitas, and, 149–50, 157
and see ***Communitas***
corporate bodies, distinguished, 149
funerals, 157

performance theory, and, 145–6
presence, and, 153–4
ritual, and, 146, 151–2
   and see **Ritual**
sacredness, and, 148, 151
social structure, and, 148
Communitas
communal bodies, and, 149–50
court proceedings, and, 159–60
   and see **Court proceedings**
interpersonal relationships, 149
nature, of, 149
performance theory, and, 145–6
presence, and, 153
ritual, and, 153–4
   and see **Ritual**
social structure, and, 148–50
Comparative equality
see also **Equality**
concept, of, 33–4
decision-making, and, 34
discrimination, and, 34, 206
egalitarianism, and, 212–5
   and see **Egalitarianism**
indeterminate ideal, as, 212–6
paradoxical ideal, as, 212–6
respectful treatment, and, 34
   and see **Respectful treatment theory**
Concepts
see **Legal concepts**
Conflict of laws
alternatives, deciding between, 45
blind experimentalism, 61–2
case law, significance of, 61–2
claims of validity, 45
cognitivism, 51
communicative plausibility, 58
compromise, 45
conciliatory formula, 43, 58
conflicting norms, 51
contradictions, 45
criticism, waiving of, 60–1
deparadoxification, 59, 61
dispute resolution, 63
   and see **Dispute resolution**
distinctions, 59–61
   and see **Distinctions**
doctrines, of, 43
historical experience, 42
institutional protection, 43–4, 58–60
law of society, 60
   and see **Law of society**
legal areas, and, 42
legal institutions, and, 42
legal norms, 42–3
   see also **Norms**
legal protection, 43–4, 58–60
normativism, 51
paradox
   ambivalent nature, 48
   deconstruction, 46–7, 49–50
   distinguished, from, 45
   legal development, and, 47
   productive potential, 46
   requirements, for, 45
   systems theory, 46–7, 49–50
   see also **Paradoxes**
paradoxical nature, 41–2, 44–5
partiality, 59
   and see **Partiality**
political legal theory, and, 55, 57–8, 61, 63, 71
private international law, 42
private law, politicisation of, 43–4
problem pressure, 58, 61
rational discourse, and, 46
reciprocity, 59
   and see **Reciprocity**
sacrificium intellectus, 60–1
self-justification, 43–4
social autonomy, and, 59–60, 62–3
social compatibility, 61
social contradictions, 43, 51
social practice, and, 44–5
social rationality, 59
social systems, and, 42
social theory, and, 41–4, 47, 51–2, 61, 63
sociology of conflict, 43
subjective rights, 43–4, 58
systems theory, and, 52
   and see **Systems theory**
transformation
   contractual constitutional law, 43–4
   organisational constitutional law, 43–4, 58–60
Consistency
coherence, 121–3
constitutional balancing, 123, 125
dispute resolution, 122, 143
   and see **Dispute resolution**
equal treatment, 120–1
fairness, and, 120–2
   and see **Fairness**
injustice, and, 120–1
interpretation, and, 128–9

law, and, 29–30
legal concepts, 120
legal paradoxes, and, 16, 30
  and see **Legal paradoxes**
legal practices, 120, 122–3
legal rules, 120
randomness, and, 138, 139
  and see **Randomness**
restoration, of, 16
Constitutional state
democracy, and, 20
legal grounding, and, 20
  and see **Legal grounding**
legal omnipotence, 20–1
legislative powers, 20–1
paradoxical nature, 20
parliamentary constraints, 21
parliamentary supremacy, 20
source of law, as, 20
Contract law
executed contracts, 75
express terms, 185
express warranties, 183–4, 186
  see also **Warranties**
frustration of contract, 75
interpretation, 183, 185
parties
  expectations, 183
  intentions, 185
  see also **Expectations**
pricing paradox
  see **Pricing paradox**
reasonable expectations, 185
unenforceable obligations, 75
warranties
  see **Warranties**
Corporate bodies
communal bodies, distinguished, 149
law-giving, and, 150
nature, of, 147–8
ritual, and, 152
  and see **Ritual**
sacredness, and, 148
social structure, and, 147–8, 150
Corporation
communal bodies
  performance theory, and, 145–6
  ritual, and, 146, 151–2
  and see **Communal bodies**
corporate personality
  founding ancestors, and, 147–8
  immortality, 147
  sovereignty, 147

social structure, and, 147
Court proceedings
adjudication
  constituent power, 159
  law-giving, 159
  legal authority, 159
authority
  clerical authority 160–4
  legal authority, 158–9
communal bodies, and, 145–6, 148
  and see **Communal bodies**
  communitas, and, 159–60
  and see **Communitas**
conflict
  ritual enactment, 160
  staged representation, 160
corporate bodies, and, 147–8, 150
fascist systems, 159–60
formalism, 160, 164
judges
  clericalisation, 161–3
  conduct, 162
  independence, 162
  judicial review, 162
  judicial speech, 162
  role, 159, 164–5
law books, and, 164
law-giving, 164
lawyers, role of, 164–5
legality, 145, 158–9
performance theory
  communal bodies, 145–6
  communitas, 145–6
  social structure, 145–6
political authority, 146
redressive interventions, 158
ritual process
  characterisation, of, 145
  deritualisation, 161–4
  founding sovereignty, 146
  ritual enactment, 160
  rule of law, and, 145, 158–9
  staged representation, 160
  use, of, 145, 158–9, 161
  see also **Ritual**
ritual structure, 146
rule of law
  realisation, of, 145
  suspension, of, 145–6, 158
sacredness, and, 159–61
sanctity, and, 147, 161–3
social structure
  communal bodies, and, 148

communitas, and, 148–50
corporate bodies, and, 147–50
ritual, and, 146–7
transcendent authority, 147
sovereignty, and, 159–61, 164
   and see **Sovereignty**
state law, 160
state power, 160
subversion, of, 159–60
theatrical nature, 146
totalitarian systems, 159–60
validity, and, 159
   and see **Validity**

Decision-making process
see also **Tort law**
deliberation costs, 24–5
heuristics, 26
information gathering, 24–5
intuitive grounds, 25–6
judicial decisions, 26
level of care, 24
optimisation, 25–6
regress problem, 25–6

Deconstruction
alternative theories, distinguished, 50–2, 55–7
ambivalence, of, 55
conflict of laws, and, 60
   and see **Conflict of laws**
deparadoxification, 50–1, 53, 56
immanence, and, 55–6
infrastructural indicators, 174
justice, and, 55, 60, 179–80
   and see **Justice**
law, deconstruction of, 55
nature, of, 55
legal argumentation, 55
legal critique, 57
legal negativism, 49
nature, of, 180
paradoxes
   paradoxification, 50, 52, 58
   paradox of decision, 55
   ultimate justification, 55
   and see **Paradoxes**
paradoxic discourse, 94
   and see **Paradoxic discourse**
political legal theory, 55, 57–8, 61, 63
political theory, 54–6
power critique, 57
religious dimension, 54, 56
rightness of law, 57

rules, calculating, 55
social contradictions, 51
social institutions, 54
socialisation, 49, 51, 56
social problems, and, 52–3, 58
social systems, and, 51–2
   and see **Social systems**
social theory, and, 51–3
substitute proposals, 61
systems theory, and, 50
   and see **Systems theory**
theologising, of, 55–6
transcendence, and, 55, 58
   and see **Transcendence**

Discrimination
see also **Gender discrimination**
equality, and, 206
   and see **Equality**
gender differences, 210–1
race-based inequalities, 220, 222–4
racial profiling, 220
unequal treatment, 209–12, 216
women pilots, 208–10, 214

Dispute resolution
see also **Disputes**
alternative dispute resolution (ADR), 34, 226–8
   and see **Alternative dispute resolution (ADR)**
conflict notion, 34
conflict of laws, and, 63
   and see **Conflict of laws**
consistency, and, 122, 143
   and see **Consistency**
justice, and, 34
   and see **Justice**
mediation, and, 34, 35
   and see **Mediation**
partiality, and, 63
   and see **Partiality**
randomness, and, 136–7, 141
   and see **Randomness**
settlement notion, 34

Disputes
see also **Alternative dispute resolution (ADR)**
dispute analysis, 225, 234
dispute culture, 235
dispute process, 236
epistemological framework, 235
legal code, governing, 235–6
legal consciousness, 235–7, 243, 245
NBC (naming/blaming/shaming) model

dispute resolution, 225–6, 234, 236–7
interpretative account, 243–5
opportunity, as, 232, 238, 242
paradox of rights, 237, 244–5
perception, importance of, 235–6, 243, 246
process orientation, 232
self-reference, and, 225–6, 235–6, 245
and see **Self-reference**
social constructs, 235
social context, 235, 240
social evolution, and, 236
social reality, and, 237
social struggle, 237
transformation, of, 234–5, 237, 241, 243

Distinctions
see also **Conflict of laws**
acts of violence, as, 84
alternative distinctions, exclusion of, 84
character
 binding character, 84
 normative character, 84
contingency, and, 91, 93
contract/organisation, 59
deconstruction, of, 60
and see **Deconstruction**
entitlements/infrastructures, 59
inaugural distinctions, 84
indeterminacy, and, 92–3
individual/restitution, 59
law/economy, 59
law/morality, 59
law/politics, 59
law/society, 59
meaning generation, 84
paradoxes, within, 61
partiality, 59–61
and see **Partiality**
public/private, 59
radically contingent, 84
reciprocity, 59–61
and see **Reciprocity**
subjective/objective rights
unfolding paradoxes, 91
univocasition, 84

Doctrine
see **Legal doctrine**

Dying
see also **Euthanasia**
ars moriendi, 254–5, 257, 271
assistance, with, 254
clergy, involvement of, 253–4, 257
funerals, 157
hope, associated with, 257–60, 266
medical hastening, 259–60, 266–7, 270
medical problem, as, 252, 256–9
medical techniques, 60, 273
medical treatment, 256, 259
nature, of, 254–5
physicians
 discretionary power, 267
 hastening death, 259–60, 266–7, 270
 hope, associated with, 257–9, 266, 270
 medical ethics, 256–7, 271
 medical techniques, 260, 273
 medical treatment, by, 256
 presence, of, 255–7, 266
 professionalism, 258–9
 prolonging life, 260, 267
 role, of, 256–7, 266, 270–1
 unjustified killing, 267
prolonging life, 260, 267
publications, on, 254
regulation, of, 271–2
religious influence, 253, 272–3
ritual, and, 157, 253–4
and see **Ritual**
suicide
see **Suicide**

Egalitarianism
see also **Equality**
absolute equality, 213
comparative egalitarianism, 212–4, 216–7, 221–3
comparative equality, and, 212–5
and see **Comparative equality**
convictions, 208
gender-based inequality, 207–8, 210–1, 215–6
see also **Gender discrimination**
guiding principles, 207–8
moral judgments, 208
opportunities, equalisation of, 212, 223
respectful treatment theory
see **Respectful treatment theory**
unequal treatment, and, 211–2, 216

Emancipation
see also **Political economy**
individual rights, 66
political legal theory, and, 71
popular will, 66, 109, 113

rationality of rule, 66
Equality
  absolute equality, 213
  Aristotelian formula, 33, 205–7, 209, 210, 215–7
  comparative equality, 33, 34, 208
    and see **Comparative equality**
  comparison groups, 215
  concepts, of, 205–7
  egalitarianism
    see **Egalitarianism**
  gender-based equality, 34, 216, 220, 222
    see also **Gender discrimination**
  gender differences, 210, 211
  gender discrimination, 206, 208–1, 224
    and see **Gender discrimination**
  HIV treatment, 222, 224
  inequality
    comparative, 213–5
    measuring, 214–5
    remedial, 213
    undeserved, 222
  judicial role, 210
  law, and, 29, 30, 33
  meaning, of, 205
  moral imperative, 217
  natural distribution, 212
  opportunity, and, 212
  race
    racial classifications, 211
    racial profiling, 220
  rationality, and, 207, 209, 212, 216–7
  relevancy, and, 206, 209–10, 215
  respectful treatment theory
    see **Respectful treatment theory**
  unequal treatment, 33, 209–11, 220, 223
Euthanasia
  see also **Dying**
  autopoietic theory, and, 249–50
    see also **Autopoiesis**
  criminal law, and, 260–1
  death
    medical hastening, 259–60, 266, 270
    medical treatment, 259–60
    sanctity of life, 262
  decriminalisation, 267
  Euthanasia Society of America (ESA), 267–70
  historical conditions, 252
  justification, 249, 261, 269
  lawful killing, 249
  legalisation, 252, 262, 266–67
  legitimacy, 266
  medical technology, and, 251–2
  Nazi euthanasia, 269–70
  operative closure
    legal perspective, 266
    medical perspective, 266
  paradoxical nature, 35, 249–50
  patient rights, 251–2
  positive law, and, 249–50
  prohibition
    legal, 261
    moral, 261
    sanctity of life, 262
  regulation, of, 250, 266–9
  rise, of, 251–2
  self-closure
    legal perspective, 266
    medical perspective, 266
  self-reference
    legal self-reference, 270
    medical self-reference, 270
    metaphysics, and, 271
    nihilism, and, 271
    and see **Self-reference**
  self-regulation, 250
  suicide, and, 261–2
    and see **Suicide**
  voluntary, 269
Expectations
  circularity, 184–5
  contract law, 183–5
    and see **Contract law**
  international law, and, 183
  jurisdiction
    domicile, and, 194
    due process, and, 194
    in personam jurisdiction, 195
    minimum contacts test, 194
    subject to suit, 195
  legal doctrine, and, 183, 185, 188–9, 194, 196, 198
    and see **Legal doctrine**
  legal obligations, 196
  legal rights, 196
  legal status, and, 194–5, 197, 203
  price
    informational proxy, 183
    interpretation, of, 185
    legal rights, 196
    market price, 183–4, 189, 200, 202
    price premium, 200–3
    pricing paradox, 184

see also **Pricing paradox**
privacy rights, 183, 195
private law, and, 183
public law, and, 183
reasonable expectations, 183, 185, 194
retroactivity, 195
self-reference, and, 184
   and see **Self-reference**

Fairness
coherence, and, 121–3
constitutional balancing, 123, 125
cultural idiosyncrasies, 121
equal treatment, and, 120–1
law, and, 29–30
legal paradoxes, and, 30
   and see **Legal paradoxes**
legal practice, and, 122–3
pluralistic sensitivities, 121–2
pluralist societies, in, 29, 121–2
randomness, and, 123, 138, 142
   and see **Randomness**
vagueness, and, 123
   and see **Vagueness**
Functional legal thinking
see also **Law of society**
acquiescence, 74
arbitral awards, 75
controls, 74
executed contracts, 75
expectations, 74
   and see **Expectations**
freedoms, 74–5
frustration of contract, 75
procedures, 74
prohibitions, 74, 75
risk prevention, 74
unenforceable obligations, 75

Gender discrimination
see also **Equality**
gender-based equality, 34, 216, 220, 222
gender differences
   motivation, 210
   relevant differences, 210–1
   supervening facts, 211
   visibility, of, 211
Israeli experience, 208–10, 214
justification, 209–10
natural inequalities, 209
neutral differences, 209
reasonableness, 209, 210
relevance, and, 210–1

respectful treatment theory, 216–8, 223
   and see **Respectful treatment theory**
supervening facts, 210–1
unequal treatment, 209–11
utilitarian considerations, 209, 224
General Security Service (GSS)
see also **Israel**
authority, of, 288, 292
code of conduct, 283–4, 291
confidentiality, 292
control, of, 291–2
interrogation methods, 280, 285, 288
judicial acceptance, 284, 286, 294
judicial control, 289, 292
legal status, 288, 292
lying in court, 281, 291, 294
necessity defence, and, 288, 292
rule of law, and, 281, 288, 291
State Comptroller's Report (Israel), 290–1
torture
   see **Torture**
Grounding
see **Legal grounding**

Human rights
breaches, of, 47
fundamental rights, 47
natural law, 47
   and see **Natural law**
natural rights, 47
social contract, 47
subjective rights, 47

Inconsistency
see also **Consistency**
legal paradoxes, and, 15, 233
   and see **Legal paradoxes**
paradoxes of coherence, 6, 127–8
   and see **Paradoxes of coherence**
vagueness, and, 127–8
   and see **Vagueness**
Israel
censorship law, 280
discrimination, in, 279
gender discrimination, within, 208–10, 214
   and see **Gender discrimination**
General Security Service (GSS)
   see **General Security Service (GSS)**
humanitarian organisations, 296
human rights, 277, 279

308 *Index*

national security, 280
occupied territories, 279
public order, 280
rule of law, in, 279
  and see **Rule of law**
secrecy, within, 280
state of emergency, within, 297
torture, within, 276–8, 280, 288
  and see **Torture**

Judges
  see also **Court proceedings**
clericalisation, 161–3
conduct, 162
independence, 162
judicial review, 162
judicial speech, 162
role, 159, 164–5
torture
  judicial decisions, 283–7, 294
  judicial delay, 286
  judicial precedent, 286–7
  judicial proceedings, 284
  judicial tradition, 286
  and see **Torture**

Judicial system
  see also **Court proceedings**
disciplinary rules, 21
interpretative authority, 21
intuitive reasoning, 26
judges
  see **Judges**
judicial review, 162

Justice
alternative theories
  convergence, 168–9
  distinguished, 169–70
  divergence, 169
  paradoxology, 170
circularity, 177
consistency, and, 176–7
  and see **Consistency**
contingency, 177–8, 180
decision-making, and, 177
deconstruction, and, 55, 60, 179–80
  and see **Deconstruction**
dispute resolution, and, 34, 236
  and see **Dispute resolution**
fluctuating, 61
foundations, of, 32, 179
guarantee, of, 176
incalculable nature, 32
infinity, and, 32, 179

law, and, 31–2, 34, 36, 54, 72, 167–8, 178–80
legal fiction, as, 178, 180
legal legitimation, 168
legal system, within, 176, 178
  and see **Legal system**
mediation, and, 34, 236
  and see **Mediation**
nature, of, 54, 56, 58, 179
paradoxical epistemologies, 170
  and see **Paradoxical epistemologies**
perceptions, of, 236
religious connotations, 54
self-observation, and, 177, 180
self-reference, and, 178
  and see **Self-reference**
sociological approach, 32
utopian concepts, 168

Law
alternative theories
  convergence, 168–9
  distinguished, 169–70
  divergence, 169
  paradoxology, 170
amendment, 101–2
application, of, 103
arbiter, as, 119, 122
arbitrary force, and, 55
arbitrary nature, 57
arbitration, and, 143
  see also **Dispute resolution**
autonomy, and, 15, 19, 102, 109, 112, 169, 248
autopoiesis
  closure, 88
  system, 35–6, 101–3, 248–52, 261, 266, 271
  theory, 35–6
  and see **Autopoiesis**
binding rules, 167
cognitive openness, 248, 250
coherence, 29, 30
components, of, 77, 79
conflicting determinations, 126
conflicting pressures, 127
conflicting rules, 78
  see also **Conflict of laws**
conscience, and, 73
consistency, and, 29–30, 120
  and see **Consistency**
corporate order, and, 150
deconstruction, and, 169, 178

   and see **Deconstruction**
destabilisation, 128
dispute resolution, 143
   and see **Dispute resolution**
equality, and, 29–30, 33
and see **Equality**
equal treatment, 115, 120
events, and, 275, 276, 297
external pressures, 16
fairness, and, 29–30, 119–20, 122
   and see **Fairness**
foundations, of, 168
founding, of, 57
groundlessness, of, 21
   see also **Legal grounding**
illegality, 247
implementation, 78
infrastructural paradox, 179
interpretation, 128
judge-made law, 60
justice, and, 31–2, 36, 54, 72, 167–8, 178–80
   and see **Justice**
justification, and, 85, 101–2
lawfulness, 88, 101–2
law of society, 66, 68
   and see **Law of society**
legal authority, 57, 168
   and see **Legal authority**
legality, 247
legal norms
   and see **Norms**
legal positivism, 104, 112–4, 176, 178–9
legal reason, 72
legal system, 77–8
legitimacy, 57
meaning
   see **Meaning**
metaphysics, and, 36
morality, and, 176
natural law, 29, 88, 104
   and see **Natural law**
natural rights, 88
nature, of, 66, 72, 79, 81, 167–9
nihilism, and, 36, 250–1, 271
   and see **Nihilism**
normative closure, 248, 250, 261, 266
normative experience, 83
normativities, 59–60
objects, of, 77
observation
   philosophical, 169

sociological, 169
operative closure, 266
originary paradox
   constraining consequences, 85
   decision-making right, 85
   fundamental nature, 86
   significance, of, 85
origins, 78, 88, 102–3, 117
paradox, and, 77–9
   see also **Legal paradoxes**
paradoxity, 28
pluralistic sensitivities, 29–30
political theory, and, 102
politics, role of, 87
positive law, 71, 106–7, 109, 111, 248–50, 277
positivisation, of, 87, 102, 104
powerlessness, of, 70
process of law, 66
quasi-transcendental law, 174, 179
rational discourse, and, 57
rationality, 59
reasonableness, 30
reference, 168
regulatory law, 248, 251
rule of law, 66, 102, 104
   and see **Rule of law**
self-enforcement, 169
self-questioning, 168
self-reference, and, 16, 28–9, 32, 35, 101, 168, 247–50
   and see **Self-reference**
self-regulation, and, 35, 250–1
self-representation, and, 88
social autonomy, and, 59–60, 62–3
social conflict, and, 60, 119
social disputes, and, 143
social system, and, 4, 13, 17, 35
   see also **Social systems**
social-theory designs, 73
society, and, 66, 68
   see also **Law of society**
sources, of, 60, 78, 83
stability, 15, 128
systemic structure
   self-organising nature, 15
   self-producing nature, 15
transcendent authority, 102, 104, 116–7
   see also **Transcendence**
understanding, of, 66
universal nature, 29, 36, 67, 102–3
   see also **Legal generality**

vagueness, 123
  and see **Vagueness**
validity, 87–9
  and see **Validity**
values, relating to, 176
violence of law, 86
Law of society
  conflict of laws, and, 67, 71
    and see **Conflict of laws**
  constitutionalisation, 71–2
  emancipation, 66
    and see **Emancipation**
  freedom, and, 67
  functional legal thinking, 74–5
    and see **Functional legal thinking**
  institutional economics, 72
  justice, and, 72
    and see **Justice**
  just-ification, 71–5
  "law" *qua*
    critical philosophy, 69
    institutional economics, 70
    juridifications, 70
    observation of event, 70, 73, 75
    systems sociology, 69
    traditional alternative, 70
  legal reason, use of, 72
  modernisation, and, 68
  ownership systems, 67
  political economy
    see **Political economy**
  positive law, 71
  prerogatives
    error prerogatives, 74
    forecasting prerogatives, 74
  private law, 67
  proceduralisation, 71–2, 74–5
  promises, significance of, 71
  protection, 67
  public law, 67
  reciprocity, and, 71
    and see **Reciprocity**
  social theory, and, 74
  society, as, 67–8
  "society as society", 67
  "society" *qua*
    critical philosophy, 68
    institutional economics, 69
    systems sociology, 69
  state/society dichotomy, 67
  system
    administration of justice, 73
    autopoietic system, 72

  justification, 73
  poietic non-system, 72–3
Legal authority
  constitutional authority, 19–21
  court ritual, 31
    see also **Court proceedings**
  formalism, 31
  governing rules, 22
  interpretative authority, 21
  judicial authority, 21, 30
  judicial proceedings, 31
  lawyers, role of, 31
  natural law, and, 29
    and see **Natural law**
  parliamentary supremacy, 20
  religious origins, 29
  rule of law, 31
    and see **Rule of law**
  self-reference, and, 22, 28, 29, 106, 112–3
    and see **Self-reference**
  sovereignty, and, 31
Legal concepts
  change of meaning, 125
  coherence, of, 125
  consistency, 120, 128
    and see **Consistency**
  constitutional balancing, 125–6
  equality, and, 125
  general levels, 125
  inexactness, of, 125
  interpretation, 128–9
  nature, of, 123, 125, 127
  particular levels, 125
  systematic decoding, 126
Legal doctrine
  development, of, 33
  expectations
    expectation-based doctrine, 183, 185, 01
    private expectation, 33
    social expectation, 33
    and see **Expectations**
  flexibility, 198
  self-reference, 33, 188–9, 194, 196, 198
    and see **Self-reference**
Legal expectations
  see **Expectations**
Legal generality
  effect, of, 115
  equal treatment, and, 115
  justification, and, 103

legal authority, 115–7
   and see **Legal authority**
legal/non-legal, delineation of, 115–6
legal order, and, 115
   and see **Legal order**
origins, 115
political theory, and, 103, 115–6
rule of law, and, 115, 117
   and see **Rule of law**
uniform application, 103
Legal grounding
constitutional state, 20
   and see **Constitutional state**
judicial authority, and, 21–2
law, of, 248, 250
validity, and, 17, 19–20
   and see **Validity**
Legal order
legal generality, and, 115
   and see **Legal generality**
secularisation, 104–5, 110–1
self-referring system, 110
sovereignty, concept of, 105–6
state autonomy, 112
transcendent authority, 116
   and see **Transcendence**
validity, 88–9
   and see **Validity**
Legal paradoxes
see also **Paradoxes**
adversarial process, 5
alternative theories, distinguished, 93–4, 96–9
ambiguity, 88
ambivalent nature, 27
analysis
   linguistic, 4
   logical, 4
arguments
   proper referent, 14
   relating, to, 13–4
autopoietic systematicity, 90
   see also **Autopoiesis**
change, and, 27
coherence, 29–30
conflicting interpretations, 5, 15
consistency, and, 16, 27, 30
   and see **Consistency**
constitutionalism, 19–21
   see also **Constitutional state**
contingency, and, 28
contradictions, and, 27
decoding, 16

deconstruction, and, 94, 98
   and see **Deconstruction**
deparadoxisation, 80, 82–3, 90, 95
distinctions, 84
   and see **Distinctions**
evanescent object, as, 81
exhaustion, and, 81
fairness, and, 30
   and see **Fairness**
figural-discursive analysis, 96
generativity, 80, 82–3, 89, 173
generic paradoxes, 17
identification, of, 81–2
indicable perplexity, 83
judicial system, and, 21
   and see **Judicial system**
justification, and, 101–2
knowledge of paradox, 81
legal authority
   see **Legal authority**
legal concepts, and, 15
legal critique, 27–8
legal development, and, 27
legal generality, and, 28–9, 103
   and see **Legal generality**
legal semantics, and, 27
legal set
   conflicting interpretation, 15
   contradiction, within, 14–5
   formation, of, 14
   inconsistency, 15
   non-normative statements, within, 14
   normative statements, within, 14
   structure, of, 14
legal structure
   autonomous systems, 15, 19
   self-organising systems, 15–6
   self-producing systems, 15
   systemic structure, 15
legal theory, and, 4, 17, 27
Liar paradox, 103
local paradoxes, 17, 26, 22–3
   and see **Local paradoxes**
logical paradoxes, distinguished, 4, 13, 17
moral value, 17
nature, of, 13, 89, 95, 103
non-apophantical paradox, 90
non-dependability, 82
non-disposability, 82
non-existence, and, 82
non-logical paradox, 90
non-object, as, 80–1

non-referentiality, 96–7
normative paradoxology, 27–8
omnipotence, and, 114
ontologisation
  non-ontological objects, 93
  non-ontological thought, 93
  onticised heteroreference, 85
  spontaneous ontologisation, 91
operational role, 16–7
paradoxical apories, 96
paradoxical observation, 90
paradoxic deixis, 96
paradoxic discourse
  see **Paradoxic discourse**
paradoxity, 82–3, 96–7
paradoxology, 81–2
paralysis, and, 82
perfomative paradoxity, 98
perplexity, and, 81–3, 87, 90, 94, 95
plausibility, and, 27
pricing paradox, 33
  and see **Pricing paradox**
productive potential, 27
randomness, 30
  and see **Randomness**
repeated experience, and, 81, 87
revelatory value, 27
self-amendment, and, 101–2
self-reference, and, 28–9, 99
  and see **Self-reference**
semantical paradoxes, distinguished, 13, 17
semantic perplexity, 98
sentences
  contradiction, within, 14
  meta-propositions, in, 14
  norm-propositions, in, 14
significance, of, 248
social dynamic, 17
social justice, 28
social problems, and, 27
social structures, and, 27
social systems, and, 13
  and see **Social systems**
social value, 17
source of law, as, 83
structural innovation, 27
systematic operating, 90
systemic stability, 93
thematisation, 95–7
theologising, 28, 81–3, 87, 90–1, 94, 96, 98
theoretical incompleteness, 96

validity, 17–19
  and see **Validity**
Legal system
  circularity, 177
  closure
    normative closure, 176, 248, 250, 261, 266
    operative closure, 176, 266
  cohesion, of, 123
  communicational network, 176
  immunity, 176
  justice, within, 176, 178
    and see **Justice**
  moral neutralisation, 176
  political interests, and, 176
  radical bifurcation, 176
  religious desires, and, 176
  self-description, 177
  self-observation, 177
  self-reference, and, 16
    and see **Self-reference**
  social autonomy, 176
  social function, 176
  social subsystem, 176
  social system, 177
  stability, 123, 129
  validity, 88
    and see **Validity**
Litigation
  see **Court proceedings**
Local paradoxes
  decoding, 22
  legal understanding, and, 22
  operation, of, 17, 26
  tort law, and, 22–3
    and see **Tort law**

Malkovich
  Being John Malkovich
    Malkovich dilemma, 37–8
    paradox, illustrated by, 3–4
Meaning
  application, of, 276
  attribution, and, 275
  contingency, and, 91, 93
  contradictions, 286
  difference, as, 91
  discourse, and, 296–7, 299
  events, and, 297
  general meaning, 275–6, 298
  indeterminacy, and, 92–3
  law, and, 36
  legal context, 276

meaning generation, 84
meaning production, 92
meaning projections, 29, 84–6
nature, of, 91–2
orientation, and, 91–2
paradox, and, 47–8, 275–6, 297–8
particular meaning, 275–6, 298
performance, and, 285, 295–6, 298
positive law, 277
signification, and, 36, 275, 298–9
sources, 292, 295

Mediation
see also **Dispute resolution**
autonomy
  exercise, of, 237–8, 245
  liberal, 238
  performative, 238
  relational, 225–6, 228, 232–3, 243–6
  secondary, 238
central quality, of, 230
conflict
  conflict management, 226, 234–5
  conflict resolution, 225
  empowerment, and, 238
  positive aspects, 237
  potential for growth, 238
  process handling, 239
  recognition, and, 238
  rights acknowledgement, 237
  self-assertion, and, 237
consent, and, 225, 232
dispute settlement, 35, 225
  see also **Disputes**
empowerment, and, 232–3, 238–9
heteronomy, and, 229, 233
interpretative model
  autonomy, and, 238
  dispute settlement, 244
  distributive justice, 244
  expression of will, 244
  mediator's role, 240–1
  nature, of, 225–6, 234
  NBC model, and, 243, 246
  paradox of rights, 244, 246
  relational autonomy, 243–6
  rights sensitivities, 244
  value judgment, and, 244
judgmental quality, 240
justice, and, 34
legal intervention, and, 230
mediator
  role, of, 236, 238–41
  transformative mediator, 240–1

mutual realisation, 34
NBC (naming/blaming/claiming) model
  dispute resolution, 225–6, 234, 236–7
  interpretative account, 243–5
negotiation, and, 226
oppression, and, 231, 239
paradoxical nature, 35, 237
paradox of rights, 237
perception, significance of, 235–6, 246
pragmatic model, 35
problem solving, and, 244
process orientation, 232
relational stage, 228–30
relational world-view, 233, 238, 245
satisfaction, and, 231
self-reference, and, 240
  and see **Self-reference**
settlement, and, 244
social aspect, 240
social emphasis, 231–2
transformative dimension, 239
transformative model, 35, 228, 231–2, 236–7, 240–2

Natural law
acceptance, of, 110
application, of, 111
continuing presence, 111
decline, of, 107, 109, 111, 250
humanistic theory, 106
legal authority, 29
  and see **Legal authority**
natural rights, and, 108
political power, and, 110–1
positive law, and, 107–9, 111–2
rejection, of, 110–2
rule of law, and, 111–2
  and see **Rule of law**
secular nature, 105, 111
significance, of, 111
social order, and, 110
sovereignty, and, 111, 114
transcendent authority, 114
  see also **Transcendence**
validity, 88
  and see **Validity**
values, of, 108

Negligence
see also **Tort law**
optimum behavioural standard, 23
optimum care level, 23–4
reasonable care, 23

314 Index

standard of care, 23
units of care, 23
Nihilism
  autopoietic theory, and, 250–1
    and see **Autopoiesis**
  euthanasia, and, 271
    and see **Euthanasia**
  law, and, 250–1, 271
  self-reference, and, 272
    and see **Self-reference**
Norms
  circularity, 44
  conflict norms, 43–4
  contradictory, 14
  evaluation, of, 18
  falsity, 14
  form, as, 85
  infinite regress, 44
  legal norms, 42–3
  legal paradoxes, and, 14
    and see **Legal paradoxes**
  moral norms, 263
  normative authority, 110
  normativism, 51
  norm justification, 44
  prescriptive nature, 14
  religious norms, 263
  substantive norms, 43–4
  supreme norms, 43
  transcendent norms, 104, 110–1
  truth, 14
  universal norms, 110–1

Omnipotence
  legal omnipotence, 20–1
  legal paradoxes, and, 114
    and see **Legal paradoxes**
  meaning of, 7
Optimisation
  see also **Tort law**
  decision-making, and, 24–5
  deliberation cost, 24
  fault, and, 23, 25
  liability rules, 23
  optimal behavioural standard, 23–4
  optimal care levels, 23–4
  optimisation techniques, 25, 25
  regress problem, 25
  solution cost, 24
Paradoxes
  see also **Legal paradoxes**
  ambivalent nature, 48
  aporia, 233

autopoietic systems, 51
  and see **Autopoiesis**
coherence, and, 5
  and see **Paradoxes of coherence**
concealment, 52
conclusion, and, 5
conflict, and, 5
conflict of laws, and, 45
  and see **Conflict of laws**
consistency, and, 16, 46–7
  and see **Consistency**
constitutive nature, 172–3
contingencies, and, 48
contradiction, and, 6, 45–8
decision, paradox of, 55
deconstruction, and, 46–7, 49–50, 55
  and see **Deconstruction**
definition, 5
denial, of, 49
deparadoxification, 48, 50–3, 56, 58–9
destructive tendencies, 46
différance, 93–4, 96, 174
ethics, and, 174
generative nature, 173
historical approach, 101
inconsistency, and, 6, 233
invisibilisation, 171
justification, 55
knowledge of paradox, 81
latency, 173–6
legal development, and, 47
legal negativism, 49
logical study, 16–7
management, of, 7
meaning, 5, 47–8, 298–9
  and see **Meaning**
paradoxic discourse
  see **Paradoxic discourse**
paradoxification, 50, 52
philosophical study, 16, 101
plausibility, 52–3, 58, 61, 233
productive potential, 46
reasoning, and, 5
reparadoxification, 48, 52, 58
self-justification, 45
self-reference, and, 45, 101
  and see **Self-reference**
semantic paradoxes, 6
  and see **Semantic paradoxes**
social dynamics, 47
social evolution, and, 173, 175
socialisation, 51–2, 56
social structure, and, 173

and see **Social structure**
systems theory, and, 46–7, 49–50, 52–3
  and see **Systems theory**
transcendental necessity, 173
transformational-generative mechanism, 172
unfolding paradoxes, 91
Paradoxes of coherence
alternative understanding, 7
cognitive over-commitment, 7
contradiction, and, 7
deparadoxification, 128, 143
destabilisation, 128–9
impossibility, and, 7
inconsistency, and, 6, 127–8
omnipotence, 6–7, 19–21
plausibility, 7
pluralistic sensitivity, 127, 130–1, 143
randomness, and, 136, 143
  and see **Randomness**
vagueness, and, 127–31, 143
  and see **Vagueness**
Paradoxic discourse
analogous tendency, 97
contingency, and, 93
deconstructionist approach, 94
deixis, development of, 95–6
différance discourse, 93–4, 96, 174
grammatisation, 96
non-referentiality, 96–7
perplexity, and, 81–3, 87, 90, 94–5
theologisation, 94, 96–7
typification, 96
Paradoxical epistemologies
auto-deconstruction, 175
autopoietic systems, 171–2
  and see **Autopoiesis**
cognition, 171
deconstruction, 174
  and see **Deconstruction**
deparadoxification, 173
distinctions, use of, 175
  and see **Distinctions**
functional differentiation, 172–3
illegality, 171
information theory, 171
infrastructural indicators, 174–5
invisibilisation, 171
legality, 171
legal positivism, and, 176–9
observation
  communicational acts, 172
  displacement, 172
  modified observation, 172
  observed observation, 172
  observing operations, 171
  self-observation, 172, 177
  unity, of, 172
operations
  meaning, of, 171
  observing operations, 171–2
performativity, 174
responsibility, 174
responsiveness, 174
self-reference
  closure, and, 176
  negative, 171, 173
  social subsystems, 172
  systemic self-reference, 170, 172
  trilogy, of, 171
  and see **Self-reference**
social description, 173
social structure, and, 173
  and see **Social structure**
systematic processes, 171
systemic operations, 171–2
systems theory, and, 170, 172, 176–7
Partiality
dispute resolution, 63
  and see **Dispute resolution**
impartial partiality, 63–4, 71
impartial social theory, 61, 63
law/society relationship, 63–4
legal development, and, 63
meaning, of, 59
normativity, and, 63
reciprocity, distinguished, 59–60
  and see **Reciprocity**
relative impartiality, 63
social autonomy, and, 63–4
social-theory design, 64
Pluralist societies
cultural idiosyncrasies, 29, 121
differences, within, 121
fairness, in, 29, 121–2
law, in, 29
Political economy
democracy, and, 66
emancipation, 66
  and see **Emancipation**
historical development, 66
Rousseau, influence of, 66
rule of law, and, 66
Precautionary principle
cost-effectiveness, 135
globalisation, and, 136

risk, 131–3, 135–6
  and see **Risk**
Pricing paradox
  circularity, 185, 189, 194, 204
  contract law
    contractual environment, in, 185–6
    contractual settings, 203–4
    and see **Contract law**
  coordination value, 203
  costs, associated with, 197
  defence, of, 184–5, 197–8
  difficulties, created by, 184
  effect, of, 196
  internalised consequences, 189
  judicial precedent, 196, 198, 204
  justification, 185, 202–3
  legal doctrine, and, 184–5
  legal indeterminacy, 185, 197–8
  litigiousness, and, 185, 197, 201
  market risk, 202
  merits, of, 197–8
  nature, of, 188–9
  pre-litigation expenses, 185
  property law
    regulatory takings, 189–90
    takings jurisprudence, 183, 189
  regulatory settings, 203
  self-reference, and, 188–9
    and see **Self-reference**
  strategic behaviour, 197
  tangible costs, and, 185
  undesirable cycling, 202
  utilitarian efficiency, 197
  volatile environments, 202–4

Randomness
  arbitrariness, 136–7
  class actions, 141
  classification, and, 141–2
  coherence, and, 136, 143
  competing claims, 141
  consistency, and, 138–9
    and see **Consistency**
  constitutional rights, 140
  decision-making, and, 136–8, 141–2
  dispute resolution, and, 136, 137, 141
    and see **Dispute resolution**
  exemption rights, 140
  fairness, and, 138, 142
    and see **Fairness**
  incompressibility, 137–8
  Israeli experience, 139–40
  land allocation, 139

  legal decisions, and, 138
  military service, 140, 142
  planning decisions, 140
  pluralistic sensitivity, and, 136, 139, 143
  rationality, 136
  risk regulation, 140
  unpredictability, 137–8
  USA experience, 139
  value, of, 140
Reciprocity
  individual relations, and, 62
  meaning, of, 59
  networks
    intersystem networks, 63
    network phenomena, 62–3
  partiality, distinguished, 59–61
    and see **Partiality**
  purpose, of, 71
  social autonomy, and, 62
  social relations, and, 62
  society-wide, 62–3
  sub-autonomies, 62
Reference of paradox
  deconstruction, and, 94, 98
    and see **Deconstruction**
  deparadoxisation, 80, 90, 95
  evanescent object, as, 79–83
  foundational paradox, 83–6
  generating paradoxes, 80
  law
    cognitivisation, 78
    components, 77, 79
    empirical approach, 77–9
    functional approach, 77–8
    generative process, 79–80
    implementation, 78
    institutional approach, 78
    lawful action, 78
    lawful expectations, 78
    lawfulness, 78
    objects, of, 77, 79
    paradox, and, 77–9
    phenomenological approach, 77–8
    positivisation, 78
    validity, 78
    and see **Law**
  legal paradoxes, 80–83
    and see **Legal paradoxes**
  legal system, operation of, 80–81
  paradoxisation, 80
  paradoxity, 81–2, 87, 90
  search, for, 77–9

social communication, 80
systems theory, and, 79–80, 89, 98
 and see **Systems theory**
urparadox
 see **Urparadox**
validity
 see **Validity**
Regulatory undertakings
 pricing paradox, and, 189–93
  and see **Pricing paradox**
 property
  compensation, 192
  economic impact, 190–2
  expectations, interference with, 190–2, 199
  future use, 200
  governmental action, 190–1
  market value, 191
  overbidding, 200–1
  price terms, 200
  restriction on use, 190–2
  short-term use, 193
  strategic overpayment, 197, 200–1
  "total takings", 192–3
  value, 199
 public interest considerations, 191
Respectful treatment theory
 application, of, 216, 224
 Aristotelian formula, and, 216, 219–21
 arrest, and, 223
 comparative egalitarianism, 221–3
  and see Egalitarianism
 criminal activity, and, 220
 disrespectful treatment, 218, 223
 distinctive feature, of, 218–9
 educational selection, and, 223
 equality, and, 221
  and see **Equality**
 exclusionary reasons, 220–2
 gender-based inequality
  equality, and, 216, 220, 222
  morally permissible, 216
  morally wrong, 216
 gender discrimination, and, 216–8, 223
  and see **Gender discrimination**
 HIV treatment, and, 222, 224
 humiliation, and, 218, 222–4
 immoral deeds, 218
 individual welfare, and, 219
 moral wrong, 218–9
 motivation, and, 216
 race

  race-based inequalities, 220–4
  racial profiling, and, 220
 rationality, and, 216–7
 relevance, and, 216, 220
 respect
  moral respect, 217
  psychological respect, 217
 unequal treatment, 216, 220, 223–4
Risk
 see also **Precautionary principle**
 climate change, and, 136
 conflicting interpretations, 132–3
 criteria
  moral, 133
  psychological, 134
  ranking criteria, 133–5
  welfare-based, 134
 damage
  irreversible damage, 133
  serious damage, 133
 environmentalism, 131
 environmental risk, 135–6
 evidence, of, 135
 exceptional risk, 133
 fluid nature, 132–3, 136
 formulation, of, 132
 industrial capitalism, 131
 meaning, of, 132–3
 ordinary risk, 133
 regulative action, and, 132–3, 136
 risk regulation, 131–3, 135–6, 140
 scientific certainty, 134–5
 uncertainty
  effect, of, 134
  ontological uncertainty, 135
  time uncertainty, 135
 vagueness, and, 133–4, 136
  and see **Vagueness**
Ritual
 communal bodies, and, 146, 151–2, 155
  and see **Communal bodies**
 communitas, and, 153–4
 corporate structure, and, 152
 court proceedings, 31, 145–7, 158–9, 161
  and see **Court proceedings**
 crisis, and, 152–3
 death, and, 157
 funerals, 157
 moral licence, 151
 nature, of, 157
 normative regeneration, 151

performance, and, 155
periodical ritual, 152–3
presence, and, 152–5
protective rituals, 152
purpose, of, 151–2, 154
redress, and, 151, 154,
rule of law, and, 145
sacrifice, and, 157–8
sacrificial killing, 157–8
sacrificial rites, 151
social structure, and, 146–7, 151, 154–5
  and see **Social structure**
theatre, distinguished, 154–6
  and see **Theatre**
theatrical transformation, 154–5
transformative power, 152, 154
Rule of law
court proceedings, and, 145–6, 158–9
legal authority, and, 31
  and see **Legal authority**
legal generality, and, 115, 117
natural law, and, 111–2
  and see **Natural law**
political economy, and, 66
  and see **Political economy**
realisation, of, 145
ritual, and, 145, 151
self-reference, and, 102, 104, 109
  and see **Self-reference**
suspension, of, 145–6, 158

Self-organisation
environmental perturbations, 15
internal order, and, 15
legal paradoxes, and, 15–7
  and see **Legal paradoxes**
non-linear dynamics, 16
regulated behaviour, 15
self-organising systems, 15–6
Self-production
see **Autopoiesis**
Self-reference
amendment, 112
autopoietic theory, and, 248–50
  see also **Autopoiesis**
civil contract, 106
closure, and, 176
disputes, and, 235, 236, 245
  and see **Disputes**
duty, concept of, 108
equity, 109
euthanasia, and, 270–1
  and see **Euthanasia**

expectations, 184
  and see **Expectations**
extra-positive laws, 108
historical background, 104, 113
infinite regress, 3
justice, and, 178
  and see **Justice**
justification, 112, 116
lawfulness, 108
legal authority, and, 102–4, 106, 112–3
  and see **Legal authority**
legal doctrine, 188–9, 194, 196, 198
  and see **Legal doctrine**
legality, 108–9
legal order
  secularisation, 104–5, 110–1
  self-referring system, 110
  sovereignty, concept of, 105–6
legal paradoxes, and, 28–9
  and see **Legal paradoxes**
legal positivism, 104, 112–4
legislative activity, 109
legislative authority, 112–3
Liar paradox, 8
liberty, 113
mediation, 240
  and see **Mediation**
metaphysics, and, 271
morality, 108–9
moral law, 108
natural law, 105–8
  and see **Natural law**
natural rights, 108
negative self-reference, 171, 173
nihilism, and, 271
political ideal, as, 101–2, 113–4
political theory, and, 104, 106–7, 109, 112–4
popular will, 109, 113
positive law, 106–7, 109, 111
re-entry, and, 3
reflexive enfoldment, 3
rule of law, and, 102, 104, 109, 111–4
  and see **Rule of law**
social contract, 109
social subsystems, and, 172
sovereignty, 113–4
  and see **Sovereignty**
state power, 106–7, 109, 111
systemic self-reference, 170, 172
systems
  legal system, 16

self-organising systems, 15
self-producing systems, 15
systems theory, and, 249, 272
and see **Systems theory**
theory of right, 108
theory of virtue, 108
transcendent authority, 102, 104–6, 109, 111–2, 114
see also Transcendence
trilogy, of, 171
Semantical paradoxes
evaluation process, 12
grammatical structure, 11–2
groundlessness, and, 10–2
hetero-referential notions
falsity, 8–9, 12
reference, 8–9
truth, 8–9, 12
intuition
linguistic, 8
logical, 8
Liar paradox, 8–9
naïve semantics, 12–3, 17, 19
resolution, of, 11
self-reference, and, 12
and see **Self-reference**
semantic instability, 9–10, 12
truth
see **Truth**
Truth-teller paradox, 10, 18
valuation pattern, 13
Social structure
communal bodies, and, 148
communitas, and, 148–50
corporate bodies, and, 147–8, 150
paradox, and, 173
performance theory, and, 145–6
ritual, and, 146–7, 151, 154
and see **Ritual**
transcendent authority, and, 147
Social systems
deconstruction, and, 51, 52
and see **Deconstruction**
law, and, 4, 13, 17
legal paradoxes, and, 13
and see **Legal paradoxes**
pressures, on, 51
self-organising, 13
self-producing, 13
self-referential, 13
social communication, 52
social plausibility, 52–3, 58, 61
social problems, 52–3, 58

social theory, 51–3
stability, 51
systems theory, and, 52–3
and see **Systems theory**
Society
see also **Law of society**
coordination, 72
nature, of, 72
subordination, 72
Sovereignty
concept, of, 105–6
corporate personality, and, 147
court proceedings, and, 159–61, 164
and see **Court proceedings**
emergence, of, 113–4
limits, on, 114
natural law, and, 111, 114
and see **Natural law**
self-reference, and, 113–4
and see **Self-reference**
Suicide
criminal character, 262–3
decriminalisation, 262–4, 270
insanity, and, 265
legalisation, 262
norms
moral norms, 263
religious norms, 263
positive legitimacy, 264
proxy, by, 262
punishment, for, 263
rationality, and, 264–6
self-murder, as, 262
social legitimacy, 264–5
sovereignty, and, 265–6
Systems theory
conflict of laws, and, 52
and see **Conflict of laws**
deconstruction, and, 50
and see **Deconstruction**
deparadoxification, 56
justice, and, 54
and see **Justice**
legal critique, 57
paradoxes, and, 46–7, 49–50
and see **Paradoxes**
paradoxical epistemologies, 170, 172, 176–7
and see **Paradoxical epistemologies**
production of knowledge, 54
political legal theory, 55, 57–8
power critique, 57
reflective levels

320 Index

meaning, and, 53–4
reflexivity of processes, 53
self-reference, 53
social theory, and, 53
system-environment relations, 53
transcendence, and, 54
religious dimension, 54, 56
rightness of law, 57
secularisation, 54
self-reference, and, 249, 272
and see **Self-reference**
self-regulation, and, 250, 272
social plausibility, 52–3, 61
social problems, 52
social theory, and, 52–3
and see **Social theory**
transcendence, and, 54–5
and see **Transcendence**
truth, and, 249
validity, within, 177
and see **Validity**

Theatre
enactment, and, 156
normative conflict, 156
participation, 156
redress, and, 154
representation, and, 156
ritual, distinguished, 154–6
and see **Ritual**
sacredness, and, 155
social drama, 156
social structure, and, 154, 156–7
spectacle, and, 155–7
spectators, 155–6
theatrical transformation, 154–5

Tort law
decision-making process, 24–6
and see **Decision-making process**
economic analysis, 22–3
enforcement mechanisms, 23
fault concept, 23, 25–6
Learned Hand formula, 23–6
liability, 23
negligence, 23
and see **Negligence**
optimisation, 23, 25
and see **Optimisation**
social costs, 23

Torture
discourse
explicity, of, 299
media discourse, 296
mediation discourse, 296
political discourse, 296
torturers' testimony, 296
International Conventions, on, 277–8
interrogation methods, 283, 285–8, 293
Israeli legal system
abstract interdiction, 289–90
authorisation, 277, 279, 285
code of conduct, 281–3
confessions, 283
criminal liability, 282
denial, of, 276, 281
discursive taboo, 279
evidence, under, 295–6
explicit interdiction, 276
humanitarian organisations, 296
implied authorisation, 276
interrogation, under, 281, 283, 285–8, 293
judicial attitude, 276, 282–3, 285
judicial decisions, 283–7, 293–4
judicial delay, 286
judicial precedent, 286–7
judicial proceedings, 284
judicial tradition, 286
justification, 280, 282
Landau Commission, 281–3, 290–1
legal meaning, 285–6
necessity defence, 281–2, 288, 293, 297
performative contradiction, 280–1
petitions, under, 295–6
physical pressure, use of, 280–4, 286, 290
prohibition, under, 36, 277–8, 288
socio-political influences, 287, 289, 291
testimonies, under, 295–6
see also **Israel**
PCAT II Decision (Israel)
effect, of, 289–90
interrogation methods, 287–8
judicial precedent, and, 286
necessity defence, 288
significance, of, 286, 294
socio-political influences, 287, 289
torture interdiction, 289–90

Transcendence
awareness, of, 54
deconstruction, and, 55, 58
exteriority, 58
political theory, and, 54–5
reflection, of, 54

significance, 54–5
systems theory, and, 54–5
  and see **Systems theory**
transcendent authority
  law, and, 102, 116–7
  legal authority, and, 104
  natural law, and, 105
  rejection, of, 106, 111
  ritual, and, 147
  self-reference, and, 112, 114
  social history, and, 106, 111
Truth
  hierarchical conception, 11, 19
  linguistic expression, 11
  linguistic framework, 11
  meta-language, 11
  multiple truth predicates, 11
  object-language, 11
  truth-incompetent sentences, 11–2
  Truth-teller paradox, 10, 18

Urparadox
  see also **Reference of paradox**
  alternative projections, 84–5
  binding, 84–5
  cognitivisation, 85
  contents, 84–5
  decisions, 87
  external constraints, 83
  forming, 84
  formulation, of, 83
  inaugural distinctions, 84
  justifiability, 85
  meaning
    meaning generation, 84
    meaning projection, 84–6
    and see **Meaning**
  non-contents, 84–5
  normative qualification, 85
  onticised heteroreference, 85
  partial paradoxes, 87–91
  positive law, and, 87
  radical contingency, 84–6
  rules, 87
  social validity, 86
  univocisation, 84, 86
  valid projections, 85

Vagueness
  coherence, and, 123, 125, 127–31, 143
  communication
    communicative capability, 128, 130
    communicative disorder, 125–6

conflicting determinations, 126
deparadoxification, 128, 143
destabilisation, and, 128–9
disordered vagueness, 127, 129–30
effect, of, 127–9
equality, and, 125
incoherence
  sensitivity, to, 131
  topological quality, 129
  transient phenomenon, 128–9
inconsistency, 127–8
legal concepts, and, 123, 125
  and see **Legal concepts**
legal inexactness
  ambiguity, 124, 125–6
  fluid nature, 125
  fuzziness, 124–5
  general terms, 124–5
  legal concepts, 125
  legal rules, 125
legal interpretation, 128–30
meaning
  loss of meaning, 129
  re-entry, 130
  and see **Meaning**
nature, of, 131
pluralistic pressures, 129
pluralistic sensitivity, 125, 127, 130–1, 143
precautionary principle, 125, 131
  and see **Precautionary principle**
randomness, 131
  and see **Randomness**
systematic decoding, 126
trust, loss of, 130
Validity
  anti-values, 88
  circular nature, 18–9
  court proceedings, 159
    and see **Court proceedings**
  decision-making, and, 18
  endowment, of, 18–9
  falsity, assignment of, 18–9
  hierarchical conceptualisation, 19
  law and order, 88
  law and violence, 88–9
  lawfulness, 88–9
  legal ambiguity, 88
  legal grounding, 17, 19–20
    and see **Legal grounding**
  legal norms, and, 18
  legal order, 88–9
  legal system, 88

natural law, 88
natural rights, 88
origins of law, 88
rules in force, 18
significance, of, 17–8
systems theory, and, 177
   and see **Systems theory**
transfer, of, 18–9
truth, assignment of, 18–9
Truth-teller paradox, 18–9
unlawfulness/illegality, 89
values, 88

Warranties
see also **Contract law**
actual belief, 188
due diligence, 186–7
enforceability, 188–9
express representation, 186–7
express warranties, 183–6
factual truthfulness, 188
implied warranties, 186
mergers and acquisitions, 186
product liability, 186
reliance, and, 186–8